INNOVATIVE PRACTICES

with Vulnerable Children and Families

Edited by

Alvin L. Sallee

Hal A. Lawson

Katharine Briar-Lawson

eddie bowers publishing, inc.

DEDICATION

To the family experts and students who innovate with vulnerable children and families.

Exclusive marketing and distributor rights for
U.K., Eire, and Continental Europe held by:

Gazelle Book Services Limited
Falcon House
Queen Square
Lancaster LA1 1RN U.K.

eddie bowers publishing co., inc.
P. O. Box 130
Peosta, Iowa 52068-0130 USA

www.eddiebowerspublishing.com

ISBN 1-57879-023-9

Preface

When child welfare workers receive better preparation and enhanced supports, child and family outcomes will improve. Reciprocally, as child and family outcomes improve, workers' job satisfaction, efficacy, and retention will improve. In this fundamental sense, workers and the families they serve are interdependent. And because they are interdependent, workers and families need to work together and learn from each other. In this perspective, families of all kinds, but especially the most vulnerable ones, often are the keys to unlocking the doors that bar the way to systems improvement.

Another key is developing effecting working relationships with other helping professions and their respective agencies. Inter-professional education and training and, in turn, collaborative practices are needed in response to the multiple needs of families. These needs include substance abuse, mental health challenges, child abuse and neglect, domestic violence, employment-related problems, and, in many cases, poverty and its companions. Where these co-occurring needs are concerned, child welfare professionals cannot be expected to "do it all, alone." So, in addition to their interdependence with families, child welfare workers also depend on other helping professionals who serve the same children and families. This inter-professional and inter-agency development entails cross-systems change.

This book explores fresh approaches to systems improvement and cross-systems change. It is one product of a three-year project in the inter-mountain west. Two Title IV-B Section 426 grants provided by the Children's Bureau, Administration of Children and Families, U.S. Department of Health and Human Services, supported this work. On the other hand, this funding agency is not responsible for this book or for its interpretations and conclusions.

Called child welfare training, this project promoted a more comprehensive and ambitious agenda. A core group of university faculty, helping professionals, state agency leaders, and family experts (former "clients") helped design and adapt this agenda. Ultimately this agenda benefited from the contributions of a large number of colleagues in Utah, Nevada, Colorado, and New Mexico.

This book does not tell the entire story of this initiative. It highlights some important practice challenges and presents a sample of promising innovations. Its twin aims are to improve practice and to invite others to improve on the work reported here. This invitation to others stems from the editors' and authors' awareness that every chapter is selective in the treatment it gives to topics. Some topics receive short shrift, and others are excluded. In this sense, the book's chief contribution may lie in its inclusion of such a broad array of topics, together with the claim that these topics are related and essential to improved child welfare practice.

Some books are structured to provide answers to questions the authors and editors have asked for readers. This book is structured differently. First of all, it asks readers to address the questions. Are these the right questions? Are they complete, correct, and correctly stated? Secondly, it asks readers to join the editors and authors in answering these questions. In other words, it is structured to encourage dialogue, resulting in mutually beneficial learning. Did the authors answer their questions? Are you satisfied with their approach? What would you add? What would you delete? What would you modify? This second set of questions stems from the realities of practice. Place, timing, and context matter, and so does the rapidly changing policy climate. In this perspective, this book will not train you; but it will help you learn and improve.

The editors are grateful to all of the authors for their timely and wonderful contributions and to the many individuals who contributed to the development of this book. We thank Judith Reich, the Project Officer at the Children's Bureau; Eddie Bowers for his courage in funding and publishing this book, and Tom LaMarre for his helpful ideas. Without Barbara Myers editing and typesetting, as well as, Rosa Ruiz's day-to-day assistance, this book would not have been possible. The support staff at New Mexico State University of Michelle A. Campolla, Elda "Cooky" Ortiz, Gracie Sanchez, Lucia Robinson, and Fernando Solorzano attended to the thousands of details and Jennifer Zenger of the University of Utah gave ongoing support that has been invaluable.

In addition, we wish to thank the following persons who have contributed so much in so many ways throughout this project. From Colorado, Art Atwell, David Berns, Jane Beveridge, Karen Bye, Lena Edwards, Ben Granger, Linda Kean, Levetta Love, Gary Martinez, Dedra Millich, Dolores Nelson, Charla Peteson-Castle, Ellie Pope and Sue Tungate; from Nevada, Stacey Hardy-Desmond, Esther Langston, Dean Pierce, Nancy Petersen, Stephen Shaw, and Robin Ynacaynye; from New Mexico, S. R. "Butch" Brown, Jonah Garcia, Deana Kessin, Marjorie Hinton, Deborah Hunt, Romaine Serna and Halaevalu Vakalahi; from Utah, Karla Aguirre, Dawn Anderson-Butcher, Robin Arnold-Williams, Debbie Ashton, Carenlee Barkdull, Mary Bitner, Rock Boyer, Irl Carlson, Susan Cutler-Egbert, Kay Dee, David Derezotes, Michelle Derr, Jeanette Drews, Dan Edwards, Myrna Gooden, Norma Harris, Deborah Hinton, Tracie Hoffman, Khadija Khaja, Olivia Morton, Ken Patterson, Kirk Read, Pat Rothermich, Zohreh Saunders, Naomi Silverstone, Chris Snodgress, Ernie Soto, Mary Jane Taylor, Patti Wester-Van Wagoner and Megan Wiesen. And to Joan Levy Zlotnik, Institute for Social Work Research-Council on Social Work Education and John Lanigan. Thank you.

- A. L. S.
- H. A. L.
- K. B. L.

Contents

Detailed Contents

Chapter 8

Chapter 9

Contributing Authors

Dawn Anderson-Butcher has a PhD in Exercise and Sport Sciences and a Master's in Social Work. She is an Assistant Professor at The Ohio State University in Columbus, Ohio. She has extensive practice and research experience in youth development programming and school-family-community partnerships.

Carenlee Barkdull, MSW, is a Doctoral Student in the Graduate School of Social Work at the University of Utah in Salt Lake City, Utah. She is Director of Colorado's New Century Collaborative Initiative and co-manager of a grant to improve compliance with the National Indian Child Welfare Act. Ms. Barkdull has 18 years of human services experience.

David Berns, MSW, is Director of the El Paso County Department of Human Services, in Colorado Springs, Colorado. He has been the Director since March of 1997. Prior to that, he was director of the Office of Children's Services for the Michigan Department of Social Services.

Rock Boyer, MSW, is Associate Regional Director for the Division of Child and Family Services in the Granite Region in the State of Utah. He has more than 19 years of experience in Child Welfare, 10 years in Alberta, Canada, and 9 years in the State of Utah. This experience includes frontline Child Welfare, Supervision, and Administrative positions in a variety of programs, including Foster Care, In-Home Services, and Family Supervision. Mr. Boyer currently is a member of the Regional, Four-State New Century Grant, Child Welfare Steering Committee.

Katharine Briar-Lawson is Dean of the School of Social Welfare at the University at Albany, State University of New York. She was formerly at the University of Utah, where she was Associate Dean for Research and Doctoral Studies and a co-facilitator of four intermountain west child welfare initiatives. Dr. Briar-Lawson is a lead author on a forthcoming book on Family Centered Policies and Practices: International Implications and a co-editor of *New Century Child Welfare Practice Serving Vulnerable Children and Families*. She has spearheaded University-Community partnerships and family and interprofessional collaboration in more than 40 states. In addition, she has developed award winning demonstration projects involving parent empowerment, school-based services, and school reform. She also served as Assistant for Children, Youth, and Families in the State of Washington.

Kip Coggins, PhD, has a Master's in Social Work from Michigan State University and a Doctoral degree in Social Work and Anthropology from the University of Michigan. Currently, Dr. Coggins is an Assistant Professor at the University of Texas at El Paso, teaching in the areas of human behavior and the social environment, policy, practice, theory, and field practicum. Dr. Coggins has been a licensed independent social worker with the State of New Mexico since 1990. He has worked as a correctional social worker with clients at all levels of custody, including maximum security and death row, at the Penitentiary of New Mexico. In addition, Dr. Coggins has presented on the culture of prisons at conferences and workshops, sponsored by the National Association of Social Worker, the New Mexico Department of Corrections, and the Texas Commission of Drug and Alcohol Abuse.

Deb DeNiro-Ashton is a Licensed Clinical Social Worker who is Murray Community Developer and Director of Support Services for the Murray School District in Murray, Utah. Ms. Deniro-Ashton has spent the last 15 years as an educator, social worker, and administrator in Murray School District. She implemented the FACT (Families, Agencies, and Communities Together) Interprofessional Service Delivery Initiative in the district and community. Ms. Deniro-Ashton is now leading the community organization and development efforts to strengthen families and build stronger neighbor-to-neighbor connections in Murray.

David S. Derezotes, LCSW, PhD, is Professor of Social Work at the Graduate School of Social Work, University of Utah, where he is Chair of the Clinical and Curriculum Committees. He currently is Clinical Supervisor at the Indian Walk-In Center, a therapist at the Family Counseling Center, and in private practice in Salt Lake City. Dr. Derezotes' publications are in the areas of practice, children and families, and spirituality and religion, including his recent textbook, *Advanced Generalist Social Work Practice*. He has practiced social work for more than 25 years.

Michelle K. Derr, PhD, is a Policy Researcher for Mathematica Policy Research, Inc., in Washington, DC. Dr. Derr's work focuses on understanding the types of personal and family challenges among welfare recipients and low-income families, particularly those who are hard to employ. In addition, she develops and implements strategies for helping these populations obtain and maintain work,

Roger S. Friedman, PhD, is a Licensed Psychologist and a Licensed Clinical Social Worker. He is a Clinical and Organizational Psychologist and a Human Services Consultant. Dr. Friedman serves as Consultant to the State of Maryland Department of Human Resources, and is an Adjunct Faculty member at the University of Maryland School of Social Work. He has more than 20 years of experience as a clinician, educator, and human services consultant. Dr. Friedman provides program consultation, training, and organizational development services to child welfare, family preservation, and mental health services across the Unites States.

Myrna A. Gooden, MSW, is Co-Project Manager of the Social Research Institute at the University of Utah Graduate School of Social Work. She is a doctoral student in social work with a specialization if Indian child welfare. Ms. Gooden presents and provides training to Indians and non-Indians nationally.

Stacey Hardy-Desmond, PhD, is Field Director/Clinical Assistant Professor at the School of Social Work at the University of Nevada, Las, Vegas, Nevada. She has extensive background in direct practice and supervision, emphasizing cultural awareness. Her clinical work with populations includes home health, adult and child in-patient psychiatric, outpatient therapy, intensive case management, residential, and crisis settings.

Judith C. Hilbert, PhD, is Assistant Professor in the School of Social Work at New Mexico State University in Las Cruces, New Mexico. Dr. Hilbert's research interest in domestic violence began with her dissertation in 1984. Since that time, she has simultaneously focused on practice with battered women and research related to issues of family violence. She is completing an NIJ grant on domestic violence in Southwestern New Mexico and has presented extensively internationally, nationally, and locally.

Tracie L. Hoffman, PhD, is an Assistant Professor/Lecturer in the Graduate School of Social Work at the University of Utah in Salt Lake City, Utah. Dr. Hoffman has worked in criminal justice and acute psychiatric settings with children and their families. She has studied minority populations in connection with mental health issues. While primarily a clinician, Dr. Hoffman considers herself a generalist with experience in client advocacy and policy practice.

Lynn C. Holley, PhD, is Assistant Professor in the School of Social Work at Arizona State University in Tempe, Arizona. Dr. Holley's teaching and research interests include diversity, oppression, and social change. She has participated in research about ethnic agencies, intergroup dialogues, and racism in the juvenile justice system.

Deborah Esquibel Hunt, PhD, is a Community Research Consultant with the Social Research Institute at the University of Utah in Salt Lake City, Utah. Dr. Hunt, who is a Cherokee of Northeast Alabama, consults with universities and tribes, mentors native graduate students, presents nationally, and designs culturally appropriate curricula. Her scholarly focus is on Indian child welfare policy.

Khadija Khaja, MSW, is a PhD student in the School of Social Work at the University of Utah in Salt Lake City, Utah. She is teaching research and working on Child Welfare And Disability Research Grants. Ms. Khaja has extensive child welfare background from Canada, where she worked as a frontline social worker, intake telephone social worker, investigating child abuse and neglect. She developed community development grants to make child welfare services more culturally sensitive. In addition, Ms. Khaja developed and co-led groups to support female adolescents who had been sexually abused. She was appointed by the Honorable Minister Elaine Ziambe to serve on the Multicultural Advisory Committee for the Department of Citizenship and Multiculturalism of Ontario, Canada.

Esther Jones Langston, PhD, is Director of the School of Social Work at the University of Nevada Las Vegas. She has been a Social Work Educator for 30 years and a Social Work Practitioner for 35 years. Dr. Langston's areas of expertise include curriculum development, women's issues, cultural diversity, gerontology (African American aging), and administration.

Hal A. Lawson, PhD, is Professor of Social Welfare and Education and Special Assistant to the Provost at the University of Albany, State University of New York. Dr. Lawson promotes university-school-family-community partnerships, and he studies and participates in complex change initiatives that improve child and family well-being. Dr. Lawson consults regularly in schools, community agencies, and universities.

Nancy Peterson, MSW, is Training Coordinator and Assistant Professor in the School of Social Work at the University of Nevada in Reno. She has more than 20 years of experience in child welfare, including agency service and university-based training. Ms. Peterson's areas of expertise include training, curriculum development, adult learning, interprofessional collaboration, and adoption.

Dean Pierce is Professor and Director of the University of Nevada, Reno, School of Social Work. An active member of the Council on Social Work Education, he serves on the Commission of Accreditation and was Co-Chair of the Commission on Gay Men and Lesbian Women. He also is active with the Nevada Chapter of the National Association of Social Workers, having served as president, board member, and chair of the Western Coalition for the 1996 Delegate Assembly. Dr. Pierce serves on Nevada's Social Work Licensing Board. He is the author of *Social Work and Society* and *Policy for the Social Work Practitioner*, and has presented dozens of refereed and invitational papers and workshops dealing with gay and lesbian issues.

Thom Reilly, DPA, MSW, is Associate Professor at the University of Nevada, Las Vegas. He is the former Director of Administrative Services for Clark County, Nevada (population 1.3 million), where he was responsible for the county's legislative initiatives, franchise agreements, policy development, and strategic planning efforts. He also was responsible for the county's neighborhood services program, labor negotiations (for more than 6,000 employees), and code compliance. Dr. Reilly also was the Administrator for the Nevada Division of Child and Family Services overseeing the State's child welfare system. In addition, he was the administrator for the State's income maintenance, food stamps, and employment and training programs.

Alvin L. Sallee, ACSW, LISW, is Professor and Director of the Family Preservation Institute in the School of Social Work of New Mexico State University in Las Cruces, New Mexico. As Head of the Department of Social Work from 1976 to 1994, he guided the BSW and MSW programs to CSWE accreditation and began the Family Preservation Institute. He has authored and administered $15 million in grants and contracts. Mr. Sallee has published more than 30 articles and co-authored three texts. He has served as a consultant to more than 30 universities, states, and countries on curriculum design, grants, and program design and evaluation. He has staffed more than 2,000 cases and often serves as an expert witness. Professionally, Mr. Sallee has served on the Board of Directors of the National Association of Social Workers, the Council on Social Work Education, and as President of the Baccalaureate Program Directors. In New Mexico, he has chaired two Governor's Committees and the Social Work Licensure Board.

Brenda D. Smith, PhD, is an Assistant Professor in the School of Social Work at the University of Albany, State University of New York. She received her PhD in 1999. Dr. Smith's dissertation focused on families with child welfare cases in Cook County, Illinois. She looked at how and why parental drug use and drug treatment compliance affect the likelihood of family reunification.

Halaevalu F. Vakalahi, PhD, is an Assistant Professor in the School of Social Work at New Mexico State University in Las Cruces, New Mexico. Her areas of interest include adolescent substance use/abuse and juvenile delinquency in the context of the family as a source of risk or protection.

Patti Western VanWagoner, MSW, is Clinical Instructor for Practicum Students from the University of Utah and is Associate Regional Director for the Division of Child and Family Services, Cottonwood Region, Utah Department of Human Services, in Murray, Utah. She has 10 years of experience with DCFS. Ms. VanWagoner has a strong commitment to children and families and remains involved with community building activities to support families.

Megan Wiesen, LCSW, is Salt Lake City, Utah, Associate Director for the Division of Child and Family Services. She began with DCFS in January 1991. Ms. Wiesen's experience includes case management, family and individual therapy, and community organization. She developed a community model of Child Protection, which was implemented in Salt Lake City.

Blanca M. Ramos, PhD, MSW, CSW, is Assistant Professor at the School of Social Welfare at the University of Albany, State University of New York. She is a licensed social worker with extensive clinical experience with diverse families. Her research interests focus on the family and cross-cultural mental health, especially concerning caregiving and domestic violence.

Chapter 1

Charlotte's Web: The Present and Future of Family Services

by Roger Friedman and Alvin L. Sallee

Introduction

The Web

What a tangled web we weave for families, social workers, administrators, and policy makers. Imagine an illustration. A hundred people are sitting around tables randomly placed throughout a large ballroom. These people represent every possible agency or program with which a vulnerable family may come in contact—law enforcement, the courts, the school system, income maintenance programs, health services (both physical and mental), child protective services, shelters—up to a hundred programs. Imagine a vulnerable family, the Jones family, standing in the middle of this distinguished group with their ecological map portrayed on a large screen (see Figure 1). The map identifies all of the services and programs with which individuals in this family interact.

As the family members call out the agencies they use, they throw a different colored ball of yarn to each worker. For example, Todd, the 13 year old boy, was picked up by the police at 1:00 a.m. for curfew violation. After the police officer stands, Todd throws his ball of yarn to the officer, while still holding the end. The next morning, Todd's case was referred to the Juvenile Probation Officer (JPO) for follow-up. When the JPO stands, the police officer throws the ball of yarn to the JPO while still holding on to the string. As each member of the family goes through this process, a large web of yarn grows around the family. A facilitator standing with the family then asks the family and each of the professionals how they feel about this web of yarn. The family is overwhelmed and choked, professionals are unaware of all of the involvement and complexity, and everyone agrees this is not the best way to serve families.

This chapter introduces the reader not only to the challenges facing vulnerable children and families, particularly concerning poverty and child welfare policy, but also where we need to go and some suggestions of how to get there. Throughout this chapter, the other chapters of this book are referenced, thus providing an overview of the total text. In the first half of this book, children's and families' vulnerabilities are explored, while the second half of the book examines innovative practices. While the chapters and the authors open many critical challenges, it is impossible for one text to cover all of them. We do believe the chapters will facilitate further self-directed learning.

Figure 1. Jones Family

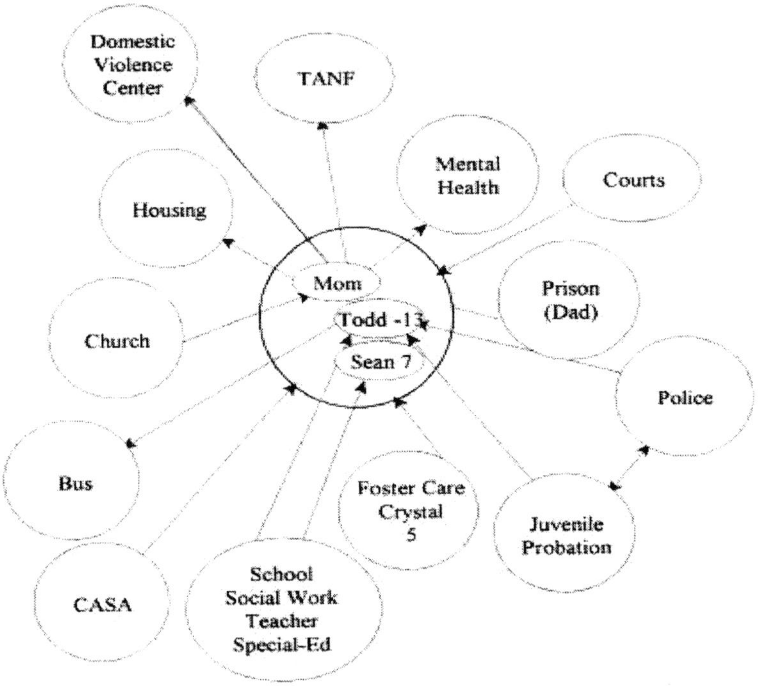

Child Welfare Legislation

Recent policies have contributed to the web the Jones family faces; therefore, we present this brief review. In 1978, to improve child welfare decisions made in regard to Native American children and families, the Indian Child Welfare Act (ICWA) (P.L. 95-608) was implemented. The Adoption and Child Welfare Assistance Act (P.L. 96-272) attempted to institutionalize permanency planning nationally in 1980. In 1993, in an effort to provide families pre-placement and in-home services, the Family Preservation and Family Support Act (P.L. 103-66) was funded for five years at almost $1 billion dollars.

Then, in 1994, as concerns about the delay in the adoption of minority children grew, the Multiethnic Placement Act (MEPA) (P.L. 103-82) passed and in 1996, the Interethnic Adoption Provisions (IEP) (P.L. 104-88). Both eliminated discrimination on the basis of race, color, or national origin of the child and the adoptive parent. In other words, ethnic criteria could not be used in the placement of a child.

In fulfilling his campaign promise to end welfare as we know it, the Personal Responsibility and Work Opportunity Reconciliation Act of 1996 (P.L. 104-193) was signed by President Clinton. This after two vetoes, one against block granting child welfare programs to the states. Commonly known as Temporary Assistance to Needy Families (TANF), the Act replaced Aid to Families with Dependent Children (AFDC). The Adoption and Safe Families Act (ASFA) of 1997 (P.L. 105-89) shortened the timelines for out-of-home placements of children and reauthorized (and renamed, to Safe and Stable Families) the Family Preservation Act of 1993.

Each piece of legislation brings a new set of regulations, with interpretations both formal and informal. Is it any wonder families and workers feel caught in the web of services and programs?

Challenges

What is the future of family services? Will we not recognize the policies, organizations, and models of practice in twenty years or will it be more of the same? The purpose of this book is not so much to predict the future, but rather to examine the tangled web of conservative and progressive trends which vulnerable families and workers face today, and to bring to light the pattern of innovations that we think are hopeful precursors of what services to vulnerable children and families can become. The challenges are to systems, programs, and practice as well as to each practitioner and family.

In this multi-layered web, we are trying to see more clearly not just an ideological debate of "what's right and what's wrong," but also the practical impact policies and programs have on families. There is no subject which people believe they are more expert on than family issues. Herein lies one of the challenges to those who support and understand family-centered principles and values. The child welfare system cannot be fixed, or even improved by child welfare alone. As McCroskey and Meezan (1998, pg. 68) write, "The basic social problems that are at the core of the nation's malaise are also at the core of child welfare problems. Poverty, violence, and drugs affect almost every family..."

Mental health assessment and environmentally inclusive treatment for children and families is addressed in Chapter 4 by Tracie Hoffman. The impact of the Criminal Justice System upon families is explored by Halaevalu Vakalahi, Lynn Holley, and Kip Coggins in Chapter 5. The critical issue of violence is explained as a story in need of an ending by Judy Hilbert in Chapter 6. Substance abuse, or drugs are cited as one of the top two concerns of child welfare. Brenda D. Smith in Chapter 7 suggests partnerships with parents and communities as an important response. Finally, without culturally competent practitioners and policies we will not be able to stem the tide of racism, sexism, and heterosexism. Two chapters, 8 and 9, speak to cultural competent practice and Indian child welfare.

Temporary Assistance for Needy Families

At the beginning of the 21st century, our ever evolving national policy debate over human services has become dominated by conservative political voices. On the national scene, there has been little if any strong, progressive advocacy for family services in the past few years. The debate itself has been narrowed to focus on blaming the "bandage" of social programs for society's ills, rather than addressing the deeper economic and social wounds that fester in our country. A conservative Congress has encouraged legal remedies over social remedies; offenders are to be punished and banished rather than treated or rehabilitated; financial support to the poor is no longer an entitlement. The many-sided ongoing debate of what is the best interest of children has, for the time being, come down on the side of protection through termination of parental rights as opposed to redoubling our efforts to support and preserve families. These trends are embodied in the Temporary Assistance for Needy Families (TANF) and Adoption and Safe Families Act (ASFA) legislation. It is more complicated than this, however, because this policy shift has intended and unintended influences and a mix of positive and negatives effects—a complex web.

The positive effects of TANF include an increasing awareness that economic survival for low income and impoverished families must be connected to job opportunity rather than long-term, meager government entitlements. David Berns presents, in Chapter 3, different options that Temporary Assistance for Needy Families should support family preservation through the integration of prevention programs in coordination with the community. He suggests more and better coordination with different systems can prevent and address poverty issues. He also suggests unified services for families, such as extended services for grandparents who are raising grandchildren, and provision of child care and transportation for those that are failing under TANF.

The unintended effects of TANF include, (1) overwhelmed county financial assistance divisions of social services, (2) the general chaos over how to prepare former welfare recipients for work, and (3) how to find jobs in an economy that continues to grow for the middle and upper classes, but is stagnant and lacks opportunity for the poor and unskilled (Pelton, 1999). Moreover, many families that once relied on cash, medical, and food benefits for survival are increasingly displaced and at increased risk for child maltreatment and family crises (LeVine and Sallee, 1999). In this respect, Katharine Briar-Lawson (in Chapter 2) addresses multiple barriers that families on welfare experience in order to retain a permanent job and integrate other economic supports and family capacity building.

Adoption and Safe Families Act

ASFA has had a similar mix of intended and unintended effects. The legislation has once again reminded us that the state is not the best parent and that we must work even harder to stop long-term foster care drift. In addition, the legislation underscores what social workers need to remember, that there are some families that are so destructive or not present that children need to be removed and protected permanently from their toxic influences. However, ASFA has also had a chilling effect on family preservation programs around the country, making workers and administrators very cautious about committing the resources it takes to help a family rebuild itself when there are organizational incentives to do otherwise and significant time restraints for service delivery.

Several state administrators do not realize the potential impact that keeping children in their own home has in regard to the child's development or ASFA policy. If nothing else, Safe Family programs, formerly known as family preservation, keep the clock from beginning for these children. The maintenance of the children in their own home is cost effective, not only in terms of out-of-home placement costs but also the large number of persons who must work with that child as soon as they are removed from their home. These include CASAs, attorneys, including the guardian ad litem, placement workers, treatment workers, supervisors, Citizen Review Board members, and often Federal Court monitors.

While the state faces these barriers, at the same time, practice wisdom points to the reality that humane excellence in child welfare practice is only achievable through skilled professional balancing of protection, preservation, and permanency. We are faced with critical questions.

First, what is the role of family-centered practice in achieving the balance between protection and preservation? Secondly, what are the necessary components of the service system capable of accomplishing this balance and how are they funded?

To help us answer these questions, we must provide the following information to agency administrators and program designers: (1) Options to reinvigorate and refine the implementation of child and family programs in light of current political and legislative mandates. (2) Service system designs that employ the values and principles of family-centered practice to protect, preserve, and to provide permanency for children. (3) A critical and forthright review of the research (facts and myths) and their implications for family practice. Which values and principles remain relevant and what does the research really suggest? And, (4) Which human service system designs are successfully combating drift, assuring safety, and moving families through the various systems to closure (Sallee, 2000)?

ASFA and the conservative political perspective has, for the time being, defined child protection and family preservation as largely irreconcilable goals rather than seeing them as complementary values that together can guide a humane and family-centered program. These new policies have moved practice from "saving families for children" to "saving children from families" (Meezan, 2000).

Managed Care

The trend toward managed care and privatization of service has brought new service delivery structures into play and has encouraged a wave of management reform into family services organizations around the country. The creation of a competitive local market place for human service "vendors" has certainly increased the level of creativity and available services in many parts of the country. The unintended effect of these developments is that coordination of programs for a single family, inclusion of families in the process of services, access to services, and establishing a family-centered model have become all the more difficult.

Much of this reform has been borrowed from the private sector and takes the form of quality control departments, use of technology and information systems to monitor services and costs, and outcome-based budgeting as opposed to salaries as the only way to determine expenditures. The use of strategic planning techniques for managers, marketing, thinking of clients as "customers to be served," and management team decision making are all part of the behavioral changes that are taking place in state and county agencies. Some of these trends are positive in that they are helping managers become more team oriented and less hierarchical, and more strategic and proactive rather than driven by the operational crises of the moment.

Katharine Briar-Lawson and Megan Wiesen provide in Chapter 12 many examples involving former clients as "family experts," from a different perspective on how to design service plans, to provide a more effective approach with the needs of the families, and collaboration as a team training with professional workers. Another factor, often overlooked with families is spirituality. David Derezotes and Tracie Hoffman in Chapter 10 explain that spiritual practice is applicable in both direct and indirect practice.

In managed care, the concern about costs and really measuring services helps everyone know what is actually being done by the many workers who are always busy but often unclear about their actual tasks. In this aspect, Hal Lawson and Carenlee Barkdull suggest, in Chapter 13, the promotion of collaboration between social worker, mental health, and other health professionals in order to integrate new ways of sharing knowledge, language, and skills. The managed care trends have a negative effect as well since they often are not adapted to the human service environment and tend to focus on the quantitative nature of services and not on measuring and supporting the qualitative, relationship side of services. The intrinsic values of family service, of helping others, caring for children, and building a better society tend to get lost as family services become seen as a another product to be marketed, evaluated, and provided in as efficient a manner as possible. And while, as

Blanca M. Ramos presents in Chapter 11, the role of caregivers is critical and stressful, there seems to be little attention to how to balance the private-sector excesses of these reforms with the intrinsic, relationship-oriented nature of the work.

Program Trends

The web of broad-based positive and negative trends we are discussing tend to distract from what we see as the most progressive, though often less noticeable area of program development. At the local and state levels, within community-based, county, or non-profit agencies, there is a growing interest in cross-system partnerships, empowering families, in thinking and behaving in a more ecological and family-centered way. This kind of progressive practice is emerging along the entire continuum of services: from investigating child sex abuse, crimes, delinquency and helping foster and biological families be more of a team, to residential programs reaching out to families and neighborhoods, to faith communities and businesses partnering up with social service agencies, to families asserting themselves in decision-making and team work with professionals.

Many of these programs are being developed on shoe-string budgets, through foundation support or through creative managers, workers, and families believing in this approach, seeing the need, and just getting started. As Chapter 14 points out, self- help and mutual support groups are the most prevalent formal support groups in American today. It is clear that the old way of providing services through larger, federally funded and supervised agencies is over. But what will the new models look like? Will they follow the private sector in a fragmented, competitive, and cost-driven manage care market place? Or can ecological, family-centered, and community-based efforts provide the outline for the future? We see these latter developments as the most hopeful direction for the future and are described throughout this book. Chapter 16 provides an in-depth case study from Utah on neighborhood teams that promote collaboration and community-based systems of care.

Where Do We Go from Here?

Quietly, often out of the limelight of media and political attention, ecological and family-centered innovations are occurring within programs across the continuum of services. An initial example is in Child Protective Services (CPS), a service that has historically been overwhelmed by increasing referrals, lack of resources, isolated, traumatized workers, and a "fishbowl" existence. This leaves staff anxious about lawsuits, political scapegoating, and negative press coverage. In almost every state, child welfare systems are being sued or are operating under federal court orders (Adams, Sallee, and Shaening, 1995).

The development and proliferation of Child Advocacy Centers (CACs), beginning in Alabama (Wilson, 1998) and now sprouting up in twenty states, is a significant ecological innovation in child protection. CACs function as partnerships between protective services, police/detectives, and medical staff. Inter-disciplinary teams, usually co-located in an office in the community, or within the social services agency, are designed to investigate, interview, and engage families where serious physical and sexual abuse has been reported. Repeated interviewing that re-traumatizes children and parents is kept to a minimum since many CACs have one-way mirrors or video-taping capacity so that the team can observe while the interviews take place. The inter-disciplinary team receives joint training, that support each other in debriefing traumatic situations, and try to make the service family-centered in regard to working with children, non-offending parents, and the offender as well.

A more macro-ecological perspective about community/family partnerships for child protection is developing in Michigan, Florida, Georgia, and several other states supported by the Edna McConnell Clark Foundation and the Center for Social Policy Studies (CPS) in Washington, D.C. (Farrow, 1997). These pilot projects are focused on the assumption that one state or county agency like social services can no longer be expected to be responsible for all child protective services.

Community partnerships are being formed where multi-agency planning and family-team meetings are being held regularly to address families needs and child safety as illustrated in Chapter 16. Networks of neighborhood supports are being organized to broaden the "eyes and ears" of CPS, to develop community support agreements to aid the family and ensure child safety, and eventually local inter-agency and family councils will be formed to review the progress and effects of these new approaches.

In addition to the increasing use of kinship care placements for child maltreatment, foster care reform with a decidedly family-centered and ecological perspective, is occurring in a number of states including Pennsylvania, Ohio, and Maryland. These initiatives supported in part by Annie E. Casey Foundation (Braziel, 1998), have led to a new emphasis on family team meetings that include foster families, biological families, and social workers to mediate the process of foster care, to help the biological family increase their competency, and to make recommendations about permanency plans. In a number of states, foster families are being seen as more central providers of services to not only the foster child but the biological family itself.

How shifting from conventional training to empowering design teams allows for collaboration and systems change is explained in Chapter 17 by Hal Lawson, Nancy Petersen, and Katharine Briar-Lawson. Joint training with social workers, foster parents, and biological parents are occurring to develop a continuing network of support and safety for the child rather than the isolation and hostility that historically has formed between the various roles.

Family preservation and family-reunification efforts continue throughout the country often with reduced resources, but with increased efforts to network with churches, community centers, juvenile justice, and mental health services. Service integration and collaboration are critical to offer an array of family preservation services from prevention to intensive in-home services (Lloyd and Sallee, 1994).

Selected programs, such as working with children and teenagers that have experienced serious abuse in-home and have multiple emotional educational needs are beginning to embrace a community-centered, wraparound approach to planning. Youth development is examined as a child welfare resource and support in Chapter 15 by Hal Lawson and Dawn Anderson-Butcher. These approaches are working to make aftercare an ongoing commitment to organizing a network of service and kinship supports in the youngster's community.

Again, as presented in Chapter 3, the implementation of TANF has brought about creative, new cross-system partnerships to find jobs and training for employment, housing opportunities, mentoring, tutors, and child care. The business community and the faith community are being mobilized in parts of the country to team up with social services and family services and provide more direct support for impoverished families and children at risk of maltreatment.

We think that, even with the complex web of policy in the field today, exciting and hopeful patterns of innovation across many traditionally isolated child and family services is taking shape. These patterns emphasize ecological thinking that explores new perspectives for family involvement in their cultural environment, cross-system partnerships, collaborative approaches, and mobilization of the community to support impoverished families where children are at high risk for abuse and neglect. We believe that the patterns presented in this book offer a family centered, humane, and effective outline for a future service delivery system.

How Do We Get There from Here?

Innovation

The challenge of the future is how to focus attention and build support today for the progressive trends that are present in the current family services environment. It is far too easy to just join in the limited debate of national policy alternatives. We need to break out of the old dichotomies of safety vs. preservation, public vs. private, federal vs. state/local, and, extend the debate to new possibilities of service delivery. The focus of these new possibilities are the ecological innovations we are highlighting in this book.

Education

This challenge should begin "at home," with social work and other human service practitioners and educators documenting, evaluating, and promoting ecological initiatives. Schools of social work should play a leading role in this task. Current students in Baccalaureate of Social Work, Masters of Social Work, and Doctoral programs need to gain "ecological and collaborative experiences" and support these initiatives through inter-professional placements, internships, and research projects. Schools of social work need to find ways to partner with administrators and managers in family services to experiment with ecological efforts, even as they confront their operational challenge of keeping up with crises in a context of shrinking resources. This kind of proactive, strategic leadership is never easy, but will be essential if we are to help these new ideas grow.

Media

There is much work to be done with the media and with political processes at the state and local levels. Journalists must be re-directed to pay attention not just to the high-profile child abuse cases that frighten and anger communities, but also to the need for partnership and community involvement when it comes to child protection and family support. We can no longer afford to create the impression to the media that child protection can be done successfully by one state or county agency. We are all in it together, and if this means a shifting of the organizational structures, more community and family involvement, so be it. Can local media be called in to cover family centered success stories? Can the traumatic side of working child maltreatment be portrayed in ways that humanize social work to the community? Can journalists be exposed to the complex, Solomon like permanency planning decisions that are made each day in county offices? For too long social work agencies have seen the media as a hostile force, waiting to pounce and scapegoat when something goes wrong. In many parts of the country, this is true about the local media. It is also true that social workers invite this kind of criticism by claiming too much responsibility for child protection, by failing to reach out and form partnerships with others in the community, and, in the name of confidentiality, putting up a wall of silence around the agency until a terrible crisis takes place.

Policy Making

Given that the media informs or at least justifies the policy makers, this arena requires careful attention too. The political collaboration among social work, lobbyists, practitioners, and state legislatures in Texas is an example of an exciting model for mobilizing support for improved family services (Sallee, C., 2000). There are some counties where County Commissioners (Berns, Chapter 3) are brought to the social services agencies, they go out on home visits, see foster children, hear about traumatic investigations, and get a real sense of how complex child protection is. This kind of "street education" helps politicians shift away from the sort of scapegoating that often takes the place of real analysis and community building for children and families.

The mobilization of experience, knowledge, political support and community involvement to support families and children is always an uphill battle. If we aim to bring real innovation into family services of the future, these tasks represent the real challenge of the next decade.

Conclusion

We are hopeful about the future of family services, not because we think the changes required will be easy, but because the nature of the innovations, as outlined in the following chapters, seem to offer so much promise. Hal Lawson, in the last chapter (18), offers us a blue print for the future rooted in the history of social work's leadership. His focus on the shared responsibilities for vulnerable children and families is tied to the very basic democratic ideals. As we move into the 21st century, family services is operating in the historical context of fifty years of federal programming, devolution of funding to states and localities, a shifting back and forth of conservative and political agendas, and a politicized schism between child safety and family preservation. What is more, our culture continues to idealize children and families but has yet to make a sustained commitment to their welfare. If we can build on the current pattern of innovations and the values implicit in ecological and family-centered practice, we can move our service delivery system to a new level of effectiveness. What more exciting challenge could there be for the 21st century?

References

Adams, A., Sallee, A. L., and Shaening, M. A. (1995). Child Welfare System Reform Litigation: Achieving Substantial Compliance. *Journal of Law and Social Work*, 2(1).

Adoption & Child Welfare Act. Public Law 96-272. (1980).

Adoption & Safe Families Act (ASFA). Public Law 105-89. (1997).

Braziel, D. J (1998). Collaboration for Change. *Annie E. Casey Foundation*. Available:**http://www.aecf.org**.

Family Preservation & Family Support Act. Public Law 103-66. (1993).

Farrow, F. (1997). Building Community Partnerships for Child Protection. *Child Protective Clearinghouse*. Center for the Study of Social Policy. Washington, D.C. Available: **http://www.cssp.ort/Kd20htm.**

Indian Child Welfare Act (ICWA). Public Law 95-608. (1978).

Inter-ethnic Adoptions Provision (IAP). Public Law 104-88. (1996).

LeVine, E. S., and Sallee, A. L.(1999). *Child Welfare: Clinical Theory and Practice.* Iowa: Eddie Bowers Publishing,

Lloyd, J. C., and Sallee, A. L. (1994). The Challenge and Potential of Family Preservation Services in the Public Child Welfare System. *Family Preservation Journal, 10*(3).

Meezan, W. (2000). Translating Rhetoric to Reality: The Future of Family and Children's Services. *Family Preservation Journal, 5*(1).

Multiethnic Placement Act (MEPA). Public Law 103-82. (1994).

Annie E. Casey Foundation.(2000). *Overview.* Available:**http://www.aecf.org/familytofamily/overview.htm.**

Pelton, L. H. (1999, Mar.). *Welfare Discrimination and Child Welfare.* Paper presented at the conference on the Implications of Welfare Reform for Children Conference, Columbus, Ohio.

Personal Responsibility and Work Opportunity Reconciliation Act. Public Law 104-193. TANF. (1996).

Sallee, A. L. (1998). Editorial. The Role of Families, *Family Preservation Journal, 3*(1).

Sallee, A. L. (2000). Editorial. The Demands of Protection, Preservation and Permanency: Where has Family Preservation Gone? *Family Preservation Journal, 5*(1).

Sallee, C. A. (2000). Personal Communication.

Wilson, C. (1998, Sep.). Implication of Public Fear and Distrust of Child Protective Services. *National Children's Advocacy Center.* Available: **http://www.ncac-hsv.org/Wash/sld001.html**

Chapter 2

Integrating Employment, Economic Supports and Family Capacity Building

Katharine Briar-Lawson

Sharma is the oldest of three children. She and her siblings live with their mother and grandmother. Sharma and her two younger siblings suffer daily from hunger and malnourishment. They live in a two room apartment. All three children are asthmatic.

Sharma's mother, Dora, suffered from sexual abuse as a child. She is also a recent victim of severe beatings by her boyfriend. Sharma was also victimized by his frequent molestations of her. Their victimization has gone unaddressed and untreated. Dora is fearful and even phobic about leaving her apartment.

Dora and her family were recently dropped from welfare because she did not follow through with job search expectations. The only source of funds for her family is the grandmother's small social security check. Sharma and her sisters may be sent to live with their her aunt until times get better for Dora. Sharma has been unable to concentrate on her school work and is so frightened about her future that she has persistent stomach pains and asthmatic attacks.

Introduction

Sharma and her siblings are joined by 15 million other children in the U.S. who are poor and whose lives are very tenuous (Sherman, 1997). Their plight is worsened by the fact the poverty rate among U.S. children is one third higher than 25 years ago. The National Center for Children in Poverty (1998) reports that eight states have experienced steep increases in child poverty for children under age six. Yet supports for poor children like Sharma and her siblings are unraveling, if not ruptured by the elimination of welfare entitlements (Cook, Vener, et al., 1998). Despite rising challenges facing poor children and families, many social workers and related health and human service providers are ill prepared to address the causes and consequences of Sharma's poverty or to integrate social services, employment, and occupational supports. This practice gap stems in part from rapid rollbacks in entitlements. For nearly 60 years, welfare guarantees served as a "rock bottom" income base upon which health, human service, and educational providers built their helping practice. Now, with the demise of welfare as an entitlement and a "protective" foundation for helping technologies, impoverished families and those who serve them face enormous challenges.

The chapter focuses on some of the conditions that create the pernicious predicament faced by Sharma's family. It addresses the growth of "double jeopardy" families. It explores some of the risk factors associated with poverty, such as abuse and neglect. Finally, the chapter sketches areas for expanded practice, programming, and financing strategies. The aim is to center human service practices around more economically, occupationally, and educationally integrative approaches, programs, and investments. Integrative practice involves the joining of social service strategies with employment, occupational, and income generating approaches. The urgency for such integrative practices derives not just from rollbacks in welfare entitlements but also from broader policy changes affecting welfare policy worldwide.

Twenty-First Century Contexts for Childhood Poverty and Consequences

Poverty

Sharma's and her siblings' impoverishment stems from many sources. Politicians might blame her mother as the cause of their impoverishment. They might cite the fact that "there are plenty of jobs." In other words, they might argue that any job is a way out of poverty and a means for Dora to be a provider for her children. They might argue that if Dora intended to be a good parent, she would be working to support her family. Some politicians might even claim that if Dora is not working and has no other means for being a provider for them, she does not deserve to keep her children. Health and human service practitioners might blame sanctioning practices or the time limits placed on the receipt of welfare brought about by the replacement of the income entitlement of Aid to Families with Dependent Children(AFDC) with time-limited aid of Temporary Assistance for Needy Families (TANF).

Sharma's and her siblings' poverty and the threatening future they face also need to be framed against the backdrop of economic globalization. Economic globalization includes the restructuring and downsizing of welfare states and the freeing of capital so that profits can be maximized (Dominelli, 1999; Glennerster, 1999; Briar-Lawson, Lawson, Hennon, et al., 2000). Such globalization penetrates the world with beliefs that economic investments will "trickle down" and lift families like Sharma's out of poverty. The relevance of this "trickle down" theory has long been debated. In fact, the limits of the economy and its capacity to serve as a foundation for human well-being gave rise to the creation of welfare states. Nonetheless, the "mean and lean" race to the bottom practices that undergird U.S. policy changes can be seen in other welfare states as well (Henderson, 1966).

For example, the shift from welfare state to market-based approaches to human welfare has accelerated the restructuring and downgrading of welfare programs in Western Europe and in Canada. Familiar patterns are emerging in all these nations. Welfare states are being replaced with a form of market-based "welfare." In the U.S., market-based approaches to welfare and other social and health services can be seen in a variety of programs and approaches. These include managed care and time-limit-driven programs, such as TANF. Lifetime limits with TANF are five years, with some states limiting TANF to just two to three years.

Paralleling TANF in welfare is the new child welfare law, the Adoption and Safe Families Act (ASFA). Time limits in ASFA require that a child be in a permanent home within 12-15 months once a child is in out of home care. This essentially limits the time parents and families can build their own capacities to be safe and stable resources for their children. The enactment of ASFA coincides with a national focus on accelerated adoption goals for the nation. Adoption rates are expected to double and incentives for expedited adoptions are now available to states.

Few would argue with the need for efficient use of resources and more intensive services for poor families (Golden, 1992; Gueron & Pauley, 1991; National Research Council, 1997). These service "improvements" may be desirable as long as child and family welfare is not compromised. For example, TANF's replacement of income guarantees with job seeking assistance is expected to help an estimated third of welfare families to become better off (Pavetti, 1998). It is expected that work-ready parents will access sound wage and benefit packages.

In fact, TANF has made it possible for some families with work-ready parents to be able to skid on and off of welfare with fewer impediments than in the past. This subset is able to sustain themselves with living wages and related supports, such as childcare and Medicaid. Moreover, good jobs and wages may serve, for some, as antidotes for family stresses and challenges (Briar, 1988).

In contrast to this subset of parents who get decent jobs are the two thirds of TANF parents who are expected to face barriers in finding decent paying jobs (Pavetti, 1998). Even if working full-time, they may lack health and related benefits. They may still be poor. In addition, underemployment, stemming from the lack of work commensurate with one's skills or from substandard wages, can exacerbate the hardships of these already vulnerable populations (Briar, 1988). For up to two thirds of TANF families and children, and the thousands like them in the future needing income supports, TANF may cause harm. Such harms stem from market failures in "lifting" vulnerable children and families out of poverty, the "clock" driven denial of income entitlements forcing families to place their children with relatives or to skid into abject conditions, and the TANF disregard for familial or parental barriers to employment. For example, Dora cannot work at this time because she is phobic and traumatized from untreated abuse. Moreover, two thirds of TANF recipients are children like Sharma; they are too young to work and thus cannot use "market mechanisms" to survive. Poverty has a long reach and can shape a life course for children like Sharma that is fraught with co-occurring and debilitating conditions (Duncan & Brooks-Gunn, 1997).

Risk Factors for Children

Child poverty affects 1 in 5 children (Sherman, 1997). Risks faced by poor versus non-poor children are striking. For example, poor children are more at risk for being reported for child abuse and neglect, more at risk for lead poisoning, more at risk for experiencing violent crime, more at risk for experiencing grade repetition and high school drop out behavior, more at risk for low birth weight, and more at risk for child mortality (Sherman, 1997). Poor children suffer from emotional and behavioral problems more frequently than do non-poor children. Poverty in early childhood affects brain and behavioral development.

Child poverty is related to entry into child welfare, juvenile justice, and adult poverty. In addition, child poverty and risk factors for abuse and neglect may trigger mental health problems and substance abuse in later years. In one study, it was found that up to 90% of women alcoholics had experienced childhood sexual abuse and 80% had experienced childhood physical abuse (Ladwig & Anderson, 1992). Among homeless (Herman, Susser, Struening, et al., 1997; Sosin, Piliavin, and Westerfelt, 1991) and prison populations, there are disproportionate numbers who have experienced childhood abuse and neglect (Piliavin, Sosin, Westerfelt, et al., 1993).

Childhood abuse and "household dysfunction" are related to co-occurring challenges of substance abuse and mental health problems (Keller & Gillis-Light, et al., 1997). Childhood trauma and household dysfunction are leading causes of death in adults. According to Felliti, Anda, Nordenberg, et al., (1998), such adverse childhood experiences may involve social, emotional, cognitive impairment; the adoption of health-risk behaviors (smoking, alcohol, drug abuse, overeating); disease (emphysema, cardiovascular disease, malignancy, STDs); disability; social problems (depression, suicide attempts, eating disorders); and early death.

Given the potentially compounding effects of poverty and its correlates, such as abuse and neglect, it is not surprising that at least one third of parents on welfare, primarily adult women like Dora, manifest multiple barriers to employment. Many of these barriers stem from the consequences of their childhood abuse, marginalization, related patterns of victimization, and coping responses in their youth and adulthood (Briar-Lawson, Lawson, et al., 1999; Taylor & Derr, 1998).

Long Term Welfare Families Facing Multiple Barriers to Employment

As is suggested by Dora's situation, traumas from both child and adulthood may affect parental capacities to seek and retain jobs (Derr & Hill, 2000; Taylor, 2000). Welfare, in fact, has served as a safety net for many parents who may be untreated victims of childhood and adult abuse and related trauma. Parents like Dora face barriers to employment because they need help in addressing domestic violence, depression, substance abuse, disabilities, and care giving stress (Taylor & Derr,1998)— not just getting a job. In fact, they require integrative supports and services that address the multiple barriers to their employability.

Time-limit exemptions are allowable for only up to twenty percent of persons receiving TANF. States are thus forced to keep the criteria for exemption from termination very narrow; otherwise, they would be retaining more than twenty percent of TANF recipients on welfare (Barkdull, Briar-Lawson, et al.,2000). States are also forced to sanction families prior to their time limit terminations. Otherwise the political fall-out from massive terminations might be too problematic for policy makers. Consequently, families like Sharma's may quietly disappear from the welfare rolls. Some of these parents and children face not only the loss of a grant but compounding risks.

Without rock bottom TANF income supports, parents are less able to be providers for their children. Homelessness and other coping, which may erode their capacity to parent, may result in referrals to child welfare systems for neglect or abuse. Parents may simultaneously appear in domestic violence, mental health, and substance abuse programs.

It is expected that child welfare referrals will increase due to TANF terminations (Courtney, 1997; Edelman, 1997; Digre, 1997; Shook, 1998). This is especially true as welfare comes to an end for families who face persistent barriers to work. Such predictions are not surprising. Attributes of long-term welfare families and those of child welfare families look strikingly similar, as Table 1 suggests (Taylor & Derr, 1998). In fact, the only thing that separates the two groups may be the presence of a welfare grant.

Skidding from TANF into child welfare should not have to be potentially catastrophic for these women and children. Yet, because of the time limits in both systems, these welfare- to-child welfare families now may face "double jeopardy." Time limits in both welfare and child welfare may result first in welfare grant loss and then loss of children to foster care and even adoption. Accelerating such losses in child welfare is the fact that without welfare, reunification from out-of-home care may be impeded (Wells, Guo & Sloan, 2000).

Table 1. Attributes of Long-Term Welfare and Child Welfare Families

Long -Term Welfare Families	Child Welfare Families
• Mental health challenges • Substance abuse • Domestic violence • Known to child welfare system in the recent past • Adults abused as children • Persistent, employment barriers	• Depression and related mental health issues • Addictions, substance abuse, self medicating behaviors • Domestic violence • Intergenerational abuse and neglect • Poverty, economic insecurity • Persistent employment barriers • Poverty is best predictor of out of home placement • Receipt of welfare may be a protective factor fostering child and family reunification rather than adoption
(Taylor & Derr, 1998)	(Wells, Guo, & Sloan, 2000)

Double Jeopardy or Second Chance Investment Families?

New expanded practice strategies are needed to turn these potentially "double jeopardy families" into "second chance investment families." As Table 2 suggests, TANF time limits of a maximum of 5 years and ASFA time limits of 1-½ years may create a "family dissolution time line" that is a de facto policy consequence of time-limited services. Time limits are like legal clocks that may have little relevance to human need. Time limits may be inadvertently creating "family dissolution clocks." This dissolution clock could be 1 and ½ years if the family is on welfare and child welfare at the same time. This is because ASFA time limits for permanency will take precedence over TANF time limits. The "family dissolution time line" could be 7 years if the family immediately skids from TANF termination into child welfare and hits the ASFA clock of 1 and ½ years. Families themselves may initiate a form of "family dissolution" in reaction to their termination from TANF. Parents may cope with the loss of welfare grants by placing their children with relatives and other guardians where they receive "child" only grants. This inventive reaction to terminations may do little to build the kind of family supports so critical to children's developmental needs for permanence and stability.

TANF "employment" time clocks and ASFA "permanency" time clocks may not coincide with parental "human recovery clocks" involving trauma, self medicating behaviors, mental health problems, and consequent coping problems. In effect, the "family dissolution time line" competes with some human recovery time lines. Thus, new pressures are placed on helping professionals to intensify counseling and related treatment services while integrating them with employment, income and related family supportive strategies.

**Table 2. Time lines Creating Double Jeopardy or Second Chance Investment
Families**

Welfare-TANF	Child Welfare-ASFA
Maximum lifetime receipt involving time limits of 5 years, with some states and counties limiting TANF to two and three years. States and counties also use sanctions to terminate families earlier than the time limits for nonparticipation in employment-related mandates.	Child must be in permanent home or have permanency plan in 12-15 months after out-of-home placement. This imposes time limits for services for parents of 12-15 months while child in is out-of-home care. Will these services for parents include income and employment supports along with protective parenting and related treatment services?

New Integrative Practices and Investments in Children, Families and Communities

It is critical that a series of innovations be developed to integrate social services with occupational, economic, and employment ladders for poor parents. As child welfare and related human service workers work to aid parents with domestic violence, mental health, and substance abuse challenges, they are in effect eliminating the barriers to employment. They need to simultaneously support economic and job development strategies. In fact, many helping professionals are better positioned to assist with welfare-to-work strategies than TANF workers. This is because TANF workers may lack human service and related counseling skills, as well as the integrative capacity to address social service needs along with employment and occupational supports. In Dora's case, her TANF worker did not have the skills or training to recognize phobias, traumas, and untreated victimization as work barriers. Dora was terminated through sanctions because she was seen as non-cooperative rather than impeded by trauma and phobias.

One hallmark of 21st-century human service providers who serve welfare and child welfare families will be an integrative service capacity involving the mobilization of social services with income, employment, and economic supports to foster permanence, safety, and child and family well-being. Such an integrative capacity is not new. There was a time in child welfare, prior to the separation of income maintenance from social services in the 1960s, when practice involved the integration of services with welfare and employment support. Some of the components of new integrative practices are discussed below and also depicted in the inventory in Table 3.

Table 3. Inventory of Selected Income, Related Supports, and Initiatives for Vulnerable Families

Income supports
- TANF and related benefits, e.g., food stamps, Medicaid
- SSI for disabilities
- Child Support
- Child care supplements, vouchers
- Earned Income Tax Credits (EITC). Every school could be helping all low-income working parents qualify. It could increase income by several thousand dollars each year
- Individual development accounts (IDAs) for every child and adult-matching and maximizing of savings
- Creating campaigns for care giver allowances or demogrants; more effective in human and fiscal terms than foster care, adoption subsidies, and adoption disruption

Income alternatives
- Time dollar barter programs

Employment and occupational ladders
- Public sector jobs created by TANF surpluses for parents and youth
- Stipends for Title I parents, creating occupational ladders into full-time jobs
- Creating internships and occupational ladders for individuals who are in recovery, moving out of help-seeking roles to help giving capacity; serving as paraprofessionals

Microenterprises, Job creation
- School stores run by youth selling their microenterprises, receiving contracts that otherwise would go to multinational corporations
- Microloan funds for microcredit (credit collateral can be other people) to start microenterprises.
- Sponsorship of former clients and low income parents to receive training to be child care providers, creating new child care options and resources for moving them from welfare to work
- Sponsorship of parents to run school and community family resource centers using federal funds

Job seeking supports
- Providing job clubs, job search workshops
- Promoting job placement

Community Development Opportunities
- Housing and Urban Development and other supports for community development, housing development.
- Community Development Block grants for low income communities for community development

Job creation community campaigns
- Creating campaigns for full employment with living wages
- Joining forces with labor and other groups on wage increases, more small business and microloan funds
- Creating new norms and rights for shorter work weeks, use of overtime to increase jobs, fostering of job sharing to increase jobs

Educational ladders
- Ensuring that individuals have choices between GED completion (and test taking) or community college enrollment in lieu of GED completion
- Providing youth in the middle school years with "work-learn-serve" options and the promise of college if they complete high school
- Creating educational plans that reinforce job and career options
- Providing information on loans, special stipends for school
- Local colleges and universities waive application fees and provide enrollment for increasing numbers of the poorest of the poor from the community
- Saving seats in college classrooms for indigenous leaders of local communities

Families as Investments

There is a need for neighborhood-community-based economic and human investments that can be built on a new relationship between families—not as drains on the resources—but as untapped investment sites. For example, some parents, like Dora, can be offered intensive services along with roles as front-line service providers for others in similar situations (Briar-Lawson, 1998). In some cases, parents who receive treatment and who are in recovery may be prime candidates for helping others. They can help to fill many of the service gaps that harmed them. Such roles may involve the building of indigenous neighborhood supports.

In some cases, parents can simultaneously be "interning" in jobs and roles that help them in their recovery as they receive and find employability on occupational ladders as human service and support workers. Such roles may help to address growing prevention gaps. In addition, parents in recovery can reach out to one another building neighborhood Narcotics Anonymous and Alcoholic Anonymous groups. Neighborhood support groups addressing domestic violence, children's safety, and drug problems can be mobilized. Teaming with helping professionals, some of these "hard to employ" parents may become major resources in the helping fields. If Dora were in a neighborhood with Time-Dollar or other barter exchanges, she might be able to access services to meet needs while donating her own services in return (Cahn & Rowe, 1992).

Paradoxically, the growing need to build neighborhoods and communities, to lift all families out of poverty, and to reduce risk factors associated with their impoverishment can be addressed by many families themselves in collaboration with professionals. The War on Poverty in the 1960s focused in part on the strengths of the poor. This led to the creation of "new careers." New Careers was a program that invested in occupational, educational, employment, and recovery supports subsidized through public sector employment. Such investments are warranted again. TANF surplus funds create a vast funding base to invest in these new careers for these "hard to employ" parents like Dora.

Neighborhood teams of child welfare and related health and human service workers can be capacity builders with parents recruited for work in Parent's Anonymous, as case aides, and family advocates in 24-hour care systems in communities and neighborhoods. Examples abound of communities in which the poor are given occupational ladders to address community needs, creating effective synergy between indigenous and professional service delivery systems (Grace Hill Settlement House, 1995).

Some of the roles leading to occupational ladders include:

- Outreach workers for parents who are pregnant and need related supports

- Parent aides providing respite for exhausted parents or for parents in relapse

- Homemakers and home aides, providing simple cleaning, cooking, and related household functions

- Child care

- Assisting parents in following through with their health and related services and supports

- Transportation aides helping children, youth, and families who need assistance getting to services, court

- Social service aides
- Foster care aides, helping foster parents with respite

- Teacher Aides, Absenteeism outreach workers

- Leaders of neighborhood information and referral systems

- Leaders of family and neighborhood support centers

- Tutors

- Safety workers—addressing drug dealing, child abuse and neglect, domestic violence

- Neighborhood policing

- Promoting barter systems

These roles need to be embedded in educational and occupational ladders in which beginning positions offer opportunities to move into higher levels of jobs and to acquire educational supports commensurate with advancement (Gittel & Coving, 1993). Integrated into these roles and jobs may be NA or AA groups, or related support groups for persons in recovery from domestic violence, or struggling with depression or trauma.

Similar supports are needed for children and youth. For example, older youth might receive stipends to help younger ones with homework, absenteeism in school, and even assist with homework clubs. If warranted, these older youth may simultaneously be in drug treatment programs. A work-recover-learn-serve foundation for such youth must lead to advancement in school, in work and service roles, and in recovery.

Successful entrepreneurial work can also be fostered. After school projects could include micro enterprises and school stores run by the youth. In one inner city school, children clear over $40,000 a year in earnings from their school store, which features their micro enterprises (The Children's Aid Society, 1993).

Drop out rates as high as 50% or more in high schools need to be reframed as missed investment opportunities. Wasted human talent and untapped investment opportunities compound pronounced needs. Instead of being dropouts or push outs, such youth might have received special supports to advance in careers in neighborhood and micro enterprise development or technology centers similar to those run by the 100 Black Men. Such youth could also work with local schools and universities in jointly sponsored family resource centers or in local child care centers. Instead, some of these youth who drop out of school become statistics as pregnant teens, juvenile delinquents and, in some cases, victims of premature death (Briar-Lawson, Lawson, et al., 1997).

Serving Dual or Multi System Parents and Children

Child welfare workers and related human service workers need to maximize income and in-kind entitlements for the families they serve. Families who are in the welfare and child welfare system and related services should be protected from TANF grant loss whenever possible.

At this time, few child welfare workers or welfare workers know who their shared families are. As referrals come into the child welfare intake system, the question must be asked about parental TANF status, including TANF sanctions and time limit termination of grants. Such information about TANF status can further alert child welfare workers to opportunities for intensive employment and economic-related supports (Warner-Kearney,2000; Ynacay-Nye,2000). Diversion units consisting of social workers and others providing intensive services and occupational supports may be needed in both TANF and child welfare to prevent families from losing children to foster care and even adoption.

SSI and Related Income Support Eligibility Screening

Screening parents like Dora for Supplemental Security Income (SSI) eligibility is an essential component of income generating activities. SSI would provide parents with a very modest income floor perhaps preventing dissolution of the family. Frightened TANF parents, like Dora, are often unable to disclose the level of depression, trauma, phobic reactions, and the like to practitioners who do not have relationship building and culturally responsive skills. Thus, SSI screening requires the most skilled and culturally congruent human service workers.

Along with SSI entitlements, many welfare and child welfare parents are not accessing the services to which they are entitled, such as food stamps, Medicaid, and child support payments. Child welfare and related human service workers need to be vigilant in their attempts to mobilize these resources.

Federal options exist for families who have been victims of domestic violence They can be exempted from TANF time limit terminations. Few states are implementing this option at this time (Barkdull, Briar-Lawson, et al., 2000). However, at the local level, human service workers can advocate for women and reference the federal provision that protects these domestic violence victims.

Parents who have been successful in obtaining full-time jobs may need help in accessing a wage supplement called an Earned Income Tax Credit (EITC). EITC is often critical to improved financial functioning. EITC is an underutilized entitlement that can bring the income floor up for a family several thousand dollars more each year. EITC should be a standard support mobilized for families through every school, health, and human service helping station in the community.

Stipends, IDAs, Micro Loans

Other untapped funds include Title I resources allocated to schools. High poverty schools are designated as Title I schools. They receive additional resources for enrichment programs along with free and reduced cost lunches. By mandate, one percent of Title I funds must be used for parent investments. However, parents are rarely mobilized to access these funds. They are thus unable to acquire stipends and accompanying roles that might create needed occupational, employment, and recovery ladders.

In some communities, banks, corporations, social service agencies, and others have mobilized Individual Development Accounts (IDAs) to create savings incentives for children and parents (Sherraden, 1991). Banks, social service agencies, and other community-based organizations often match these savings, dollar for dollar. Savings behaviors are rewarded as children and families are seen as good investments.

Micro loan funds are designated for the poor (Otero & Rhyne, 1994). Yet, micro lenders often have a difficult time giving grants to the most in need because the collaborative mechanisms to reach low income populations have not been fostered. In Salt Lake City, for example, the School of Social Work helped to connect the micro loan providers with TANF program leaders and hosted a workshop to help expand access to micro loan funds for TANF families.

Job-Seeking Technologies

Many job seeking tools, such as job clubs, might be adopted in all social service agencies. Job clubs have placement rates that are very high among welfare parents (Azrin, 1980). Using a buddy system, job clubs work at enhancing motivational supports and success in interviewing. Job clubs and related job search strategies need to be in the repertoire of the vast numbers of helping professionals who touch the lives of public sector families.

Human service providers also need to be at the vanguard in promoting job and wage reforms. Supports for full employment coalitions, shared jobs, improved job creation through reduced overtime, reduced week work opportunities all can be advanced by the often silent human service community.

Educational Partnerships

Partnerships among universities and inner city and poor rural communities also help to advantage poor and marginalized parents and youth (Briar-Lawson & Wiesen, 2000). For example, many high school drop outs struggle to acquire a GED. For those daunted by such work, the alternative pathway of enrolling in a community college (even with a high school or GED) may be an option. Few know about this option.

Other pathways into college can be created, such as subsidized or waived tuition for indigenous community leaders or former TANF parents. Seats can be saved in classrooms when there are insufficient numbers of regularly enrolled students. Community residents can take courses in grant writing, in interviewing skills, in addictions, and in family violence. Action research can also engage parents in relevant studies that help them document their needs and rights to improved and tailored services, economic, and housing supports (Lawson & Briar-Lawson, 2000). Such studies can then be used for community development projects and funds from Housing and Urban Development or Community Economic Development can be accessed.

Data-driven reforms involve new research and demonstration project partnerships among helping disciplines such as social work, public health, education, and nursing. Partnerships between universities and agencies can spawn innovations with pilots serving as "systems change" tools. For example, fieldwork agencies and students along with faculty can test new neighborhood service strategies by fostering incubators of 24-hour neighborhood service delivery models. New front-line practices need to be built in welfare and child welfare, which address these double jeopardy families. Staffed by social workers, these model units can demonstrate and test inventive new policies and practices that help to prevent the irreversible harms to families and children when welfare sanctions, terminations, and loss of children ensue.

All these potential family capacity building, economic, and employment supports require more innovative policy supports ensuring that social workers and related human service professionals incorporate them in their practice repertoire. It also requires that such helping professionals help design the 21st-century welfare state.

A 21st-Century Investment-Based Welfare State

The 21st century can be shaped by new kinds of thinking about families and their untapped capacities to be resources not only for their own children and other members but also for their communities and society as a whole. In fact, new thinking is required that calculates the costs of failure versus returns on investments

(Bruner,1993). For example, the benefits of aiding long-term welfare families with their complex challenges through integrative occupational, educational employment, and recovery strategies may far outweigh the costs associated with the preventable sequelae.

Currently, fifteen million disadvantaged children face barriers to adult citizenry. The human costs may be so vast that they are difficult to calculate. The fiscal costs are $130 billion per year in future lost earnings, health, educational gains (Sherman, 1997). The $130 billion could have been invested in strategic supports. Such supports might involve occupational, educational, economic, and recovery ladders discussed earlier.

Most notable work on early childhood interventions and cost savings has been done by an interdisciplinary team at the RAND Corporation (Karoly, et al., 1999). After reviewing credible data from nine early childhood programs, Karoly, et al., (1999) estimate the costs and savings to society. They show the benefits of cost-savings analysis and conclude that early childhood programs will save dollars.

While it may be impossible to turn all family supportive programs into relevant cost-savings-oriented studies, such evaluative capacity may need to be within the repertoire of practitioners and program leaders serving impoverished and vulnerable children and families. Social workers and other health and human service professionals need to ensure that social welfare programs have the evaluation characteristics needed to estimate cost effectiveness and cost savings. This requires that social workers and other human service professionals move beyond some of the natural abhorrence of monetizing outcomes. This will mean compromise as many of the most substantive human outcomes and societal social welfare impacts cannot be monetized. If social work educators and practitioners do not join forces in this work, it will be done by others, such as budget analysts, who may less able to do appropriate valuations of relevant outcomes and impacts.

It may also prove helpful to health and human service providers and especially social workers in calculating costs of failure and cost savings analyses by addressing unrecoverable costs, irreparable human damage, and jeopardy multipliers. For example, time limits in welfare and in child welfare can be studied as "jeopardy multipliers" for some families. Moreover, these phenomena need to be calculated in program outcome and fiscal cost studies. Thus, the loss of a grant may lead to homelessness, followed by charges of neglect against a family, which then may be followed by costly out-of-home care and then adoption.

Instead of multiplying jeopardy, it is possible to use data on irreparable costs (both human and fiscal) to argue for services and investments that essentially "front-load" systems. For example, as David Berns' chapter suggests, in counties like El Paso, Colorado, TANF funds and services are being used as the family preservation arm of the child welfare system. Workers are being trained to provide intensive services to divert families from skidding into the child welfare system. Elsewhere, the influx of new families in already beleaguered child welfare systems may create an adoption crisis. The $130 billion lost each year to the nation because of children like Sharma who are unable to have successful life courses might have been invested in prevention.

Solutions to some of these preventable problems also exist in such models as the Swedish Family Contact Program, in which stressed families are provided respite and mentor families (Hort & Olsson, 1997).) Other solutions include care giver grants, far less costly than foster care and adoption subsidies. The funds paid to foster parents could be paid to parents as "care giver grants" to enhance children's development and to prevent loss of children into foster care and adoption.

A return-on-investment framework must guide the new thinking that develops a 21st-century welfare state. Poor and vulnerable children and families can serve as sources of major 21st-century investments. Rather than being seen as drains on the economy, they can be reframed as vastly enriching investments. Without such investment, their contributions and indigenous knowledge, skills, and capacities are lost. Each human service practitioner can be part of this design and investment work in building and advancing integrative approaches to social services, income, and occupational supports. Each integrative intervention is a building block for a 21st-century investment-based welfare state.

References

Azrin, N. H. (1980). *Job counselor's manual: A behavioral approach to vocational counseling.* Austin, TX: Pro-Ed.

Barkdull, C., Briar-Lawson, K., Johnson-Berry, S., Kelley, N., and Abu-Bader, S. (2000, January). Criteria for exemption from welfare terminations: Implications for child welfare systems. Paper presented at the Society for Social Work and Research, Charleston, SC.

Berns, D. (1998). *Working papers on TANF, family preservation and poverty eradication.* Colorado Springs, CO: The El Paso County Department of Human Services.

Briar, K. (1988). *Social work with unemployed.* Silver Springs, MD: National Association of Social Workers.

Briar-Lawson, K. (1998). Capacity–building for family centered services and supports. *Social Work, 43,*539-550.

Briar-Lawson, K., Lawson, H., Collier, C., and Joseph, A.(1997). School-linked comprehensive services: Promising beginnings, lessons learned, and future challenges. *Social Work in Education, 19,* 136-148.

Briar-Lawson, K., Lawson, H., Derezotes, D., Hoffman, T., Petersen, N., Harris, N., and Sallee, A. (1999, January). *Serving Families with Substance Abuse, Mental Health, Domestic Violence, and Employment Challenges.* Paper presented at the Society for Social Work and Research Conference, Austin, TX.

Briar-Lawson, K. and Wiesen, M. (1999, June). *Model Partnerships between child welfare and universities.* Paper presented at the Partnership Symposium, Washington D.C.: U.S. Children's Bureau.

Bruner, C. (1993). *Toward outcome-based accountability: Readings on constructing cost-of-failure/return on investment analysis of prevention initiatives.* Des Moines: Child and Family Center.

The Children's Aid Society. (1993). *Building a community school.* New York: Author.

Cahn, E. and Rowe, J. (1998). *Time dollars: The new currency that enables Americans to turn their hidden resource time into personal security and community renewal.* Chicago, IL: Family Resource Coalition.

Cook, J., Vener, S., and Brown, L. (1998). *Are states improving the lives of poor families.* Boston: Tufts University, Center on Hunger and Poverty.

Courtney, M. E. (1995). The foster care crisis and welfare reform. *Public Welfare 53,*(3), 27-33.

Derr, M. and Hill, H. (2000, January). *How family violence influences employment and mental health: Comparing long-term welfare recipients based on experiences with adult and child abuse.* Paper presented at the Society for Social Work and Research Conference, Charleston, SC.

Digre, P. (1997). *Impact of proposed federal welfare changes on child protection: Executive summary.* Los Angeles, CA.: Department of Children's Services.

Dominelli, L. (1999). Neo-liberalism, social exclusion and welfare clients in a global economy. *International Journal of Social Welfare 8*(1), 14-22.

Duncan, G. and Brooks-Gunn, J. (1997). (Eds.). *Consequences of growing up poor.* New York: Russell Sage.

Edelman, P. (1997). The worst thing Bill Clinton has done. *The Atlantic Monthly,* March, 43-58.

Fellitti, V., Anda, R., Nordenberg, D., Williamson, D., Spitz, A., Edwards, V., Koss, M., and Marks, J. (1998). Relationship of childhood abuse and household dysfunction to many of the leading causes of death in adults. *American Journal of Preventive Medicine, 14,* 245-258.

Gittell, M. and Covington, S. (1993). *Higher education in JOBS: An option or opportunity.* New York: City University of New York, Howard Samuels State Management and Policy Center.

Glennerster, H. (1999). Which welfare states are most likely to survive? *International Journal of Social Welfare 8*(1), 2-13.

Golden, O. (1992). *Poor children and welfare reform.* Westport, CT: Auburn House.

Grace Hill Settlement House. (1995). *M.O.R.E, Member organized resource exchange.* St Louis: Author.

Gueron, J. and Pauley, E. (1991). *From welfare to work.* New York: Russell Sage.

Henderson, H. (1996). *Building a win-win world: Life beyond global economic warfare.* San Francisco: Berrett-Koehler.

Herman, D., Susser, E., Struening, E., and Link, B. (1997). Adverse childhood experiences: Are they risk factors for adult homelessness? *American Journal of Public Health, 87,* 249-255.

Hort, S. and Olsson, E. (1997). Sweden: towards a deresidualization of Swedish child welfare policy and practice? In N. Gilbert (Ed.). *Combating Child Abuse: International Perspectives and Trends* (pp. 105 – 124). New York & Oxford: Oxford University Press.

Ladwig, G. and Andersen, G. (1992). Substance Abuse in Women: Relationship between chemical dependency of women and reports of physical and/or sexual abuse. In C. M. Sampelle (Ed). *Violence against women: Nursing, research, education and practice issues* (pp. 167-180). New York: Hemisphere Publishing Company.

Lawson, H. and Briar-Lawson, K. (2000, January). *Addressing TANF and child welfare challenges using action research methodologies: Selected findings and a new model for research and research utilization.* Symposium Presentation, Society for Social Work and Research, Charleston, SC.

Karoly, L., Greenwood, P., Everingham, S., Hoube, J., Kilburn, M., Rydell, C., Sanders, M., and Chiesa, J. (1999). *Investing in our children.* Santa Monica: RAND.

Kessler, R., Gillis-Light, J., Magee, W., Kendeler, K., and Eaves, L. (1997). Childhood adversity and adult psychopathology. In I. Gotlib & B. Wheaton (Eds.). *Stress and adversity over the life course: Trajectories and turning points* (pp. 29-49). New York & Cambridge: Cambridge University Press.

National Center for Children in Poverty. (1998). Child poverty in many states takes a turn for the worse. http://cpmcnet.columbia.edu/dept//nccp/news/sufa98/1sufa98.html.

National Research Council. (1997). *New findings on welfare and children's development.* Washington D.C. National Academy Press.

Pavetti, D. (1998, November). Colloquium on Welfare Research, Salt Lake City, UT: Graduate School of Social Work, Institute for Social Research.

Piliavin, L., Sosin, M., Westerfelt, A., and Matsueda, R. (1993). The duration of homeless careers: an exploratory study. *Social Service Review, 67,* 576-598.

Sherman, A. (1997). *The cost of poverty in America*. Washington DC: Children's
Defense Fund.

Sherraden, M. (1991). *Assets and the poor: A new American welfare policy*. Amonk,
NY: Sharpe.

Shook, K. (1998). Assessing the consequences of welfare reform for child welfare,
Poverty Research News, *2*(1), 1-7.

Sosin, M. R., Piliavin, L., and Westerfelt H. (1991). Toward a longitudinal analysis
of homelessness. *Journal of Social Issues*, *46*,157-174.

Taylor, M. J. (2000, January). *Involvement of long-term welfare recipients in the
child welfare system*. Paper presented at the Society for Social Work and
Research, Charleston, SC.

Taylor, M. J. and Derr, M. (1998). *Understanding families with multiple barriers
to self-sufficiency*. Salt Lake City, UT: Graduate School of Social Work, Social
Research Institute.

Otero, M. and Rhyne, E. (1994). (Eds.). *The new world of microenterprise finance*.
West Hartford, CT: Kumarian Press.

Vehelda, B. and Haverman, J. (1999). Untouched by reform, *The Washington Post
National Weekly Edition*, January 11.

Warner-Kearney, D. (2000). *Overview of Pilot*. Salt Lake City, UT: Utah Division
of Children and Family Services.

Wells, K.,Guo, S., and Sloan, J. (2000, January). *Impact of welfare reform on the
child welfare system*. Paper presented at the Society for Social Work and
Research, Charleston, SC.

Ynacay-Nye, R. (2000). *Child welfare training and planning priorities*. Carson
City, NV: Division of Children and Family Services.

Chapter 3

Addressing Poverty Issues in Child Welfare: Effective Use of TANF as a Prevention Resource

David A. Berns

Introduction

Child Welfare professionals often emphasize the risk to families facing a reduction or elimination of their welfare benefits. Staff may fear that children will be placed into foster care because families have lost economic supports. These fears, while reasonable and possibly justified, do little to improve conditions for the families involved. They may even lead to self-fulfilling prophecies. As an example, a worker investigating an allegation of neglect by a homeless parent may assume that there are no economic supports through the welfare system to help the family. Based on this assumption, whether true or not, the worker may proceed with placement as the only known solution. Indeed, some states or localities may have designed their new welfare systems in a punitive manner with the primary goal of eliminating people from public assistance. In those instances, the child welfare worker may have few choices in providing for the economic needs required to keep the family together.

This chapter explores the opportunities and potentials for uniting child welfare and public assistance. It suggests that Temporary Assistance to Needy Families (TANF) and other public assistance programs should be reengineered to become the primary prevention programs for child welfare (Berns & Drake, 1999). It also shows how child welfare can reframe its mission and redefine itself as an anti- poverty program.

These changes in perception and practice are possible by developing a common set of guiding principles that govern both child welfare and public assistance programs. This chapter will be useful to those wanting to change the system to be more responsive to the needs of children and families in their communities.

The processes suggested in this chapter have been successfully implemented in El Paso County, Colorado, with very favorable results.

Outcomes

On July 1, 1997, El Paso County, Colorado (Colorado Springs area) welfare reform blended child welfare and public assistance into a unified system. Since that time, and based on information through December 31, 1999, the following outcomes should be noted:

Foster Care

- There has been a 7.2% decline in the number of children in family foster care from 580 on July 1, 1997, to 538 on December 31, 1999.

Residential Treatment

- The number of youth in high cost residential treatment facilities declined from 145 to 91 during the same period.

TANF

- The number of employable adults on the Temporary Assistance to Needy Families (TANF) has declined from 2388 to 1222. This is even more impressive when considering that welfare reform actually started under a federal waiver and that the decline from that period is from about 4600 cases to 1222. This is a 73.4% decline from the peak number of cases.

Sanctions

- The decline in welfare cases should also be considered in light of the fact that cases are infrequently closed due to sanctions. In fact, sanctions (the process of closing a case for failure to comply with rules or requirements) are viewed as a mutual failure of the agency and the client. A process including home calls and renegotiations of expectations is used to remove sanctions before or shortly after they are implemented.

Childcare

- Childcare payments have quadrupled from a $3M per year program in 1997 to projected over $12M in the year 2000. This has included a considerable emphasis on improving quality, access and payment levels to providers.

Adoptions

- Special needs adoptions have more than quadrupled from 49 in 1996 to 230 in 1998 and 216 in 1999. Much of this growth is attributable to the expansion of community partnerships made possible through TANF, medicaid, and other programs traditionally outside of the child welfare system.

CPS Intake

- The county has experienced a 15% decline in families taken to court through the Children's Protective Services Intake system, and yet 20% more families are receiving in-home, family-based services. In other words, resources and processes have been changed to serve more families and to protect more children without court involvement.

Employment

- Almost 90% of the employers working with the county's primary employment contractor (Goodwill Industries) provide benefits, including health benefits for their employees. This is crucial because welfare recipients who obtain jobs with such benefits are more likely to retain their jobs, to advance financially, and are not nearly as likely to return to welfare in the event of an economic downturn.

Fund Blending

- Using a blending of TANF and child welfare funds, comprehensive teen parent services have been developed. A variety of local agencies have united around a common mission to keep teen parents in school while providing for the economic and safety needs of the children. The flexibility provided under TANF has allowed these programs to grow and develop in a seamless manner.

Family Supports

- Comprehensive services to grandparents raising their grandchildren have been developed using TANF to fund both the staff and the family-based supports. More than 500 families are served per month, resulting in a significant decline in the need for more intrusive child welfare services.

Teenagers

- Both the child welfare system and economic support programs serve many teenagers transitioning to adulthood. By combining resources and expertise, a comprehensive system of services supports their transition. The strengths of the welfare system in employment, training, and economic support combine with the expertise and relationships in Child Welfare's Independent Living Programs, resulting in expanded opportunities for both populations.

All of the above were accomplished while maintaining or improving safety indicators in the child welfare system, and while implementing what the National Center for Children in Poverty has cited as "the most creative, sophisticated and child friendly implementation of welfare reform that we have seen around the country" (As quoted in the Gazette Telegraph Newspaper dated July 4, 1999). Furthermore, this was accomplished while living within the constraints of the TANF block grant and a cap on child welfare expenditures.

Guiding Principles

Several tools and processes were developed to aid in the implementation of policies and programs that would result in the types of outcomes noted above. The most important of these are the guiding principles. El Paso County Department of Human Services selected guiding principles found in Figure 1 for programs such as TANF, Children's Protective Services, out- of-home care, adoptions, employment, or child care.

Asking questions such as those found in Table 1 expands understanding of how the principles can guide operations. Answers have resulted in massive changes in virtually all aspects of the system. Although not always used in a structured or formal process, questions are asked in relation to every program area to determine how well they measure up to the guiding principles.

Figure 1. Guiding Principles

Vision: To eliminate poverty and family violence in El Paso County.

Mission: To strengthen families, assure safety, promote self-sufficiency, eliminate poverty, and improve the quality of life in our community.

Guiding Principles:

System of care must:

- be family-driven
- protect the rights of families
- allow smooth transitions between programs
- build community capacity to serve families
- emphasize prevention and early intervention
- be effectively integrated and coordinated across systems

Services must:

- be culturally respectful
- be evaluated for outcomes continually
- be delivered by competent staff
- be accessible, accountable, and comprehensive
- be individualized to meet the needs of families
- be strength-based and delivered in the least intrusive manner

Table 1. Principles of Public Human Services Workbook and Assessment Tool

I. The system of care must be family driven and include extensive family leadership.

    A. How are the views and priorities of families included in this program currently? Describe family roles in oversight and administration, policy department, program development, case planning, and collaborative delivery of services.

    B. How would consumers view their roles in these areas? If the agency's views of consumer participation is different from the views of the consumers, how would you resolve the differences?

    C. What barriers do you see to expanding family leadership and involvement?

    D. What other strategies or opportunities could be used to expand family involvement in this program?

II System of care must protect the rights of families.

    A. Why do your customers come to your agency? Do they have a choice in providers?

    B. What rights do your consumers have to choose the level, type or quality of services which you provide?

    C. If a customer is not satisfied with the level, type, quality or other aspect of your service, how would you know?

    D. What laws or policies restrict or limit our ability to deliver services in a manner or level desired by your customers?

    E. What laws or policies mandate the level or quality of your services? What avenues are available to require your compliance?

    F. What avenues are available to consumers who feel their rights have been violated?

    G. How are complaints addressed? To what extent are consumers satisfied that their concerns are appropriately handled?

    H. What other strategies could you use to increase your accountability to your customers?

III Smooth and seamless transition between programs must accompany families as they develop.

    A. What other systems served your customers before they reached your program?

    B. What plans or strategies were used to coordinate your activities with those of previous systems?

    C. When families leave your services or programs, who will continue to see them or serve them?

    D. What strategies do you use to plan with other programs and services that serve your customers before or after your involvement?

    E. What new strategies could you use to provide for a smoother or seamless transition into your programs?

    F.   What new strategies could you use to provide for a smoother or more seamless transition when customers enter your services, programs or agencies?

IV. The community must build capacity to serve families.

    A.   Describe gaps in quantity, quality or access to the services provided through this program.

    B.   List the key agencies and individuals who have a stake in assuring sufficient capacity.

    C.   Describe what the key stakeholders are currently doing to assure adequate capacity.

    D.   Describe new or innovative approaches to expanding capacity not currently being used.

    E.   Identify new strategies that may expand capacity to meet the level of need.

    F.   Explore how the current resources (funding, staff, community support, etc.) could be used in a way to leverage additional capacity.

    G.   Describe additional advocacy issues that could be used to increase resources including staffing to a level that meets the customer's needs.

V. The system of care must emphasize prevention and early intervention.

    A.   What could have been done to prevent the need for this service?

    B.   What services could have been provided earlier that would have reduced the severity of the problem?

    C.   How may this service help to prevent even more serious problems in the future?

    D.   What partnerships will help establish a better prevention network? If the community knew about the problems you are dealing with, who would they say is in the best position to prevent them? How are you working with those entities?

    E.   As the community looks at the whole range of social issues, what role would they say you play in preventing problems in other systems? How well are you living up to those expectations?

    F.   What strategies can you encourage to help the community to deal with issues in a fashion that avoids the need for your service?

    G.   What strategies can you offer to make your program more effective in preventing problems in other systems?

VI. Systems and programs must be effectively integrated and coordinated.

    A.   What other programs or agencies are often involved with this same target population?

    B.   Describe current linkages between key programs.

    C.   Describe how customers may view the integration of programs that they receive.

    D.   Describe how staff interacts with staff from other programs.

    E.   Describe any mechanisms that you currently use to pool or blend funding and other resources with other agencies serving common customers.

F. Explore additional linkages that may help improve services and outcomes for families, i.e., collocation of staff, blended funding, computer linkages, etc.

VII. All services must be culturally respectful.

A. Who do you serve?
B. Are your services located in the areas where your customers live?
C. What actions are taken to assure that staff looks like the customer population?
D. How do you use the indigenous leaders and supports in your customer's communities?
E. Has your staff participated in diversity training? If so, how do you know if they practice as trained?
F. Have you conducted an analysis to identify any continuing issues of institutional bias in your organization?
G. How would your customers rate the cultural competence of your agency? Of individual staff:
H. What systemic changes beyond training can you take to improve the cultural competence of your agency and of each staff member?

VIII.   Outcomes of services must be evaluated continually.

A. How do you know if the current program is successful? If the current program were eliminated, what would happen?
B. What is your criteria for success? Would your customers use the same criteria? If not, how would they know if your program is successful?
C. How would your community partners know if you were successful? How do they evaluate your success or failure?
D. Assess if your evaluations measure activities rather than outcomes. Are you looking at outcomes for individuals, families, community and agency?
E. What other ways can outcomes be evaluated from the customer's and community's perspective?
F. Explain how your improved assessment of outcomes may be used to change and improve your services.

IX. All services must be delivered by competent staff.

A. What criteria do you use to determine if your staff is competent?
B. Discuss the adequacy of the criteria and qualifications for new staff and for promotions.
C. What training and educational opportunities are provided to increase the competency of staff?
D. What aspect of your staff's competence would your customers say are adequate or good? What aspects would they say are deficient?
E. What systems do you use to gain input from consumers and community partners regarding staff performance?
F. What other strategies can you use to bolster your assessment of staff?

G. What other strategies can you use to increase the competence of staff?

X. Services must be accessible, accountable, and comprehensive.

    A. Describe how your customers would describe the ease of accessing this service.
    B. Who reviews the quality of the service? How is this done?
    C. Is the service included in a comprehensive plan that addresses the consumer's top priorities?
    D. What changes would make it easier for consumers to use the service?
    E. How could quality review be improved? Can consumer ratings be expanded and better used?
    F. Are there other services and strategies that need to be added or coordinated to improve the effectiveness of this program?

XI. Services must meet the individualized needs of families.

    A. How rigid or defined is the current program or service? Is access to the service defined by rigid eligibility criteria?
    B. What changes will a potential recipient need to make to adapt to the program guidelines?
    C. How well would your customers say your services meet their needs and priorities?
    D. Can eligibility be expanded based on needs for the service?
    E. What strategies would make the program more flexible? How can services be developed more fully around the accessed needs and desires of the consumer?

XII. Services must be strength based and delivered in the least intrusive manner possible.

    A. How are the strengths of individuals, families and the community assessed currently? Are assessments primarily based on deficits and problems?
    B. What techniques are used to design programs or services around strengths?
    C. To what extent do services reflect the wants and desires of the recipients?
    D. How would participants rate the degree of intrusion of disruption in their lives needed to participate in the services?
    E. What additional strategies could be used to assess strengths?
    F. What strategies could be used to decrease intrusion or disruption?

Workbook written and developed by David Berns, Veronica Spaulding, and Bonnie Abernathy.

El Paso County 7 "Ps"

El Paso County implemented more than 70 distinct initiatives to address one or more of the described outcomes. Each initiative proceeded individually but was always guided by a common vision and by the entire set of principles. This approach still leaves the task of massive systems' reform overwhelming and seemingly impossible.

The county needed a framework illustrating how all of the initiatives fit into an overall system. The El Paso County 7 "Ps" provided a visible and easily understood model that demonstrated the integration of child welfare and welfare reform.

The 7 "Ps" as illustrated in Table 2 begins with the premise that the primary mission of the department is one of "protection." This protection includes safety for children and adults, issues of domestic violence, protection of the community from juvenile delinquency, and protection of the economic well being for the most vulnerable in the community.

Table 2. The Seven "P's" Protection System

Prevention	Preservation	Placement	Permanency
TANF Family Support MEDICAID Maternal & Infant Support Services Food Stamps	Forensic Interviewing Risk Assessment	Structured Risk Assessments Solution-Based Model	Foster Care Supportive Services Reunification Services
School Attendance Projects	Community Protection System	Standardized Payments to Foster Homes	Expedited Permanency Planning
Flexible Payments	Wrap Around	Managed Care for Behavioral Health	Adoptive Placement
Minor Parent Services Grandparent Support	Kinship	Flexibility in Service & Placement Options	Post Adoption Service
Day Care Child Support	Intensive Family Preservation Services	Expanded Role of Private Agencies	Funded Guardianships
Housing Assistance Employment Services Child Death Review Panels	Strength-Based Assessments	Coordinated Medical Care for Child & Family	
Transportation	Life Skills Training Economic Assistance Day Treatment		
Partnerships Schools - Consumers - Substance Abuse Treatment - Sexual Abuse Services - Respite Care - Domestic Violence Intervention - Extended Family - Mental Health			

Proficiency
Training - Automation - Staffing
Performance Monitoring/Outcome Bases - Legal Representation
Confidentiality/Public Right to Know - Cultural Competence - Quality Enhancement

The department carries out its mission of protection through an array of services, including Prevention, Preservation, Placement, and Permanency. These constitute the next 4 "Ps" in the model. Because the tasks are too important and too complex for any one agency, strategies must be done in "Partnerships" with families, other agencies, and the entire community. Finally, the entire system is undergirded through approaches that assure Proficiency. Strategies that include cultural diversity, outcome measurement, training, and enhanced automation provide the tools necessary to make the rest of the initiatives effective.

Everyone in the agency is directly involved in at least one of the systems' changes, but no one plays a leadership role in all of them. Each initiative has champions and workers that design and implement their portion in accordance with the guiding principles. Everyone can readily see where they and their priorities fit into the overall structure of the agency.

Each of the 7 "Ps" and indeed most of the individual initiatives could be the topic of an entire paper. Much has been written and published related to El Paso County's strategies for adoptions, kinship care, child care, teen parent services, community-based protective services systems, and child welfare managed care.

Prevention best exemplifies unification of child welfare and assistance payments programs in El Paso County. Changes in this area required a reframing of traditional views and approaches. In fact, child welfare staff now see their services as an anti-poverty program. Assistance payments workers now understand their role as the primary prevention strategy for child welfare.

Using Welfare Reform Programs for Prevention in Child Welfare

Over the years as a child welfare administrator, the author lamented that there was very little money devoted to prevention. All of the funds seemed to go to foster care, institutional placements, and other services after a child had been abused or neglected.

As we dreamed about the possibility of providing prevention services, we asked what services would help to prevent child abuse or neglect. The answers were always the same. We need to address poverty, employment, housing, nutrition, domestic violence, substance abuse, education, and training. Resources need to be devoted to child care, transportation, and medical care. When we looked at this list of elements, we noted that almost all of them were fundable under TANF, Medicaid, food stamps, or other programs handled by assistance payments staff.

We also noted that most of the families served in our child welfare systems have very low incomes. The U.S. Department of Health and Human Services confirmed this connection in the National Incidence Study of Child Abuse and Neglect. In that report, it was noted that families with incomes of $15,000 or less per year were more than 22 times more likely to be in the child welfare systems as families with incomes of $30,000 per year or more. We postulated that raising people out of poverty would go a long way toward reducing their need for and involvement with child welfare services.

As noted in an article in the March 1999 issue of the *Journal of Policy and Practice*, Barbara Drake, Deputy Director in El Paso County, and the author talked to child welfare staff in the county. All confirmed that poverty was a huge issue. Unfortunately, they were so overwhelmed with concerns about safety and permanence, they did not have the time or the opportunity to routinely address employment, child support, or other strategies that could help alleviate poverty.

At the same time, workers expressed concern that counseling, therapy, parenting skills, and drug treatment were not sufficient by themselves to keep children safe. Often, parents did not complete their treatment because of problems with transportation, childcare, housing, or other poverty-related issues.

It was also noted that even middle-income families can face financial crises when they become involved with child welfare. As an example, if a stepfather sexually abuses his stepdaughter, he may be removed from the home. If he is the major source of income for the family, mother and daughter are left without that income. The child may feel that she is responsible for their financial plight and may feel pressure to recant. Unless we adequately address the financial needs of this family, they may be prematurely and inappropriately reunited with the perpetrator.

When TANF was signed into law in 1996, only a few of us predicted the massive drop in caseloads and federal expenditures. Indeed, most of the discussion focused on the crisis that would result from inadequate funding for TANF. Many predicted that children would migrate to the child welfare system because TANF funds would no longer meet family needs. Nationally and statistically, these predictions have not materialized—at least not yet. In fact, not only have TANF caseloads dropped but, in some instances, so have child welfare caseloads.

We know, however, that our communities and families still have many needs. The low-paying jobs many former recipients obtained may provide more money than their TANF payment but still not be sufficient to move them out of poverty. More needs to be done to support their self-sufficiency goals and to develop long-term skills that move them into better-paying jobs.

In Colorado, most of the flexibility granted to states under federal welfare reform was, in turn, granted to counties. Each county was given a block grant of federal and state TANF funds. Counties must also pay their portions of the Maintenance-of-Effort (MOE) funds. In other words, counties must spend their money first before they can gain access to state and federal TANF funds. Any expenditure above the county's share is 100 percent state and federal funds.

In El Paso County, the TANF budget is approximately $20 million, of which about $3.6 million is county money. Due to declining caseloads, about $10 million is spent on direct TANF payments. This means that about $10 million of federal money will go unspent unless an appropriate use for it is found. The money can either be left on reserve with the hope that it will remain available for bad times or be invested in families and the community. The El Paso Board of County Commissioners elected to invest the money in families now.

It was not easy to change the frame of reference to see how prevention could be provided by TANF staff or by anyone outside of the child welfare system. Child Welfare administrators had to accept the following points:

- Just because prevention is not being done within the child welfare system does not mean that it is not being done at all.

- Just because prevention is not being done sufficiently or adequately does not mean that child welfare staff should increase, expand, or add prevention activities into their programs. Someone else may be able to do prevention much better outside the child welfare system.

- Every program or service, regardless of how intensive or how late in the process, is still a prevention program for some other program. Substance abuse treatment for chronic abusers is still a prevention service for child welfare, which in turn is a prevention program for juvenile delinquency services. Of course, juvenile delinquency services should prevent entry into adult corrections. The prison and parole system should prevent crime and promote the rehabilitation of the inmates.

Those people designing a new service system under welfare reform struggled to keep these points in mind. Not everyone readily accepted these premises. It was hard for child welfare to accept that prevention would be someone else's responsibility. Even though child welfare workers seldom had the time to concentrate on prevention, they often felt responsible and guilty for the deficit. Guilt is a hard emotion to give up.

In another portion of our office, TANF staff had been hired as eligibility technicians. They gathered information, matched it against eligibility criteria, and determined what, if any benefits the client would receive. They found it difficult to toss out years of training and accept a new role facilitating and promoting a client's progress toward economic self-sufficiency. Workers hesitated in throwing out the rule book and authorizing services or assistance without a detailed eligibility rule book.

Unifying the system began by asking several task forces to identify what needed to be included in welfare reform. Employers, consumers, childcare advocates, faith-based organizations, private agencies, child welfare professionals, schools, and other community members described what they saw as important. Focus groups with recipients asked what the agency had done in the past that hurt and what was done that helped. The agency pledged to stop doing things that hurt and to do more of what helps. Front-line staff took the community's vision and determined how it could be implemented. Management trusted staff's professional experience and wisdom to put the ideas into a legal, practical, efficient, and effective system. With the flexibility granted under federal and state law for TANF, never before opportunities were identified, reviewed against the guiding principles, and implemented. Most of the structured changes were developed and implemented within a couple of months of passage of Colorado's welfare reform legislation.

The structure of welfare reform fell primarily into three categories. First, the community wanted processes that assured that work paid. The system needed to provide incentives so that anyone with a job was better off financially and psychologically than they would have been without a job. Second, the community recognized the need to enhance support financially, psychologically, and physically from both parents. Programs were designed around ways to increase all of these aspects of support from non-custodial parents whenever possible and appropriate and in the most strength-based and supportive manner possible. Third, the stakeholders wanted to expand supports for families so that they could reach their own dreams and be successful in their own manner toward self-sufficiency.

The El Paso County Board of Commissioners made these plans possible when they defined the mission of welfare reform. They publicly acknowledged that their goal was not to eliminate welfare but rather to work with the community to eliminate poverty. They knew that welfare roles would plummet if clients escaped the bonds of poverty. Obviously, if clients were no longer poor, they would no longer need to receive TANF. The commissioners challenged the community to identify any punitive, repressive, or unhelpful elements in the plan and assured that they would be eliminated or modified to the maximum extent within their discretion. Although the initial plan was very well received, a few suggestions were received and changes were made accordingly.

Staff recommended several strategies to make sure that employment would be rewarded. Some of these strategies included expanded income disregards so that clients could keep more of their earnings without drastically reducing their welfare check. They also suggested a $500 bonus once a client obtained a job sufficient to cancel their grant. Diversion programs allowed applicants to obtain services immediately, even before eligibility was determined. This allowed applicants to receive the support they needed to obtain or retain employment without ever officially receiving TANF and without using any of their lifetime time limits for receipt of TANF benefits. Job descriptions and caseloads were modified to allow more time and attention to the individual needs of consumers. Specialized contractual services were created to assist individuals with multiple challenges to receive the unique supports they needed. Processes were created to allow recipients to be the principal creators of their own plans. Ownership of the plans by the consumers led to little use or need for sanctions. Those not following the agreed upon plan were offered opportunities to renegotiate. If new barriers were discovered, additional supports were developed and provided.

A second strategy under welfare reform involved additional supports for non-custodial parents. National and state legislation concentrated on strategies and tools to enforce child support orders. Income tax intercepts, revocation of professional licenses, employer registration of new hires, and several other strategies helped to obtain financial support from employed parents but did little to foster emotional support. They also were of little use if the non-custodial parent was unemployed.

The El Paso County strategy recognized the importance of both parents being involved financially and emotionally in the lives of their children. The county collaborated with the private child support agency, the Center on Fathering, the Women's Resource Agency, and Goodwill Industries to provide employment services to unemployed non-custodial parents. In addition, parenting classes, mediation, flexibility in enforcement of child support orders, and a central focus on the best interests of the child were infused into the system. Hospitals, the business community, faith-based organizations, and others were brought together to develop a strength-based, family-focused approach to the financial and emotional support of children.

The third focus of welfare reform in El Paso County centered on additional supports to strengthen families. The savings resulting from declining caseloads provided wonderful new resources. Rather than leaving huge reserves or transferring the money to other programs, new services and opportunities were developed within the assistance payments structure. The money was used to leverage other resources within the department and within the community. None of the money was spent. It was all invested in better outcomes for children and families.

Barbara Drake and the author of this chapter published several descriptions of the supportive services developed under welfare reform in El Paso County (Berns & Drake, 1999). A few of those descriptions are summarized below.

El Paso County's Approach

Kinship care. Through TANF, the department provides kinship services to grandparents who are raising their grandchildren—in the form of both increased financial assistance and support services aimed at keeping the extended family intact.

Kinship families who are eligible for these "child only" TANF grants make up 30% of the welfare caseload in El Paso County—similar to caseloads throughout the country. Many of these families are identical to those who enter the child welfare system, except that relatives, typically grandparents, have stepped in before the child welfare agency becomes involved. Providing strength-based support to families decreases the likelihood they will become more deeply involved in the system. The families receive services based on what they determine they need to maintain the children in their homes.

This effort required specific organizational changes. When Colorado's welfare reform law was implemented in 1997, the county transferred several of their best child welfare staff to TANF, matching them with talented technicians to create a team specially designed to serve grandparents and other relative caretakers. Funded entirely by TANF, the unit established grandparent support groups that connect families with community resources and help grandparents establish legal guardianships, allowing them to approve medical treatment and school enrollment. Staff has access to flexible funding to assist families, akin to wraparound services in child welfare, but funded by TANF. The program is an alternative to child welfare. TANF pays for preventive services for children at low to moderate risk, intervening before escalating crises require intensive services.

El Paso County is expanding this approach to provide services to families in ongoing child welfare cases. The county approach asks what it would take to enable these relatives to care for children in a safe, family-empowering environment. Services are designed and delivered accordingly.

Domestic Violence. Nearly one-third of El Paso County welfare recipients surveyed responded that they have been victims of domestic violence. In response, the department contracted to have a staff member from the local Center for Prevention of Domestic Violence located in welfare office. This domestic violence professional provides client services and staff training and serves as a resource to staff on individual cases. Funded as part of the welfare reform initiatives, this contract helps develop additional domestic violence related community resources, such as emergency housing and treatment-support groups. Services are culturally relevant and include Latino and Asian-Pacific focuses. These domestic violence services help link child protection, protection of adult victims, and opportunities for economic independence.

Child Care. The Alliance for Kids works for quality early childhood care and education in El Paso County. With significant consumer leadership, this broad-based community organization was the impetus behind a number of child care strategies that our agency implemented. These are

- Increased provider-reimbursement rates for child care services to low-income and child welfare families.

- On-site enrollment for low-income child care programs at child care centers and in-home providers.

- A child care referral database matching available resources with the needs of all families served by the agency, including those receiving child welfare services.

- Helping the community apply for child care grants aimed at improving quality and building capacity for low-income children, based on priorities identified by the Alliance for Kids.

- Increased payments for guaranteed child care slots and full-day/full-year child care so parents can choose quality care and move more effectively from welfare to work. This care is provided in partnership with the local Head Start, child care providers, and school district preschool programs.

Child care dollars bundled with welfare reform dollars at the local level are improving availability and quality of child care, making this a vital element in prevention and early intervention approaches to child welfare.

Support for Teen Parents. Locally, 319 girls age 10-17 gave birth in 1997—12% of total births in El Paso County. Pregnant and parenting teens face numerous risks: insufficient education, poor job skills, poverty, homelessness, dependence on welfare, domestic violence, and future unplanned pregnancies. Their children are at risk for neglect and abuse, abandonment, poor parenting, unstable home lives, poverty, lack of stimulation and education, poor nutrition and development, and the absence of stable father figures.

Under the auspices of TANF, a team of eligibility specialists, caseworkers, and community partners serve pregnant and parenting teens that come to the agency's attention. Teen-parent families receive assessments and case management services, home visits, parenting instruction, continuing education, job training, and mentoring. Outcomes are gauged by measuring educational achievement, individual and family functioning, and level of self-sufficiency.

Employment Support. El Paso County developed an employment support program to serve children aging out of foster care and those who are growing out of welfare dependence. Collaborating with employment programs typically associated with welfare reform, the program coordinates with the teen-parent program around independence issues. Although these support services address two different populations, both focus on building assets and setting goals, educational achievements, and self-sufficiency strategies that lead to employment. Foster care children currently in the agency's Independent Living program are served by caseworkers and employment counselors working in concert. A teen resource center housing many community partners recently opened to promote self-sufficiency.

Joint Family Preservation and TANF Services. Family preservation services for preventing foster care placements combine with "prevention" focused TANF services. This approach provides families who are entering the system with comprehensive, strength-based services with the least intrusion upon the family. It also addresses concerns about the impact of welfare reform on the child welfare system, particularly as the time-limit clock expires on people's benefits. Further, in El Paso County, TANF dollars support casework plans that provide, for example, domestic-violence services or drug and alcohol treatment. Services are coordinated by including them in both the child welfare treatment plan and the TANF individual responsibility or employability plan.

Joint Training. In collaboration with the University of Utah School of Social Work, four states, and several other universities, El Paso County is implementing cross-systems training, assessment, and services. This effort includes child welfare and TANF and incorporates substance abuse, domestic violence, and the mental health system. A design team with a large number of consumer representatives guides much of the system's reform efforts in the agency and helps develop training to assure success of the changes.

Facilitating Community Partnerships. With the flexible use of TANF funds, services expand through community partnerships. Working with community groups, the county helped sponsor a biannual haircut, clothing, and support event; community-wide faith-based mentoring; vocational rehabilitation services for eligible TANF families, and employment services through Goodwill Industries and one-stop career centers. Over 90 staff from numerous agencies are collocated at the DHS office. Dozens of agency staff are outstationed into community locations.

Conclusions

El Paso County made many changes in its child welfare and public assistance payments programs that contributed to ongoing success. No single strategy accounts for all of the improvement in any given program. The elements working together provide a synergy. Every change opens new challenges and opportunities.

Many might say these approaches would never work in their state or community. The political leaders may not have the will. The agency leaders may not have the vision or the community may be too entrenched in the status quo. All these may be true and if we accept them as reality, there likely will be little positive change.

On the other hand, we may assume another reality. We may decide that the current system generates poor outcomes. We may realize that poor outcomes cost more than good outcomes. We may decide to invest in strategies that result in better outcomes for children and families.

Policymakers, agencies, communities and families design and build our systems and our society. The question remains: will we design, consolidate, and build a system that meets the needs of our children and families?

References

Berns, D. and Drake, B. (1999). Combining child welfare and welfare reform at a local level. *Policy and Practice, The Journal of the American Public Human Services Association, 57*(1), 26-34.

Chapter 4

Mental Health Assessment and Environmentally Inclusive Treatment for Abused Children And Low-Income, Multiethnic, and/or Multiproblem Families

Tracie L. Hoffman

Introduction

The Fourth Edition of *The Diagnostic and Statistical Manual of Mental Disorders* (American Psychiatric Association, 1994), often referred to as "The DSM-IV," is a compendium of assessment categories compiled mostly by psychiatric professionals. Contemporary psychiatry is a division of modern medicine and adheres to a disease model. In other words, the DSM-IV is a volume of psychiatric "illnesses," which are considered disorders, and which have biological causes and, ideally, medical cures. Social workers conceptualize mental health problems as being influenced not only by biological concerns but also by environmental variables, such as socioeconomic status, culture, religious/spiritual orientation, family functioning, as well as man-made trauma and natural disasters. Thus, social workers, when compared to the psychiatric ideologies of the DSM-IV, tend to have a broader perspective on the origins and dimensions of mental health concerns. Therefore, social workers often differ from psychiatrists in their ideas on how to assess, research, and provide mental health services.

These differences were brought home to me while working in a public psychiatric hospital. I had a conversation with my good friend, the attending psychiatrist of our adolescent inpatient mental health unit. We were discussing our multiethnic, abused young clients of whom 85% were suicidal, 9% were dangerous to others due to an emotional disturbance, and 6% were gravely disabled. These clients largely hailed from indigent families with interrelated problems of drug abuse, unemployment, domestic violence, and familial mental health problems. "You know," he said, recognizing the dearth of literature addressing our particular client population, "It would be great to do research with these families and the kids. The problem with them is that they don't fit criteria for diagnoses in The DSM-IV."

Expecting no controversy, I replied with what I thought was obvious: "That's not *their* problem. The problem lies with the inability of the DSM-IV to account for the environmentally influenced symptoms of diverse, low-income, multi-problem families and their kids." I was quite surprised when my intelligent, typically open-minded friend began to argue that I had no concept of what "a psychiatric diagnosis" was, of how it was scientifically established, and how psychosocial circumstances were inconsequential to the emergence of indisputably biological, medically based symptom constellations. Suddenly, two people, who routinely agreed on a variety of issues, (and were previously able to discuss disagreements civilly) were polarized by respective ecological and exclusively medical-model theoretical orientations. As a social worker, I had always held to a "person-in-environment" orientation and my resolve to validate this perspective has been galvanized by the provocative conversation with my psychiatrist colleague.

The following chapter unfolds in three major sections related to mental health and abuse: (1) The need for the social work person-in-environment perspective and the challenges of the medical model and the DSM-IV; (2) Relevant research on the multiple environmental facets of abuse and mental health, which concern child welfare and related systems; (3) Multimethod micro, meso, and macro level interventions.

The Need For the Social Work Person-in-Environment Perspective and the Challenges of The Medical Model and The DSM-IV

The Person-in-Environment Perspective on Mental Health Issues

Many researchers and theorists have also noted the unique reciprocal relationship between stress in environments and mental health (Achenbach, 1985; Aldwin, 1994; Bloom, 1979; Lazarus & Folkman, 1984; Parad, 1965; Williams, Karls, & Wandrei, 1989). Social workers have long been committed to seeing human problems as resulting from, and being addressed within, a complex context composed of intra-individual concerns and his/her external circumstances (Germain & Gittelman, 1980; National Association of Social Workers, 1995; Richmond, 1917). However, as mentioned, the person-in-environment paradigm is not predominantly embraced by all mental health professionals (Henk, 1985; Karls & Wandrei, 1992a; Klerman, Valliant, Spitzer, & Michels, 1984).

The Medical Model

A "medical model" dominated the birth of psychiatry (Greenblatt, 1957; Grob, 1973; World Health Organization, 1978). Contemporarily, the medical model continues to thrive in mental health settings (Callicutt, 1987) and, as mentioned, its influence is evident in the *Diagnostic and Statistical Manual of Mental Disorders, Fourth Edition* (DSM-IV) (American Psychiatric Association, 1994). The DSM-IV is the most commonly used mental health classification volume in the United States today (Adelman, 1995). Vega, Zimmerman, et al. (1994) speculated that the lack of well-integrated environmental considerations in assessment has limited, and continues to limit, the empirical study of low-income, multi-problem, and/or multi-ethnic clients in the following closed cycle: *DSM diagnostic categories have been developed without adequate incorporation of environmental influences* (Rogler, 1996).

It is not likely, therefore, that DSM-IV criteria will adequately match the symptoms of marginalized groups whose environmental circumstances may largely differ from those of originally studied groups (Fabrega, 1994; Mezzich & Saavedra, 1994; Roberts, 1994). "Measures of distress and disorder . . . have been taken from mainstream research with little if any modification for use in studying [those who were not included in research samples]" (Lopez, 1994, p. 110). Thus, if a particular group was not included in the development of a DSM-IV diagnostic category, that group would not likely meet the criteria for the developed diagnosis.

Previously established notions of mental health, including most assessment and treatment plan formulations, have not fully integrated ethnic and related socioeconomic factors (Durant, Cadenhead, Pendergrast, Slavens, & Linden, 1994; Lopez, 1994; Mezzich & Saavedra, 1994; Padilla, 1994). Ironically, the very factors that place a minority family and child at risk for mental problems (poor socioeconomic conditions within which minority groups are statistically more likely to live, National Institute of Mental Health, 1990) exclude that child and family, retroactively, from inclusion in the original groups observed from which ideas about mental health and disorders were developed: groups of Anglo, middle-class individuals (Goldstein, 1987; Guthrie, 1976; Iijima-Hall, 1997).

Through this process, an "establishment psychiatry" orientation is reinforced in which low-income, multi-problem, and/or minority group members are circularly excluded from established criteria and, thus, accurate diagnosis (Fabrega, 1994, p. 140). This circular process effectively precludes many marginalized groups from qualifying for mental health diagnoses, which can result in inappropriate or complete lack of mental health treatment. Of relevance, the validity and reliability of the Diagnostic Interview for Children and Adolescents (DICA), through which DSM-IV diagnoses are often identified in research, "has not yet been sufficiently established, particularly as it relates to...ethnic populations in the United States" (Vega,

Zimmerman, et al., 1994, p. 48). Goldstein (1987) noted, "Theories of personality and psychopathology [were] based largely on observations of Caucasian, middle-class . . . individuals" (p. 109). Guthrie (1976) reviewed the treatment of ethnicity in psychiatric research, literature, and treatment protocols, and then summarized his findings in a book descriptively titled, *Even The Rat Was White*.

Many authors (e.g., Karls & Wandrei, 1992a; Karls & Wandrei, 1992b; Nash & Fraser, 1997; Roberts, 1994) suggest that an ecological, person-in-environment framework facilitates the appropriate assessment of client-specific symptoms within diverse groups. Unfortunately, research, as well as contingent funding, and services are not often based on ecological theories. Rather, they are also predicated on medically based models (Callicutt, 1987) and/or diagnoses derived from the DSM-IV (Adelman, 1995) which, in the United States, is "nearly universally [used] among mental health workers" (Karls & Wandrei, 1995, p. 1826). Thus, empirical research utilizing DSM-IV categories may overlook, misinterpret, and distort the factors associated with the mental health symptoms of low-income, multi-problem, and/or minority groups (Mezzich & Saavedra, 1994). Therefore, by using many DSM-IV diagnostic categories in research and in service provision, the accurate scientific study of, and provision of services to, low-income, multi-problem, and/or minority-group mental health needs may be inadvertently precluded (Fabrega, 1994; Martinez, 1994).

The Need to Incorporate Environmental Considerations in Mental Health Assessment

Many professionals have articulated the need to include environmental considerations in the assessment of multi-ethnic, low-income, and/or multiproblem clients (Fabrega, 1994; Guarnaccia, Good, & Kleinman, 1990; Lopez, 1994; Martinez, 1994; Mezzich & Saavedra, 1994). Recent studies have included issues of ethnicity and mental health, but such inclusion is a relatively new phenomenon (Telles & Karno, 1994). As ethnic demographics in the U.S. have changed, and continue to change dramatically, the study and treatment of mulitproblem, low-income, and/or minority clients must concurrently change in order to accurately address the burgeoning needs of previously ignored groups.

For example, even though child maltreatment is a formidable concern among many Latino health professionals (National Coalition of Hispanic Health and Human Services Organizations, 1997), abuse among Latino youth has not been a well-researched topic. The lack of research in this field may be due, in part, to a previous lack of funding for studying Latino children (National Institute of Mental Health, 1990). These youth have been considered to be in a small minority group and, thus, of relatively little importance (Karno, 1994). However, the U.S. Census Bureau (1995) predicts that Latinos will "soon be the nation's largest ethnic minority group [and are] already per capita the most abundant in children and youth" (Karno, 1994,

p. 14). Relatedly, "Latino youth comprise 11.7 of all youth in the United States. The size of Latino youth will grow to 19 million in 2020, about 25% of all U.S. youth" (Gonzalez, 1997, pp. 99-100). Relevantly, Iijima-Hall (1997) noted that the helping professionals need to incorporate ethnicity (and often associated socioeconomic and multiproblem concerns) into research, assessment, and treatment or become obsolete in the context of changing U.S. demographics, representing increasing proportions of people of color.

Multiaxial Diagnoses

Throughout the evolution of the DSM, many changes have been made (American Psychiatric Association, 1952, 1968, 1980, 1987). Still, the mental health concerns of multi-ethnic, low-income, and/or multiproblem children and families remain largely unaddressed.

The most recent edition of the DSM (DSM-IV, American Psychiatric Association, 1994) has made some movement toward environmentally inclusive assessment via a "multiaxial diagnostic system." This multi-axial system includes five "Axes" or distinct areas of assessment: Axis I is reserved for the identification of major mental disorders; Mental retardation and personality disorders are listed under Axis II; Axis III is where major medical conditions are recorded; Life stresses are listed under Axis IV; and one's level of functioning is recorded under Axis V via a 100 point scale known as "The Global Assessment of Functioning (or GAF). Although "this [multiaxial] system [the DSM-IV] includes a dimension acknowledging 'psychosocial stressors,' [Axis IV] this dimension is used mostly to deal with the environment as a contributing factor (i.e., such stressors are not usually specified as primary [etiologic] causes)" (Adelman, 1995, p. 34). Also, the DSM-IV implicitly devalues the importance of multiaxial assessment of stress and adaptation noting that, "Clinicians who do not wish to use the multiaxial format may simply list the [primary Axis I and/or II] appropriate diagnoses...[being certain to include] general medical conditions" (American Psychiatric Association, 1994, p. 35). In the assessment of psychiatric conditions, many believe that further consideration needs to be given to the etiological contributions of environmental trauma, including the requisite evaluation of clients' adaptation to environmental stress (e.g., Cervantes & Arroya, 1994; Fraser & Galinsky, 1997).

Obstacles in Redesigning Assessment Schemes

Many social workers have called for a revisioning of assessment schemes within the social work profession (Karls & Wandrei, 1992b; Mattani & Kirk, 1992). In reaction to the primarily intrapersonal focus of the DSM, the National Association of Social

Workers funded the development of a formally codified "Person-In-Environment Assessment Scheme (P.I.E.)" (Karls & Wandrei, 1995). However, the prospects for unanimous, interprofessional adoption of a social work generated diagnostic framework are uncertain at best (Callicutt, 1987; Kirk, Saporin, & Kutchincs, 1989). Thus, rather than attempting to replace the DSM-IV, Mezzich and Saavedra (1994) suggested that professionals recognize, apply, and refine the few environmentally inclusive diagnoses (symptoms related to environmentally inclusive diagnoses) contained in the DSM-IV. This "strengths-based" strategy, thus, may promote positive DSM revisions by emphasizing the value of existing environmentally inclusive DSM-IV diagnoses (Mezzich & Saavedra, 1994).

Environmentally Inclusive DSM-IV Diagnoses

Very few DSM diagnoses link environmental stressors with the etiology of diagnoses. V-Code categories include "Relational Problems" and "Problems Related to Abuse or Neglect" (American Psychiatric Association, 1994, pp. 680-682). However, V-Codes are not actually categorized as diagnoses but, rather, as "Other Conditions That May Be a Focus of Clinical Attention." Post Traumatic Stress Disorder (PTSD), Adjustment Disorders, and Acute Stress Disorder are the only three DSM-IV diagnoses that include environmental considerations in primary etiologic formulations (American Psychiatric Association, 1994). However, only one set of DSM-IV symptoms (those comprising PTSD) are etiologically linked to environmental stressors associated with a specific combination of persistent, severe psychiatric symptoms (American Psychiatric Association, 1994). PTSD symptoms uniquely focus on "the 'fit' between the person and environmental circumstances in understanding adaptation to stress" (Green, Lindy, & Grace, 1985, p. 407).

DSM-IV Adjustment Disorder diagnoses also acknowledge an environmentally based "stressor" yet specify that the "adjustment disordered person's [reaction be] in excess of what would be expected from exposure to the stressor" (American Psychiatric Association, 1994, p. 626). Alternatively, a PTSD diagnosis requires that the stressor must be of an extreme nature while, in contrast, in Adjustment Disorders, the stressor can be "of any severity" (American Psychiatric Association, 1994, p. 626). Thus, in an adjustment disorder, a person's intrapsychic reaction may be seen as the true root of the disorder rather than the severity of the stressor (American Psychiatric Association, 1994.)

The Acute Stress Reaction is defined, operationally, as a short version of PTSD, with stressors and symptoms being identical. "For individuals with the diagnoses of Acute Stress Disorder whose symptoms persist for longer than 1 month, the diagnosis of PTSD should be considered" (American Psychiatric Association, 1994, p. 431). Acute Stress Disorder is required to remit within 1 month and Adjustment Disorders are required to abate within 6 months. Thus, these diagnoses would, by definition, be inadequate enough to address all postchild abuse sequelae since many related trauma reactions persist well into childhood (Finkelhor, 1992; Krammer & Green, 1991; Mc Leer, Deblinger, Henry, & Orvaschel, 1992; Callaghan, Henry, & Wallen, 1994; Perez & Windom, 1994) and, often, into adulthood (Briere, 1992; Briere & Runtz, 1988; Janoff-Bulman, 1985; Silverman, Reinherz, & Giaconia, 1996; Terr, 1994). In PTSD, there is no inherent end time limit included in symptom criteria. Thus, the study of PTSD symptoms seems to be well-suited in examining a broad range of post-abuse reactions that may last over an extended period of time. Though PTSD fits the medical model's requirement that the cause (traumatic stress) precedes an effect (the *post* traumatic stress *syndrome)*, symptoms of PTSD also uniquely focus on "the 'fit' between the person and environmental circumstances in understanding adaptation to stress" (Green, Lindy, & Grace, 1985, p. 407).

Mezzich and Saavedra (1994), in work sponsored by the National Institute of Mental Health, examined psychiatric assessment considerations, noting, "Sociocultural stressors are highly relevant to [minority group] mental health and illness" (p. 176). Roberts (1994) noted, "A fuller understanding of the etiology of [ethnic minority] psychological disorders will require explanatory models which reflect the presumed multifactorial nature of the phenomenon being studied. " (p. 32)".

Mental Health Research on the Multiple Environmental Facets of Abuse

The Environmental Factor of Abuse

There are innumerable, multifactorial dimensions of one's personal environment (such as socioeconomic circumstances, traumatic occurrences, social support or lack there of, relative lack of access to resources, etc.). The complexity and variety of environmental factors has often been used to justify the lack of empirical mental health research regarding specific environmental dimensions (Germain & Gittelman, 1994). Frequently, environmental conditions are relegated to an amorphous realm of nonlinearly related, unidentifiable, and potentially intervening variables (Kachigan, 1986).

Child abuse, however, is very often the primary reason why vulnerable families are identified and brought into public service systems (Trupin, Tarico, Low, Jemelka, & Mc Clellan, 1993) and, thus, is logically a very important environmental variable to consider when working with such families. In addition, when abuse reports are confirmed, protective service workers are more likely to refer children for supportive, public clinical services than if abuse remains unsubstantiated (Garland, Lansverk,

Hough, & Ellis-Macleod, 1996). It is also important to note that minority children are more likely to be overrepresented in child protective service caseloads (Hogan & Sui, 1988).

Child abuse is recognized as an environmental stressor affiliated with PTSD symptoms (American Psychiatric Association, 1994). Many have revealed an association between posttraumatic stress symptoms and child physical abuse (Green, 1983, 1985; Hullings-Catalano, 1996; Straus, 1994; Sumner, 1996; van der Kolk & Fisler, 1994; Veltkamp & Miller, 1994) and child sexual abuse (Astin, Ogland-Hand, Coleman, & Foy, 1995; Greg & Parks, 1995; Kiser, Heston, Millsap, & Pruitt, 1991; Levine, 1996). However, the majority of research regarding abused children and trauma symptoms does not focus on ethnicity and examines predominantly Anglo subjects (Cherepon & Prinzhorn, 1994; Goldstein, 1987; Guthrie, 1976; Iijima-Hall, 1997; National Institute of Mental Health, 1990).

In addition, there is a body of literature that indicates a largely positive association between child abuse, PTSD symptoms, and the severity of other psychiatric problems suggesting a link between the environmental traumatic symptoms and various emotional difficulties (Conte, 1995; Finkelhor & Browne, 1985; Iverson & Segal, 1990; Mc Leer, et al., 1994; Moscarello, 1991; Terr, 1991). Child abuse has been associated with anxiety reactions (Bernstein & Borchardt, 1991; Green, 1995; Mennen & Meadow, 1993, 1994). Behavioral problems have also been linked to child abuse (Adams, McClellan, Douglass, & McCurry, 1995; Ellason, Ross, Sainton, & Mayran, 1996; Harmon & Riggs, 1996). Relationships have been uncovered between child abuse and depression (Cherepon & Prinzhorn, 1994; De-Bellis, Lefter, Trickett, & Putnam, 1994). In addition, disassociative features are often significantly related to abuse (Lawrence, Cozolino, & Foy, 1995; Midgow, 1994; van der Kolk, Pelcovitz, Roth, & Mandel, 1996).

Child Abuse Prevalence. The concept of "prevalence" refers to the extent to which a particular phenomenon exists. The prevalence of child abuse is a growing concern, and contemporary mental health assessment schemes would thus be remiss in ignoring the relationship between mental health and child abuse. In 1962, approximately 10,000 child abuse reports were filed in the United States (Fontana, 1971). The number of reports increased astronomically in the 1970s and 1980s, with 1.4 million reports of child abuse logged in 1986 (Wells, 1995). That figure more than doubled by 1992, with a record 2.9 million children being reported as abused (National Center on Child Abuse and Neglect, 1994). Some believe that the recent explosion in child abuse reports may be strictly an artifact of increased awareness; whereas, others believe that the incidence of actual child abuse may have increased as well (Daro, Jones, & McCurdy, 1990). While not all reports are substantiated (Sedlak & Broadhurst, 1996), it is estimated that more than 1.5 million U.S. children experience serious physical abuse annually (Hullings-Catalano, 1996).

Sexual abuse is the subject of approximately one-sixth of U.S. child abuse reports (Sedlak, 1991). Estimates of the prevalence of childhood sexual abuse vary dramatically. In 1986, Peters, Wyatt, and Finkelhor estimated that between 6% and 62% of females had been sexually abused; whereas, 3% to 31% of males had been molested. Subsequently, Finkelhor, Hotaling, Lewis, and Smith (1990) conducted a national telephone survey and found that 27% of women and 16% of men reported having experienced childhood sexual abuse. Differing estimates are the result of many factors, including differing definitions of what constitutes sexual abuse, the under reporting of child molestation, what actually is reported when reports are filed, and whether or not figures are based on child abuse reports or retrospective accounts of adult survivors (National Center on Child Abuse and Neglect, 1994). Generally, reports based on retrospective accounts reflect higher estimates of sexual abuse prevalence as child maltreatment, near the time of abuse, is seriously under reported, even by professionals who recognize the abuse (National Center on Child Abuse and Neglect, 1994). Veltkamp and Miller (1994) estimated that only one-fifth of identified child abuse is formally reported by professionals in child treatment institutions. In addition, child abuse is often under reported in rural communities where Child Protective Service Agencies may not be as accessible as in Urban settings (Spence, 1984).

Parental Factors, Child Abuse, and Children's Mental Health. Unfortunately, the research in this area is limited. The available research suggests that different environmental features, such as cultural factors (Egami, Ford, Greenfield, & Crum, 1996; Hong & Hong, 1991) and parental influences (Connelly & Straus, 1992; Hussey & Singer, 1993; Zuravin, 1989) compile, in part, variables that affect the risk of child maltreatment.

In the DSM-IV, it is noted that PTSD symptoms may be more severe and long lasting if the stressor is of human design (American Psychiatric Association, 1994). Child abuse is of human design, with the perpetrator often being a member of the child's family (Hullings-Catalano, 1996). When trauma is inflicted by a person, the appearance of PTSD symptoms is related to the identity of the person inflicting the stress. Deblinger, Henry, and Orvaschel (1992), as well as Mc Leer, et al. (1992), found that PTSD symptom severity and prevalence increased when an abuser was a member of the child's family. In a review of empirical literature, Browne and Finkelhor (1987) found that symptoms of distress increase when the perpetrator is a father figure. Unfortunately, the National Center on Child Abuse and Neglect (1994) found that the majority of reported perpetrators (79%) were parents (12% relatives other than parents, 4.6% noncaregivers, 1.4% child care providers, 0.5% foster parents, 0.3% residential care personnel, and 2.3% unknown).

Intergenerational Patterns. The phrase, "intergenerational patterns," refers to family patterns that persist from generation to generation. It is important to study these patterns as they tend to be quite persistent and thus, where dysfunctional, are important targets of reparative interventions.

In a study of 2,000 youngsters, aged 10-16, Boney-McCoy and Finkelhor (1995) found that the early victimization of a family member was positively correlated with that family member subsequently perpetrating child sexual abuse. Green and Kaplan (1994) studied maternal child abusers and found that most had been abused, themselves, as children. Green, Coupe, Fernandez, and Stevens (1995) studied mothers who had sexually abused their children and found that all subjects had been victims of child molestation. Further, Famularo, Fenton, Kinscherff, and Ayoub (1994) studied 109 pairs of mothers-who-had-been-abused and the children that they abused. The authors found that 37% of the mothers had met the criteria for PTSD while 36% of the children met PTSD criteria—and those children whose mothers had PTSD were over represented in the group of children experiencing PTSD. Sumner (1996) looks at the long-term impact of child physical abuse. Along with the likelihood of perpetrating abuse on one's own children, the adult-abused-as-a-child may develop symptoms of PTSD. Intrusive thoughts, panic attacks, withdrawal symptoms and behavior problems can manifest in the adult who was physically abused in childhood. Busby (1996) noted that adults who were sexually and physically abused as children exhibited "both primary and secondary symptoms associated with trauma. . . . They were experiencing higher levels of primary symptoms (depression, avoidance, and anxiety) and secondary symptoms (borderline and passive-aggressive behavior patterns) commonly found in clients diagnosed with PTSD" (p. 216). Given the links between abusive parental behavior, a history of parents being abused as children and PTSD, an argument might be made that parent-to-child abuse may be a behavioral symptom of PTSD in the formerly abused parent.

Poverty and Perpetration. A history of abuse is not the only predictor for abuse perpetration among parents. Many researchers note a high correlation between child maltreatment and poverty (Egami, et al., 1996; Sedlak & Broadhurst, 1996; Whipple, 1991). "When [parents] are exhausted from low-paying jobs...[they] find it harder to be consistent in discipline..." (Fraser, 1997, p. 1). Frighteningly, Sedlak and Broadhurst (1996) noted (in data derived from child abuse reports), "Children from families with annual incomes below $15,000, as compared to children from families with annual incomes above $30,000, were over 22 times more likely to experience some form of maltreatment . . . and 18 times more likely to be sexually abused" (p. xviii). Sedlak and Broadhurst also reported that "children of single parents have a 77% greater risk of being harmed by physical abuse . . . than children living with both parents" (Sedlak & Broadhurst, 1996, p. xviii). These combined statistics suggest that minority youth may be at increased risk for child abuse due to socioeconomic conditions (Herrenkohl, Herrenkohl, Rupert, & Egolf, 1995; Kotulak, 1996; Singer, Singer, & Anglin, 1993; Telles, 1994; Walsh, 1990).

Child Abuse and Parental Unemployment. Results from studies reveal "evidence that links unemployment with increasing rates of child abuse" (e.g. Briar, 1988; Gelles & Straus, 1979; Jones, 1990, p. 579). This relationship is attributed to the environmental stress that a family encounters during times of joblessness. However, it is important to note that some research suggests:

> Contrary to expectation, the unemployment rate, when differentiated from the loss of income, was either insignificant or negatively associated with child maltreatment. These findings provide a basis for recommending two broad changes in child welfare policy: The spreading of the financial burden of parenthood among all taxpayers and the creation of neighborhood family centers offering an array of health, social, and emergency services (McNicoll, 1989, p. 1).

Wolfner and Gelles (1993) noted child abuse was associated with paternal unemployment; whereas, poverty increased the likelihood of child abuse regardless of a parent's gender. Relatedly, Spence (1997) sampled 254 child abuse cases in Texas and conducted a log linear statistical analysis of variables finding that the factor of maternal employment most accurately predicted the existence of child abuse within the home. Thus, while welfare reform proponents may extol the virtues of parental employment, it may be, in many cases, that poverty (which often accompanies joblessness) is more powerfully associated with child abuse, and that employment, especially in female-headed households, could actually exacerbate familial stress.

Child Abuse and Parental Substance Abuse. Some researchers have explored the relationship between parental substance use, child abuse, and features associated with the protectiveness of a parent when a child is being mistreated (e.g., Rutherford, Cacciola, Alterman, Mc Kay, & Cook, 1997). Hindman (1979) notes that child abuse is highly associated with parental alcohol abuse. Holzhauser (1979) also notes the correlation between child abuse and parental alcohol and drug abuse, calling for a coordination of services to treat the spectrum of associated problems.

Child Abuse and Parental Mental Illness. A number of researchers have examined the association between parental mental health problems and child abuse (e.g., Bools, Neale, and Meadow, 1994; Louis, Condon, Shute, & Elzinga, 1997). Stroud (1997) even noted the presence of certain parental mental illnesses were associated with the killing of offspring. Interestingly, a study conducted by the Social Research Institute at the University of Utah (1998) found that maternal mental illness was the strongest predictor among factors resulting in out-of-home placement for abused children.

Interactive Factors Associated with Parent-to-Child Abuse

In noting the association between child abuse and poverty, parental substance abuse, and parental mental illness, respectively, one may logically question whether or not these factors are interrelated. In fact, research has been conducted which suggests that, indeed, these environmental factors do tend to exist in interactive clusters characterizing the "multiproblem family" (Dore, 1993). These clusters are often composed of environmental factors associated with abuse in a child's life, including economic stress, parental mental illness, and parental substance abuse (Gelles & Straus, 1979; Junewicz, 1983).

Resistance to Environmentally Inclusive Diagnoses such as PTSD

Even though many researchers have documented the impact of child maltreatment, environmental stress, and symptoms throughout the life span (Barahal, Waterman, & Martin, 1981; Gislason & Call, 1982; Howling, Wodarski, et al., 1993; Kurtz, Gaudin, Wodarski, & Howling, 1993; Pynoos, 1993; Trickett, 1993; van der Kolk, 1987a), skepticism regarding the enduring impact of environmental stressors, such as child abuse, continues to thrive (Campbell, 1992; Molton, 1996; Yapko, 1994). For example, some resist the reality of child trauma by suggesting that children often lie about abuse. However, research has demonstrated that children infrequently lie about abuse (Berlinger, 1995; Jones & McGraw, 1987). The Harvard Medical School (1993) reported that "only 5% to 10% of reports are judged to be false" and that "false retractions [of child abuse] are understood to be far more common than true ones" (p. 6).

Further, far from inventing artificial connections between past abuse and current troubles, Figley, Scrignar, and Smith (1992) noted that the opposite is often true, with patients and clinicians frequently failing to make the connection between prior trauma and symptom presentation. In addition, many researchers and theorists have examined the phenomenon of memory, and the cognitive processing of child abuse as protective, adaptive mechanisms in posttrauma coping strategies (Creamer, Burgess, & Pattison, 1990; Dodge, Pettit, et al., 1995; Forman, 1993; Hartman & Burgess, 1993; Pynoos & Nader, 1989; Rhue, Lynn, & Sandberg, 1995; Rogosch, Cicchetti, & Aber, 1995). Many claim that lack of memory and/or the cognitive repression of actual traumatic events are far more likely in troubled individuals than the retrospective invention of fictional torture (Branscomb & Fagan, 1992; Bremmer, Randall, Scott, & Campbell, 1995; Musicar & Josefowitz, 1996; Niederland, 1964).

In addition, some also argue that cognitive interventions can help to mitigate against problems associated with memory gaps and repressed recollections throughout the life span (Chemtob, Roiblat, et al., 1988; Deblinger, Mc Leer, & Henry, 1990), thus lending credibility to the reality of memories successfully recovered and addressed (Kreitler & Kreitler, 1988). Many researchers have also not only documented the connection between child trauma and PTSD but have explored the particular types of stressors that precipitate particular trauma responses (Feinstein, 1989; Feinstein & Dolan, 1991; Saigh, 1991; van der Kolk, 1984, 1987b, 1988). Others have documented links between child maltreatment and other psychiatric and behavioral problems (Famularo, Kinscherff, & Fenton, 1991; Famularo, Kinscherff, et al., 1990; National Research Council, 1993; Stevens-Simon & McAnarney, 1994). Some have even examined the empirical connection between biological conditions and child abuse, as well as PTSD (Bowman, 1993; Carrey, Butler, et al., 1995; Charney, Deutch, et al., 1993; Shalev, Orr, et al., 1992; van der Kolk, Greenberg, Boyd, & Krystal, 1985).

Still, Patten, Gatz, et al. (1989) found that many therapists prefer to overlook trauma-based diagnoses in order to use less environmentally based symptom clusters, such as depression, psychotic disorder NOS, and borderline personality disorder despite the fact that child physical and sexual abuse is included in the histories of up to 75% of studied clients. In fact, the initial DSM-III PTSD diagnostic criteria did not include child abuse as a possible precursor or children as potential sufferers in spite of previously documented postabuse symptomatology (Brett, Spitzer, & Williams, 1988; Green 1983, 1985; Kempe, Silverman, Steele, Droegemueller, & Silver, 1962; Mc Leer et al., 1992; Terr, 1983). Benedek (1985) noted that fellow psychiatric professionals responded with hostility when Terr (1994) addressed colleagues regarding the association between trauma and psychiatric symptoms.

> The audience's response of disbelief, in the face of carefully collected documentation, might have been so intense because it was difficult for professionals to accept that traumatic events, caused by fellow human beings, in the lives of children might color and shape their lives for years to come. . . . A review of the literature in regard to children, psychic trauma, and disaster supports the concept of clinical denial (p. 4).

Not only has it been difficult to establish child abuse as a valid stressor related to PTSD, but it also was difficult for PTSD to gain recognition as a legitimate diagnosis at all, even for war veterans, though many researchers documented the existence of battle trauma-related symptoms (Horowitz, 1976; Kardiner & Spiegel,

1947; Newman, 1976). It was not until 1980 that PTSD became a "real" diagnosis in the DSM-III (American Psychiatric Association, 1980). Herman (1992) maintained that the emergence of the PTSD diagnosis found its support in the political context of a collapsing "cult of war" and the growth of an antiwar movement. With the Vietnam War at its height, many trauma-related support coalitions emerged. By the mid-1970s, hundreds of informal rap groups had been organized, and by the end of the decade, political pressure from veterans' organizations resulted in a legal mandate for a psychological treatment program called "Operation Outreach" within the Veterans Administration. In the years following the war, the Veterans Administration commissioned research that traced the legacies of Vietnam veterans and demonstrated the direct relationship of posttraumatic symptoms to combat experience. Due to political pressure, continuous documentation, and compelling research, the medically based DSM-III included the environmentally based PTSD diagnosis (American Psychiatric Association, 1980).

It was equally, if not more difficult, to gain the formal inclusion of child abuse as a factor in PTSD, even though research demonstrates a strong similarity between the symptoms of PTSD war veterans and child abuse victims (Mc New & Abell, 1995). Yet, in historical context, this is not surprising as the tendency to doubt that child abuse, or any form of environmental trauma, may contribute to psychiatric problems is not a new phenomenon (Benedek, 1985; Finkelhor, 1988).

Lieberman (1987) noted that children have only recently been thought to be vulnerable to any form of mental illness and that the term "emotionally disturbed child" is a product of the 20th century. Previously, mentally disordered youths were considered to be "possessed," "wicked," "insubordinate," or "incorrigible" (Lieberman, 1987, p. 111). Child abuse was not seen as a precursor to emotional difficulties. In fact, in biblical times, it was written that "He that spareth his rod, hateth his son: But he that loveth him chastenteth him betimes." (Proverbs, 13: 24). Thus, physical punishment has been long associated with "good parenting" and "love," rather than "abuse" and "trauma related symptoms."

Diagnosis Driven Treatment

In the field of mental health practice today, mental health services are "means tested" in both public and private sectors. "The DSM Diagnosis" is the basis upon which mental health services are delivered and reimbursed (Sykes-Wylie (1995) Thus, the diagnosis has become our means test. Callicutt noted that, "The issues regarding reimbursement related to diagnostic categories for psychiatric inpatient care in pyschiatric hospitals, as well as psychiatric units in general hospitals, is undergoing examination and may be expected to affect future legislation" (1987, p. 134). Jansson asserts that mental health policy is "defined by diagnostic considerations" (1984, p. 436).

"Managed Care" is the latest system to be introduced into the arena of mental health policy. Public and private delivery systems are being modified to operate within managed care philosophies. Phrases such as:

'medically necessary'...now are used to justify reimbursable [mental health] service delivery. Managed care systems require that clinicians explain and demonstrate that their methods are being effective and are needed...Clinicians need to be concise as to what an improve[ment] will 'look like,' how they are going to help the client achieve the goal, and what the termination criteria are. Many clinicians will have to dust off a book on behaviorism they read in graduate school and begin to define problems in terms of frequency, rate, and duration" (Todd, 1994, pp.2-3).

While ostensibly pragmatic, managed care logic assumes that all mental health problems are medically based, amenable to brief, goal-directed therapies. "Once the DSM had wedged open the door of 'medical necessity,' managed care administrators found they could play fast and loose with its categories, choosing which disorders were more or less truly 'medical,' which did or did not deserve the reimbursable status of illness" (Sykes-Wiley, 1995, p. 30). Managed care logic also assumes that all problems can be operationalized, that progress is unilinearly upward rather than subject to fits and starts, and that there is necessarily an end point to treatment.

Unfortunately, not all emotional and mental problems lend themselves to tidy "cures." Again, the medical model has been applied to the mental health realm and the dimensions of mental health problems are, thus, expected to fit within the constraints of the medical model. The underlying ideology is circular: In order to justify treatment, we must be able to precisely identify the sole problem (via diagnosis), and improve, if not cure it. If we can't identify the specifics of the problem, much less improve or cure it, we can't justify treatment. Obviously, this thinking precludes treatment for those whose problems don't fit into neat diagnostic categories, those whose problems are enigmatic, and/or those who need maintenance support long-term therapy, or services for integrally involved family members.

Of course, many mental health concerns do not fit neatly into medical explanations. As mentioned, PTSD is the only DSM diagnostic category that clearly stresses environmental factors as pivotal to the etiology of long-term psychiatric problems and only recently has PTSD been recognized as a legitimate DSM diagnosis. Effective treatment strategies for PTSD are only beginning to be explored, and many require the consistent participation of a trusted therapist over a substantial period of time and service in a variety of environmental venues. Progress is not universally upward, as often the PTSD sufferer experiences increased symptoms as problems are explored. For example, Finkelhor and Browne (1985) *found that, as the recovery process unfolds, some related traumatic related symptoms often emerge. The emergence of such symptoms should not be viewed as setbacks but rather as inherent parts of recovery.* Thus, it is difficult to "justify" the predictably erratic treatment course of PTSD within a medical, managed care model.

The consideration of PTSD and associated symptoms is particularly important when working with minority and/or multiproblem families who are more likely to experience environmental problems, such as poverty, and related concerns, such as child abuse (Gonzalez, 1997; Heffernan, 1988; National Advisory Mental Health Council, 1990; National Institute of Mental Health, 1990; Sedlak & Broadhurst, 1996). However, Cervantes and Arroya (1994) noted that many clinicians routinely ascribe only a limited number of DSM symptoms to minority clients from low-income, multiproblem families. Gonzalez, Castillo-Canez, Tarke, Soriano, Garcia, and Valasquez, (1997), encouraged clinicians and researchers to explore the symptoms of more environmentally inclusive DSM-IV symptom groups when working with minority and/or multiproblem clients. These authors emphasized that the conceptualization of symptoms has "social, economic, and political implications" (p. 160).

Yet, Baca and Koss-Chioino (1997), as well as Hack, Osachuck, and de Luca (1984), reported that treatment for youth, including minority youngsters, is largely group treatment focusing on reimbursable diagnoses. Sykes-Wiley notes that, for reimbursement purposes, "the diagnoses usually accepted are those with symptoms that take the least time to ameliorate, which most quickly respond to standardized treatment models... Current good shots for reimbursement include depressive, anxiety and learning disorders, but not post-traumatic stress disorder..."(Sykes-Wiley, 1995, p. 30).

Therefore, one is not likely, under managed care to be reimbursed for being diagnosed with PTSD even though the DSM-IV (American Psychiatric Association, 1994) blatantly proclaims that "Studies of at risk individuals... have yielded prevalence rates...[up to] 58%" (p. 426). As demonstrated through research cited earlier in this chapter, those who are at risk include those exposed to poverty, child abuse, domestic violence, familial substance abuse, and familial mental illness.

Despite or perhaps because of limited funding for environmentally based diagnoses, managed care model is prevalent in the public mental health services today (Todd, 1994). Wineburgh (1998) notes that even the 75% of U.S. citizens who have private health insurance were enrolled in managed care health maintenance organizations. "However, the notion that mental health services might be 'manageable' is immediately challenged by the complexity of mental illness...the ideological and conceptual disagreements about diagnosis and treatment, [and] unclear success and/or outcome criteria" (Wineburgh, 1998, p. 433).

Thus, it is critical for social workers, rooted in a "person-in-environment" model (Karls & Wandrel, 1995) to explore the assignment, when criteria have been met, of environmentally inclusive diagnoses. As vulnerable families often enter the service systems in association with intrafamilial child abuse, it is important for social workers to compile an assessment that would support the justification for the coordination of services to all those involved in the environment of perpetration. Unfortunately, as mentioned in the DSM-IV, PTSD alone includes environmental trauma as etiologically essential to long-term assessment considerations and treatment plans. Social workers must advocate for agencies to fund the PTSD diagnosis. In addition, the social work profession must advocate for syndromes with ecological etiologies to be more comprehensively included in the DSM-IV. In this way, social workers can continue to demonstrate the importance of emphasizing environmental considerations in both assessment and in treatment planning for vulnerable families.

Micro, Meso, and Macro Level Interventions for Low-Income, Multiethnic, and/or Multiproblem Children and Families

Treatment Strategies for Trauma Related Symptoms

Diagnostic labels have serious implications for treatment. Thus, there are dangers in ignoring environmental factors in diagnostic assessment, especially when treatment options are being considered. There are many approaches recommended for the treatment of trauma symptoms. Some authors speak to the value of community and social support; other authors focus on specific phases of treatment; some speak to the length and timing of treatment; and still other authors present multiphase, multimodality models to treatment. Nearly all authors speak to the importance of including environmental features into treatment. The following is an attempt to overview the various treatment recommendations for traumatized children. There are many approaches recommended for the treatment of trauma symptoms in children. Some authors speak to the value of community and social support; other authors focus on specific phases of treatment; some speak to the length and timing of treatment; and still other authors present multi-phase, multi-modality models to treatment. Near all authors speak to the importance of including environmental features into treatment. The following is an attempt to overview the various treatment recommendations for traumatized children.

As the mental health concerns of low-income, multiethnic, and/or multiproblem families and abused children have not been adequately researched, nor addressed, it is important to include such individuals and families in their own assessment and treatment plans across micro, meso, and macro interventions. The following are therapeutic strategies designed to guide individuals and families through the challenge of healing while ideally allowing clients to be the stewards of their own treatment.

Micro, Multiphase/Multimodality Therapeutic Models. As abuse trauma resonates throughout the many dimensions of life, a single type of treatment is typically inadequate in comprehensively addressing client needs. Thus, many trauma treatments do not focus on simply one phase or method of intervention. The multiphase/multimodality strategies are designed to address the many stages and many dimensions of trauma reactions. Most of these models stress the incorporation of a child's environment in healing strategies, including where and **when** appropriate, family participation. While these models largely focus on micro-level therapeutic interventions, the importance of a child's readaptation to his or her community is often emphasized as well.

Susan G. Forman (1993), in discussing stress reactions in children, recommends a combination of therapeutic techniques. These techniques are a collection of body/mind interventions, including relaxation exercises, problem solving methods, social skills and assertiveness training, the teaching of self-instruction skills, reframing irrational ideas, promoting stress-reducing cognitions, altering beliefs about success and failure, and encouraging behavioral self-control. Numerous forums can be utilized to employ these interventions, including individual, group, and family therapy, as well as incorporating integral community institutions, such as one's school and/or church. This multi-method, multi-forum therapy is designed to help the traumatized child renegotiate his or her environment in a healthy way.

Herman (1992) writes about developing a safe, healing relationship between the therapist and client. In the context of the establishment of this safety, the recollection and mourning of trauma can begin. Then, the safe one-on-one relationship can be parlayed into other modalities, such as family therapy, in promoting a reconnection with other significant people. Also, group therapy can promote a sense of commonality and a normalizing of common reaction symptoms to trauma. Ultimately, the goal is to generalize the principles of the trusting therapeutic relationship for use in the rest of the client's environment.

Jerome Kroll (1993) recommends a multi-phase model in treating PTSD. This model involves many aspects of re-exploring the environmental trauma. The therapist first attempts to assist the client to deal with their past environmental trauma by exploring the nature of post-traumatic symptoms, feelings of disillusionment, feelings of guilt regarding any perceptions of shared blame, and then the possibility of forgiveness. Next, the therapist helps the client interpret how the past trauma may dictate the future by examining any disassociative symptoms, self-contempt, repetition compulsions, and mistrust of self and/or others. The therapist then proceeds to examine how the past trauma interplays in therapeutic transference by permitting the client to "test" the therapist for rejection, seduction, victimization, and exploitation. When the therapist successfully "passes" these tests, the therapeutic relationship is thought to be proved a safe microcosm of the environment. This safety provides the space in which a client can integrate environmental traumatic experiences into a restored sense of self.

Block (1991) sees the healing process an in five stages. The first stage emerges from feelings of hopelessness and promotes the following resolution: "I won't be hurt again!" The therapist supports the client in making this resolution. The second stage revolves around a theory that the client has what is known as a "traumatic boundary" or "safe zone." This zone is thought to be erected to defend the client against a re-experiencing of environmental assaults. The second stage of Block's treatment involves the therapist's being invited into the client's safe zone. The third stage involves a quest for 're-understanding' of the trauma. In this stage, the therapist attempts to help reframe the negative messages that the client may have created spontaneously to make sense of the traumatic situation. Many of these messages contain self-condemning themes, which the therapist seeks to de-and-recode. In the fourth stage, the therapist seeks to support the client by creating a "Bystander Phenomenon." In this stage, the therapist tries to recreate the trauma and convey a sense of "objective outrage" at the client's victimization. In the fifth stage, the therapist attempts to help the client examine and reverse feelings of shame and guilt. Thus, Block's therapy systematically seeks to unravel the mystery of the client's reaction to environmental trauma and then helps the client reweave a safe life-perception.

Frank M. Ochberg (1991) proposes a model of post-traumatic therapy that strives to help the victim regain a sense of normalcy. Ochberg states, "Since traumatized and victimized individuals are reacting to abnormal events, they may confuse the abnormality of the trauma with the abnormality of themselves" (p. 5). Thus, Ochberg attempts to employ the "normalization principles," which include the following: PTSD is a normal reaction to extremely stressful environmental trauma; the therapist is integral in helping the client feel re-empowered as an adaptive human being; and every individual has an idiosyncratic path toward recovery. Ochberg stresses strategies in employing these principles, such as role playing, hypnotherapy, education, nutrition, humor, and exercise. The therapeutic experiences can include working through grief and extinguishing fear responses through desensitization, medication, and telling the trauma story. Ochberg stresses the importance of social support and integration of the client into a nurturing environment.

Carolyn M. Aldwin (1994) also sees adaptation to stress as a normal part of development. Aldwin, in fact, views childhood trauma reactions as revisable blueprints from which more adaptive, adult coping styles can be developed. Through Transactional Analysis, Aldwin feels that individuals can reassign meaning, reaction, and patterns of coping in adapting to a changing, variably stressful environment.

van der Veer (1992) incorporates five theoretical approaches in treatment recommendations: The psychiatric approach (in which medications use is considered); the psychodynamic approach; the family therapy approach; the learning theory approach; and the cognitive approach. van der Veer feels that it is important to treat the survivor of trauma with an eye to the various dimensions of the post-traumatic sequelae—the various ways in which environmental trauma can intrude upon an individual's ability to function.

Community and Social Support in the Treatment of Trauma Related Symptoms

Most all treatment strategies stress the importance of initially removing the youngster from traumatic stressors, or removing the stressors from the child, as the first essential feature of treatment. In fact, in some cases, such removal may significantly lessen symptoms in and of itself. Many trauma symptoms lessen spontaneously over time in stressor free environments (Sack, Clarke, et al., 1993). Goodwin (1985) notes that increased fear could be indicative of "failures in environmental protection" that may require active further protection intervention prior to continuing work on dynamic issues.

However, removal of the child from the environment wherein the stress took place is not uniformly useful. Mennen (1993) found that anxiety actually tends to increase when a child is removed from the home if the perpetrator is not a family member. This may speak to the importance of lobbying for legislation that, in many cases, removes the stress (including the perpetrator) from the child rather than the child from the stress-containing environment. The importance of social and community support is stressed by many authors.

Krammer and Green (1991) report that the use of an informal support network was negatively correlated with the intensity of PTSD symptoms though the presence of PTSD was not affected. Terr (1991) conducted a 4-year follow-up study of school bus kidnaping victims. Symptom severity was related to the youngster's previous vulnerabilities, family dysfunction, and community bonding, again pointing to the importance of social and community support as factors in treatment.

Wilson and Lindy (1994) speak to a person-environment approach to traumatic stress reactions. Wilson examines the individual's subjective response to trauma, (affective, and cognitive and neurophysiological) as well as the post traumatic milieu. Wilson charges the therapist in assisting the client in making adaptations in the post-trauma community and social environment.

Janoff-Bulman (1985) stresses the need to utilize coping strategies in treatment —strategies that focus on helping the "victim" regain a sense of power in the community. Janoff-Bulman (1985) speaks to the need to reconstruct "shattered assumptions" after the trauma. Janoff-Bulman feels that PTSD symptoms largely result from the demolition of an individual's underlying assumptions about life. After a serious trauma or series of traumas, a person may feel excessively vulnerable, may no longer see life as having meaning, and may lose a positive self-perception. Janoff-Bulman makes suggestions about how to incorporate specific coping strategies in therapy. The therapist should help the client redefine the event, find meaning in the trauma, change debilitating behaviors, seek social support, and counteract self-blame. Janoff-Bullman extols utilizing social support in undoing self-blame as a "coping strategy that is surprisingly adaptive in terms of reestablishing shattered assumptions" (p. 15). The importance of utilizing environmental support in treatment is underscored.

Some authors recommend creative ways to bring the social environment into the treatment setting. Group therapy is often used as a way of bringing a microcosm of society into therapy. van der Kolk (1985) found "although controlled studies are lacking, clinical experience suggests that group therapy is the treatment of choice for many patients with PTSD... Group psychotherapy allows for partial recreation of the peer group, and the sharing and reliving of common experiences may facilitate entrance into the world of adult relationships, a process that was arrested by the trauma" (p. 369). Thus, van der Kolk sees group therapy as a way of simulating the client's social environment in treatment.

Successful experience dealing with traumatic episodes in the past has been correlated with a positive prognosis for those who have experienced trauma (Martini, Ryan, et al., 1989). As young persons, by definition, do not have a considerable amount of previous life experience, psychoeducational methods/techniques about others' successful experience in dealing with trauma can be vicariously therapeutic. An inclusion of community members who have had such successful experiences can also be a helpful feature in treatment.

Specific Examples of Meso Level Interventions

In Utah, as part of a Children's Bureau Initiative, a wide range of service providers and clients met to collectively design coordinated treatment strategies, which would include environmental services for those with mental health, child abuse, substance abuse, unemployment, and domestic violence concerns. A consortium of mental health professionals, child protective service administrators, substance abuse treatment providers, and Workforce Service (TANF) staff, meet monthly with "family experts." Family experts are largely mental health clients from low-income, ethnically representative groups. The consortium, also known as "The Utah Design Team," has monthly meetings with client consultants about the improvement of services. Also, client family experts are involved as guest lecturers in courses at the University of Utah, Graduate School of Social Work (GSSW), to discuss the importance of including cultural, socioeconomic, and traumatic factors in mental health assessment and treatment. Recently, family experts have been included in the GSSW's curriculum committee to consult on the creation of culturally and socioeconomically inclusive social work curricula.

Examples of Macro Level Interventions

In addition, in coordination with the Utah Chapter of the National Association of Social Workers (UCNASW), family experts were afforded the opportunity to learn how to influence the state legislature at UCNASW's annual lobby day. One family expert joined UCNASW's Political Action Committee. In an effort to reach a national audience, another client family expert detailed experiences of mental illness, abuse, familial substance use, domestic violence, and poverty in a now completed novel. Yet another family expert, based on her experiences, developed an informative one-woman-show involving the multifactorial struggles of homeless mentally ill women (Browne, 1993). Her solo performance was showcased at a function involving the entire Utah State Legislature, followed by a standing ovation from legislators.

Summary

The previous chapter explored the importance of including environmental factors in diagnostic formulations when working with low-income, multi-problem, and/or ethnically diverse children and families. The link between diagnostic assessment and funding for services was underscored (Jansson, 1995).

While PTSD criteria might not address all of the nuances of understudied, abused, low-income, minority, and/or multiproblem children and families, the inclusion of environmental considerations is particularly important in the mental health assessment of such children and families. As discussed, PTSD is the only DSM-IV diagnosis which specifically cites environmental factors as integral in the etiology of persistent, serious symptoms (American Psychiatric Association, 1994). Thus, in cases involving abuse, arguably one litmus test for familial vulnerability, clinicians are encouraged to consider environmentally inclusive diagnoses as primary Axis I diagnostic labels, such as PTSD, when criteria has been met.

Social workers should also fight for the funding of the PTSD diagnosis, as well as for the development and DSM-IV adoption of other environmentally triggered diagnoses. The PTSD Diagnosis legitimizes funding for services to the child victim, the family, and for conditions associated with abuse perpetration such as poverty, unemployment, substance abuse, and perpetrator mental illness. As low-income, multiethnic, and/or multiproblem individuals' and families' mental health concerns have not been sufficiently studied or included in treatment, clients should be encouraged and given opportunities for empowerment to influence their own treatment plans, meso-level service system providers and educators, and macro-level legislation and public perceptions.

The social work voice is required to combat "clinical denial" as well as reinforce the burgeoning public awareness of environmental factors, such as child abuse, and mental health diagnoses. As has been seen, diagnostic conceptualizations often direct treatment plans and policies. Thus, it is extremely important for social workers to document the relationship between environmental trauma, such as child abuse, and mental health problems. It is also important for social workers to remember minority and/or disadvantaged groups in researching the nuances of this relationship. Mc New & Abell (1995) note that the lack of connection between environmental stressors and diagnoses may result in "an inappropriate use of institutionalization or counter-therapeutic" interventions (p. 123). Thus, research is required that investigates the association between environmental trauma and psychiatric symptoms to ensure that treatment plans and funding include those who have problems associated with abuse and/or other trauma.

As social workers with a person-in-environment perspective, we must speak to the external issues (largely ignored by the DSM IV) that face our clientele. It is extremely important that social workers voice a need to include environmental factors in diagnostic decisions and contingent treatment plans and policies; it is critical that we retain a keen awareness of the environmental conditions which can impact upon mental and emotional functioning. We must be prepared to argue that symptomatology can include factors that are generated and sustained in part by external, as well as internal, difficulties. Framed in this way, such problems are able to be addressed rather than simply condemned. Social workers must be willing to voice opposition to the trend to narrow our understanding of mental illness to the most simple, manageable, and exclusively medically treatable concepts. We must retain our person-in-environment perspective.

References

Achenbach, T. M. (1985). *Assessment and taxonomy of child and adolescent psychopathology: Developmental clinical psychology and psychiatry* (Vol. 3). Beverly Hills, CA: Sage Publications.

Adams, J., McClellan, J., Douglass, D., and McCurry, S. (1995). Sexually inappropriate behaviors in seriously mentally ill children and adolescents. *Child Abuse and Neglect, 19*(5), 555-568.

Adelman, H. S. (1995). Clinical psychology: Beyond psychopathology and clinical interventions. *Clinical Psychology: Science and Practice, 2*(1), 28-44.

Aldwin, C. M. (1994). *Stress, coping and development: An integrative perspective.* New York: The Guilford Press.

American Psychiatric Association. (1952). *Diagnostic and statistical manual of mental disorders.* Washington, DC: Author.

American Psychiatric Association. (1968). *Diagnostic and statistical manual of mental disorders* (2nd ed.). Washington, DC: Author.

American Psychiatric Association. (1980). *Diagnostic and statistical manual of mental disorders* (3rd ed.). Washington, DC: Author.

American Psychiatric Association. (1987). *Diagnostic and statistical manual of mental disorders* (3rd ed., rev.). Washington, DC: Author.

American Psychiatric Association. (1994). *Diagnostic and statistical manual of mental disorders* (4th ed.). Washington, DC: Author.

Antler, S. (1978). Child abuse: an emerging social priority. *Social Work, 23*(1), 58-61.

Astin, M. C., Ogland-Hand, S. M., Coleman, E. M., and Foy, D. W. (1995). Posttraumatic stress disorder and childhood abuse in battered women: Comparisons with maritally distressed women. *Journal of Consulting and Clinical Psychology, 63*(2), 308-312.

Baca, L. M., and Koss-Chioino, J. D. (1997). Development of a culturally responsive group counselling model for Mexican American adolescents. *Journal of Multicultural Counseling and Development, 25*(2), 130-141.

Barahal, R. M., Waterman, J., and Martin, H. P. (1981). The social cognitive development of abused children. *Journal of Consulting and Clinical Psychology, 49*(4), 508-516.

Benedek, E. P. (1985). Children and psychic trauma: A brief review of contemporary thinking. In S. Eth & R. S. Pynoos (Eds.). *Posttraumatic stress disorder in children* (pp. 1-16). Washington, DC: American Psychiatric Association.

Berlinger, L. (1995). Child sexual abuse: Direct practice. In National Association of Social Workers (Ed.). *Encyclopedia of social work* (pp. 408-417). Washington, DC: National Association of Social Workers Press.

Bernstein, G. A. and Borchardt, C. M. (1991). Anxiety disorders of childhood and adolescence: A critical review. *Journal of the American Academy of Child and Adolescent Psychiatry, 30*(4), 519-532.

Block E. L. (1991). Post-Traumatic Stress Disorder—Therapeutic approach avoidance: an illustrative case. *Psychotherapy, 28,* 1, 162-167.

Bloom, B. (1979). Prevention of mental disorders: Recent advances in theory and practice. *Community Mental Health Journal, 15,* 179-191.

Boney-McCoy, S. and Finkelhor, D. (1995). Prior victimization: A risk factor for child sexual abuse and for PTSD-related symptomatology among sexually abused youth. *Child Abuse and Neglect, 19*(12), 1401-1421.

Bools, C. Neale, B., and Meadow, R. (1994). Munchausen Syndrome by Proxy: a study of psychopathology. *Child Abuse and Neglect, 18*(9), 773-788.

Bowman, E. S. (1993). Etiology and clinical course of pseudoseizures: Relationship to trauma, depression, and dissociation. *Psychosomatics, 34*(4), 333-342.

Branscomb, L. P. and Fagan, J. (1992). Development and validation of a scale measuring childhood dissociation in adults: The Childhood Disassociative Predictor Scale. *Dissociation Progress in the Disassociative Disorders, 5*(2), 80-86.

Bremmer, J. D., Randall, P., Scott, T., and Capelli, S. (1995). Deficits in short-term memory in adult survivors of childhood sexual abuse. *Psychiatry Research, 59*(1-2), 97-102.

Brett, E. A., Spitzer, R. L., and Williams, B. W. (1988). DSM-III criteria for posttraumatic stress disorder. *American Journal of Psychiatry, 145*(10), 1232-1236.

Briere, J. N. (1992). *Child abuse trauma: Theory and treatment of lasting effects.* Newbury Park, CA: Sage Publications.

Briere, J. N. and Runtz, M. (1988). Postsexual abuse trauma: Data and implications for clinical practice. *Journal of Interpersonal Violence, 2,* 367-379.

Briar, K. (1988). *Social work and the unemployed.* National Association of Social Workers Press.

Browne, A. (1993). Family violence and homelessness: The relevance of trauma histories in the lives of homeless women. *American Journal of Orthopsychiatry, 63*(3), 370-384.

Browne, A. and Finkelhor, D. (1987). Impact of child sexual abuse: A review of the research. *Psychological Bulletin, 99,* 66-77.

Busby, D. M. (1996). Symptoms of survivors of physical and sexual abuse. In D. M. Busby (Ed.). *The impact of violence on the family* (pp. 213-227). Needham Heights, MA: Allyn & Bacon.

Callicutt, J. W. (1987). Mental health services. In *Encyclopedia of social work* (Vol. 2, pp. 125-135). Silver Spring, MD: National Association of Social Workers.

Campbell, T. W. (1992). False allegations of sexual abuse and their apparent credibility. *American Journal of Forensic Psychology, 10*(4), 21-35.

Carrey, N. J., Butter, H. J., Persinger, M. A., and Bialik, R. J. (1995). Physiological and cognitive correlates of child abuse. *Journal of the American Academy of Child and Adolescent Psychiatry, 34*(8), 1067-1075.

Cervantes, R. C. and Arroya, W. (1994). DSM-IV: Implications for Hispanic children and adolescents. *Hispanic Journal of Behavioral Sciences, 5,* 93-103.

Charney, D. S., Deutch, A. Y., Krystal, J. H., Southwick, S. M., and Davis, M. (1993). Psychobiologic mechanisms of posttraumatic stress disorder. *Archives of General Psychiatry, 50,* 294-305.

Chemtob, C., Roiblat, H. L., Hamada, R. S., Carlson, J. G., and Twentyman, C. T. (1988). A cognitive action theory of posttraumatic stress disorder. *Journal of Anxiety Disorders, 2,* 253-275.

Cherepon, J. A. and Prinzhorn, B. (1994). Personality Assessment Inventory (PAI) profiles of adult female abuse survivors. *Assessment, 1*(4), 393-399.

Connelly, C. D. and Straus, M. A. (1992). Mother's age and risk for physical abuse. *Child Abuse and Neglect, 16*(5), 709-718.

Conte, J. R. (1995). Child sexual abuse overview. In National Association of Social Work (Ed.). *Encyclopedia of social work* (pp. 402-408). Washington, DC: National Association of Social Workers Press.

Creamer, M., Burgess, P., and Pattison, P. (1990). Cognitive processing in posttrauma reactions: Some preliminary findings. *Psychological Medicine, 20,* 597-604.

Daro, D., Jones, E., and McCurdy, K. (1990). Reliability and validity of the National Incidence Study conducted by Westat Associates in 1988: Methodological review. In S. J. Wells (Ed.), *Child abuse and neglect overview* (pp. 346-353). Washington, DC: National Association of Social Workers Press.

De-Bellis, M. D., Lefter, L., Trickett, P. K., and Putnam, F. (1994). Urinary catecholamine excretion in sexually abused girls. *Journal of the American Academy of Child and Adolescent Psychiatry, 33*(3), 320-327.

Deblinger, E., Mc Leer, S. V., Atkins, M. S., Ralphe, D., and Foa, E. (1989). Posttraumatic stress in sexually abused, physically abused, and nonabused children. *Child Abuse and Neglect, 13*(3), 403-408.

Deblinger, E., Mc Leer, S. V., and Henry, D. (1990). Cognitive behavioral treatment for sexually abused children suffering posttraumatic stress: Preliminary findings. *Journal of the American Academy of Child and Adolescent Psychiatry, 29*(5), 747-752.

Dodge, K. A., Pettit, G. S., Bates, J. E., and Valente, E. (1995). Social information-processing patterns partially mediate the effect of early physical abuse on later conduct problems. *Journal of Abnormal Psychology, 104*(4), 632-643.

Durant, R. H., Cadenhead, C., Pendergrast, R. A., Slavens, G., and Linden, C. W. (1994). Factors associated with the use of violence among urban Black adolescents. *American Journal of Public Health, 84,* 612-617.

Egami, Y., Ford, D. E., Greenfield, S. F., and Crum, R. M. (1996). Psychiatric profile and sociodemographic characteristics of adults who report physically abusing or neglecting children. *American Journal of Psychiatry, 153*(7), 921-928.

Ellason, J. W., Ross, C. A., Sainton, K., and Mayran, L. W. (1996). Axis I and II comorbidity and childhood trauma history in chemical dependency. *Bulletin of the Menninger Clinic, 60*(1), 39-51.

Fabrega, H. (1994). Hispanic mental health research: A case for cultural psychiatry. In C. Telles and M. Karno (Eds.). *Latino mental health: Current research and policy perspectives* (pp. 139-169). Los Angeles: Neuropsychiatric Institute, University of California at Los Angeles and The National Institute of Mental Health.

Famularo, R., Fenton, T., Kinscherff, R., and Ayoub, C. (1994). Maternal and child posttraumatic stress disorder in cases of child maltreatment. *Child Abuse and Neglect, 18*(1), 27-36.

Famularo, R., Kinscherff, R., and Fenton, T. (1991). Posttraumatic stress disorder among children clinically diagnosed as borderline personality disorder. *The Journal of Nervous and Mental Disease, 179*, 428-431.

Famularo, R., Kinscherff, R., Fenton, T., and Bolduc, S. M. (1990). Child maltreatment histories among runaway and delinquent children. *Clinical Pediatrics, 29*(12), 713-718.

Feinstein, A. (1989). Posttraumatic stress disorder: A descriptive study supporting DSM-III-R criteria. *American Journal of Psychiatry, 146*(5), 665-666.

Feinstein, A. and Dolan, R. (1991). Predictors of posttraumatic stress disorder following physical trauma: An examination of the stressor criterion. *Psychological Medicine, 21*, 85-91.

Figley, C. R., Scrignar, C. B., and Smith, W. H. (1992, March). The aftershocks of trauma: Posttraumatic stress disorder encompasses a wide spectrum of psychiatric diagnoses. Can you identify it even when your patient doesn't make the connection between the trauma and the symptoms? *Patient Care*, pp. 121-148.

Finkelhor, D. (1988). The trauma of child sexual abuse: Two models. *Journal of Interpersonal Violence, 2*(4), 348-366.

Finkelhor, D. (1992). *Child abuse trauma: Theory and treatment of the lasting effects*. Newbury Park, CA: Sage Publications.

Finkelhor D. and Browne, A. (1985). The traumatic impact of child sexual abuse: A conceptualization. *American Journal of Orthopsychiatry, 55*(44), 530-541.

Finkelhor, D., Hotaling, G., Lewis, I. A., and Smith, C. (1990). Sexual abuse in a national survey of adult men and women: Prevalence, characteristics, and risk factors. *Child Abuse and Neglect, 14*, 19-28.

Fontana, V. J. (1971). *The maltreated child*. Springfield, MA: Charles C. Thomas.

Forman, S. G. (1993). *Coping skills interventions for children and adolescents*. San Francisco: Jossey-Bass Publishers.

Fraser, M. W. (1997). The ecology of childhood: A multisystems perspective. In M. W. Fraser (Ed.), *Risk and resilience in childhood: An ecological perspective* (pp. 1-9). Washington, DC: National Association of Social Workers Press.

Fraser, M. W. and Galinsky, M. J. (1997). Toward a resilience-based model of practice. In M. W. Fraser (Ed.). *Risk and resilience in childhood: An ecological perspective* (pp. 265-275). Washington, DC: National Association of Social Workers Press.

Garland, A. F., Lansverk, J. L., Hough, R. L., and Ellis-Macleod, E. (1996). Type of maltreatment as a predicator of mental health service use for children in foster care. *Child Abuse and Neglect, 20*(8), 675-688.

Gelles, R. J. and Straus, M.A. (1979). Violence and the American family. *Journal of Social Issues, 35*(2), 15-39.

Germain, C. and Gittelman, A. (1980). *Life model of social work practice.* New York: Columbia University Press.

Germain, C. and Gittelman, A. (1994). Ecological perspective. In National Association of Social Workers (Ed.). *Encyclopedia of social work* (pp. 816-824). Silver Spring, MD: National Association of Social Workers Press.

Gislason, I. L. and Call, J. D. (1982). Dog bite in infancy: Trauma and personality development. *Journal of the American Academy of Child Psychiatry, 21*, 203-207.

Goldstein, E. G. (1987). Mental health and illness. In National Association of Social Workers (Ed.). *Encyclopedia of social work* (18th ed., pp. 102-111). Silver Spring, MD: National Association of Social Workers Press.

Goodwin, J. (1985). Post traumatic symptoms in incest victims. pp. 157-167. In S. Eth, and R. S. Pynoos (Eds.). *Post-traumatic stress disorder in children.* Washington, D.C.: American Psychiatric Association.

Gonzalez, G. M. (1997). The emergence of Chicanos in the twenty-first century: Implications for counseling, research, and policy. *Journal of Multicultural Counseling and Development, 25*(2), 94-106.

Gonzalez, G. M., Castillo-Canez, I., Tarke, J., Soriano, F., Garcia, P., and Valasquez, R. J. (1997). Promoting the culturally sensitive diagnosis of Mexican Americans: Some personal insights. *Journal of Multicultural and Counseling Development, 25*(2), 156-161.

Green, A. H. (1983). Dimension of psychological trauma in abused children. *Journal of the American Academy of Child Psychiatry, 22*(3), 231-237.

Green, A. H. (1985). Children traumatized by physical abuse. In S. Eth and R. S. Pynoos (Eds.). *Posttraumatic stress disorder in children* (pp. 135-154). Washington, DC: American Psychiatric Association.

Green, A. H. (1995). Comparing child victims and adult survivors: Clues to the pathogenesis of child sexual abuse. *Journal of the American Academy of Psychoanalysis, 23*(4), 655-670.

Green, B. L., Lindy, J. D., and Grace, M. (1985). Posttraumatic stress disorder toward DSM-IV. *Journal of Nervous and Mental Disease, 173*(1), 406-411.

Greenblatt, M. (1957). Implications for psychiatry and hospital practice: The movement from custodial hospital to therapeutic community. In M. Greenblatt, D. J. Levinson, and R. H. Williams (Eds.). *The patient and the mental hospital: Contributions of research in the science of social behavior* (pp. 611-619). Glencoe, MA: The Free Press.

Greg, G. R. and Parks, E. D. (1995). Selected Minnesota Multiphasic Personality Inventory-2 Scales for identifying women with a history of sexual abuse. *Journal of Nervous and Mental Disease, 183*(1), 53-56.

Grob, G. N. (1973). *Mental institutions in America: Social policy to 1875.* New York: The Free Press.

Guarnaccia, P. J., Good, B. J., and Kleinman, A. (1990). A critical review of epidemiological studies of Puerto Rican mental health. *American Journal of Psychiatry, 147*(11), 1449-1456.

Guthrie, R. (1976). *Even the rat was white.* New York: Harper & Row.

Hack, T. F., Osachuck, T. A. G., and de Luca, R. V. (1994). Group treatment for sexually abused preadolescent boys. *Families in Society, 75*(4), 217-228.

Harmon, R. J. and Riggs, P. D. (1996). Clonidine for posttraumatic stress disorder in preschool children. *Journal of the American Academy of Child and Adolescent Psychiatry, 35*(9), 1247-1249.

Hartman, C. R. and Burgess, A. W. (1993). Information processing of trauma. *Child Abuse and Neglect, 17*(1), 47-58.

Harvard Medical School. (1993, July). Child abuse: Parts I and II, special supplement. *The Harvard Mental Health Letter,* p. 6.

Heffernan, J. (1988). *Social welfare and social work: An introduction.* St. Paul, MN: West Publishing.

Henk, M. (1985). Developing codes and classifications for social workers in health care. In J. M. Karls and K. E. Wandrel (Eds.). *Person-in-environment: Encyclopedia of social work* (Vol. 3, pp. 1818-1827). Washington, DC: National Association of Social Work.

Herman, J. L. (1992). *Trauma and recovery: The aftermath of violence—from domestic abuse to political terror.* New York: Basic Books.

Herrenkohl, E. C., Herrenkohl, R. C., Rupert, L. J., and Egolf, B. P. (1995). Risk factors for behavioral dysfunction: The relative impact of maltreatment, socioeconomic status, physical health problems, cognitive ability, and quality of parent-child interaction. *Child Abuse and Neglect, 19*(2), 191-203.

Hindman, M. H. (1979). Family violence: an overview. *Alcohol Health and Research World, 4*(1), 2-11.

Hogan, P. T. and Siu, S. F. (1988). Minority children and the child welfare system: An historical perspective. *Social Work, 33*(6), 493-498.

Holzhauser, R.A. (1979). The addiction syndrome---A model training program for counselors. *Alcohol Health and Research World, 4*(1), 28-30.

Hong, G. K. and Hong, L. K. (1991). Comparative perspectives on child abuse and neglect: Chinese versus Hispanics and Whites. *Child Welfare, 70*(4), 463-475.

Horowitz, M. J. (1976). *Stress response syndromes.* New York: Jason Aronson.

Howling, P. T., Wodarski, J. S., Kurtz, D. P., and Gaudin, J. M. (1993). *Maltreatment and the school-age child: Developmental outcomes and system issues.* New York: The Haworth Press.

Hullings-Catalano, V. (1996). Physical abuse of children by parents. In D. M. Busby (Ed.). *The impact of violence on the family* (pp. 43-74). Needham Heights: Allyn & Bacon.

Hussey, D. L. and Singer, M. (1993). Psychological distress, problem behaviors, and family functioning of sexually abused adolescent inpatients. *Journal of the American Academy of Child and Adolescent Psychiatry, 32*(5), 954-961.

Iijima-Hall, C. C. (1997). Cultural malpractice: The growing obsolescence of psychology with the changing U.S. population. *American Psychologist, 52*(6), 642-651.

Iverson, T. J. and Segal, M. (1990). *Child abuse and neglect: An information and reference guide.* New York: Garland and Publishing, Inc.

Janoff-Bulman, R. (1985). The aftermath of victimization: Rebuilding shattered assumptions. In C. Figley (Ed.). *Trauma and its wake: The study of posttraumatic stress disorders* (pp. 1-24). New York: Brunner/Mazel.

Jansson, B. (1994). *Social policy: From theory to practice.* Pacific Grove, CA: Brooks/Cole Publishing.

Jones, L. (1990). Unemployment and child abuse. *Families in Society: The Journal of Contemporary Human Services*, 71(10), 579-87.

Junewicz, W. J. (1983). A protective posture toward emotional neglect and abuse. *Child Welfare, 62*(3), 243-252.

Kachigan, S. K. (1986). *Statistical analysis: An interdisciplinary introduction to univariate and multivariate methods.* New York: Radius Press.

Kardiner, A. and Spiegel, H. (1947). *War, stress, and neurotic illness: The traumatic neuroses of war* (rev. ed.). New York: Hoeber Press.

Karls, J. M. and Wandrei, K. E. (1992a). PIE: A new language for social work. *Social Work, 37*, 80-85.

Karls, J. M. and Wandrei, K. E. (1992b). The person-in-environment system for classifying client problems. *Journal of Case Management, 1*(3), 90-95.

Karls, J. M. and Wandrei, K. E. (1995). *Person-in-environment system: The PIE classification system for social functioning problems.* Washington, DC: National Association of Social Workers Press.

Karno, M. (1994). The prevalence of mental disorders among persons of Mexican birth or origin. In C. Telles and M. Karno (Eds.). *Latino mental health: Current research and policy perspectives* (pp. 3-16). Los Angeles: Neuropsychiatric Institute, University of California at Los Angeles and The National Institute of Mental Health.

Kempe, C. H., Silverman, F. N., Steele, B. F., Droegemueller, W., and Silver, H. K. (1962). The battered child syndrome. *Journal of the American Medical Association, 181*(1), 17-24.

Kirk, S., Saporin, M., and Kutchincs, H. (1989). The prognosis for social work diagnosis. *Social Casework, 68*(5), 295-304.

Kiser, L. J., Heston, J., Millsap, P., and Pruitt, D. (1991). Physical and sexual abuse in childhood: Relationship with posttraumatic stress disorder. *Journal of the American Academy of Child and Adolescent Psychiatry, 30*(5), 776-783.

Klerman, G. L., Valliant, G. E., Spitzer, R. L., and Michels, R. (1984). A debate on DSM-III. *American Journal of Psychiatry, 141*(4), 539-553.

Kotulak, R. (1996). Why some kids turn violent. In R. Kotulak (Ed.), *Inside the brain: Revolutionary discoveries of how the mind works* (pp. 77-86). Kansas City: Andrews and McMeel Publishing.

Krammer, T. and Green, B. L. (1991). Posttraumatic stress disorder as an early response to sexual assault. *Journal of Interpersonal Violence, 6*(2), 160-173.

Kreitler, S. and Kreitler, H. (1988). Trauma and anxiety: The cognitive approach. *Journal of Traumatic Stress, 1*(1), 35-56.

Kroll, J. (1993). *P.T.S.D./Borderlines in therapy: Finding the balance.* (Chapters 1-4). New York: W. W. Norton & Company.

Kurtz, P. D., Gaudin, J. M., Wodarski, J. S., and Howling, P. T. (1993). Maltreatment and the school-aged child: School performance consequences. *Child Abuse and Neglect, 17*(5), 581-589.

Lawrence, K. J., Cozolino, L., and Foy, D. W. (1995). Psychological sequelae in adult females reporting childhood ritualistic abuse. *Child Abuse and Neglect, 19*(8), 975-984.

Lazarus, R. S. and Folkman, S. (1984). *Stress, appraisal, and coping.* New York: Springer Publishing Company.

Levine, L. B. (1996). Adult survivors of incest. In D. M. Busby (Ed.), *The impact of violence on the family* (pp. 185-212). Needham Heights, MA: Allyn & Bacon.

Lieberman, F. (1987). Mental health and mental illness. In National Association of Social Workers (Ed.), *Encyclopedia of social work* (18th ed., pp. 111-125). Silver Spring, MD: National Association of Social Workers Press.

Lopez, S. R. (1994). Latinos and the expression of psychopathology: A call for the direct assessment of cultural influences. In C. Telles and M. Karno (Eds.), *Latino mental health: Current research and policy perspectives* (pp. 109-127). Los Angeles: Neuropsychiatric Institute, University of California at Los Angeles and The National Institute of Mental Health.

Louis, Condon, Shute, and Elzinga. (1997). The development of the Louis MACRO (mother and child risk observation forms: assessing parent-infant-child risk in the presence of maternal mental illness. *Child Abuse and Neglect, 2*(7), 589-606.

Martinez, C. (1994). Psychiatric treatment of Mexican Americans: A review. In C. Telles and M. Karno (Eds.), *Latino mental health: Current research and policy perspectives* (pp. 227-239). Martinez, F. (1994). Mental health research in the public sector and its impact on Hispanic clients. In C. Telles and M. Karno (Eds.), *Latino mental health: Current research and policy perspectives.*(pp. 243-248). Los Angeles: Neuropsychiatric Institute, University of California at Los Angeles and The National Institute of Mental Health.

Mattani, M. and Kirk, S. (1992). Assessing assessment in social work. *Social Work, 36,* 260-266.

Martini, R. D., Ryan, C., Nakayama, D., and Ramenofsky, M. (1989). Psychiatric sequelae after traumatic injury: The Pittsburgh Regatta accident. *The Journal of the American Academy of Child and Adolescent Psychiatry. 29* (1): 70-75.

Mc Leer, S. V., Callaghan, M., Henry, C., and Wallen, J. (1994). Psychiatric disorders in sexually abused children. *Journal of the American Academy of Child and Adolescent Psychiatry, 33*(3), 313-319.

Mc Leer, S. V., Deblinger, E., Henry, D., and Orvaschel, H. (1992). Sexually abused children at high risk for posttraumatic stress disorder. *Journal of the American Academy of Child Psychiatry, 31*(5), 875-879.

McNew, J. A. and Abell, N. (1995). Posttraumatic stress symptomatology: Similarities and differences between Vietnam veterans and adult survivors of sexual abuse. *Social Work, 40*(1), 115-126.

McNicoll, P. M. A. (1989). The social and economic precursors of child maltreatment: a study of the ecosystem. Doctoral Dissertation, University of Washington, 1989). *Social Work Abstracts,* 23075.

Mennen, F. E. (1993). Evaluation of risk factors in childhood sexual abuse. *The Journal of the American Academy of Child and Adolescent Psychiatry, 32,* (5) 934-939.

Mennen, F. E. and Meadow, D. (1993). The relationship of sexual abuse to symptom levels in emotionally disturbed girls. *Child and Adolescent Social Work Journal, 10*(4), 319-328.

Mennen, F. E. and Meadow, D. (1994). A preliminary study of the factors related to trauma in childhood sexual abuse. *Journal of Family Violence, 9*(2), 125-142.

Mezzich, J. E. and Saavedra, J. (1994). DSM-IV development and Hispanic issues. In C. Telles and M. Karno (Eds.). *Latino mental health: Current research and policy perspectives* (pp. 171-180). Los Angeles: Neuropsychiatric Institute, University of California at Los Angeles and The National Institute of Mental Health.

Midgow, J. (1994). Silencing the child. *Transactional Analysis Journal, 24*(3), 178-184.

Molton, P. (1996). Incest, false accusations of incest and false denials of incest: Discerning the truth in the debates about recovered memory. *Journal of Mental Health, 5*(2), 167-172.

Moscarello, R. (1991). Posttraumatic stress disorder after sexual assault: Its Psychodynamic and treatment. *Journal of the American Academy of Psychoanalysis, 19*(2), 235-253.

Musicar, L. and Josefowitz, N. (1996). Flashback phenomenon in survivors of childhood sexual abuse: A four-stage treatment model. *Journal of Contemporary Psychotherapy, 26*(2), 177-191.

Nash, J. K. and Fraser, M. V. (1997). Methods in the analysis of risk and protective factors: Lessons from epidemiology. In M. W. Fraser (Ed.). *Risk and resilience in childhood: An ecological perspective* (pp. 34-49). Washington, DC: National Association of Social Workers Press.

National Advisory Mental Health Council. (1990). *National plan for research on child and adolescent mental disorders* (DHS Publication No. ADL 90-1683). Washington, DC: Alcohol, Drug Abuse, and Mental Health Administration.

National Association of Social Workers. (1995). *Encyclopedia of social work* (19th ed.). Washington, DC: Author.

National Center on Child Abuse and Neglect. (1994). *Child maltreatment, 1992: Reports from the states to the National Center on Child Abuse and Neglect.* Washington, DC: U.S. Government Printing Office.

National Coalition of Hispanic Health and Human Services Organizations. (1997). *Office of Minority Health Resource Center database record.* Washington, DC: Author.

National Institute of Mental Health. (1990). *Congressional child and adolescent mental health hearings: Summary of October 9, 1990, testimony.* Washington: DC: U.S. Government Printing Office

National Research Council. (1993). *Understanding child abuse and neglect.* Washington, DC: U.S. Government Printing Office.

Newman, J. C. (1976). Children of disaster: Clinical observations at Buffalo Creek. *American Journal of Psychiatry, 133*(3), 306-312.

Niederland, W. G. (1964, December). *The role of the ego in the recovery of early memories*. Paper presented at the meeting of the American Psychoanalytic Association, New York.

Ochberg, F.M. (1991). Post-traumatic therapy. *Psychotherapy, 28*,1, pp. 5-15.

Padilla, S. (1994). Systems change in public mental health. In C. Telles and M. Karno (Eds.), *Latino mental health: Current research and policy perspectives* (pp. 249-256). Los Angeles: Neuropsychiatric Institute, University of California at Los Angeles and The National Institute of Mental Health.

Parad, H. (Ed.). (1965). *Crisis intervention*. New York: Family Service Association of America.

Patten, S. B., Gatz, Y. K., Jones, B., and Thomas, D. L. (1989, May). Posttraumatic stress disorder and the treatment of sexual abuse. *Social Work*, pp. 297-203.

Perez, C. M. and Windom, C. S. (1994). Childhood victimization and long-term intellectual and academic outcomes. *Child Abuse and Neglect, 18*(8), 617-633.

Peters, S. D., Wyatt, G. E., and Finkelhor, D. (1986). Prevalence. In D. Finkelhor (Ed.), *A sourcebook on child sexual abuse* (pp. 15-59). Newbury Park, CA: Sage Publications.

Pynoos, R. S. (1993). Traumatic stress and developmental psychopathology in children and adolescents. In J. M. Oldham, M. B. Rib, and A. Tasman (Eds.). *Review of psychiatry* (Vol. 12, pp. 205-238). Washington, DC: American Psychiatric Press.

Pynoos, R. S. and Nader, K. (1989). Children's memory and proximity to violence. *Journal of the American Academy of Child and Adolescent Psychiatry, 28*(2), 236-241.

Rhue, J. W., Lynn, S. J., and Sandberg, D. (1995). Dissociation, fantasy, and imagination in childhood: A comparison of physically abused, sexually abused, and nonabused children. *Contemporary Hypnosis, 12*(2), 131-136.

Richmond, M. E. (1917). *Social diagnosis*. New York: Russell Sage Foundation.

Roberts, R. E. (1994). Research on the mental health of Mexican origin children and adolescents. In C. Telles and M. Karno (Eds.). *Latino mental health: Current research and policy perspectives* (pp. 17-39). Los Angeles: Neuropsychiatric Institute, University of California at Los Angeles and The National Institute of Mental Health.

Rogler, L. H. (1996). Framing research on culture in psychiatric diagnosis: The case of the DSM-IV. *Psychiatry, 59*, 145-155.

Rogosch, F. A., Cicchetti, D., and Aber, J. L. (1995). The role of child maltreatment in early deviations in cognitive and affective processing abilities and later peer relationship problems. *Development and Psychopathology, 7*(4), 591-609.

Rutherford, M. J., Cacciola, J. S., Alterman, A. I., Mc Kay, J. R. and Cook, T. J. (1997). Young men's perceived quality of parenting based on familial history of alcoholism. *Journal of Child and Adolescent Substance Abuse, 6*(3), 43-56.

Sack, W. H., Clarke, G., Him, C., Dickason, D., Goff, B., Lanham, K., and Kinzie, D. (1993). A 6-year follow-up of Cambodian refugee adolescents traumatized as children. *The Journal of the American Academy of Child and Adolescent Psychiatry. 32*, (2): 431-437.

Saigh, P. A. (1991). The development of posttraumatic stress disorder following four different types of traumatization. *Behavioral Research Therapy, 29*(3), 213-216.

Sedlak, A. J. (1991). *National incidence and prevalence of child abuse and neglect: 1988.* Rockville, MD: Westat.

Sedlak, A. J. and Broadhurst, M. L. A. (1996). *The Third National Incidence Study of child abused and neglect: (NIS-3)*. Washington, DC: U.S. Department of Health and Human Services.

Shalev, A. Y., Orr, S. P., Peri, T., Schreiber, S., and Pitman, R. K. (1992). Physiologic responses to loud tones in Israeli patients with posttraumatic stress disorder. *Archives of General Psychiatry, 49.* 870-875.

Silverman, A. B., Reinherz, H. Z., and Giaconia, R. M. (1996). The long-term sequelae of child and adolescent abuse: A longitudinal community study. *Child Abuse and Neglect, 20*(8), 709-723.

Singer, M. I., Singer, L. T., and Anglin, T. M. (Eds.). (1993). *Handbook for screening adolescents at psychosocial risk.* New York: Lexington Books.

Spence, R. T. (1984). An analysis of ecological risk for child abuse. (Doctoral Dissertation, Austin, Texas, 1984). *Social Work Abstracts*, 12906.

Stevens-Simon, C. and McAnarney, E. R. (1994). Childhood victimization: Relationship to adolescent pregnancy outcome. *Child Abuse and Neglect, 18*(7), 569-575.

Straus, M. B. (1994). *Violence in the lives of adolescents.* New York: W. W. Norton and Company.

Stroud, J. (1997). Mental disorder and the homicide of children: a review. *Social Work and Social Sciences Review, 6*(3), 149-162.

Sumner, K. L. (1996). Adult survivors of childhood physical abuse. In D. M. Busby (Ed.). *The impact of violence on the family* (pp. 149-183). Needham Heights, MA: Allyn & Bacon.

Sykes-Wiley, M. (1995). The power of DSM-IV: Diagnosing for dollars? *The Family Therapy Networker*, (3) 23-37

Telles, C. (1994). Hispanic immigration and socioeconomic status: A review of psychiatric epidemiologic findings. In C. Telles and M. Karno (Eds.). *Latino mental health: Current research and policy perspectives* (pp. 63-71). Los Angeles: Neuropsychiatric Institute, University of California at Los Angeles and The National Institute of Mental Health.

Telles, C. and Karno, M. (Eds.). (1994). *Latino mental health: Current research and policy perspectives.* Los Angeles: Neuropsychiatric Institute, University of California at Los Angeles and The National Institute of Mental Health.

Terr, L. C. (1983). Time sense following psychic trauma: A clinical study of ten adults and twenty children. *American Journal of Orthopsychiatry, 53*(2), 244-261.

Terr, L. C. (1991). Childhood traumas: An outline and overview. *American Journal of Psychiatry, 148*, 10-20.

Terr, L. C. (1994). *Unchained memories: True stories of traumatic memories, lost and found.* New York: Basic Books.

Todd, T. (1994). *Surviving and prospering in the managed mental health care marketplace.* Sarasota: Professional Resource Press.

Trickett, P. K. (1993). Maladaptive development of school-aged, physically abused children: Relationships with the child-rearing context. *Journal of Family Psychology, 7*(1), 134-147.

Trupin, E. W., Tarico, V. S., Low, B. P., Jemelka, R. and Mc Clellan. (1993). Children on protective service caseloads: Prevalence and nature of serious emotional disturbance. *Child Abuse and Neglect, 17*(3), 345-355.

U.S. Bureau of the Census. (1995). *Statistical abstracts of the United States* (115th ed.). Washington, DC: Author. van der Kolk, B. A. (1984). Adolescent vulnerability to posttraumatic stress disorder. *Psychiatry, 48*, 365-370.

van der Kolk, B. A. (1987a). The psychological consequences of overwhelming life experiences. In B. A. van der Kolk (Ed.). *Psychological trauma* (pp. 1-29). Washington, DC: American Psychiatric Press.

van der Kolk, B. A. (1987b). The separation cry and the trauma response: Developmental issues in the psychobiology of attachment and separation. In B. A. van der Kolk (Ed.), *Psychological trauma* (pp. 31-62). Washington, DC: American Psychiatric Press.

van der Kolk, B. A. (1988). The trauma spectrum: The interaction of biological and social events in the genesis of the trauma response. *Journal of Traumatic Stress, 1*(3), 273-290.

van der Kolk, B. A. and Fisler, R. E. (1994). Childhood abuse and neglect and loss of self-regulation. *Bulletin of the Menninger Clinic, 58*(2), 145-168.

van der Kolk, B. A., Greenberg, M. S., Boyd, H., and Krystal, J. (1985). Inescapable shock, neurotransmitters, and addiction to trauma: Toward a psychology of post traumatic stress. *Biological Psychiatry, 20*, 314-325.

van der Kolk, B. A., Pelcovitz, D., Roth, S., and Mandel, F. (1996). Dissociation, somatization, and affect dysregulation: The complexity of adaptation to trauma. *American Journal of Psychiatry, 153*, 83-93.

van der Veer, G. (1992). *Counseling and therapy with refugees: Psychological problems of victims of war, torture, and repression.* (Chapters 1, 2, & 9-12). Chichester: John Wiley & Sons Ltd.

Vega, W. A., Zimmerman, R. S., Warheit, G. J., Jackson, D., Gil, A., and Sokol-Katz, J. (1994). The role of cultural factors in mental health problems of Hispanic adolescents. In C. Telles and M. Karno (Eds.), *Latino mental health: Current research and policy perspectives* (pp. 41-61). Los Angeles: Neuropsychiatric Institute, University of California at Los Angeles and The National Institute of Mental Health.

Veltkamp, L. J. and Miller, T. W. (1994). *Clinical handbook of child abuse and neglect.* Madison: International Universities Press.

Walker, A. J. (1985). The psychobiology of trauma. In J. P. Wilson (Ed.), *Trauma, transformation, and healing: An integrative approach to theory, research, and posttraumatic therapy* (pp. 21-37). New York: Brunner/Mazel.

Chapter 5

Issues of Crime and Delinquency for Child Welfare

Halaevalu F. Vakalahi, Kip Coggins, and Lynn C. Holley

Introduction

Crime and delinquency have led to the destruction of the lives of children, their families and the communities in which they live. As a national social problem, crime and delinquency have stricken all sectors of society including our most vulnerable populations of children and youth. Likewise, the social and emotional status of families and communities are disrupted and often disintegrated as a result of experiences of crime and delinquency and the involvement of parents in the criminal justice systems.

As a profession that promotes social justice and the protection of individual rights, both of victims and perpetrators, social work has a role in the fight against the destructive impacts of crime and delinquency. Social workers, with their expertise in prevention and rehabilitation through individual and group work, administration, policy, and research need to play an important role in the criminal and juvenile justice systems, especially in terms of addressing the needs of juvenile offenders and children with parents in prison.

The number of people in correctional facilities in the United States has increased from 400,000 in 1982 to 1.6 million in 1996, with a projection of 4 million by the end of the year 2000 (U.S. Department of Justice, 1998; Gendreau, Goggin, & Law, 1997). In 1998, over 4 million adult men and women were on probation or parole, an increase of 131,000 over the previous year. In 1983, of the 108,580 persons released from prisons in 11 states, an estimated 63 percent were re-arrested for a felony or serious misdemeanor within 3 years, 47 percent were re-convicted, and 41 percent were returned to prison or jail (U.S. Department of Justice, 1998).

In 1997, about 1 in every 5 arrests involved a juvenile. The major growth in juvenile arrests during the past decade has been for violence, weapons, drugs, and curfew violations. In 1997, juvenile homicides were at their lowest point in the decade, but still 21 percent above the average of the 1980's. Of all victims killed by juveniles between 1980 and 1997, 14 percent were family members; of the number of murders, 43 percent were either a family member or an acquaintance. In 1997, about 106,000 juvenile offenders were in residential facilities (Snyder & Sickmund, 1999). In 1996, about 306,900 delinquent juvenile cases were placed on probation, an increase of 58 percent from 1987 (Stahl, Sickmund, Finnegan, Snyder, Poole, & Tierney, 1999).

This chapter discusses critical issues of crime and delinquency that must be considered by child welfare system personnel in working with children and their families. Information provided in this chapter would assist child welfare personnel in designing systems and services that will better meet the needs of these families. Particular attention is given to multi-systemic collaboration strategies for working with the children of families impacted by incarceration.

Race, Social Class, Gender and Incarceration

People of Color

A social justice concern for social workers lies in the fact that people of color and those who are from lower socioeconomic groups are disproportionately represented in our nation's jails and prisons (Young, 1998). Almost half of jail inmates in 1996 reported incomes during the month prior to being arrested that would result in less than $7, 200 annually (Harlow, 1998).

Further, approximately 63 percent of jail inmates in 1996 were people of color, a dramatic increase from 54 percent in 1983. The non-Hispanic black population was six times more likely than non-Hispanic whites to be in a jail in 1998 (Gilliard, 1999). The majority of inmates in state prisons in 1991 were people of color (64 percent of women and 65 percent of men), an increase from their proportion in 1986 (60 percent of women and 60 percent of men). The U.S. Department of Justice predicts that, if incarceration rates remain stable, more than one in four black men and one in six Hispanic men will be incarcerated at some point in their lives. Likewise, the U.S. Bureau of Justice for 1997 indicates that the rate of incarceration for Native Americans is 38 percent higher than the national average. Moreover, these rates of incarceration for people of color compare to a lifetime likelihood of incarceration of one in 23 for White non-Hispanic American males (Bonczar & Beck, 1997).

Incarcerated Women

Ninety percent of inmates in the U.S. are male, but the number of incarcerated females is rising dramatically. Women comprised about 10 percent of jail inmates in 1996, compared to 7 percent in 1983 (Harlow, 1998). The number of female inmates in state prisons grew 75 percent between the end of 1986 and June 1991; more than half of this growth was due to increased numbers of those charged with drug offenses (Snell & Morton, 1994). Women inmates were more likely to be incarcerated in state prisons and/or jails due to a drug offense than were men, and were less likely than men to be incarcerated due to a violent offense (Harlow, 1998; Snell & Morton, 1994). In 1999, 7 percent of federal prison inmates were women. In 1998, more than 950,000 women were under correctional supervision—about one percent of the female population (U.S. Department of Justice, 1998).

As with men, women of color are over represented among incarcerated populations. Black women have almost the same chance of serving time in prison as white men, and are more than twice as likely as Hispanic women to serve time in a prison and about seven times as likely as white women to serve time in a prison (Bonczar & Beck, 1997).

It is important that child welfare workers realize that women involved in the justice system are more likely than men, and more likely than women in the general population, to have been physically or sexually abused. According to the U.S. Department of Justice, 57 percent of female and 16 percent of male state inmates have been physically or sexually abused, as have 40 percent of female and 7 percent of male federal prison inmates; 48 percent of female and 13 percent of male jail inmates; and 40 percent of female and 9 percent of male probationers (Harlow, 1999). Over 71 percent of the incarcerated women in Young's (1998) Washington state sample reported that they had experienced such abuse. While men reported being abused as children, women reported being abused both in childhood and adulthood; those who reported being abused were more likely to report use of illegal drugs and regular use of alcohol (Harlow, 1999). Women reporting abuse were more likely than other women to be serving a sentence for a violent crime (Snell & Morton, 1994).

The increase in the proportion of women and people of color involved with the justice system has been, in large, the result of the manner in which the "war on drugs" has been waged. There is evidence that enforcement of drug laws is racially biased. Research indicates that black youth are *less* likely than white youth to use legal and illegal drugs (SAMHSA, 1996, cited in Covington, 1997). Further, the 1991 Household Survey reported that 52 percent of respondents who reported using crack cocaine were white and only 38 percent were black (as cited in Schneider, 1998). In spite of these self-report figures, 14 percent of white jail inmates in 1996 had a drug offense as their most serious charge, compared to 27 percent of black inmates and 28 percent of Hispanic inmates (Harlow, 1998). When drug detection efforts are concentrated in poor communities of color, rather than in white or middle-class communities (Harris, 1999; Schneider, 1998), residents will be arrested at higher rates.

The practice of racial profiling by law enforcement also leads to a higher arrest rate for people of color outside of poor neighborhoods. Racial profiling is based on the assumption that people of color, particularly African Americans and Latinos, are more likely than European Americans to be involved in drug trafficking. Although there is no evidence that this assumption is accurate, it leads law enforcement to target people of color for traffic stops, during which their cars are searched. Increased searches of African Americans and Latinos lead to increased arrests and convictions, thus creating the perception that African Americans and Latinos are more likely to carry illegal drugs (Harris, 1999).

The American Civil Liberties Union (ACLU) reports that Hispanics comprise 30 percent of drivers stopped by police in Illinois, even though they comprise only 8 percent of the population; Hispanic and African American drivers in Illinois are searched at rates greatly exceeding their percentage in the population (Harris, 1999). The ACLU also reports that 73 percent of drivers who were searched between January 1995 and September 1996 on Interstate 95 north of Baltimore were black, while black drivers comprised only 17 percent of all drivers on this highway (Harris, 1999).

Impacts of Neighborhood Crime on Families

In addition to experiencing the ramifications of having a family member involved with the justice system, many families endure the effects of neighborhood violence. Neighborhood crime is a known risk factor for juvenile disruptive and delinquent behaviors (Bilchik, 1998). Families of all ethnic and socioeconomic groups may have direct experience with community violence (Guterman & Cameron, 1997). While families in both middle-class and low-income communities worry about family safety and crime in general, people living in low-income neighborhoods are also concerned about drugs and gangs (e.g., see Nandi & Harris, 1999). Families of color and low-income families also often fear harassment by police. For some families, exposure to neighborhood violence is a "chronic feature of life" (Guterman & Cameron, 1997, p. 496).

In their literature review of the effects of witnessing or experiencing violent neighborhood crime, Guterman and Cameron (1997), note that studies have indicated that survivors and witnesses of crime may experience posttraumatic stress disorder, depression, cognitive delays, and/or aggression. Some youth may respond to neighborhood violence by either developing close peer groups (viewed by many as "gangs") or by limiting their activities (Madriz, 1997).

Impacts of Incarceration on Families

As incarceration rates increase, the number of children with parents who are incarcerated continues to grow. There are approximately 10 million children in the United States who have been impacted by parental involvement in the criminal justice system (Weissman & LaRue, 1998). About 80 percent of female inmates and 50 percent of male inmates have children under age 18, which translates to more than 1.5

million minors having a parent behind bars (Dallao, 1997; Henriques, 1996). While children of male inmates often live with their mothers, more than half of the minor children of female inmates were residing with grandparents during their mothers' incarceration, and approximately one fourth were living with their fathers (Snell & Morton, 1994).

The incarceration of parents precipitates many family crises, including possible permanent damage of parent-child and inmate-partner relationships, emotional and financial burdens, and stigmatization (Coggins & Fresquez, 2000; Gabel, 1995; Girshick, 1996). When a parent is incarcerated, particularly the male member of the family, the financial status of the family is impacted and there is almost always a reduction in the family's income (Carr, 1999; Watts & Nightingale, 1996). Unfortunately, it is often the case that the families with parents who are incarcerated were lacking proper resources in the first place that would have helped them cope with the loss (Phillips and Bloom, 1998).

Incarcerated parents fear losing their roles as parents, attachment with their children, and rejection which sometimes leads to hostility and alienation (Henriques, 1996). Among many possible results, children with incarcerated parents experience stigmatization from members of the community who express disapproval of their parents' criminal activities. They become lonely, and may have feelings of anxiety, guilt, shame, fear, insecurity and instability which may lead to behavioral problems such as teen pregnancy, truancy, isolation, violence, and sometimes incarceration (Carr, 1999; Hungerford, 1993; Sutton, 1996; Weissman & LaRue, 1998). As noted by Couturier (1995), the best predictor of a male child being incarcerated is the incarceration of his father.

Discussion

Implications for Practice

Any discussion of crime and delinquency issues has implications for the child welfare system and the families served. This is especially true when we consider the service needs of the children of incarcerated parents. The number of children with parents in prison is growing and will continue to increase as long as incarceration rates continue to rise (Coggins & Fresquez, 2000). As stated earlier, the incarceration of a parent generally results in the reduction of overall family income. However, the children of parents in prison experience a multitude of other disruptions in their lives as well. Social workers working with the children of incarcerated parents need to keep in mind that these children are likely to be placed out of their homes through kinship foster care arrangements or in traditional non-relative foster care settings. Furthermore, these children are also more likely to experience emotional and behavioral problems resulting from the family disruption that is caused by parental involvement in criminal behavior and subsequent parental incarceration.

The reaction of children to parental imprisonment can be highly variable, and mixed. This is due to variations in the strength of the parent-child bond and the capacity of the child's natural familial network to provide support. A strong natural support network, or lack thereof, plays an important role in the severity of the trauma a child will experience as a result of parental imprisonment (Coggins & Fresquez, 2000). In addition, the relationship between child and parent prior to incarceration will have an influence on the manner in which a child experiences parental imprisonment. If the pre-incarceration parent-child relationship was characterized by little or no contact, the impact on the child will undoubtedly be less than would be the case in a close relationship, especially if that relationship was warm and nurturing (Block and Potthast, 1998).

When parents are imprisoned, their children often experience feelings of abandonment, loss, anger and loneliness (Henriques, 1982; Hungerford, 1993). Children of parents in prison may become withdrawn and isolate themselves, or they may engage in disruptive behaviors such as running away from home or refusing to attend school (Coggins & Fresquez, 2000). In addition, children of parents in correctional facilities often experience difficulty when it comes to issues of trust (Weissman and LaRue, 1998). Therefore, those social workers working with the children of incarcerated parents need to be prepared for children who exhibit a broad range of emotions and behaviors in response to the incarceration of their parents.

Permanency Planning. Incarceration of a parent may be viewed by some as evidence that a parent is unfit. However, incarceration alone does not constitute grounds for the termination of parent-child relationships. Courts regularly find that imprisonment itself is not sufficient grounds for the termination of parental rights (Genty, 1991/92). Therefore, child welfare workers need to be prepared to take on the role of making certain that children of incarcerated parents maintain parental contact. Since most individuals in prison will one day be released, parents who are incarcerated need to be taken into consideration in the formulation of long term permanency plans.

Permanency planning for children of parents in correctional facilities requires that child welfare workers consider several important factors that simply do not arise in work with the families of non-offenders. In developing permanency plans, child welfare workers must, first consider the length of a parent's sentence. If a long period of incarceration is a factor, especially in the case of female inmates, permanency plans will need to include longer-term placement options. Second, child care workers working with the children of incarcerated parents must consider the stability of any placement that might be recommended during the period of incarceration, and the support that potential caregivers might need to ensure the viability of a placement until the parent's release. Finally, the date for family reunification and the services that will be needed at that time must also be made a part of permanency plans for minor children of incarcerated parents.

Preparing parents in correctional facilities for transition back to the community and family reunification needs to begin long before the release date. The inclusion of mothers in permanency planning is a valuable mechanism for increasing empowerment involvement in decisions that will affect the lives of their children (Katz, 1998). Likewise, the involvement of incarcerated fathers in permanency planning decisions keeps them involved in the lives of their children, and has also been shown to improve the feelings of self-worth and efficacy during incarceration (Hairston, 1998). Therefore, social workers working with families impacted by incarceration need to foster parent-child relationships with long term permanency and reunification goals in mind. This means making certain that intervention goes well beyond simply assuring that regular visits occur (Coggins & Fresquez, 2000).

There are of course those obvious situations in which reunification will not be possible. Incarcerated parents who have been given a death sentence, or a life sentence without parole, will never transition back into the community. However, for more than 90 percent of inmates this is not the case. Therefore, those involved in the cases of children with incarcerated parents need to work collaboratively with those parents and corrections departments to determine the feasibility and viability of eventual parent-child reunification during the formulation of permanency plans (Beckerman, 1998).

Implications for Policy

First, child welfare workers serving families in which a member is incarcerated can advocate on behalf of clients to encourage the continuation of family relationships. An appropriate place to begin this effort is the creation of "family-friendly" visitation areas within jails and prisons. In addition, social workers involved with families impacted by incarceration can work to ensure that children placed in foster care have the opportunity to visit, telephone, and write to their incarcerated parents.

Second, working with corrections departments and human service providers social workers can help create a smoother transition for offenders from the correctional facility to the home community. Since many inmates in correctional settings are from economically disadvantaged families and communities, they will likely be in need of a wide range of support services upon release. Some will need ongoing chemical dependency treatment. Others will need ongoing mental health services. Nearly all will need financial and employment assistance to help them support their families (Coggins & Fresquez, 2000). However, social workers attempting to assist families in which a parent has been incarcerated soon find that barriers to social reintegration exist. Criminal records create difficulties in securing employment, housing, and even public assistance. Persons who have felony convictions related to the use or sale of certain types of drugs may be banned from receiving TANF or food stamps for the rest of their lives (Phillips and Bloom, 1998, p. 536). Since many mothers in prison have been convicted of drug related crimes, the potential for limited assistance upon release is a reality for which they must plan, and an area in which social workers can play a key role (Coggins and Fresquez, 2000).

Third, because the "war on drugs" has led to the increased arrest, conviction, and incarceration of women and people of color, it is important that social workers advocate for changes in our nation's response to drug related offenses. These changes might include, for example, equalizing the penalties for "crack" and other forms of cocaine as well as the use of drug treatment programs as alternatives to mandatory incarceration. In addition, as a profession social work must become involved in strategies focused on fairer treatment of minority and economically disadvantaged individuals. For instance, community education and efforts directed toward the elimination of practices such as racial profiling by police.

Finally, both micro and macro level interventions on behalf of children and families impacted by incarceration must be provided in a culturally and linguistically relevant manner. Service providers need to be familiar with the cultures of communities and sensitive to individual and family differences and preferences in the areas of cultural expressions, traditions, and values. For instance, providers need to know whether families prefer individual treatment, family treatment, or inclusion of other significant individuals and groups (e.g., church community, ethnic community) in the helping process. The time taken to understand and develop culturally relevant and appropriate services will indeed be time well spent.

Safety and Security. Aside from the initial trauma children face when their parents are incarcerated, correctional facilities themselves present a very real source of ongoing stress. When family members visit loved ones in correctional facilities, issues of safety and security must be taken into consideration. Security issues and precautions often create an unwelcome environment for families. Generally, families view correctional environments as hostile, complicated and seldom inviting (Carr, 1999). Furthermore, within correctional facilities the concern with safety and security takes precedence over the needs of families to visit and interact with their incarcerated loved ones (Coggins & Fresquez, 2000).

Although correctional officials often understand and believe in the importance of maintaining the parent-child relationships during incarceration, inmate visitation does not and cannot take priority over safety and security (Hairston, 1998). Given the opposing needs of correctional facilities and families, correctional social workers need to find ways to help families while assuring adherence to proper procedures for facility security and safety.

Implications for Research

Without a doubt current criminal justice and corrections policies have had a profound impact on economically disadvantaged families and communities of color. Research has shown that youth from nurturing families of high socioeconomic status with few psychosocial stressors are far less likely to experience problems as they reach adolescence and early adulthood (McWhirter, et al., 1998). Given that economically disadvantaged children are already at greater risk for problems, the addition of stress related to parental incarceration can push them into a high-risk category. The indicators of high-risk youth are depression, anxiety, anger and feelings of hopelessness, all of which are found in children whose parents are incarcerated. Moreover, these characteristics frequently lead to self-destructive and delinquent behavior.

Social workers committed to advocating for families impacted by incarceration must direct efforts toward conducting sound research. Simply stating that families ought to remain in contact during periods of parental incarceration is not enough to change the attitudes or practices of lawmakers and corrections department administrators. Demonstrating through research that the maintenance of strong family ties can reduce later delinquent behavior in the youth of incarcerated parents will be necessary if policy and program change is to become a reality. Although some programs at selected correctional facilities look promising, the need to conduct research on a larger scale will further the efforts of social workers and other helping professionals to advocate for effective programming that has the potential to produce long lasting and positive results for the children who have been impacted by parental involvement in the criminal justice system.

Conclusion

Child welfare and criminal justice systems often serve the same families. This chapter has described those aspects of the criminal justice system that are most critical for child welfare system personnel to understand, and has offered strategies for serving these families more effectively. Evidently, a more effective approach to working with the children of families impacted by incarceration can only occur if helping professionals work collectively to coordinate services. Releasing vulnerable and socially stigmatized parents from correctional facilities to résumé parenting responsibilities without support, places children at risk and sets parents up for failure (Coggins & Fresquez, 2000).

Consequently, social workers need to be at the forefront of advocating for and developing services for this particularly needy client population (Johnson, Selber, and

Lauderdale, 1998). Social workers can advocate for offenders and society together by helping offenders and communities fulfill their respective responsibilities. They can lead in developing economic opportunities and help offenders find alternatives to illegitimate means of meeting their needs. They may provide social skills building programs, mental health treatment, pre-release planning services, and post-release follow-up for incarcerated offenders. Social workers can advocate for regular contact and interaction between incarcerated parents and their children and families (Coggins & Fresquez, 2000). They can help make visiting areas and visiting policies more able to maintain and strengthen family ties without compromising safety and security. Social workers can help in maintaining contact and reunifying inmates in correctional facilities with their families, upon release. They can also help families to begin coping with the transition of their incarcerated loved ones from jail/prison to the community (Carr, 1999). Likewise, social workers can link inmates and their families with multiple service systems within their home communities.

References

Beckerman, A. (1998). Charting a Course: Meeting the Challenge of Permanency Planning for Children with Incarcerated Mothers. *Child Welfare, LXXVII*(5), 513-529.

Bilchik, S. (1998). *Serious and violent juvenile offenders*. Washington, DC: Office of Juvenile Justice and Delinquency Prevention.

Block, K. J. and Potthast, M. J. (1998). Girl Scouts beyond bars: Facilitating parent-child contact in correctional settings. *Child Welfare, LXXVII*(5), 561-578.

Bonczar, T. P. and Beck, A. J. (1997, March). *Bureau of Justice statistics special report: Lifetime likelihood of going to State or Federal prison*. Washington, DC: U.S. Department of Justice.

Carr, C. (1999). *A network of support for offenders*. Ottawa: Correctional Service of Canada.

Coggins, K. and Fresquez, J. E. (2000). *Working With Clients in Correctional Settings: A Guide for Social Workers and Corrections Professionals*. Dubuque, IA: Eddie Bowers Publishing, Inc.

Couturier, L.C. (1995). Inmates benefit from family services programs. *Corrections Today, 57*(7), 100-107.

Covington, J. (1997). The social construction of the minority drug problem. *Social Justice, 24*(4), 117-X.

Dallao, M. (1997). Coping with incarceration from the other side of the bars. *Corrections Today, 59*(6), 96-98.

Donziger, S. R. (1996). *The real war on crime: The report of the National Criminal Justice Commission*. New York: Harper Perennial.

Estrin, A. (1994). Family support and criminal justice. In S. Kagan & B. Wessbourd, B. (Eds.). *Putting families first*. San Francisco, CA: Josey-Bass Publishers.

Fox, V. (1972). *Introduction to corrections*. Englewood Cliffs, NJ: Prentice Hall.

Fresquez, J. E., Khalsa, S. S., and Bell, C. (1998). *Application of social work methods in corrections*. An unpublished paper presented at the National Association of Social Workers Conference: New Mexico Chapter, Feb. 26.

Gabel, S. (1995). Behavioural problems in children of incarcerated parents. *Forum on Corrections Research, 7*(2), 37-39.

Garvin, C. and Tropman, J. E. (1992). *Social work in contemporary society*. Englewood Cliffs, NJ: Prentice Hall.

Garvin, C. & Tropman, J. E. (1998). *Social work in contemporary society: Second Edition*. Needham Heights, MA: Allyn & Bacon.

Gendreau, P., Goggin, C. and Law, A. (1997). Predicting prison misconducts. *Criminal Justice and Behavior, 24*(4), 414-431.

Genty, P. (1991/92). Procedural Due Process Rights of Incarcerated Parents in Termination of Parental Rights Proceedings: A Fifty State Analysis. *Journal of Family Law, 34*, 757-846.

Gilliard, D. K. (1999). *Bureau of Justice statistics bulletin: Prison and jail inmates at midyear 1998*. Washington, DC: U.S. Department of Justice.

Girshick, L. B. (1996). *Soledad women: Wives of prisoners speak out*. Westport, CT: Praeger Publishers.

Goebel, J. (1976) [1937]. *Felony and misdemeanor*. Philadelphia, PA: University of Pennsylvania Press.

Guterman, N. B. and Cameron, M. (1997). Assessing the impact of community violence on children and youth. *Social Work, 42*(5), 495-505.

Hairston, C. F. (1998). The Forgotten Parent: Understanding the Forces that Influence Incarcerated Fathers' Relationships with Their Children. *Child Welfare, LXXVII*(5), 617-639.

Harlow, C. W. (1998). *Bureau of Justice statistics special report: Profile of jail inmates 1996*. Washington, DC: U.S. Department of Justice (Revised 6/04/98).

Harris, D. A. (1999). *Driving while black: Racial profiling on our nation's highways*. An American Civil Liberties Union Special Report. [On-line] available: http://www.aclu.org/profiling/report/index.html.

Heffernan, J., Shuttlesworth, G. and Ambrosino, R. (1997). *Social work and social welfare: An introduction* [Third Edition]. St. Paul, MN: West Publishing Company.

Henriques, Z. W. (1996). Imprisoned mothers and their children: Separation-reunion syndrome dual impact. *Women and Criminal Justice, 8*(1), 77-95.

Hungerford, G. P. (1993). *The children of inmate mothers: An exploratory study of children, caregivers and inmate mothers in Ohio* (Ohio State University Doctoral Dissertation).

Johnson, T., Selber, K., and Lauderdale, M. (1998). Developing Quality Services for Offenders and Families: An Innovative Partnership. *Child Welfare, LXXVII*(5), 595-615.

Katz, P. C. (1998). Supporting Families and Children of Mothers in Jail: An Integrated Child Welfare and Criminal Justice Strategy. *Child Welfare, LXXVII*(5), 495-511.

Madriz, E. (1997). Latina teenagers: Victimization, identity, and fear of crime. *Social Justice, 24*(4), 39-X.

McWhiter, J. J., McWhiter, B. T., McWhiter, A. M., and McWhiter, E. H. (1998). *At Risk Youth: A Comprehensive Response* [2nd Edition]. Pacific Grove California: Brooks/Cole Publishing.

Morris, N. and Rothman, D. J. (Eds.). (1995). *The Oxford history of the prison: The practice of punishment in western society.* New York: Oxford University Press.

Myers, W. C., Scott, K., Burgess, A. W., & Burgess, A. G. (1995). Psychotherapy, biopsychosocial factors, crime characteristics, and classification of 25 homicidal youths. *Journal of the American Academy of Child and Adolescent Psychiatry, 34*(11), 1483(7).

Nandi, P. K. and Harris, H. (1999). The social world of female-headed black families: A study of quality of life in a marginalized neighborhood. *International Journal of Comparative Sociology, 40*(2), 195-X.

Phillips, S. and Bloom, B. (1998). In whose best interest? The impact of changing public policy on relatives caring for children with incarcerated parents. *Child Welfare, 77*(5), 531-541.

Rohn, W. and Ostroski, T. (1991). Advances in technology make it easier to monitor inmates. *Corrections Today, 53*(4), 142-145.

Rotman, E. (1995). The failure of reform. In N. Morris & D.J. Rothman (Eds.), *The Oxford history of the prison.* New York: Oxford University Press.

Rusche, G. and Kirchheimer, O. (1968). *Punishment and social structure.* New York: Russell and Russell.

Schneider, C. L. (1998). Racism, drug policy, and AIDS. *Political Science Quarterly, 113*(3), 427-X.

Seymour, C. (1998). Children of parents in prison. *Child Welfare, LXXVII*(5), 469-493.

Snell, T. and Morton, D. C. (1994). *Bureau of Justice statistics special report: Women in prison. Survey of State Prison Inmates, 1991.* Washington, DC: U.S. Department of Justice.

Snyder, H. N. and Sickmund, M. (1999). *Juvenile offenders and victims: 1999 National report.* Washington, DC: Office of Juvenile Justice and Delinquency Prevention.

Stahl, A., Sickmund, M., Finnegan, T., Snyder, H., Poole, R., and Tierney, N. (1999). *Juvenile court statistics 1996.* Washington, DC: Office of Juvenile Justice and Delinquency Prevention.

Sutton, M. (1996). *Breaking the cycle of despair: Children of incarcerated mothers.* Annie E. Casey Foundation Technical Assistance Reports.

Szostak, E. W. (1998). Maintaining safety and security by managing contraband. *American Jails, 12*(3), 62-64.

Taylor, S. (1999, April). Racial profiling: The liberals are right. *National Journal, 31*(17), 1084.

U.S. Department of Justice Bureau of Justice Statistics. (1998). *National Corrections Reporting Program,* 1-18.

Watts, H. and Nightingale, D.S. (1996). Adding it up: The economic impact of incarceration on individuals, families, and communities. *Journal of the Oklahoma Criminal Justice Research Consortium, 3,* 55-62.

Weissman, M. and LaRue, C.M. (1998). Earning trust from youths with none to spare. *Child Welfare, 77*(5), 579-594.

Young, D. S. (1998). Health status and service use among incarcerated women. *Family and Community Health, 21*(3), 16-X.

Chapter 6
Violence in the Family:
A Story in Need of an Ending

Judith C. Hilbert

Introduction

Best practices with families who experience multiple challenges *must* include a close evaluation and examination of violence within each family member's life, as well as the family as a whole. All too often, issues of family violence, particularly with respect to the relevant meaning to each family member, are overlooked or minimized due to preconceived or theory driven notions of what needs to be done. This chapter will address how family members' stories themselves may *best* tell us how to practice, how to intervene, and how to truly be of help to those who experience violence within their families. A family case history will be utilized as a teaching tool.

Story Telling and Listening

Story telling is a powerful and informative way of communicating and sending messages. Listening to the richness of a story gives the listener an opportunity to close one's eyes and see through the eyes of the story teller. It offers the listener a chance to enter into the story-teller's experience of life. Listening without judgement means that the listener must be accepting, quiet, and humble. For many people, including helping professionals like social workers, just listening is not familiar. People want to help. The professional is often guided by a need to act, to solve, to direct, and to be an expert. For helping professionals, assuming a listening role may be foreign to the way in which they were trained. Quietly listening may appear foolish or silly, or non-expert. Yet, who is more expert about his or her own situation than the one who has experienced it.

A practitioner's expertise derives from professional experience, knowledge of resources and alternatives, and knowledge of sources of support not known to the client. The practitioner must have another ability, however, the ability to assist clients to discover their own resources, their own strengths and limitations, and to develop insight and awareness of their behavior and the interactive influence of this upon those around them. Assisting clients in this manner is particularly critical when working with a family who is experiencing domestic violence. For domestic violence includes a set of behaviors contributed to, influenced by, and felt by each and every member of the family. Each and every family member has their own personal, unique and meaningful rendition of the story of their family's violence.

Just Listening

It is especially difficult for novice social workers initially to do nothing but listen to the violent stories of their clients. First of all, these stories are filled with anguish, fear, pain, suffering, rage, and abandonment. As helpers, we serve to reduce these feelings with our clients. Yet, they must be told. So, the social worker needs to learn to assist and collaborate with the story teller. And, the stories must be heard—in all their detail and horror. For it is through stories that we can attribute meaning to the events in life. And through meanings, helpers may begin to derive practice interventions.

A Short Story about the History of Family Violence

Domestic violence is a story. Originally, it was not a social problem or a political or public health problem. In fact, domestic assault only became a legal problem once one violated the laws regulating the parameters of the assault. In the United States, the story begins with the colonists.

Historically, violence perpetrated against wives has been a part of the development of this country, documented and sanctioned in some of the early records of the colonists. As families immigrated to the New World and began to set up a system of order, reliance on English Common Law seemed suitable. Keeping order was most necessary if this group of families were to establish a social system which functioned smoothly, justly, and successfully for the purpose of the survival of the entire group. Given that husbands and fathers were totally responsible for their families, it was their duty to keep wives and children in line. In line meant behaving in the manner which was determined by the founding fathers of the colonies.

Del Martin (1977), one of the major historians of spousal assault, reports that based on old English common-law doctrine, wife beating was explicitly permitted for correctional purposes. Davidson (1978) suggests that wives have been subjected to extreme forms of cruelty from their husbands for hundreds of years and certainly is an integral part of this country's development from the time in which wives were considered chattel. Historical and legal data are available which demonstrate that women have been subjected to brutal and often lethal forms of violence in their own home (Strauss, Gelles, and Steinmetz, 1980). This behavior was considered legal and just, provided it was contained within the limits of the law. These limits suggested that sticks no bigger in diameter than one's thumb were acceptable weapons for corrective beatings. Domestic violence only became a legal problem when one used too large a stick.

Violence against Children

Children, too, were beaten as a common form of punishment. Although child abuse was being studied in the 17th century in France, it was not until the 20th century that Dr. Kempe and his colleagues (1962) brought the issue of child abuse in this country to the attention of the medical profession in his seminal article on the Battered Child Syndrome. For close to two hundred years after the Colonists came to the New World, beating children was not considered a legal or social problem. And it was not until another decade that *wife* abuse was finally recognized as a social problem in need of legal solutions.

The Beginning of Change—A Social Problem

During the 60s, with the advent of the women's movement, women began to meet and share their life stories. In these consciousness raising groups, more and more women for the first time revealed they were living in homes where violence was the common form of family interaction. Not only were children being abused, but wives too spoke of the violence they suffered at the hands of their partners.

Yet, the violence described by these women was different in nature from that of the Colonist wives. While the Colonists sought to sanction and control the violence, wives in the 20th century experienced domestic assault that was often for 'no apparent reason', with little regard to type and degree of abuse, and with no legal prohibitions for this behavior. Violent behavior had as many meanings to the perpetrator as there were perpetrators. They were not as a group attempting to fulfill their duties and obligations for keeping their 'chattel' in line for the sake of the greater community. Instead the violence in families was now kept 'behind closed doors', unpredictable, indiscriminate and severe. There were no laws to protect the victims of domestic or family assault.

It was not until the 1970s that the phenomenon of domestic violence was identified as a social problem. Through the early research efforts of Straus, Gelles, and Steinmetz (1980), it was determined that domestic violence did exist. It crossed racial, educational, economic, religious, and social class boundaries, and although this form of behavior was prevalent among the U.S. public, it was not considered a problem at the societal level. This early survey research done across the U.S. reinforced the stories of the women in the 60s consciousness raising groups. Such stories were not fabrications of 'women libbers', but were representative of the lives of many such women in the cities and backwoods of this country. No longer could these stories be quieted. Domestic violence, meaning violence against wives and children, became a concern of the American public.

The Influence of Culture

Often one asks if domestic violence is not simply a problem in all cultures. The answer is yes and no. In the U.S., this is a particularly difficult question to answer. Miller and Wellford (in Cardarelli, 1997) offer an extensive review of the literature regarding the influence of culture. They suggest there are a number of problems in determining cultural factors as contributing to domestic violence.

For example, research instruments used to measure domestic violence may be biased toward the dominant culture's understanding of the definition of abuse. Few studies have been done with instruments designed and developed for validity and reliability in culturally sensitive ways. Further, language barriers may contribute to victims' inability to describe and report violence accurately to researchers and service providers. Moreover, in some cultures, while domestic violence may not be acceptable, maintaining the honor of the family by keeping this secret prohibits victims from seeking help. Finally, studies have shown that immigrants who become highly acculturated to the U.S. way of life, reveal high rates of domestic assault as compared with those who are less acculturated (Sorenson & Telles, 1991). We can conclude, however, from this mixed picture that indeed in some cultures, including the U.S., violence is commonplace and tacitly sanctioned.

Legal Responses

With the identification of domestic violence as a social problem, legal reforms were slowly instituted across the country. Such legal reforms were intended to do more than simply regulate the extent, rationale, and type of assault against wives. They were intended to address assaults and threats of assaults against any household member. This would broaden the definition of domestic abuse to include spouse, person living as a spouse, ex-spouse, ex-living together partner, children, parents, siblings, and/or persons related by consanguinity or affinity. It would also open the door for a number of legal and social services to be created, along with the misunderstandings, confusions, and stereotypic responses of competing helping paradigms.

A Contemporary Tale about Family Violence

Let's consider the Romito family. Their story is quite representative of contemporary families who experience domestic violence. Each family member has his/her own perception and reaction to the violence within the family. Let's start with Carol—the battered woman in this case.

Carol's Story

Another long night. Why does he keep at me so? No matter what I do he isn't happy. He is overworked, I know. But still. I used to think that he would begin to relax, to quit getting so mad. I used to think in time our relationship would change and he would realize that I am not his enemy, or his punching bag. That I did not do any of those bad things to him that his own family did. That I did not protest against the war he fought. That I did not do anything other than love him and want a long life with him and our 2 kids. But then, here I am again—bleeding, alone, and scared. I am glad he finally passed out but worry about his mood in the morning. I must get sleep. The kids will be awake soon, and I don't want them to see me with puffy, crying eyes. Maybe I should take one of his sleeping pills. Maybe the whole bottle...

In the morning, Carol awoke and quickly started breakfast. A good hot meal might mitigate the hangover quesies Tony would be feeling. And she hustled to get the kids up, fed, and out to the bus stop. She had a plan for the day. He would be starting his long distance run with a load to Loudon, Tennessee, and wouldn't be back for 4 days. She had to take good advantage of this time. Yet she was so weary. Was it worth it?

After Tony left and the kids went off to school, Carol sat down with her cup of coffee. She was 35 years old, a housewife with a son, Art, a daughter, Lupe, and a husband who made good money as a long distance trucker. While he carefully gave her money for groceries, he kept the remainder and paid all their bills himself. Their modest home in rural West Virginia was surrounded by beautiful rolling hills and forest. The nearest neighbors were 10 miles away. Her family lived nearby but were unaware of Carol's beatings. She didn't want to worry them what with Daddy having a heart condition and all. Mama too was not in the best of health, and, living on social security, they certainly could not help financially at all. Her sister Barbara Ann was in a marriage similar to Carol's, although an unspoken agreement between the two prohibited them from sharing their burden.

Carol tried to sort out her options. Over the 8 years of her marriage, she had first spoken to the Pastor about Tony's behavior. Carefully and gingerly, she told how he first used to call her names, dirty names and put down names. Then he began to push her around. One time he pulled a bunch of her hair out. Ultimately he began to beat her with his fists although lately he often sat, yelling at her while he 'played' with his knife. And he was using a lot of pills to stay awake on the road and then sleep at night. Sometimes he drank a six pack when he got home.

The Pastor listened all right but then made her feel like it was somehow her fault. He told her she must become a better wife and mother, that she must try harder to be good and kind to Tony. He said she should pray a lot and ask for God's forgiveness for being so self-centered. He reminded her how difficult Tony's family life had been, and how she didn't want to break up their marriage and subject her kids to a broken home and life of shame. She walked out of church feeling lost and more alone. The solace she expected from the Church was not forthcoming.

Carol remembered how she talked with her doctor about her situation once. She went for a routine check up and the doctor found an old fracture that was healing poorly. When he asked how it happened, Carol started weeping. She told him the whole story of years of abuse and pain. He prescribed tranquilizers for her and suggested she see a therapist. With a diagnosis of depression, Carol did have one appointment with this therapist. Although a woman, gender made little difference for Carol. The female therapist immediately focused on Carol's growing up relationship with her father and explored conflicts Carol had with her mother. As the oldest of 6 children, Carol assumed considerable responsibility for her younger siblings. Somehow, the therapist found this most interesting and even went so far as to suggest that perhaps Carol was trying to take over her mother's role. Carol left and never returned for her second visit.

The most recent helper Carol sought was the volunteer at the local battered woman's shelter. Their relationship was over the phone as Carol was far too frightened to really go into town and be seen going to the shelter. The volunteer seemed to understand. After all, she too had been a battered wife. They talked about getting together informally with other battered women to see how they could help themselves and each other. What a thought! The volunteer also suggested that Carol go to the shelter although she warned her that the helpers there may strongly insist that she blame Tony and get away from him forever. Or they could offer couple counseling if Carol insisted on staying with Tony. Then, both she and Tony would have to examine the dynamics of their relationship to see who played what part in the violence. Carol did not believe that was even an option. Imagine—Tony who insisted he was right and she was stupid and wrong—going for help to own his part in their problems.

Carol sat for quite a while. She didn't have to hurry. Before she could decide what to do she had to decide who to turn to for help. Right now, there seemed to be no one who could truly understand what it meant to her to be a wife who was battered. As she sat, she quietly wept.

Co-Occurring Challenges

Carol's tale underscores two major issues common to many battered women who seek help. First, she is confronted with various options from helpers but each helper also brings competing paradigms and meanings. Not one listens and searches non-judgmentally for the meaning of life as Carol experiences it. Each is eager to give direction, advice, interpretation, and counsel, based upon their own professional (and perhaps personal) perspective. Such competing and often conflicting paradigms of help contribute to the meaninglessness, confusion, and suffering experienced by the battered woman. More dangerously, this continued existence in hopelessness and despair supports the continuance of the violence itself.

The second major issue involved in Carol's situation is the co-occurring difficulties to which she alludes—substance abuse and suicidal ideation. Carol's abusive relationship has progressed in intensity and severity as has her depression and sense of despair. The chronicity of both circumstances contribute to heightening the risk of Carol becoming substance dependent and/or overtly suicidal.

Children and Domestic Violence

Lastly, we must not overlook Carol's children who are suffering and at risk as well. While she does not make mention of them as effected by the abuse, current thinking recognizes that each family member feels the effects of violence perpetrated upon their loved ones. Even the perpetrator is affected by his behavior. For the moment, let's consider the 'invisible victims'—child witnesses of family violence.

Effects of Violence on Children. Far too often the children involved in families where Mom is being battered become the victims of abuse themselves. Early research (Carlson, 1984) as well as contemporary studies (Straus, Williams, & Corrigan, 1992) consistently reveal the significant impacts of witnessing parental abuse on the children. In 1984, Carlson's study indicated that more than 3 million American children were exposed to violence between their parents every year. This number continues to rise with the increase in violence in American homes. Today the number may be as high as ten million children each year. In fact, Akukwe's literature review (1998) suggests that child abuse is fifteen times more likely to occur in families where the mother is being battered and that these abused children themselves are more likely to become abusers as adults.

Unfortunately, unless children are physically abused, the effects of witnessing a parent's abuse are dangerously overlooked. Children who suffer psychological and emotional effects are often the invisible victims of a violent home.

Effects-Immediate. Tutty, Weaver, and Rothery (1999) suggest as social workers have learned more about the extent and seriousness of wife abuse, they have become especially aware that when women are abused, children are also likely victims. The effects of living in a home where Moms and Dads engage in domestic violence may be understood as immediate and/or chronic; direct and/or indirect.

The most obvious effects on children who live with parental violence is the physical abuse they also may endure. Often they become the direct victims of parental assault. The literature attests to the prevalence of this phenomenon. While not the primary target of the violence, children become the secondary victims of the assault as the batterer wields his power and control over the entire family. However, they may become the accidental victims of physical abuse as well. Far too often babies held by the battered woman may receive blows intended for her.

Effects-Situational. Less obvious but nonetheless immediate are the effects of domestic violence that may be categorized as situational. For example, women with children fleeing from their batterers are becoming the fastest growing segment of the homeless population today. According to the National Coalition for the Homeless (NCH), families now comprise 40% of the nation's homeless population and studies suggest as many as 50% of all homeless women and children are fleeing from domestic violence (Krishnan, & Hilbert, 1998). Homelessness brings with it additional difficulties for the children. In addition to losing their own home, they may no longer be welcomed in their relatives' homes as well. Often relatives become the targets of stalking and harassment perpetrated by batterers in search of their families. The children, if found, may be abducted and used as leverage for Mom to return to her abuser. Leaving home and the batterer may relieve children of their fears of becoming hurt or witnessing their Mom's assault, but may be replaced with fear of reprisals if found.

When battered women can no longer rely on friends and family for a place to stay, they may take their children to live in shelters—either homeless or domestic violence shelters (Krishnan & Hilbert, 1998). Often crowded and hectic given the continual entry and departure of the residents, children are then subjected to the confusion and chaos of life among large groups of residents with their own personal and poignant difficulties. Socially, they are distanced from the familiar school and play surroundings, often isolated without close friends. Academically, they may be withdrawn from school while "on the run." Economically, they may be unable to have the usual and customary 'luxuries' afforded through life "at home with Papa." The transient lifestyle of the homeless battered woman and her children creates situational consequences that affect the children socially, academically, familially, financially, and physically. To gain safety from violence, the battered woman and her children who flee suffer enormous losses—losses which must be recognized by those who seek to help them.

 Neglect. For those children who are not physically abused and whose Moms do not flee from the batterer, other forms of abuse occur. Clearly, they are benignly 'neglected' as their Moms seek to focus attention on the batterer in order to avoid a beating. Carol could not attend to her children other than to get them out of harm's way. While this may be the best she could do at the time, many women who live with on-going abuse remain preoccupied and distracted day after day as they struggle simply to survive. Little energy, time, direction, and comfort can be offered to children by Moms when Moms are concerned with their very own existence. As a result, children often are left with ambivalent feelings toward *both* adults in their home and remain confused about what is happening. Sometimes they feel responsible for the violence as they are frequently the target of the argument. Or they may have been "parentified," asked to assume the inappropriate role of caretaker or parent substitute for their siblings and/or parent(s).

Children may be fearful of expressing their own feelings (especially anger), and worry about issues of divorce, separation, the unknown, the "outside" world. They, like their Moms, may feel powerless, helpless, and depressed. In fact, frequently they may believe that such violence does not occur in other families and for this they carry the burden of keeping the secret and the shame of living within a violent family.

Physically, these children may experience somatic complaints in the forms of headaches or stomach aches. They may seem tired, lethargic, and may be seen as "lazy" by their teachers. Frequently they appear nervous, anxious, and with a short attention span. They may regress in their developmental accomplishments. Often they are sick with colds and may neglect their personal hygiene. Given that most children keep the secret of their family violence, and do not explain the cause of their behaviors, they may become misdiagnosed with psychiatric disorders or academically misassessed as learning disabled, ADHD, or the like (Kendall-Tackett & Eckenrode, in Kantor & Jasinski, 1997).

Behaviorally, children who witness parental abuse may themselves act out or withdraw, become the overachiever or underachiever, reacting in extremes to ordinary situations. They may refuse to go to school, fearful that something terrible may happen at home. Attention-seeking behaviors are not uncommon as these children attempt to divert the batterer from beating their mom. They may wet the bed, have trouble sleeping, experience nightmares and in some cases develop serious psychological symptoms.

While children's advocates in domestic violence shelters have led the way in paying attention to these forgotten victims of domestic abuse, research is just beginning to discern the enormity and specificity of the effects on children who witness parental violence. Studies indicate that these children significantly display more behavioral problems and less social competence than do children from non-violent families and from children who do not witness the abuse (Jaffe, Wolfe, et al., 1986).

Effects-Chronic. Peled (in Edelson & Eisikovits, Eds., 1996) suggests that subjecting children to the victimization of their mothers is a severe form of psychological maltreatment. In fact, Post Traumatic Stress Disorder is frequently experienced by children as result of growing up terrorized, witness to rigid and destructive behaviors, and exposed to limited role models (Graham-Berman & Levendovsky, 1992).

Children who have witnessed parental violence are at risk for delayed effects as they develop into adulthood. Psychologically, these children may set rigid defenses for themselves, appearing aloof, sarcastic, blaming, and defensive. They may experience difficulties forming attachments and/or trusting others in intimate relationships, often attempting to exert absolute control so as to mitigate potential for violence. Relationships may start intensely and end abruptly due to poor conflict resolution skills. As dating teens, they know either passive or aggressive methods of dealing with conflict (Tutty & Wagar, 1994) and struggle with replicating the behaviors that they despised at home. Abuse of drugs and alcohol, and depressive behaviors and suicidal ideation are major risk factors. As young adults, they too may act out the violence in their search for committed, intimate life-long adult relationships.

Linking Theory with Practice

Social learning theory and the inter-generational transmission of violence process suggest that children model behaviors they observed growing up, and those in violent homes will most likely become victims or perpetrators of domestic violence themselves. In common language the idea is that violence begets violence. This perspective gives little attention to the influences beyond the parent-child and parent-parent dyads. Influences, such as peers, non-parental caring adults, community consciousness and sanctions, and individual choice and responsibility, are disregarded for the most part. Interventions, then, based on an intergenerational transmission perspective, reflect psycho-educational models, behavioral management models, and cognitive-emotional approaches. Often interventions are directed solely on the child rather than on the family unit or on a more comprehensive, holistic approach that includes informal and formal support systems within the community.

A contemporary theoretical perspective that offers a more hopeful prognosis for children who experience parental violence is social bonding theory (Hirschi in Dutton, 1998). Social bonding suggests that even if one grows up witnessing abuse, the intergenerational transmission perspective can be challenged by the number of those who are not abusive in adult intimate relationships. The individual's bond to society rather than to his/her family history of violence explains whether one will become violent in adult intimate partner relationships. Bonding to society includes the dimensions of attachment to significant others, commitment to personal investments in conventional lines of conduct, involvement in conventional activities, and belief in the moral validity of social rules. This perspective allows for an explanation of cross-generational *cessation* of family violence. This view is a shift from a family of origin experience of parental violence upon which children as adults will imitate violent behavior to the idea that a cessation of violence is possible and can be based upon the influences of the greater social order. In other words, among men reared in violent homes, the greater the bond to society, the less likely one is to engage in domestic violence. Initial research (Lackey & Williams, 1995) indicates that forming strong social bonds in adulthood influences the cessation of intimate partner violence across generations. This research is promising as it implies that one is not destined to replicate the violence experienced in childhood. It offers hope that children as adults can and do become non-violent with the intervening factors of societal influences.

Practice Principles for Best Practice Interventions

Given the number and variety of services available for families who experience domestic violence, it is common for competing helping paradigms and turf issues to arise. The Romito 's story points to this. However, the continuance, progression, and dangerousness of life within a family where there is violence dictates that early intervention is necessary—especially for the sake of the children. Most research supports the idea that boys who witness their fathers abusing their mothers are at high risk of becoming abusers themselves. Davies (1991) discusses the need to intervene with male toddlers who have witnessed parental violence. Tutty and Wagar (1994) agree that early intervention holds the promise for short cutting the inter-generational transmission of violence and work with school-aged children toward that end. Whether one subscribes to the inter-generational transmission of violence perspective or a social bonding approach, early intervention is required to offer these children a chance to survive and to thrive as they develop into adulthood.

Practice Principles

1. Helping Children. Helpers can solicit the *child's meaning* of living with parents who are violent. In all likelihood, the children will raise issues of secrecy, shame, conflicting loyalties, feelings of abandonment, loneliness, anxiety, and/or guilt. .

Practice Skills:

    A. *Use practice techniques that are age and developmentally appropriate* to introduce the idea that not all families are violent. In such a way, the worker can assist with non-violent ways to solve problems and resolve conflicts. Practice techniques that may be useful include story telling. Having the children tell their stories of their families help to introduce the important issues most meaningful to the child.

    B. *Avoid interpretation of children's stories.* Helpers must be wary of interpreting these stories, however. Quiet listening and undivided attention to these children is particularly imperative given they may have had little opportunity for this centered attention.

C. *Attend to issues of abandonment with children.* Research indicates that not only are children affected directly by the violence in their homes, but they react to their Mom's stress of being battered (Levendovsky & Graham-Berman, 1998) and to the phenomenon of feeling alone and abandoned during this time (Margolin & John, in Kantor & Jasinski, 1997). On-going issues of grief & loss of both parents must be addressed.

D. *Foster a sense of empowerment.* As children receive the attention and focus from help givers, a budding sense of empowerment may occur. Often children have not progressed developmentally toward mastery of the usual and customary developmental tasks. Being preoccupied with parental behavior, these children cannot focus on accomplishing those activities common to children their age. To feel empowered against the backdrop of fear, helplessness, and powerlessness these children have experienced in their homes is particularly necessary along all developmental stages.

A Reminder: It is critically important to remember that children in families that experience domestic violence are not only children of battered women, but also children of battering fathers. No other activity between two individuals in love raises as great a set of powerful and ambivalent emotions among the entire family. As such, these children are continuously faced with conflicting loyalties. In most cases, the mother's relationship with the father becomes fractured along with the consequent splintering of relationships throughout the family structure. The fractured relationship between the mother and father must not camouflage the pain of the children's loss of relationship with their father. Whether these children feel love for their father, they may have been attracted to his demonstrated strength and power. Peled (1997) indicates that while child witnesses may identify with their mother's pain, they struggle with the attraction of siding with the one who has power and control in the family. They need to have the opportunity and assistance from professionals to maintain the best relationship possible with their father. Children of battered women and battering fathers must be given the attention for their emotional needs and relational rebuilding with both parents.

2. Family Focus. While it is imperative that children's needs not be overlooked, it is also imperative to address the needs and concerns of the entire family. Each member suffers in his/her own way and generally wishes to remain a family—without the violence.

Practice Skills:

Interventions need to focus on 4 areas:

- conflict resolution

- problem solving skill development

- safety skill development

- relational re-building.

Social workers must be comfortable and able to *make home visits* where they can assist with breaking the silence, developing norms for rule setting, and offering respite for the victim. Using this time to discuss the meaning of the violence within the family from each member's perspective is extremely valuable in reducing the distancing between "perpetrator" and "victims."

3. Community/collaborative Interventions. To effectively interrupt family violence, community wide interventions and inter-professional collaborations are mandatory. We find, for example, services outside the home for children may include non-residency children's programs in shelters. Shelter programs may be limited by mom's willingness and availability to have children attend, however. Schools, then, are in the unique position to offer violence awareness and prevention programs directly to children. Murray Straus' most recent work focuses on corporal punishment as precursors to family violence, and he firmly believes family violence could be diminished if churches get involved (Straus, in Barnett, Miller-Perrin, & Perrin, 1997).

The story of violence within a family such as the Romito's demonstrates two major issues. First, each and every member of a family in which there is violence suffers. All become victims, so to speak, and want the violence to stop. Each story must be heard and respected without blame or disgust on the helper's part. Secondly, the need for collaborative, community-level intervention becomes obvious. Multiple agencies and services may be called upon to offer specialized services to various members of this family. As in Carol's experience, however, the tendency to partialize and specialize in treatment with victims, perpetrators, and/or witness/victims may be great. As a worker committed to the preservation and enrichment of families, a collaborative and family-focused holistic approach is much more sound, provided that preserving the family not be at the expense of a battered woman. On the other hand, with strong monitoring and appropriate safety measures, if the family wishes to stay together and address the violence, a family preservation perspective may be useful.

Home visits with all family members present, concrete behavioral contracting with specified consequences, and intervention techniques that allow for each family member's story to be heard with respect is imperative. Encouraging and assisting each family member to bond with extended family and community members may indeed contribute to the interruption of "the cycle of violence" within a family.

The Story's Ending

We cannot predict what will happen to the Romito family. Left alone, in all probability, the violence will escalate in frequency and severity. Each family member will continue to suffer silently and alone. Someone may die.

As helpers who wish to participate in this story's ending, we must listen, assess, join with this family, and work collaboratively towards meeting the various needs and co-occurring challenges this family presents. We must actively yet patiently await the unfolding richness of detail as family members speak to us. Our very presence offers a modicum of hope that something will change for this family. Our goal is to maximize and energize this hope in service to a non-violent resolution of family stress and conflict. We must become part of the story's ending.

References

Akukwe, C. (1998). The potential impact of the 1996 welfare reforms on intimate partner violence. *Family and Community Health, 20*(4), 54-62.

Davidson, T. (1978). *Conjugal crime: Understanding and changing the wife beating pattern.* New York: Ballentine Books.

Davies, D. (1991) Intervention with male toddlers who have witnessed parental violence. *Families in Society. 72,* 515-524.

Dutton, D. (1998). *The abusive personality: Violence and control in intimate relationships.* New York: The Guilford Press.

Graham-Berman, S. and Levendovosky, A. (Feb. 1992). Traumatic stress symptoms in children of battered women. *Journal of Interpersonal Violence, 13,* 111-128.

The Healing House Inc. (1998). Walking away from abuse--embracing empowerment (1st edition). Deming, NM.

Jaffe, P., Wolfe, Wilson, S., and Wolfe, D. (1986). Promoting changes in attitudes and understanding of conflict resolution among child witnesses of family violence. *Canadian Journal of Behavior Science,* (18) 4.

Jaffe, P., Wolfe, Wilson, S., and Wolfe, D. (Jan. 1986). *American Journal of Psychiatry, 143*:1.

Kempe, C. H., Silverman, F. N., Steele, B. F., Droegemueller, W., and Silver, H. K. (1961). The battered child syndrome. *Journal of the American Medical Association, 181*, 107-112.

Kendall-Tackert and Eckenrode (1997). The effects of neglect on academic achievement and disciplinary problems: A developmental perspective. In Kantor and Jasinski, *Out of the Darkness: Contemporary Perspectives on Family Violence*. Thousand Oaks, SAGE Pub.

Krishnan, S. and Hilbert, J. (Sept/Oct 1998). In search of sanctuary: Addressing issues of domestic violence and homelessness at shelters. *Women's Health Issues. 8*(5).

Lackey, C. and Williams, K. (1995). Social bonding and the cessation of partner violence across generations. *Journal of Marriage and the Family. 57*(2) 295-306.

Levendovsky, A. and Graham-Berman, S. (Jun 1998). The moderating effects of stress on children's adjustment in women-abusing families. *Journal of Interpersonal Violence, 13*, 383-397.

Margolin and John (1997). Children's exposure to marital aggression: Direct and mediated effects. In Kantor and Jasinski, *Out of the Darkness: Contemporary Perspectives on Family Violence*. Thousand Oaks, SAGE Pub.

Marker, A., Kemmelmeier, M., and Peterson, C. (Oct. 1998). Long-term psychological consequences in women witnessing parental physical use and experiencing abuse in childhood. *Journal of Interpersonal Violence 13*, 574-589.

Markward, M. (1997). The impact of domestic violence on children. *Families in Society: The Journal of Contemporary Human Services, 78*, 66-70.

Martin, D. (1977). *Battered wives*. New York: Pocket Books.

Miller, S. and Wellford, C. (In Cardarelli, a. p. , Ed. 1997). Patterns and correlates of interpersonal violence. *Violence between Intimate Partners*. Boston, Allyn and Bacon.

Peled, E. (1997). The battered women's movement response to children of battered women: A critical analysis. *Violence against Women. 3*, 424-446.

Peled, E. (In Edelson, J. and Eisikovits, Z. Eds., 1996). Secondary victims no more: Refocusing intervention with children. *Future Interventions with Battered Women and their Families.* Thousand Oaks. SAGE Pub.

Sorenson, S. and Telles, C. (1991). Self-reports of spousal violence in a Mexican-American and Non-Hispanic White population. *Violence and Victims. 6*: 3-15.

Straus, M. (1997). In Barnett, Miller-Perrin, and Perrin. *Family violence across the lifespan*. Thousand Oaks, SAGE, 41.

Straus, M. A., Williams, O. B., and Corrigan, P. W. (1992). The differential effects of parental alcoholism and mental illness on their adult children. *Journal of Clinical Psychology, 48*, 406-414.

Straus, M. A., Gelles, R. J., and Steinmetz, S. K. (1980). *Behind closed doors: Violence in the American Family.* Garden City, NY: Doubleday.

Tutty, L. and Wagar, J. (1994). The evolution of a group for young children who have witnessed family violence. *Social Work with Groups. 17*(2), 89-104.

Tutty, L., Weaver, G., and Rothery, M. (1999). Residents' views of the efficacy of shelter services for assaulted women. Paper presented at the Third Annual Conference of the Society for Social Work and Research, Austin TX Jan 22-24, 1999. In press in *Violence and Women.*

Chapter 7

Child Welfare and Substance Abuse: Toward Partnerships with Parents and Communities

Brenda D. Smith

Introduction

As we transition to a new century, parental substance abuse continues to challenge child welfare policy makers and service providers. Eighty percent of state child welfare administrators cite parental substance abuse and family poverty as the top two child welfare issues (CWLA, 1998). Frustration with parental substance abuse and, in particular, the difficult and lengthy process of overcoming addiction, inspired the 1997 Adoption and Safe Families Act (ASFA). ASFA shortens the time frame in which parents must comply with reunification requirements. The implementation of ASFA raises questions about the potential consequences of shorter permanency time lines for families affected by substance abuse. Will parents with substance abuse problems be able to comply with treatment requirements within the shortened time lines? Given the lengthy recovery times associated with addiction, do families affected by substance abuse have any real chance for reunification? Will more parents with substance abuse problems have their parental rights terminated?

Such questions highlight the importance of providing effective services to families, which are both affected by substance abuse and involved with the child welfare system. Yet, recent experience affirms the difficulty in effectively reaching such families. We still lack information about the relationships between parental substance abuse and involvement with the child welfare system. We still lack information about the most effective ways to engage clients with substance abuse problems in services. What's more, as we focus attention on the overlap between substance abuse treatment and involvement with the child welfare system, we learn more about conflicts between the two service systems—conflicts which, in themselves, pose a barrier to services. Fortunately, we have also made some progress in outlining ways to overcome these barriers through innovative collaborative partnerships.

After summarizing what is known about the links between parental substance abuse and involvement with the child welfare system, this chapter (1) outlines conflicts between the child welfare and the substance abuse treatment service systems; (2) describes some innovative ways to overcome the conflicts between the two service systems; and, (3) lists some remaining problems faced by both service systems. The chapter concludes by offering some guidelines for approaching parental substance abuse in the new century.

Links Between Child Welfare and Substance Abuse

The Percentage of Child Welfare Cases Involving Parental Substance Abuse

Given the amount of attention devoted to parental substance abuse, it is surprising to note the lack of solid data on the prevalence of parental substance abuse among families involved with the child welfare system. Most state child welfare systems are only beginning to systematically collect data on parental substance abuse, and a national data reporting system has only recently been developed. Consequently, we must rely on prevalence estimates. Studies have attempted to obtain estimates of the prevalence of parental substance abuse in child welfare cases through a variety of methods, including surveys of state administrators (CWLA, 1998) and surveys of caseworkers (GAO, 1998). One study involved a telephone survey of caseworkers and reviewed a sample of case files (Children's Bureau, 1997). In addition, estimates of the prevalence rate have been based upon reports to newly developing data systems, such as the Adoption and Foster Care Analysis and Reporting System (AFCARS) and the Multistate Foster Care Data Archive (Goerge & Hardin, 1993; Goerge, Wulczyn, & Hardin, 1996).

Estimates of the problem range as low as 10 percent of child abuse reports (SAMHSA, 1999) and 26 percent of open child welfare cases (Children's Bureau, 1997), to as high as 78 percent of foster care cases (GAO, 1994). Perhaps the most scientifically sound estimate comes from a study which used probability sampling and asked caseworkers about the incidence of substance abuse in their cases. This study found that 26 percent of open cases in 1994 involved caretaker substance abuse (Children's Bureau, 1997). Some researchers question these findings, however, due to the possibility that caseworkers are unaware of parental substance abuse. As recently as 1991, only 68 percent of child welfare agency survey respondents indicated that they routinely screened for substance abuse issues during maltreatment investigations, and only 31 percent of respondent agencies felt that their risk assessment tools adequately assessed substance abuse issues (Young & Gardner, 1997). Thus, despite wide-ranging findings and the absence of systematic data collection, it is routinely reported, and generally accepted, that one to two thirds of child welfare cases involve parental substance abuse (SAMHSA, 1999). Indeed, administrators and service providers are convinced that the vast majority of child welfare cases involve substance abuse. Clearly, however, we need more systematic means of collecting data on the problem.

The Effect of Substance-Exposed Infants

One contributor to the portion of child welfare cases involving substance abuse was the crack cocaine epidemic of the late 1980s and early 1990s. Whereas researchers had devoted attention to the effects of parental substance abuse for decades, the crack epidemic brought heightened attention to the phenomenon of prenatal drug exposure. Early studies of cocaine-exposed infants suggested that prenatal drug exposure led to serious and chronic developmental and behavioral problems. Later research has tempered these early predictions (Mayes, Granger, Bornstein, & Zuckerman,1992). The early studies did not adequately account for conditions associated with illicit drug, use such as poverty, poor nutrition and inadequate parental care. In addition, the effects of substances such as alcohol, tobacco and environmental toxins had not been isolated from the effects of illicit drugs. Moreover, recent studies conclude that the effects of prenatal substance exposure can be mitigated by a child's environment as she grows (Lester, Freir, & LaGasse, 1995).

Concern about substance-exposed infants affected child welfare caseloads in several ways. Some states mandated reports of substance-exposed infants to child protective authorities. Some states considered prenatal substance exposure prima facie evidence of child neglect and opened child welfare cases for all positive drug screens. Finally, fearful of the risks that prenatal substance abuse posed to subsequent child safety and well-being, some states opened child welfare cases or removed children from families under "risk of harm" allegations. As a consequence, more infants were placed in substitute care, and the age distribution of admissions to foster care shifted downward (Goerge, Wulczyn, & Hardin, 1996). Prenatal substance exposure has had important effects upon child welfare policy, services, and caseload dynamics. However, substance-exposed infant cases comprise a minority of child welfare cases involving parental substance abuse (Young & Gardner, 1997).

The Percentage of Families with Substance Abuse Problems Involved with the Child Welfare System

Whereas the portion of child welfare clients with substance abuse problems seems substantial, the overlap is not reciprocal. The portion of families with substance abuse problems who become involved with the child welfare system appears to be quite small. Estimates suggest that in 1995, 7.5 million children, or 10 percent of children under age 17, lived with a parent who was dependent on alcohol or illicit drugs; 8.3 million children, or 11 percent of children under age 17, lived with a parent who was dependent on alcohol and/or in need of treatment for illicit drug use (Huang, Cerbone, & Gfroerer, 1998). These figures provide a cross-sectional picture of parental substance abuse; estimating the exposure to parental substance abuse over the course of childhood is more difficult. However, one study using sophisticated methodology estimates that about 28 percent of children under age 17 are exposed in their lifetime to alcohol abuse or dependency in their family (Grant, 2000).

By contrast, in 1996, 970,000 children were included in substantiated maltreatment reports, and there were about 500,000 children in foster care (Children's Bureau, 1998; Children's Bureau, 1997). Thus, even if every child involved with the child welfare system that year came from a family with a substance abuse problem, the number would constitute less than 12 percent of all children living with a parent with a substance abuse problem.

Based on the estimates that about half of substantiated child abuse reports involve parental substance abuse, we would estimate that *about 6 percent* of the children living with a parent with a substance abuse problem were involved with the child welfare system in 1996. Again, this figure provides a cross-sectional picture of parental substance abuse and child welfare involvement; we lack estimates of the likelihood of child welfare involvement over the course of childhood for children living in families with substance abuse problems. That percentage may be higher. Still, despite evidence that substance abuse can impair parental functioning, it is clear that most families with substance abuse problems avoid involvement with the child welfare system. Factors such as economic resources, family structure, and social and community support all contribute to helping families avoid involvement with the child welfare system. Substance abuse, per se, does not result in child welfare involvement.

The Percentage of Child Welfare Clients Who Obtain Substance Abuse Treatment Services

One area of concern related to the overlap between child welfare and parental substance abuse is the delivery of substance abuse treatment services. Service providers question the availability, accessability, quality, and effectiveness of substance abuse treatment for families involved with the child welfare system. A 1998 Child Welfare League of America study suggested that two thirds of parents involved with child welfare services need substance abuse treatment, yet treatment services were available for only 31 percent of all parents, or about half of those in need (Leiderman, 1998). Likewise, a study focusing exclusively on parents with substance abuse problems involved with child welfare services also found that about half of such parents received substance abuse treatment; 23 percent had treatment offered but did not receive it; and 23 percent had no treatment services offered (Children's Bureau, 1997). Finally, a study focusing on parents with substance abuse problems (whether or not they were involved with the child welfare system) found that 37 percent had received substance abuse treatment in the past year; 63 percent had not received treatment (SAMHSA, 1997).

Comparisons between these studies can be merely suggestive as we are unable to control for important variables, such as the severity of drug use among the different study groups. The collective findings suggest that among parents with substance abuse problems, involvement with child welfare services may be associated with receiving substance abuse treatment. This possible association merits investigation.

The Percentage of Substance Abuse Treatment Clients Involved with Child Welfare Services

Although the statistics suggest that only a small portion of parents with substance abuse problems become involved with child welfare services, the extent of child welfare involvement among female clients of substance abuse treatment facilities is substantially higher. Several studies summarized by the Substance Abuse and Mental Health Services Administration (SAMHSA) suggest that 20 to 40 percent of mothers attending substance abuse treatment programs have some type of involvement with child welfare services. A study of a SAMHSA-sponsored residential treatment program for pregnant women and mothers found that 20 percent of the clients had been referred for services by a child welfare agency, and 40 percent had a child in foster care (Dowell and Roberts, 1998, cited in SAMHSA, 1999). Several other treatment program evaluations have found child welfare involvement in about one-third of the mothers attending treatment (Stevens & Arbiter, 1995; Wobie, et al., 1997). Finally, SAMHSA's National Treatment Improvement Evaluation Study (SAMHSA, 1996) found that 44 percent of mothers having children under age 18, and 15 percent of fathers having children under age 18, said that they entered treatment to maintain or regain child custody. Of the mothers entering treatment within a year of their most recent birth, two thirds reported doing so to keep or regain child custody (SAMHSA, 1999).

Thus, though the majority of parents with substance abuse problems have no involvement with the child welfare system, of the parenting women who attend substance abuse treatment programs, the rate of child welfare involvement is much higher. Again, this suggests an association, at least among parenting women, between involvement with child welfare services and involvement with substance abuse treatment services.

Child Welfare Correlates of Parental Substance Abuse

In addition to establishing the prevalence of parental substance abuse among the child welfare population, researchers have attempted to identify other child welfare correlates of parental substance abuse. Parental substance abuse has been associated with longer foster care stays for children (Fanshel, 1975; Walker, Zangrillo & Smith, 1991; Murphy, et al., 1991), noncompliance with child welfare treatment plans (Famularo, Kinscherff, Bunshaft, Spivak, & Fenton, 1989; Butler, Radia, &

Magnata, 1994; Murphy, et al., 1991), subsequent maltreatment allegations (Wolock & Magura, 1996; Jaudes, Edem, & Van Voorhis, 1995), and a reduced likelihood of family reunification (Murphy, et al., 1991; Walker, Zangrillo, & Smith, 1991).

Efforts to understand the correlates of parental substance abuse have been hindered by the limited use of multivariate research.[1] With bivariate associations, we cannot discern the extent to which outcome factors associated with substance abuse stem from substance abuse, per se, or from other factors associated with substance abuse. It is likely that outcomes associated with substance abuse are substantially influenced by factors that tend to accompany substance abuse, especially among parents involved with the child welfare system. Such factors include neighborhood hazards (violence, crime, environmental toxins), mental health issues, lack of social support, lack of support services, social stigma, and poverty. The social and economic factors which often accompany substance abuse and child welfare involvement make it difficult to assess the consequences of substance abuse, per se (National Research Council, 1993). Thus, just as early research on the effects of prenatal cocaine exposure exaggerated the consequences of cocaine exposure because the research failed to account for the effects of other substances and other social and economic factors associated with poor developmental outcomes, much of the research on the child welfare outcomes associated with parental substance abuse is subject to the same type of misinterpretation.

Even research which attempts to use matched comparison groups is sometimes difficult to interpret. For example, Jaudes, Edem, and Van Voorhis (1995) compare the subsequent maltreatment risk among infants with SEI allegations to the maltreatment risk among infants from the general population living in the same neighborhood. Certainly, a history of parental substance abuse may be one factor which places substance-exposed infants at greater risk of subsequent harm. Yet, it is likely that such infants are exposed to multiple influences which place them at increased risk of child welfare involvement as compared to infants from the general population, even those in the same neighborhood. Frank (1995) notes that even if matched on socioeconomic characteristics, children involved with child welfare services tend to have more developmental problems than children who aren't involved. To answer questions about the consequences of parental substance abuse, per se, we need more research including multivariate controls and studies using stronger research designs.

Conflicts Between the Two Systems

Increasing attention to the overlap between child welfare and substance abuse has prompted increased recognition and a more sophisticated understanding of some fundamental differences between the two service systems. Nancy Young (Young & Gardner, 1997) and Laura Feig (Feig, 1998) have conducted important conceptual work to explain the fundamental differences between the two service systems. Below I summarize the two service systems' contrasting conceptions of (1) the client; (2) substance abuse, addiction and relapse; (3) success; and, of increasing relevance since ASFA, (4) time.

Contrasting Conceptions of the Client

Although much of the attention in child welfare cases is devoted to parents' behavior, child safety is the primary concern of the child welfare system. Hence, children are the primary clients. When a service plan calls for reunification, or when working with intact families, good case workers may see strengthening families as their primary objective and, thus, consider entire families as their clients. Still, work load assignments typically reinforce the notion that children are the primary clients. In Illinois, for example, a case worker's case load size is measured by the number of children in his or her case load. The number of biological parents with which a case worker may be working is not taken into account when computing the work load. Similarly, the number of foster parents or prospective adoptive parents with which a case worker may be working are typically not calculated as part of a "case load size" (Smith, 1999).

Importantly, the child welfare system works with adults based on their status as *parents*. The ultimate goal of services for parents, at least in theory, whether the services be substance abuse treatment, parenting classes, or counseling, is simply to improve parenting. Also, the vast majority of the adult clients with whom the system works are women.

Substance abuse treatment providers, on the other hand, typically do not inquire about the parent status of their adult clients, most of whom are men. Typical treatment providers do not consider children, entire families, or "parents" to be their clients; they typically work with adults as individuals.[2] Just as adults are not counted among the case loads of child welfare workers, parent status is not included among the standardized data collected by substance abuse treatment centers (Young and Gardner, 1997).

Providers in these two service systems need to collaborate, but often they do not. Clearly, it is easy to envision a scenario in which a child welfare case worker prioritizes visits and services to a child in foster care. Meanwhile, the child's biological parent attends substance abuse treatment. Yet the service systems fail to collaborate to reunite and strengthen the entire family. Lack of collaboration is compounded when substance abuse treatment professionals fail to understand that a parent may not be considered the "client" of a child welfare worker. Substance abuse treatment professionals may assume that parents receive support and advocacy from child welfare workers, when child welfare workers may not consider that to be part of their job.

Another potential consequence of the two service systems' contrasting notions of the client is that both service systems may construe the interests of parents and children as competing (Brindis & Theidon, 1997). Child welfare workers may primarily view parents with substance abuse problems as potential threats to their children, while substance abuse treatment providers may primarily view children as obstacles to parents' recovery. Some child welfare workers discourage family visitation in cases involving substance abuse; some traditional treatment models force parents to pursue recovery without their children. Different practices would likely evolve if both service systems considered whole families to be their clients.

Contrasting Conceptions of Substance Abuse, Addiction and Relapse

Different theories to explain addiction inspire different responses to it. At the heart of the conflict between the two service systems are different notions of substance abuse and addiction. Most substance abuse treatment services adhere to the disease theory of addiction. According to this conceptualization, addiction is like a disease in that it is chronic and something over which an individual has limited control. Like other diseases, it has symptoms, follows a predictable course, and can be treated but not cured (Feig, 1998). The disease of substance abuse does not reflect upon an individual's moral character. Recovery from addiction is expected to be a slow-moving, arduous process characterized by small steps forward and set-backs; relapse is expected, and sometimes even valued, as part of the process.

Although child welfare workers are likely to be familiar with this conceptualization of addiction and may even adhere to it to some extent, a different conceptualization of addiction prevails in the child welfare system. In the child welfare system, substance abuse and addiction can end up being conceptualized as willful destructive behavior. Addicted parents, at best, lack strength and, at worst, care about substance use more than their children. Continued substance abuse is viewed as an indicator of insufficient motivation, and if faced with the prospect of losing child custody, insufficient motivation is considered an indicator of insufficient love. In the child welfare system, relapse, contrary to being expected and accepted, is viewed as "non-compliance." Children will not be reunited with parents who "fail to comply" with treatment plans. Hence, while child welfare decision makers may be familiar with the notion that substance abuse is a disease, the system responds to substance abuse as a choice. Substance use patterns reflect an individual's motivation, character, and capacity to parent.

Contrasting Conceptions of Success

The primary objective of substance abuse treatment is to decrease or stop substance use. This objective is measured through self-reports and attendance at treatment sessions and follow-up meetings.

In child welfare, in theory, the primary objective is healthy family functioning as indicated by child safety, permanency, and well-being. Success indicated by these objectives is difficult to achieve, however, because the objectives can conflict with one another. For example, child safety may be best achieved in a foster care placement, but the placement may not provide either permanency or well-being. In addition, these child welfare outcome objectives can be quite difficult to measure. Due to the difficulty of measuring the outcomes; and due, at least in part, to court influence, child welfare services have increasingly turned to specific, concrete, and easily obtained indicators of success, such as drug-free urine screens and diplomas indicating completion of services. As a consequence, some argue that the ultimate purpose of services, such as family functioning or parenting capacity, is not being measured. The need for more meaningful measures of success is discussed below.

While the two service systems' conceptions of success may differ more in theory than in practice, the theoretical differences are important. For example, it is possible to end or reduce substance abuse without achieving healthy family functioning, child safety, permanency, or well-being. Yet achieving abstinence, even under such circumstances, would likely be considered a success to most substance abuse treatment providers. Likewise, it is possible to use substances to some extent and still maintain family functioning, child safety, permanency, and well-being. In theory, this achievement should be considered a success by the child welfare system. If family functioning and child safety were upheld as the primary goal and measures were in place to maintain them, the child welfare system could declare success even if some parental substance use continues. In practice, despite its intended focus on child safety, the child welfare system often focuses on parental abstinence, per se, as its goal.

Contrasting Time Lines

One of the most obvious conflicts between the two service systems is their different orientation to time. Substance abuse treatment is provided according to the client's readiness. Recovery is expected to be a slow, perhaps life-long, process involving relapses and fresh starts. In contrast, the child welfare system pays attention to the time frames of children. Although the child welfare system has not succeeded in moving quickly, and has been condemned for the phenomenon of "foster care drift," child welfare policy has increasingly implemented measures to shorten the amount of time children spend involved with child welfare services and not in permanent homes.

ASFA constitutes the most recent example of such measures. It shortens the amount of time from 18 to 12 months in which permanency hearings must be held and requires states to begin efforts to terminate parental rights when a child has been in substitute care for 15 of the past 22 months.

The implementation of ASFA, along with the implementation of new time lines accompanying the 1996 welfare reforms, have prompted the notion that many families involved with the child welfare system are subject to "four clocks" (Young & Gardner, 1997). The four clocks are: (1) the child welfare system's six-month case reviews and permanency time lines newly shortened with ASFA; (2) the new TANF time lines which vary state by state, but which limit receipt of public benefits to at most 5 years and require work within 2 years; (3) the slow process of recovery; and, (4) children's developmental time lines. Some families may be subject to a fifth clock as some public housing programs implement five-year time limits for public housing stays (HUD, 1999; Pitcoff, 1999).

Substance abuse treatment providers may expect and be patient with client relapses and slow progress toward recovery. However, a slow recovery process will conflict with children's needs as well as the shortened child welfare and public assistance time lines. Even if parents engage in services, they may fail to recover sufficiently within a time period which enables them to (1) progress toward reunification; (2) enter the labor force as an alternative to, or condition of, receiving TANF benefits; and, (3) safely parent. Some parents face the prospect of accomplishing the arduous work in overcoming addiction only to find that they may still permanently lose custody of their children due to the length of recovery time. The conflicting time lines also raise the possibility that added demands, such as TANF work requirements, will complicate and extend substance abuse recovery time.

Up to now, the child welfare system has generally taken a "zero tolerance" approach to parental substance abuse. In a zero tolerance environment, a relapse can indicate non-compliance with reunification plans. With the shortened ASFA time lines, a poorly timed relapse could result in a decision to terminate parental rights. Another potential hazard of the shortened ASFA time lines is that children may be reunified with recovering parents before the parents are ready. Expedited reunifications could increase the likelihood of disrupted reunification. The potential hazards associated with the conflicting time lines starkly highlight the need for service system collaboration in order to help cross-system clients.

Progress in Overcoming the Conflicts

In recent years, some progress has been made in identifying steps needed to overcome the conflicts between the child welfare and substance abuse treatment service systems. Progress has been made both conceptually, through descriptions of ways to overcome system-based barriers, and practically, through the implementation of model intervention programs. Two key themes of common prescriptions for overcoming service system barriers are collaboration and comprehensiveness.

Collaboration

Prescriptions suggest that to overcome their conflicts, the child welfare and substance abuse treatment service systems must move toward *inter-organizational collaboration* (Lawson & Barkdull, this volume). The systems must collaborate through joint goal setting, joint training, and joint funding efforts (Feig, 1998). Rather than criticizing each other for not working according to the desired time table or not reaching the desired results, the service systems must work together toward common goals. As the service systems identify shared goals, they can more easily work cooperatively to achieve the goals. In addition, joint training of service system staff could help the service systems to better understand one another and to see more clearly some commonalities in their objectives. Finally, both service systems must become financially committed to shared objectives so they will be more likely to 'own' responsibility for shared outcomes (Feig, 1998; Lawson & Barkdull, this volume). Joint funding might help reduce the inclination of each service system to regard the other as attempting to take advantage of its resources. As described by Lawson and Barkdull (this volume), the key to inter-organizational collaboration is shared accountability for outcomes.

Comprehensiveness

Clearly, the child welfare and substance abuse treatment systems must work more effectively together. Yet, for truly effective service systems to develop—systems that will prevent parental substance abuse as well as treat it—additional collaboration, such as family-centered and community collaboration, will be needed (Lawson & Barkdull, this volume). Certainly, families involved with both child welfare and substance abuse treatment services are often involved with other service systems as well, including schools and adult education, mental health, criminal justice, public health, and public assistance. Thus, collaborative efforts may need to involve multiple systems. Moreover, the communities in which families live, like the families themselves, are often condemned as poverty-stricken, violent, and resource-poor. Yet the communities and families have strengths that can be identified and built upon. A preventive, comprehensive, responsive service system will involve partnerships with traditional service providers as well as informal support systems and indigenous helpers who may be clients of the systems as well. Collaboration between and professionals and community members may promote the development of communal norms, including empathy and solution-focused language (Lawson, this volume).

Model Programs

A number of states and counties have developed new collaborative initiatives to overcome some of the cross-systems barriers between child welfare and substance abuse treatment. Such programs typically include joint-funded programs and joint training of providers from both systems. In addition to promoting collaboration between child welfare and substance abuse providers, such programs include empirically based treatment methods (NIDA, 1999) and often provide comprehensive services, including outreach, transportation, and child care (Smith, Marsh, & D'Aunno, 1998; Guza, Wilson, & Thompson, 1998; Walsh & Young, 1998). The most innovative programs have engaged community-based organizations and natural helping networks including informal networks of recovering parents (Van Wagoner, et al., this volume). Community-based helping networks have provided substance abuse aftercare services, child safety monitoring, parent support, and reunification respite care (Young & Gardner, 1997).

Remaining Problems in Both Systems

Considerable progress has been made, not only in conceptualizing the conflicts between child welfare and substance abuse treatment services, but in conceptualizing what is needed to move toward overcoming many of these conflicts. Still, both service systems have some remaining problems which can hinder cross-systems change. In this section of the chapter, I describe some of these remaining obstacles.

Micro-Level Conceptions of the Problem

In our efforts to understand social problems and responses to them, our attention is selective. Certain aspects of problems receive more attention than other aspects; some aspects of problems go unnoticed. We can deepen our understanding of problems and their solutions by explicitly seeking out overlooked and obscured dimensions.

Service system responses to parental substance abuse tend to focus on individual or sometimes family-level conceptions of the problem. We say that parents with substance abuse problems involved with the child welfare system come from "multiple vulnerable" families (Halpern, 1997). We point out the co-existence of problems such as mental illness, depression, and domestic violence. We note that many parents indicated for child maltreatment were abused or neglected themselves. Sometimes we also note that such families tend to be poor and live in poor or violent neighborhoods.

Rarely, however, do discussions of parental substance abuse point to the systemic, structural nature of the influences on such families. It is easy to develop a picture of each individual family struggling in isolation with poverty, neighborhood violence, and consequent family problems. And it is easy to lose sight of the collective experiences of oppression experienced by such families and the institutionalized and structural contributors to the problems they face. Both service systems are subject to the tendency to individualize and de-politicize their clients' experiences. Both systems should focus more attention on issues of social justice and distributive justice, including good jobs and meaningful work, income supports, quality education and health services, housing, community development, and environmental quality (Hooper-Briar & Lawson, 1994).

Insufficient Attention to Gender

One of the institutionalized and structural contributors to the joint problems of parental substance abuse and involvement with the child welfare system relates to the status of women. Involvement with the child welfare system and, indeed, the concept of child neglect, though typically discussed in gender-neutral ways, are primarily associated with women. The "parents" involved with the child welfare system are, by and large, mothers (Swift, 1995; Gordon, 1988). Likewise, concerns about parental substance abuse focus primarily on mothers' substance abuse. When we conceptualize these issues in gender neutral ways, we lose sight of the ways in which notions of appropriate gender role adherence affect our reactions to, and assessment of, the issues. Women's substance abuse carries an added stigma over men's substance abuse. Ingrained notions of appropriate female behavior, especially notions of appropriate maternal behavior, intensify a moral dimension in assessments of women's substance abuse.

Also obscured when we conceptualize parental substance abuse in gender neutral terms is the oppression of women—especially poor women—by both the larger society and the men in their lives. The rates of sexual abuse, sexual assault, and partner violence against women who abuse substances and become involved with the child welfare system are alarmingly high (Blume, 1999; Gilbert, El-Bassel, Schilling & Freidman, 1997; Paone, Chavkin, Willets, Friedman, & Jarlais, 1992). We are just beginning to understand how correlates of women's oppression, such as violence, abuse, and powerlessness, relate to subsequent substance abuse (Woodhouse, 1992; Purnell, 1998). Not only has women's substance abuse been associated with traumatic events such as violence, placement of children in foster care, and sudden drops in income, it has been associated with "stigma trauma," or trauma specifically linked to the social interactions resulting from oppression (Fullilove & Lown, 1992). Whereas pleasure and thrill seeking constitute strong motivations for substance use among males, women are more likely to use substances as self-medication, or as a way to cope with oppressive situations, difficult events, and (often consequent) psychological distress (Inciardi, Lockwood, & Pottieger,1993; Hser, Anglin, & Booth, 1987).

As life experiences and motivations for substance abuse differ by gender, so might the effectiveness of different treatment modalities (Peugh & Belenko, 1999). Confrontational techniques typically used in treatment for men, may only reinforce feelings of self-blame among women (Ramsey, 1980). Whereas men may be socialized toward defense mechanisms, such as blaming others and false bravado, women may be more inclined to withdraw. Thus, women may be served best by treatment programs which create a safe and supportive environment, promote a sense of competence, provide concrete supports, and draw attention to collective experience (Marsh & Miller, 1985; Peugh & Belenko, 1999; Young, 1995). In other words, gender neutral treatment programs may not address the particular needs of women.

Finally, a gender neutral conceptualization of parental substance abuse contributes to the dismissal of men's roles as fathers. Parent status and parenting responsibilities are rarely used as an incentive for men in substance abuse treatment. Both service systems might better meet the needs of parents if the special needs of men and women parents were explicitly addressed.

Insufficient Attention to Race

Another of the institutionalized and systemic influences upon the coexistence of parental substance abuse and involvement with the child welfare system relates to the status of African Americans and racial bias in our society. Just as gender bias is hidden when we conceptualize parental substance abuse in gender neutral ways, racial bias is hidden when we fail to acknowledge the extent to which the (mostly women) parents who are targeted by both the child welfare system and substance abuse treatment services are disproportionately African American. The racial composition of child welfare caseloads has shifted over the past 30 years from 40 percent African American in 1977 to 54 percent in 1994. The shift among out-of-home placement cases was even greater. The percentage of children in out-of-home care that is African American shifted from 30 percent in 1977 to 63 percent in 1994 (Children's Bureau, 1997).

A survey of case files (Children's Bureau, 1997) found that African American families involved with the child welfare system are more likely than white families to have substance abuse problems noted in the case record. Thirty-seven percent of African American families have substance abuse problems identified in the case record, compared to 20 percent of white families. The survey also found that African American children are more likely than white children to be placed in foster care over in-home services and, of children in foster care, African American children have longer stays in foster care than white children. The Children's Bureau study found that African American children were more likely than white children to be placed out of the home even after accounting for other family characteristics associated with out-of-home placement. Finally, an often-cited study found that despite a similar level of substance abuse among pregnant African American and white women, African American women were more likely be reported to authorities for substance abuse during pregnancy (Chasnoff, Landress, & Barrett, 1990).

If we fail to acknowledge the increased likelihood of identified parental substance abusers to be African American mothers, we fail to recognize the extent to which racial bias may contribute to both substance abuse and involvement with the child welfare system. African American women are more likely to be involved with the child welfare system because of detection bias as described by Chasnoff. Rather, systemic biases in our society result in conditions in which African American women are disproportionately subject to factors which contribute to parental substance abuse and child welfare involvement. Just as Leroy Pelton (1981) identified the "myth of classlessness" in child welfare services by pointing out associations between poverty, per se, and child maltreatment, it is also a myth to deny that at the very foundation of our approach to child maltreatment in general, and parental substance abuse in particular, are notions of race (Roberts, 1997).

Superficial Indicators of Success and Failure

Another lingering problem with both the child welfare and substance abuse treatment service systems is that both systems use superficial measures of success and failure. To indicate success and failure, both systems must rely on things that can be easily measured; both systems lack ways to measure the things that are ultimately most important. Popular measures of success include concrete documents, such as sign-in sheets, attendance certificates and, especially, lab reports from urine toxicology screens. These commonly-used indicators of success shift attention toward service participation, per se, and away from the desired result of service participation. Although the child welfare system ostensibly considers family functioning or safe parenting to be the ultimate outcomes, it often relies on superficial indicators to assess treatment compliance and successful progress.

Measures are also determined by outside authorities. For example, the demands of the courts have substantially influenced which outcome indicators are used in child welfare cases.[1] Whereas case workers report that assessments of family needs and strengths should determine service plan objectives and indicate progress, service plans largely reflect things that workers and parents will be held accountable for in court.

---

[1] The courts play a critical role in the decision-making, trajectories, timing, and outcomes of child welfare cases. In many issues related to parental substance abuse, they could be considered a third service system which needs to collaborate with the child welfare and substance abuse treatment systems.

Not only do such things tend to prioritize service participation over service outcomes, as noted above, such things tend to be quite uniform across clients rather than reflecting case workers' assessments of unique family circumstances. Emphasis on such indicators limits case worker discretion, reduces the role of individualized assessments, and deflects attention away from the goal of promoting safe parenting and, once again, from the common structural influences that families face.

Blaming Clients for Service System Failures

A final problem remaining with both service systems is the tendency to attribute failures to clients. Much has been written about the difficulty of engaging parents with substance abuse problems in treatment, the high rates of treatment drop-out, the high rates of relapse, and the difficulty of successfully overcoming addiction. We know that child welfare workers become frustrated after making progress toward family reunification only to have a parent withdraw from services. Likewise, substance abuse treatment providers become frustrated when clients drop out of treatment. Whereas parents share the responsibility for treatment outcomes, too little burden has been placed with service providers to engage clients in services.

A recent audit of New York City foster care records found that of parents who had failed to progress toward reunification, the case files did not indicate whether or not the parents had been offered reunification services (Sengupta, 2000). When service providers assume none of the responsibility for service participation, all of the responsibility falls to the client, even when the client has received no assistance to obtain services. If the service providers share none of the responsibility for engaging clients in treatment, it becomes "easier for the caseworker if the parent drops out of treatment and thus can be shown uncooperative with the case plan" (Feig, 1998).

In addition to engaging clients in treatment, service providers should assume more responsibility for providing quality services. Clients may drop out of services because they find them ineffective. Evidence suggests that client-centered comprehensive services are effective and have good retention rates (Stevens & Arbiter, 1995; Olsen, 1995). A study of women attending substance abuse treatment found that treatment retention and completion were strongly associated with treatment program type. Programs using an empowerment philosophy and offering comprehensive support services and peer alliances had better retention rates (Strantz & Welch, 1995).

Oftentimes, both service systems face problems due to insufficient knowledge, insufficient resources, and conflicts, such as those described above, which form barriers to effective collaboration and effective service delivery. Sometimes treatment services are unavailable; sometimes outreach and engagement efforts are lacking or insufficient; sometimes there are conflicts between service providers and the courts. Yet, despite the many acknowledged problems with the service system, when services fail (or fail to be provided), parents are usually held responsible. For parents involved with the child welfare system, responsibility for treatment failures can bring about serious consequences, including delayed reunification and permanent loss of child custody. Ironically, loss of child custody and the attachment of moral stigmas may intensify substance abuse or trigger a relapse. In other words, service systems may contribute inadvertently to the problems they seek to treat.

Toward a Parent- and Community-Centered Approach

This concluding section of the chapter includes some action recommendations. The recommendations are listed in three categories: action to meet concrete needs; action to understand and change systemic influences; and action to engage parents and communities.

Action to Meet Concrete Needs

- To promote stronger families, both service systems must listen to parents' descriptions of concrete needs and expand connections to concrete services such as housing, transportation, health care, child care, and economic assistance.

Women in substance abuse treatment want access to concrete services (Marsh & Miller, 1985). Inadequate transportation and child care creates a substantial barrier to women's access to, and success in, treatment. Plus, when provided, such services seem to bring some of the hardest to serve women into treatment (Marsh, D'Aunno, & Smith, forthcoming). Child welfare and substance abuse treatment centers must move beyond an "assembly line" conceptualization, each system working on its specialized part, and participate in efforts to meet comprehensive needs (Lawson & Barkdull, this volume).

Action to Understand and Change Systemic Influences

- Service providers should support the efforts of parents, workers, and community members to come together in consciousness raising groups to better see and understand the effects of social oppression as a collective experience.

- Service providers should keep and share statistics on race, poverty, and neighborhood characteristics.

Parents involved with both child welfare and substance abuse treatment services are subject to multiple oppressions based on gender, race, and social class. They constitute a group that routinely faces the consequences of inequalities and biases built into the structures of our society. Rather than continuing to focus only on the consequences of these oppressions as they manifest in individual families, both service systems must begin to note the sources of the oppressions, the strengths of families in facing them, and the commonalities in families' experiences.

Action to Engage Parents and Communities

- The child welfare system, including the courts, should sharpen its focus on safe parenting. It should focus on the consequences of substance abuse rather than substance abuse, per se.

A sharpened focus on safe parenting as the ultimate objective will expand opportunities to develop innovative ways to promote child safety in families involved with substance abuse. Parents, engaged as collaborators and unafraid of losing custody as a result of relapse, might participate in problem solving about how to keep children safe. For example, parents could participate in the development of *relapse risk reduction strategies*, which constitute concrete plans to assure child safety in the event of relapse, including the identification of a back-up caretaker.

- Both service systems must identify and use parent and community strengths as a resource for mutual help and work toward change.

Too often parents involved with child welfare and substance abuse treatment services are identified primarily by their failures—as addicts and failed parents. Yet, their identities as mothers and fathers are often something that these women and men feel proud about. Such pride and confidence should be carefully built upon rather than squelched. Parental pride might be used, and further strengthened, through helping others. Parents, engaged as "expert partners" (Hooper-Briar & Lawson, 1994), along with the two service systems, must work with other community institutions toward changes that prevent, not only treat, parental substance abuse and child welfare involvement.

Endnotes

1. In every day terms, bivariate methods look only at the association between two variables; multivariate methods account simultaneously for co-occurring influences. Researchers using only bivariate methods risk finding spurious, or apparent but false, associations. For example, coffee drinking may be associated with lung cancer. If we look only at the two variables, we may assume a causal relationship between coffee

drinking and lung cancer. However, the apparent relationship may stem from an association between coffee drinking and cigarette smoking. A multivariate model, looking simultaneously at the effects of coffee drinking and cigarette smoking on lung cancer, would likely show that the association between coffee drinking and lung cancer is accounted for by cigarette smoking.

2. This situation is changing for women as more women's treatment centers acknowledge the importance of women clients' parenting role. Treatment centers for men, however, still typically do not acknowledge the potential importance of the parenting role for men (many of whom are fathers).

References

Blume, S. (1999). Chemical dependency in women: Important issues. *American Journal of Drug and Alcohol Abuse, 16*(3-4), 297-307.

Brindis, C. D. and Theidon, K. S. (1997). The role of case management in substance abuse treatment services for women and their children. *Journal of Psychoactive Drugs, 29*(1), 79-88.

Brindis, C., Berkowitz, G., and Clayson, Z. (1997). Options for recovery: Promoting perinatal drug and alcohol recovery, child health and family stability. *Journal of Drug Issues, 27*(3), 607-624.

Butler, S. M., Radia, N., and Magnata, M. (1994). Maternal compliance to court-ordered assessment in cases of child maltreatment. *Child Abuse and Neglect, 18*(2), 203-211.

Chasnoff, I. J., Landress, H. J., and Barrett, M. E. (1990). The prevalence of illicit-drug or alcohol use during pregnancy and discrepancies in mandatory reporting in Pinellas County, Florida. *The New England Journal of Medicine, 332*(17), 1202-1206.

Child Welfare League of America. (1998). *Alcohol and Other Drug Survey of State Child Welfare Agencies.* Washington, D.C.: Child Welfare League of America.

Dowell, K. and Roberts, T. (1998). *Preliminary findings from the cross-site evaluation of the Center for Substance Abuse Treatment's Residential Women and Children and Pregnant and Postpartum Women Programs.* Unpublished paper.

Famularo, R., Kinscherff, R., Bunshaft, D., Spivak, G., and Fenton, T. (1989). Parental compliance to court-ordered treatment interventions in cases of child maltreatment. *Child Abuse and Neglect, 13*, 507-514.

Fanshel, D. (1975). Parental failure and consequences for children: The drug-abusing mother whose children are in foster care. *American Journal of Public Health, 65*(6), 604-612.

Feig, L. (1998). Understanding the problem: The gap between substance abuse programs and child welfare services. In R. L. Hampton, V. Senatore, and T. P. Gullotta (Eds.). *Substance abuse, family violence, and child welfare: Building perspectives*. Thousand Oaks, CA: Sage Publications.

Frank, E. J. (1995). Prenatally drug-exposed children in out-of-home care: Are we looking at the whole picture? *Child Welfare, 75*, 19-34.

Fullilove, M. T. and Lown, A. (1992). Crack 'hos and skeezers: Traumatic experiences of women crack users. *Journal of Sex Research, 29*(2), 275-287.

Frank, E. J. (1995). Prenatally drug-exposed children in out-of-home care: Are we looking at the whole picture? *Child Welfare, 75*, 19-34.

Gilbert, L., El-Bassel, N., Schilling, R. F., and Freidman, E. (1997). Childhood abuse as a risk for partner abuse among women in methadone maintenance. *American Journal of Drug and Alcohol Abuse, 23*(4), 581-595.

Goerge, R. M. and Harden, A. (1993). *The impact of substance-affected infants on child protection services and substitute care caseloads: 1985-1992*. Chicago: Chapin Hall Center for Children at the University of Chicago.

Goerge, R. M., Wulczyn, F. H., and Hardin, A. W. (1996). New comparative insights into states and their foster children. *Public Welfare*, Summer 1996.

Gordon, L. (1988). *Heroes of their own lives: The politics and history of family violence*. New York: Penguin Books.

Grant, B. F. (2000). Estimates of U.S. children exposed to alcohol abuse and dependence in the family. *American Journal of Public Health, 90*(1), 112-115.

Guza, K., Wilson, D., and Thompson, C. (1998). Chemical dependency services for parents involved with child welfare in Washington State. *The Source, 8*(2). Berkeley, CA: Abandoned Infants Assistance Resource Center.

Halpern, R. (1997). Good practice with multiply vulnerable young families: Challenges and principles. *Children and Youth Services Review, 19* (4), 253-275.

Hooper-Briar, K. and Lawson, H. (1994). *Serving children, youth and families through interprofessional collaboration and service integration: A framework for action*. Oxford, OH: The Institute for Educational Renewal at Miami University and the Danforth Foundation.

Hser, Y., Anglin, M. D., and Booth, M. W. (1987). Sex differences in addict careers. *American Journal of Drug and Alcohol Abuse, 13*, 231-251.

Huang, L., Cerbone, F., and Gfroerer, J. (1998). Children at risk because of parental substance abuse. In Substance Abuse and Mental Health Administration, Office of Applied Studies. *Analyses of substance abuse and treatment need issues (Analytic Series, A-7)*. Rockville, MD: Department of Health and Human Services, Substance Abuse and Mental Health Services Administration.

Inciardi, J. A., Lockwood, D., and Pottieger, A. E. (1993). *Women and crack cocaine*. New York: MacMillan Publishing Company.

Jaudes, P. K., Edem, E., and Van Voorhis, J. (1995). Association of drug abuse and child abuse. *Child Abuse and Neglect, 19*(9), 1065-1075.

Leiderman, D. S. (1998). *Breaking the link between substance abuse and child maltreatment: An issue forum.* Washington, D.C.: Child Welfare League of America.

Lester, B. M., Freier, K., and LaGasse, L. (1995). Prenatal cocaine exposure and child outcome: What do we really know?" in M. Lewis and M. Bendersky (Ed.). *Mothers, babies and cocaine: The role of toxins in development.* Hillsdale, New Jersey: Lawrence Erlbaum Associates, Inc.

Marsh, J. C., D'Aunno, T. A, and Smith, B. D. (forthcoming). Increasing access and providing social services to improve drug abuse treatment for women with children. *Addiction.*

Marsh, J. C. and Miller, N. (1985). Female clients in substance abuse treatment. *International Journal of the Addictions, 20*(6-7), 995-1019.

Mayes, L. C., Granger, R. H., Bornstein, M. H., and Zuckerman, B. (1992). The problem of prenatal cocaine exposure: A rush to judgement. *Journal of the American Medical Association, 267*(3), 406-408.

McMahon, T. J. and Luthar, S. S. (1998). Bridging the gap for children as their parents enter substance abuse treatment. In R. L. Hampton, V. Senatore, and T. P. Gullotta (Eds.). *Substance abuse, family violence, and child welfare: Building perspectives.* Thousand Oaks, CA: Sage Publications.

Murphy, J., Jellinek, M., Quinn, D., Smith, G., Poitrast, F. G., and Goshko, M. (1991). Substance abuse and serious child mistreatment: Prevalence, risk, and outcome in a court sample. *Child Abuse and Neglect, 15,* 197-211.

National Institute on Drug Abuse. (1999). *Principles of drug addiction treatment: A research-based guide.* (NIH Publication No. 99-4180). Washington, D.C.:author.

National Research Council. (1993). *Understanding child abuse and neglect.* Washington, D.C.: National Academy Press.

Olsen, L. J. (1995). Services for substance abuse-affected families: The project connect experience. *Child and Adolescent Social Work Journal, 12*(3), 183-196.

Paone, D., Chavkin, W., Willets, I., Friedman, P., and Jarlais, D. D. (1992). The impact of sexual abuse: Implications for drug treatment. *Journal of Women's Health, 1*(2), 149-153.

Pelton, L. H. (1981). *The social context of child abuse and neglect.* New York: Human Sciences Press.

Peugh, J. and Belenko, S. (1999). Substance-involved women inmates: Challenges to providing effective treatment. *Prison Journal, 79*(1), 23-44.

Pitcoff, W. (1999). New hope for public housing? Orange, NJ: National Housing Institute.

Purnell, R. (1998). Putting drug use in context: Life-lines of African American women who smoke crack. *Journal of Substance Abuse Treatment, 15*(3), 235-249.

Ramsey, M. (1980). Special features and treatment needs of female drug offenders. *Journal of Offender Counseling, Services and Rehabilitation, 44*, 357-368.

Roberts, D. (1997). *Killing the black body: Race, reproduction and the meaning of liberty.* New York: Pantheon Books.

Sengupta, S. (2000). Hevesi says children are in foster care too long. *New York Times*, March 16, B2.

Smith, B. D. (1999). Parental drug use, treatment compliance and reunification: Client classifications and the common wisdom in child welfare. Unpublished Doctoral Dissertation, University of Chicago.

Smith, B. D., Marsh, J. C., and D'Aunno, T. A. (1998). Child welfare and substance use: Findings from a collaborative services initiative in Illinois. *The Source, 8*(2). Berkeley, CA: Abandoned Infants Assistance Resource Center.

Stevens, S. and Arbiter, N. (1995). A therapeutic community for substance abusing pregnant women and women with children: Process and outcome. *Journal of Psychoactive Drugs, 27*(1), 49-56.

Strantz, I. H. and Welch, S. P. (1995). Postpartum women in outpatient drug abuse treatment: Correlates of retention/completion. *Journal of Psychoactive Drugs, 27*(4), 357-373.

Swift, K. J. (1995). *Manufacturing 'bad mothers:' A critical perspective on child neglect.* Toronto: Toronto University Press.

U.S. Department of Health and Human Services, Children's Bureau. (1997). *National study of protective, preventive and reunification services delivered to children and their families.* Washington, D.C.: U.S. Government Printing Office.

U.S. Department of Health and Human Services, Children's Bureau. (1998). *Child maltreatment 1996: Reports from the states to the national child abuse and neglect data system.* Washington, D.C.: U.S. Government Printing Office.

U.S. Department of Health and Human Services, Substance Abuse and Mental Health Services Administration. (1999). *Blending perspectives and building common ground: A report to congress on substance abuse and child protection.* Washington, D.C.: U.S. Government Printing Office.

U.S. Department of Health and Human Services, Substance Abuse and Mental Health Services Administration, Office of Applied Studies. (1997). *Substance abuse among women in the United States.* Rockville, MD: author.

U.S. Department of Health and Human Services, Substance Abuse and Mental Health Services Administration. (1996). *National treatment improvement evaluation study.* Rockville, MD: author.

U.S. Department of Housing and Urban Development. (1999). *Hope VI: Building communities, transforming lives.* Washington, D.C.: author.

U.S. General Accounting Office. (1998). *Foster care: Agencies face challenges securing stable homes for children of substance abusers.* (GAO/HEHS-98-182). Washington, D.C.: author.

U.S. General Accounting Office. (1994). *Foster care: Parental drug abuse has alarming impact on young children.* (GAO/HEHS-94-89). Washington, D.C.: author.

Walker, C., Zangrillo, P., and Smith, J. M. (1991).*Parental drug abuse and African American children in foster care.* Washington, D.C.: National Black Child Development Institute.

Walsh, M.A. and Young, J. J. (1998). Innovative strategies for strengthening systemic links between child welfare services and services for alcohol and other drug problems: The DHS IMPACT program. *The Source, 8*(2). Berkeley, CA: Abandoned Infants Assistance Resource Center.

Wobie, K., Davis-Eyler, F., Conlon, M., Clarke, L., and Behnke, X. (1997). Women and children in residential treatment: Outcomes for mothers and their infants. *Journal of Drug Issues, 27*(3), 585-606.

Wolock, I. And Magura, S. (1996). Parental substance abuse as a predictor of child maltreatment re-reports, *Child Abuse and Neglect, 20*(12), 1183-1193.

Woodhouse, L. (1992). Women with jagged edges: Voices from a culture of substance abuse. *Qualitative Health Research, 2*(3), 262-281.

Young, I. M. (1995). Punishment, treatment, empowerment: Three approaches to policy for pregnant addicts. In P. Boling (Ed.). *Expecting trouble: Surrogacy, fetal abuse & new productive technologies.* Boulder, CO: Westview Press.

Young, N. K. and Gardner, S. (1997). *Bridge-building: An action plan for state and county efforts to link child welfare services and treatment for alcohol and other drugs.* Irvine, CA: Children and Family Futures.

Chapter 8

Competent Practice: Diversity, Racism and Heterosexism

Stacey Hardy-Desmond, Esther J. Langston,
Dean Pierce, and Thom Reilly

Introduction

The Child Welfare system is founded on the noble two-fold goal of protecting children and strengthening families. The challenge to service providers and organizations that operate within the child welfare system is to meet this goal while maintaining a balance of efficiency and efficacy. Continuing changes in the demographics of American society, that is, increased heterogeneity in general, and among child welfare clients in particular, necessitates that everything from individual interventions to tactical organizational strategies, integrate attention, and action derived from multiculturalism.

The goal, then, of this chapter is to illuminate the crucial role of cultural competence in meeting the goals and mission of child welfare. The authors posit that a clear understanding of the dynamics of diversity, racism and heterosexism, culturally sound theoretical considerations, and culturally based applications are integral to developing a foundation for best practices in services to *all* children and families.

Understanding Cultural Competence

Cultural competence is the capacity to work effectively with people from a variety of ethnic, cultural, political, economic, and religious backgrounds. It is being aware and respectful of the values, beliefs, traditions, customs, and parenting styles of those we serve, while understanding that there is often as wide a range of differences within groups (e.g., Native Americans) as between them. Cultural competence is being aware of how our own culture influences how we view others.

Cultural competence is not just about "racial" differences. A white American service provider has as much need of cultural competency when working with a family of Ukrainian immigrants as when working with an African American family, perhaps more so. Cultural competency includes, but is not limited to developing skills. It includes improving one's ability to control or change one's own false beliefs, assumptions, and stereotypes; to think flexibly; to accurately find sources of information based on similarity and diversity; and to recognize that a single universal "right" way of thinking, feeling, and acting does not exist.

Cultural competence requires an open mind and heart and the willingness to accept the views of others. It may mean setting aside one's own beliefs in order to better serve others. Generally, we need to lower our defenses, take risks, and practice behaviors that may be uncomfortable or unfamiliar. All people are alike in some ways and different in others. Everyone needs to eat, have clothes and shelter, to learn, to grow, and to experience meaning and purpose in their lives (Harper & Lantz, 1996).

The Why, Who, and What of Competent Practice

This chapter is organized to address the interrogatives, "why," "who," and "what." In this case the "why" represents information, primarily ethno-racial demographics that illustrate the proportionate over-representation of children of color in various segments of the child welfare system and figures on poverty and its impact on other quality of life areas. Some general information on child abuse and neglect will be presented as the precursor to out-of-home placement/foster care.

The "who" represents the ethical and professional mandate for service providers to individually and collectively strive for a multicultural knowledge base, orientation, and method of practice. Cultural competence allows service providers to feel comfortable and be effective in their interactions with families whose cultures are different from their own. It enables families to feel good about their interactions with their service provider, and it allows the two parties to accomplish their goals (Brislin, Cushner, Cherrie, & Yong, 1986).

A service provider of white or of Anglo-European descent is part of the dominant U.S. culture, part of a group whose culture, customs, and habits have shaped American society more than any other (Lynch, 1992). Consciously and unconsciously, elements for "privilege" come with membership in the dominant culture. It is important to examine these factors when working with people of other cultures, as it can alienate clients and decrease the likelihood of positive outcomes. It does not help the client when a service provider evidences a pattern of viewing his or her own world view as correct and the client's view as problematic or pathological. Blindly encouraging clients to "give up" aspects of their cultural heritage, erroneously couched as "helping," can cause anxiety for the service provider and can hurt the client and damage the relationship (Harper & Lantz, 1996).

A model for competently creating solutions with clients and the rationale for each step will be presented in this section which focuses on micro practice. This section will also contain a more detailed discussion of working with gay, lesbian, bisexual, and transgender youth to highlight some dynamics and practical concerns that can also be applicable to children of other diverse backgrounds.

From the micro-focused "who" to the macro-focused "what" of culturally competent practice, this chapter will then cover relevant organizational issues. Williams (1997) reported that clients who perceive themselves as racial minorities expected to be negatively evaluated by the public systems that serve them. They expected to be looked down upon and discriminated against, to have their background and culture misunderstood. When culture is overlooked or when service providers and organizations do not understand what is normal in the context of the culture, harmful decisions are made by service providers and by organizations, limiting the ability to engage families and communities and build on their strengths.

The authors will not only present an argument for why cultural competence and agency performance outcomes are linked. The chapter will issue a call for multiculturally based changes in planning and training vital for effective service delivery in human service organizations.

Evidence of the Need for Culturally Competent Practice

Over-Representation

The following data focuses on ethno-racial factors; they demonstrate over-representation. The point is that ethno-racial factors and cultural factors are not interchangeable. As mentioned previously, culture is not limited to ethnicity and race; these data highlight the need to diligently attend to such cultural factors as ethnicity and the possible contribution of overt and covert racism in child welfare and human services as a whole. The most current available census data as reported by the Child Welfare League (2000) indicate that of the 69,872,059 children under 18 living in the U.S. in 1998, 65% were White, 14.6% were African-American, 15.4% were Latino, 4% were Asian/Pacific Islander, and 1% were American Indian.

With the aforementioned percentages in mind, comparative information on poverty provides a discordant context. "Every Day in America" (2000) data available through the Children's Defense Fund (CDF) provides information, by race, that illustrates this fact. The CDF estimates that each day, 1,323 White babies are born into poverty. Compare this with 723 African-American babies and 679 Latino babies born into poverty daily. One can easily see the disproportionate over-representation of children of color.

Poverty is an important child welfare issue because other quality of life factors are directly linked to it. To continue the cross-racial comparison, of White babies, 1,033 are born daily without health insurance and 275 are born to women who had late or no prenatal care. For African-American babies, 247 are born without health insurance and 114 are born to mothers who have little or no prenatal care. For Latino babies, the figures are 532 and 124 respectively for not having health care and being born to a woman who has had limited prenatal attention. The Child Welfare League (2000) cites a 1998 Kaiser Commission report in noting that up to an estimated 4.5 million children are potentially eligible for Medicaid but are not enrolled. Information on poverty, health insurance, and prenatal care were not available through the CDF on Asian or Indian American children at the time of this writing.

Poverty also has an impact on both education, and obtaining adequate child care. The CDF reports that 56 percent more is spent per student in the richest U.S. school districts than in the poorest. This gap that confirms that equal educational opportunity is not a reality. The ability of families to locate and pay for child care is yet another factor linked to poverty and socio-economic status. The CDF reports that full-day child care can range from $4,000 to $10,000 per year, while one-third of U.S. families earns less than $25,000.

The Child Welfare League of America—Children 2000 (2000), links substance abuse to many of the problems faced by families in child welfare. Substance abuse is noted as a significant contributor to child abuse, neglect, and at-risk behavior among adolescents in foster care. Most alarming is that the CWLA cites the 1999 U.S. Department of Health and Human Services in noting that 46% of parents in the child welfare system with substance abuse problems were neither offered or provided substance abuse service. To what extent lack of attention to cultural factors contributed to this statistic is not known. However, this information is presented to underline the fact that gaps between need and service delivery continue to exist and a critical consideration in closing this gap may well be the often overlooked impact of cultural factors.

On violence, the overall occurrence of youth violence appears to be declining. However, in examining arrests (which are also down), a cross-racial snapshot reveals that 126 White children are arrested for violent crimes daily, while 270 are arrested for drug abuse. For African-American children the daily figures are 105 and 143 for violent crimes and drug abuse arrests respectively. Four arrests are made in both categories for Asian American children. American Indian children are arrested twice as much for violent crimes and three times as much for drug-related incidents daily. Again, these figures, when compared to the population percentages do not match. For example, African-American children who make up about 14.6% of the general U.S. population, make up about 44% of those arrested for violent crimes.

In examining the figures on child abuse and neglect, the National Clearinghouse on Child Abuse and Neglect Information notes that in 1996 more than 2 million reports of maltreatment were made on behalf of 3 million children (U.S. Department of Health and Human Services, 1996b). Various protective service agencies across the country that year identified 1 million children as victims of substantiated maltreatment. More than half or 53% of child abuse and neglect victims are White. African American make up about 27% of these cases, and Latino children make up about 11%. American Indian children comprise 2% of these cases while 1% are Asian

American/Pacific Islander children. Here, the figures for African-American and American Indian children are disproportionately high. Abuse, neglect, and safety constitute primary reasons for referrals to the divisions of child welfare service that manage out-of-home placements or placements outside of the care of parents.

Out-of-Home Placement/Foster Care

U.S. Health and Human Services data from 1994 indicate that nearly 60,000 children were in out-of-home placements. Once out of the home, African-American and American Indian children tend to spend far more time in foster care before being adopted as compared to White children. Historically, attempts had been made by foster and adoption service providers to try to match children with racially similar caregivers and adoptive parents. The Multiethnic Placement Act (MEPA) of 1994 as amended by the Interethnic Adoption Provisions (IEP) of 1996 has three specific goals. These are to decrease the length of time that children wait to be adopted, to facilitate the recruitment and retention of foster and adoptive parents who can meet the distinctive needs of children awaiting placement, and to eliminate discrimination on the basis of the race, color, or national origin of the child or the prospective parents. MEPA-IEP is certainly not without controversy. Debate continues to focus on whether or not permanent care givers can meet the ethno-cultural needs of children from different ethno-cultural backgrounds. The authors propose that the key consideration is whether or not care givers—regardless of background—are supported by child welfare service providers and agencies in addressing all of the developmental needs of children including the cultural components of identity development.

Although family foster care, designed to provide temporary protection and nurturing for children experiencing maltreatment, has been a critical service for millions of children in the United States, the increased attention given to this service in the last two decades has focused more on its limited ability to achieve its intended outcomes than on its successes. This has resulted in a questioning and devaluing of family foster care as well as predictions of drastic reductions in its use. The reality, however, has been quite different. Though the use of the service has shifted, reflecting social and political events, family foster care remains an important child welfare service.

By 1984, P.L. 96-272 was showing some success in reducing the number of children in care and the length of time spent in care. From the mid-1980s to the late 1990s, however, a dramatic 74% increase in the number of children in out-of-home placements occurred (Petit & Curtis 1997); the length of time children remained in care and their rate of reentry into care also rose. Concurrently, the out-of-home care system found itself facing new challenges—the over representation of children of color.

In 1980, 47% of children in foster care were children of color. By 1995 61% of children in foster care were children of color. African American, Native American and Latino children and youths are disproportionately represented in the foster care system by a margin of more than two to one. In 1990, for the first time, there were more African American than Caucasian children in foster care.

In 1995, African American children represented only 15% of the U.S. population of children, but 44% of the foster care population; Latino children represented 14% of the U.S. children population, but 12% of the foster care population; and Native American and Asian or Pacific Islander children represented 5% of the total U.S. children population, and 3% of the foster care population. Data on length of time spent in a first placement show that African American children have longer duration in care than all other groups in New York, California, Michigan, and Illinois (Child Welfare League of America Foster Care, 1998).

Cultural Competence For Service Providers

Lynch and Hanson (1998) list five reasons for the difficulties that people experience when they try to understand or function in a culture other than their own:

1. Cultural understanding in one's first culture occurs early and is typically established by age 5.
2. Children learn new cultural patterns more easily than adults.
3. Values are determined by one's first culture and may have to be revised to be effective in a second culture.
4. Understanding of one's first culture introduces errors in interpreting the second culture.
5. Long-standing behavior patterns are typically used to express one's deepest values.

Therefore, to become a culturally competent practitioner, the individual must be capable of understanding the similarities and differences in cultural and behavior patterns to function effectively in the context of cultural differences.

Cross, et al. (1989) indicated five elements of cultural competence:

1. Awareness and acceptance of difference
2. Awareness of own cultural values
3. Understanding dynamics of difference
4. Development of cultural knowledge
5. Ability to adapt practice to the cultural context of the client.

These five elements are integral to each step of the "Creating Solutions" model presented later in this section. To effectively intervene in the lives of children and their families, service providers and organizations must become culturally competent and utilize the values and ethics of social work practice with all client systems.

Cultural competence is professional competence. The two are inextricably linked in the effective practice of social work. While it is generally accepted that cultural sensitivity and respect for human diversity are important, it is vital for the worker to fully accept these as necessary and fundamental components of the worker's toolbox. The culturally competent worker must however go beyond the mechanical accumulation of skills (such a superficial approach would only offer a false sense of capability) and adopt a culturally competent attitude that infiltrates the worker's entire approach to intervention.

It is appropriate at this point to differentiate between the pseudo-culturally competent service provider and the authentically culturally competent service provider. A common mistake is for service providers to equate cultural competence with some familiarity with certain ethnic groups, i.e., African-Americans, Asian Americans, Latinos, etc. In theory, and most importantly, in practice, cultural factors include such domains of human experience as gender, sexual orientation, race, ethnicity, socio-economic status, religious and spiritual issues, age, and physical ability. The very fact that some sort of "need" forms the basis of social work efforts in itself calls, loudly, for operating from the basis of cultural sensitivity.

The client, whether by choice or by mandate, enters into a relationship with the service provider "for something." Therefore, it could be said that by virtue of the helping relationship—between the service provider and the client, the professional and the consumer, the administrator and the organization—cultural differences exist.

The worker who focuses solely on the racial/ethnic sub-category of culture is limited if not blinded by this view and is also limited in his or her effectiveness as an agent of change. Too often the prevailing mind set is that culture is the "icing" when in fact it is the "cake." This applies whether the service provider is dealing with individuals, families, groups, or organizations. Micro, mezzo, and macro systems all present to the worker unique cultural values, norms, and preferences. Because of this, it is not within the scope of this chapter, nor within the capability of any writer to enumerate the various manifestations of culture. This would not only be impractical, but ineffective. Further, it would only serve to reinforce so many approaches that have, as indicated previously, given service providers a false sense of competence with regard to culture. Rather, the authors posit that it is better to bolster the strengths that have brought so many to this field and highlight a foundation that can easily be translated to protect culturally competent practice toward the goal of protecting all children and strengthening all families.

First of all, it must be understood, and it is worth repeating, that cultural competence is not an "extra." It deserves the same reverence as ethics, interviewing skills, knowledge of community resources, and clinical judgement. It is arguably at the basis of all of these. Section 1.05 of the Code of Ethics of the National Association of Social Workers (1996) addresses "cultural competence and social diversity" in parts a, b, and c. It is in the spirit of respect for culture that social work truly happens as both an ethical responsibility and professional duty. With this premise embedded deep within the service provider's marrow, the worker can begin the process of sound intervention.

Creating Solutions

The primary job of the social worker is to facilitate problem-solving, or conceptualized better, "finding solutions." The following "CREATE Solutions" steps provide a model for finding solutions congruent with operating from a culturally competent framework (Hardy-Desmond, manuscript in progress):

Step 1: "C" — "See" the Problem
Step 2: "R" — Review the Options
Step 3: "E" — Evaluate the Available Options
Step 4: "A" — Action Planning
Step 5: "T" — Trial Intervention
Step 6: "E" — Evaluate the Outcome

Illustrative Scenario. As partial fulfillment of the requirement for obtaining certification as a foster home, Mr. and Mrs. Greene, an African-American couple in their 50s, are expected to take parenting classes. These classes follow the generally accepted format of standard parenting skills and techniques, including communication, non-violent methods of discipline, measuring baselines and monitoring behavioral changes, and designing natural consequences. While the Greene's are willing to participate in the parenting training program, in the course of the initial sessions, they begin to recognize discrepancies between their own style and expectations of the class instruction. For example, they have difficulty accepting the concept of providing children with choices under certain circumstances. This method, designed to increase the child investment in the desired behavior, is in stark contrast to the more directive style of parenting to which they are accustomed. The Greenes begin to question how they will practically implement the parenting techniques proposed by "the county" for foster children while employing what they perceive as being more effective, directive techniques with the young grandchildren they also have in their care.

Beginning with step 1, effectively "seeing" the problem goes beyond the specific reasons for referral or service intake. Culturally effective service providers will appropriately consider the referral in the context of the individual, the social system, and the cultural elements of the agency in which they are working. This step requires the synthesis of multidimensional assessment skills and techniques. Assessment from a culturally aware perspective serves to broaden the service provider's view of the elements that are interfering with the family's ability to function optimally—with "optimal" being a culturally defined construct. It is the cultural perspective that provides a context for accurately ascertaining the breath and scope of problems while simultaneously highlighting strengths and resources.

This step mandates that the service provider extends the assessment process beyond substantiating pre-established suppositions (of which the service provider may or may not be fully aware). The culturally astute service provider is then open to being receptive to a range of factors that ultimately make the assessment process more accurate, substantive, and functional as a tool for guiding intervention. This is critically important in child protection, family preservation, mental health, school, and other child welfare intervention contexts when it comes to the effective and accurate documentation and transfer of information.

Lum (1999) cites "knowledge acquisition" as one of the four key areas in the constellation of generalist and advanced level cultural competencies. While Lum is referring to the general call for social workers to engage in the broad development of a body of information that fosters an understanding in terms, demographics, history, and sociological factors and values—on a practice level, this applies to the orientation from which a worker can practically conduct assessments toward the "acquisition of knowledge" about specific clients and families.

For the Greenes, assessment/intake for participation in the foster parent training certification program would be made more accurate with obtaining information about their current parenting practices and the value systems behind these practices. Both the ethno-cultural background of the prospective foster parents and their ages are potentially important factors here. It may not be unlikely for foster parents with this background to adhere to principles of parenting that are more directive. The Greenes connection to certain culturally defined belief systems around parenting would be important information to transmit to the parenting class instructors in addressing the specific needs of the Greenes and other class participants.

Steps 2 and 3 involve reviewing options and assessing which options are the most viable given the information available. Again, culture is inherent to this step as the options that are available may or may not match the options to which the client or family system may be amenable. Additional complications are introduced with abuse reporting and other legal mandates that impact subsequent steps. On a purely informational level, the service provider must be knowledgeable about what is available in his or her community and about the legal, policy, and ethical structure within which social work occurs. In reality, the worker must also modify the selection and/or presentation of these options based on the client's culturally determined receptivity. It is not that systemic mandates are ignored, rather the service provider acts as a sort of interpretive conduit through which these macro- level issues are translated for maximum effectiveness of interventions and to increase the likelihood of successful outcomes.

The understanding and consideration of options occur in the context of the helping relationship. Leigh (1998) cites Saaleby in proposing the employment of "ethnographic interviewing" and how this method may be operationalized. This, Leigh states, is an avenue through which the social worker as stranger can be interested, sincere, and trustworthy by listening to the person's narrative as he or she becomes the social worker's "cultural guide" (pg. 40).

As this applies to the case of the Greenes, options could range from the implementation of ethnically specific parenting programs that are available, to the modification of the parenting instructional material to address the culturally specific needs of the participants, to having foster parents like the Greenes participate in the standard program with supplemental support and processing with the service provider. Without consideration of cultural factors, these options become invisible —they are generally logistically possible, but may not be considered—thereby possibly alienating certain foster parents or, at best, reducing the credibility of representatives of "the system."

Step 4 involves planning for action. The culturally sensitive service provider designs and develops the most viable interventions that support a balance between the needs of the client and dictates of the organizational structure. The standpoint that, for example, the organizational dictates have to occur at the sacrifice of the client's cultural values, belief system, and norms is absurd. In fact, when skillfully executed, the integrity of organizational standards and requirements can be more effectively met with the addition of cultural sensitivity. Leigh (1998) discusses the concept of clients as "cultural guides." In this respect, *action planning is enhanced by the understanding that in spite of the expertise the service provider brings to the relationship, clients will always be experts of their own experience.* As such, the planning becomes an authentically collaborative effort.

So, continuing with our example, the organizational dictate is that those desiring to be foster parents must complete an approved parenting program can and should be maintained. But given the agency's available resources, the worker may determine that supplemental processing of the parenting class information would be the most practical option for the Greenes. The Greenes' service provider would then need to be skilled in assisting the Greenes in translating the parenting principles into techniques congruent with their culturally defined belief system of parenting, or if appropriate, supporting the Greenes as they adapt to new principles, or ascertaining if the principles are in direct and irreconcilable conflict with the ones held by the Greenes. It is the opinion of the authors that the latter, although possible, is very rare, but may be the erroneous first conclusion of a pseudo-competent worker.

Assuming that the purpose of the parenting class is to assist foster parents in providing an emotionally and socially consistent and healthy environment, and assuming that the Greenes hold the same motivation, the fundamental philosophy is not the area of conflict—it is the means of attaining the goal. The truly culturally competent service provider is able to identify this congruence and is more apt to assist the Greenes in navigating the specific techniques.

Step 5 is the stage of "Trial Intervention." All interventions can be considered "trials," not in a random sense, but in an "educated testing" sense based on all of the information available at the time. This step is the "action" component of the solution creating process—the phase in which the worker applies the intervention based on the preceding steps. This of course incorporates elements of assessment as the worker strives to ascertain the family's response to the actual intervention. Without the advantages of cultural sensitivity, the service provider is apt to jump to this step operating mechanically from a monolithic concept of interventions—a "one size fits all" approach. Continuing this metaphor, just because an agency may mandate a certain "uniform" (e.g., parenting classes) doesn't mean the service provider can't "tailor" it to fit the needs of the family. Service providers have to take care to remain faithful to the ethical standards of the profession by "tailoring" interventions with respect to human diversity.

With the Greenes, this would mean the act of purposefully integrating the processing of the parenting information in meetings and home visits (as determined from the action planning step) i.e., designating time to understand how the Greenes were experiencing the classes given possible age, ethnic, even religious and other factors. Again, the decision to make this a priority and the ability to do this skillfully would be the direct result of operating from a place of cultural competence.

Outcome evaluation is the sixth and final step in this model. Beyond being a current buzzword in current social work practice, examining outcomes takes on particular importance in (culturally) competent practice at the micro level, and as will be explained later, at the organizational level as well. Competent service providers are invested in ascertaining feedback on the effectiveness of their work—an on-going process that the service provider uses to hone his or her skills in working with client-consumers and families, and to refine his or her professional growth. The impact of cultural competence is that it makes the worker more open to a wider range of feedback that further clarifies and enhances the intervention picture.

Again, using our example with the Greene's, a worker may only look at the fact that the Greene's attended all of the parenting class sessions and evaluate that to be a "successful" outcome. But the culturally competent worker will not only consider attendance as a determination of success—the culturally competent service provider will want to obtain information about how the parenting information has been integrated into the Greenes' world view. Through processing the information with the Greenes, the culturally competent service provider is interested in the extent to which the parenting information is likely to be used on a day-to-day basis, given the cultural background the Greene's brought to the parenting class experience. The culturally competent service provider has a crisper, sharper view of the successful completion of requirements that in the short and long run have the potential for qualitatively greater success. How often might "failure to complete requirements" and "failed placement" be due to a failure to fully employ cultural sensitivity? When working with families, the benefit of cultural competence can easily outweigh the cost when one considers the allocation of time and resources to the many "corrective efforts" by workers when ill-conceived interventions don't work. While failure to consider cultural factors may not be the only culprit, given the fundamental role of culture in the human experience, one can only imagine the "savings" in time and effort gained by workers who recognize, respect and harness the power of culture in their work. (Hardy-Desmond, manuscript in progress).

Summary

In the next section, a close-up examination of work with gay, lesbian, bisexual, and transgender youth will be presented. It is note worthy that some of the dynamics and considerations that are appropriate for other diverse populations are illustrated via this comparatively detailed look at the gay, lesbian, bisexual, and transgender youth within the context of child welfare practice. Development of sexual identity can be generally compared to the larger developmental issue of identity development for all children during a critical period and, in particular, the development of ethno-cultural identity. Additionally, some of the "invisibility" issues that will be presented as they relate to gay, lesbian, bisexual, and transgender youth mirror the general lack of attention to such cultural considerations as bi- and multi-racial/cultural children, prejudice among human service professionals and agencies, and perceptions regarding mental illness which continue to carry with it a social stigma.

Gay, Lesbian, Bisexual And Transgender Youths

Youths between 13 and 18 years of age comprise roughly one-third of the population in foster care, despite the fact that they currently comprise only about 12% of the U.S. population. This is the age where youth begin the discovery of sexual identity. Social workers must have an understanding of gay, lesbian, bisexual, heterosexual, and transgender youth. Even if the number who are arguably lesbian or gay is assumed to be only two percent of all in their middle teens, there are approximately 267,000 lesbian or gay youth in this age group. That number grows to 1,333,500 at the least, if the truer proportion is ten percent (Durby, 1994, p. 13). Nonetheless, they are "invisible" to many who serve children and families (Durby, 1994, p.2). This invisibility is not necessarily the choice of lesbian, gay, bisexual, or transgender youth, nor does it imply that they do not need social and health services. The idea that these young people are, and should be, invisible is imposed on them by social, family, and religious stigma, and by scholarship that denigrates the activities of those who publicly proclaim their sexual orientation as deviant behavior or wrong choices (Durby, 1994, Herr, 1997; Mallon, 1994).

Service providers, of course, frequently deal with lesbian, gay, bisexual, and transgender youth, because these young people are over-represented among their caseload as suicides, runaways, castaways, substance abusers, and victims of peer and family violence. Unfortunately, because service providers are unaware of, or unwilling to use in their practice assessments, theories that view a lesbian, gay, bisexual, or transgender sexual orientation as healthy and positive, such young persons suffer doubly. First, they suffer as victims of violence and abuse, placing them among the most vulnerable of our youth. Second, they often are not supported in their efforts to attain a positive self-identity as a lesbian, gay, bisexual, or transgender person or in their struggles to deal with a hostile world.

Next, the vulnerability of lesbian, gay, bisexual, and transgender youth will be discussed and how service providers unwittingly use theories and values about their development and identity to further endanger these young people will be explained. Finally, an example of a different theoretical perspective and suggestions for strengths-based practice interventions and policy initiatives are offered.

Markers of Vulnerability

Suicide data offer chilling testimony of the vulnerability of lesbian, gay, bisexual, and transgender teens. A controversy has risen questioning if the rate is higher among lesbian, gay, bisexual, and transgender youth than their heterosexual peers. For example, in a review of adolescent suicide studies, Hershberger, et al. (1996) found wide variation in the estimates of lesbian, gay, bisexual, and tansgender suicide ranging from 21% to 42% of all teen suicides. Their study indicated a suicide attempt rate of 42% and a suicide ideation rate of 60%. They also discovered that higher disclosure rates, greater levels of sexual experience, and higher victimization rates were associated with those who attempted suicide. They conclude that the critical issue about lesbian, gay, bisexual, and transgender suicide is not the rate or incidence, but the factors that lead to it (Hershberger, Pilkington, & Augelli, 1996).

School life can assume the proportions of a living nightmare for lesbian, gay, bisexual, and transgender youth. They are verbally and physically threatened at an appalling rate. For example, harassment, name-calling, violence, and an unsupportive environment pose major stressors. In addition, information about their lives is not a part of the curriculum of many schools. Sex education is not a given within America's public school system. Even when courses are offered, there is no guarantee that the sexual orientation of lesbian, gay, bisexual, and transgender adolescents will be addressed. Indeed, teachers are still taught that while adolescence may be a time of same-sex experimentation, it is not a natural or equivalent alternative to heterosexual adolescent development, Therefore teachers and counselors are unprepared to recognize and deal with lesbian, gay, bisexual, and transgender children (Durby, 1994; Herr, 1997; Hunter, 1990).

Unlike other youngsters, not all lesbian, gay, bisexual, and transgender adolescents believe they can seek the support of their parents (Mallon, 1994). Parents, when faced with a child who comes out as a lesbian, gay, bisexual, or transgender person, do not respond in a supportive fashion. Rejection, grief, anger, or disgust exemplify the range of negative responses offered by parents and siblings when a lesbian, gay, bisexual, or transgender youth discloses (Rothberg & Weinstein, 1996). For parents, feelings of failure and fear often result in a family crisis that may be resolved by silencing or rejecting the youth (Strommen, 1989).

Data about the high number of runaway and throwaway lesbian, gay, bisexual, and transgender youth offer a frightening look at what happens when lesbian, gay, bisexual, and transgender children are forced out of the family. Lesbian, gay, bisexual, and transgender children end up among the homeless population living on the streets of large cities. For example, it is estimated that between 25-40% of Los Angeles homeless youth are lesbian, gay, bisexual, or transgender (Durby, 1994). They exchange sex for drugs, food, and shelter. These activities too often lead to addiction or illness (Durby, 1994; Mallon, 1994).

Lesbian, gay, bisexual, and transgender youth who turn to the health care system meet significant barriers (Durby, 1994). Lesbian youth are viewed by professionals as being less at risk and are overlooked in outreach or other programs. Sexually transmitted diseases are as real as is substance abuse in the lives of these adolescents. For example, one study found that about three-quarters of homeless youth who engaged in prostitution also had drug-related problems (Yates, et al., 1991). Few medical or social services exist to deal with their issues or concerns (Durby, 1994).

Hence, the lives of too many lesbian, gay, bisexual, and transgender youth are marked by psychological trauma, parental rejection, violence, and life threatening illnesses. Moreover, little is offered to them in the way of compassionate and competent social service programs.

A Different Theoretical Perspective

Troidan (1989) has illustrated a stage-based developmental theory that presents lesbian, gay, bisexual, and transgender adolescent development as normal. He posits four stages, including:

1. Sensitization: During pre-puberty, a generalized sense of marginalization and difference.
2. Identity Confusion: During teen years, suspicions of being a homosexual conflicts with socially imposed images.
3. Identity Assumption: During late teens or early adulthood, movement toward resolution of identity confusion leads to self and public identity as homosexual.
4. Commitment: During the remainder of adulthood, homosexuality is adopted as a way of life (Troidan, 1989).

This approach offers service providers a basis for normalizing and strengthening lesbian, gay, bisexual, and transgender youth.

Culturally competent service providers meet the needs of those adolescents who are generally outside the mainstream social service network (Durby, 1994) (i.e., Gay and Lesbian Social Services in Los Angeles, the Gay and Lesbian Community Service Center in Los Angeles, and the Sexual Minority Assistance League in Washington, D.C.). In order to provide effective services, many of these programs do not employ professionals, such as social workers. The majority of the services are delivered by paraprofessionals (Cagle, 1997).

The Code of Ethics of the National Association of Social Workers (1996), however, calls for culturally competent services for lesbian, gay, bisexual, and transgender persons and mandates social change efforts to end discrimination based on sexual orientation. All service workers, therefore, must be prepared to work with and for lesbian, gay, bisexual, and transgender young people. For many, a paradigm shift is needed for the delivery of culturally competent social services.

Cultural Competence Human Service Organizations

Organizations must know enough to be sensitive to and supportive of lesbian, gay, bisexual, and transgender youth as being functionally healthy and worthwhile. Service providers and organizations must know enough about the development and identity issues of these young people to do no harm in their practice with them. They must deal supportively with parents and network with or thoroughly understand resources, such as Parents and Families of Lesbians and Gays, that support lesbian, gay, bisexual, and transgender adolescence and their parents (Whitlock, 1989). Service providers must create a climate or environment in agencies serving families and children that is welcoming and safe for lesbian, gay, bisexual, and transgender youth (Mallon, 1994; Durby, 1994). Finally, they must advocate for social, educational, and health services that do not exacerbate the pain, loss, and trauma experienced by lesbian, gay, bisexual, and transgender adolescence but instead provide opportunities to strengthen and support their growth and development.

Performance Outcomes of Child Welfare Systems

In the past two decades, there has been an increased demand for program effectiveness and efficiency in the child welfare arena. Federal and state mandates are requiring public child welfare agencies to become more performance-based in their operations. A more coherent, focused, and defensible set of child well-being and permanency outcomes is emerging in the child welfare field. These outcome measures are being used to illustrate the varying degrees of success and shortcomings of child welfare systems nationwide.

As organizations collect the necessary data to measure the efficacy of their interventions, the poor outcomes for culturally diverse families and children are becoming glaringly apparent. Compared to their Caucasian counterparts, minority children are removed from their homes for child abuse and neglect more frequently, receive fewer services once in the system, remain in foster care for longer periods of time, and recidivate when they return home from care at higher rates (Courtney et al., 1996). While there are multidimensional reasons for the differential treatment and outcomes of minority children and families in the child welfare system, agency competence in multiculturalism is a critical component in addressing this problem.

Planning and Training

Despite the fact that minority children and families are disproportionately affected and adversely over-represented in public child welfare organizations, too little attention is focused on understanding the organizational deficits contributing to these poor outcomes. When child welfare agencies begin to realize their weaknesses in serving minority populations, their first response, more often than not, is to mandate training for staff on how to become more culturally competent. However, administrators and policy-makers are often noticeably absent from these mandated events, and the training does not become an integral part of the organizational development efforts in the agency. Furthermore, a strategic and well thought-out plan on how to mobilize necessary resources and overcome poor agency performance fails to accompany these training efforts. If child welfare agencies want improved outcomes for minority children and families, there must be a system-wide strategy that includes a commitment from all levels of the organization.

Cross, et al. (1989) conceptualized a culturally component system of care that acknowledges and incorporates improving service delivery to minority clients at multiple levels, including the policymaking, administrative, practitioner, and consumer levels. The authors purport that becoming effective in achieving more positive outcomes for minority children and families is a developmental process and should be viewed as a goal toward which professional agencies and systems can strive.

Agencies serious about overcoming organizational barriers in effectively serving minority clients should begin by formally acknowledging a commitment to culturally competent services. This is best accomplished by codifying this in the organizational vision and mission statement. Outlining the provision of culturally competent services in the organization's mission statement sets the tone for the entire organization and demonstrates to those inside and outside of the agency a commitment to address these issues.

Strategic planning linked to both tactical and operational planning is another effective way to implement culturally competent services in organizations. This allows for a planned approach and a clear understanding in the organization of what needs to be done, by whom, when, and why. Strategic planning also can be effective in identifying the opportunities and threats that may occur as the agency sets the specific goals, objectives, and strategies aimed at increased performance in cultural competence. Increasingly, resource allocations in both public and non-profit organizations are being linked to the agencies' strategic plan. Identifying specific strategies statements that address services to diverse clients and link necessary functions, such as human resources, finance, and information technology allows for an increased likelihood in achieving a system-wide and holistic response. A formal strategic planning process that incorporates a standard for improved child welfare outcomes for diverse children and families can create improved understanding inside and outside the organization about culturally diverse client needs, enhanced organizational and decision-making capabilities in addressing those needs, and increased political support for enacting authentic organizational reforms.

Conclusion

As indicated in this chapter, a multidimensional, multicultural approach is critical for meeting the needs of our diverse population. Available data seem to indicate that the proportionate populations of child welfare clients generally do not match the distribution of the general U.S. population; on various dimensions, children and families of color may be over-represented for services. This supports the premise that cultural competence—considered as equivalent to professional competence—is necessary to increase the success of interventions at the micro level, and to increase organizational successful outcomes. Providing services to meet the needs of children and families, service providers and organizations must become culturally competent in the delivery of services if positive change is to occur. This competence must not be limited to good intentions or even a repertoire of techniques, but must be founded on a value system that can translated into application at all levels of service delivery. The authors propose a variety of approaches that may serve to assist service providers and organizations in developing a culturally sound, best practices orientation and focus.

References

Brislin, R., Espeland, P., Cherrie, C., and Young, M. (1986). *Intercultural Interactions: A practical guide*. Beverly Hill: Sage Publications.

Cagle, B. (1997). *Agency-building and social work professionalization: A view from queer youth organizations*. Unpublished master's thesis, University of Nevada, Reno.

Child Welfare League of America Foster Care, Fact Sheet, January 4, 1998.

Child Welfare League of America, Demographic Fact Sheet, 2000.

Children's Defense Fund, KeyFacts, 2000.

Courtney, M., Barth, R., Berrick, J., Brooks, D., Needell, B., and Park L. (1996). Race and child welfare services: Past research and future directions. *Child Welfare 75*(2).

Cross, T., Bazron, B., Dennis, K., and Isaacs, M. (1989). Towards a culturally competent system of care. Washington, D.C.: CASSP Technical Center.

Darby, D. D. (1994). Gay, Lesbian, and Bisexual Youth. *Journal of Gay & Lesbian Social Services: Issues in Practice, Policy and Research, 1*(3-4), 1-38.

Hardy-Desmond, S. (2000). Manuscript in progress.

Harper, K. and Lantz, J. (1996). *Cross-Cultural Practice: Social work with diverse populations*. Chicago: Lyceum Books, Inc.

Herr, K. (1997). Learning lessons from school: Homophobia, heterosexism, and the construction of failure. In M. B. Harris (Ed.). *School Experiences of Gay and Lesbian Youth*. In New York: Harrington Park Press.

Hershberger, S. L., Pilkington, N. W., and Augelli, A. R. (1996). Categorization of lesbian, gay, and bisexual suicide attempts. In C. Alexander (Ed.). *Gay and Lesbian Mental Health*. New York: Harrington Park Press.

Leigh, J. W., (1998). *Communicating for Cultural Competence*. Boston: Allyn and Bacon.

Lum, D., (1999). *Culturally Competent Practice: A Framework for Growth and Action*. New York: Brooks/Cole.

Lynch, E. (1992). From culture shock to cultural learning. In E. W. Lynch and M. J. Hanson (Eds.). *Developing Cross-Cultural Competence: A Guide for Working with Young Children and Their Families*. Baltimore, MD: Paul H. Brooks Publishing Co., 35-62.

Lynch, E. and Hanson, M. (1998). *Developing Cross-Cultural competence (2nd Ed.)*. Baltimore, MD: Paul H. Brooks Publishing Co.

Mallon, G. P. (1994). Counseling strategies with gay and lesbian youth. *Journal of Gay & Lesbian Social Services: Issues in Practice, Policy and Research, 1*(3-4), 75-92.

National Association of Social Workers Delegate Assembly. (1996). *Code of Ethics* (Brochure).

Petit, M. R. and Curtis, P.A. (1997). Child abuse and neglect: A look at the states - *The 1997 CWLA stat book*. Washington, DC: Child League of America.

Rothberg, B. and Weinstein, D. L. (1996). A primer on lesbian and gay families. In M. Shemoff (Ed.). *Human Services for Gay People: Clinical and Community Practice*, New York: Harrington Park Press.

Strommen, E. F. (1989). "You're a what?": Family member reactions to the disclosure of homosexuality. *Homosexuality and the Family*.

Troiden, R. R. (1989).The formation of homosexual identity. *Journal of Homosexuality, 17*(1-2).43-73.

U.S. Department of Health and Human Services. (1996a). A Guide to the Multiethnic Placement Act of 1994 as amended by the Interethnic Adoption Provisions of 1996.

U.S. Department of Health and Human Services. (1996b). Child Maltreatment: Reports From the States to the National Child Abuse and Neglect Data System.

Whitlock, K. (1989). Bridges of Respect. Philadelphia: American Friends Service Committee.

Williams, C. (1997). Personal reflections on permanency planning and cultural competency.

Yates, G. L., MacKenzie, M.D., Pennbridge, J., and Swofford, A. (1991). A risk profile comparison of homeless youth involved in prostitution and homeless youth not involved. *Journal of Adolescent Health, 12*(7), 545-548.

Chapter 9

Walking in Moccasins: Indian Child Welfare in the 21st Century

Deborah Esquibel Hunt, Myrna Gooden, and Carenlee Barkdull

"Oh, I just love shoes," she said, as we wandered through a shopping mall. Questioning her softly, "Why, Mom?" "Oh, I don't know. I just love shoes," and she looks from store to store, buying none. The next day, while attending a summer institute class I teach, my mother speaks again about shoes. "Oh, those boarding school shoes they made us wear were awful. Big, ugly clunkers. Even when I put my brother's socks in the toes, they still didn't fit and they always hurt my tiny feet." After class, as I pack up my computer, I gently prod, "So, Mom, do you think the boarding school shoes have anything to do with you loving to shop for shoes now?" "Oh, my gosh!" she exclaims, "I never thought of it that way!" And so an elder tells a story and learns a new term to describe her boarding school memories—post-traumatic stress disorder.

Ida Houle Gooden, Turtle Mountain Ojibwe elder

Stories and Values

In the beginning, there was a story; that story is ours and that story is yours. As human beings, we carry our unique stories, which are inherent to our cultures. One approach to teaching culturally competent practice has been to create stereotypes about particular ethnic or cultural groups. We believe this approach limits our ability as helping professionals to respond in meaningful and appropriate ways.

When we speak of American Indian/Alaska Native people, we must consider the 558 federally recognized tribes and 558 tribal society stories along with numerous state-recognized and self-identified tribes. It is important to acknowledge the tremendous diversity within tribal groups and the varying levels of assimilation among generations. At the same time, it is important to recognize certain common pan-Indian values, which have endured across tribes and across attempts at cultural genocide. This chapter is dedicated to improving child welfare practice efforts with the Indigenous people of the North American continent. The authors have blended Indian and non-Indian approaches to child welfare issues in quest of instilling hope for the future of Native children. Culturally responsive practice will be defined, and key values and competencies needed to work with American Indian children and families will be illustrated. Knowledge of federal policies with American Indians and their impact on Indian families and culture is an essential component of appropriate practice. In this chapter, child welfare and welfare reform policies are analyzed along with other relevant legislation and the implications for Indian child welfare practice. Case examples of culturally responsive practices in Indian Country are included. The stories are universal, heartfelt, and add depth to the challenge of meeting multi-cultural, multi-faceted needs in Indian Country. It is hoped that *all* who engage in child welfare work will meet the challenge to put on "new moccasins" to become as *culturally responsive* as possible.

Culturally Responsive Practice and Foundational American Indian Values

There is an increasing body of social work literature addressing culturally competent practice with American Indian people (Tsoi Goodluck, 1993; Edwards & Egbert-Edwards, 1994 and 1998; Weaver, 1999). Hilary Weaver (1999) notes the change in social work literature between 1988 and 1998 as moving "from cultural sensitivity to cultural competence, the ability to integrate cultural knowledge and sensitivity with skills for a more effective and culturally appropriate helping process." Her studies focus on " ... knowledge, skills, and values necessary for culturally competent service provision." Weaver is among the American Indian social work educators who are working to fill the literature gap "by providing empirical information on culturally competent social work with Native Americans" (p. 217).

To help fill this gap, we are proposing a broader definition of *culturally responsive* practice that goes *beyond* learning history, valuing diversity, and complying with policy. We believe that all child welfare workers, agencies, educators, and policy makers must consciously choose a *change of heart* and deliberately put on a pair of *moccasins*. In this broader definition, the individual becomes a part of the collective and is re-dedicated to serve Indian children, families, communities, and nations from the *spirit* of the Indian Child Welfare Act.

The fundamental concern in culturally responsive practice is <u>values</u>. While there is great diversity among and within the various American Indian tribes, there are a number of common values which provide a foundation for culturally responsive child welfare practice. These values have been identified by a number of authors (Edwards & Edwards, 1998; Timas & Reedy, 1998; Moran, 1999; and Sachs, Harris, Morris & Hunt, 1999) and are summarized in Table 1.

Table 1. Shared Traditional American Indian Values

Value: Autonomy

American Indian people value personal freedom and autonomy.

- Each person is valued as an individual; children are sacred
- Extended families provide extensive, consistent, and loving care of infants and small children, reinforcing their value
- Children are given opportunities to be self-reliant and responsible to the welfare of the tribe early in their lives
- Children learn by observing modeling by other family, clan, and tribal members

Value: Solidarity

American Indian people value family and tribal solidarity and cohesiveness.

- Each person perceives themselves as first a member of a specific tribe (Ojibwe, Yurok, Diné, Haida); secondly, as an American Indian/Alaska Native
- Has considerable pride in clan and tribal lineage and heritage
- Is expected to bring honor and respect to their families, clans, and tribes; individual behavior reflects the whole
- Respects all tribal members: children, youth, adults, and elders
- Is prepared to sacrifice with humility for the collective
- Is generous with one's talents and material goods

Value: Competence

American Indian people value attainment of knowledge and skills.

- Each person is encouraged to develop unique talents, knowledge and skills that will benefit themselves and the group
- As the people learn from their environments and animals, the knowledge is passed on
- Each skill acquired by young people is positively noted without any "fanfare" – reinforcing personal satisfaction for a job well done
- Self-improvement is valued over comparison with others; thus, competition is discouraged

Value: Spirituality

American Indian people believe in a Supreme Being and the continuity of life.

- Each person strives to maintain a positive balance and harmony with their Supreme Being and all living things
- The people believe that all of the Creator's works have spirits and are to be treated respectfully
- Many tribes have detailed accounts of their "creation" or "origin" stories

- It is important to show respect and reverence for the land, their homelands, and those areas sacred to them
- Spirituality and religious practices are routinely integrated throughout each day's activities
- Every thought and action is powerful and affects the past, present, and future of all

Value: Balance
American Indian people value harmony and balance.

- Each person demonstrates appreciation for life by the way in which they positively regard and reinforce their physical, mental, emotional, and spiritual health
- Each person is appreciated for what they contribute to the well being of the group
- Industry is valued; so is time for leisure, fun, social development, and social interaction
- Appreciating balance and harmony leads to understanding the appropriate times for hunting, harvesting, and utilization of nature's bounties, and for the appropriate use of all natural resources

Value: Wisdom
As all other values are achieved, wisdom is acquired.

- Much wisdom is transmitted to American Indian people through their elders
- When one lives in harmony with the cultural wisdom, people experience contentment and physical and emotional well being
- The roles of men and women are highly valued and complementary
- When people are secure within themselves and their culture, they are better able to contribute positively to the well being of others, in particular the children

With regards to children, it is generally considered the responsibility of the entire tribe or community to protect the children by carefully watching, witnessing, and intervening according to custom when the child is in danger (Sachs, et al., 1999). Individual cultural identity is an extension of the tribal and family identity, with each child having a unique place in the collective.

In other words, from the Indian perspective, the child does not "belong" to only the parents, but is a treasured resource for the whole tribe. The extended network of kin, non-kin and clan comprise the Indian child's "family." Therefore, decisions about child safety and well-being are likely to be based on criteria different from U.S. mainstream child welfare assumptions and include an expanded set of resources beyond the nuclear family. For Indian people, the termination of parental rights would equate to the termination of tribal membership because the "parents" are all those who are invested in the child's happiness. Likewise, "foster care" is an unknown concept in most native languages (National Indian Child Welfare Association, 1996).

Therefore, when making Indian child welfare decisions, there are differing cultural standards that must be considered. Culturally appropriate decisions are in the long term in the best interest of the lifetime development of the Indian child. These decisions are guided by the standards developed under the Indian Child Welfare Act of 1978 (ICWA). Table 2 is an example of the cultural differences that might be encountered by Indian and non-Indian workers.

Table 2: Cultural Differences in Indian Child Welfare Decision-Making

Decisions About:	Indian Perspective	Non-Indian Perspective
Safety	In a general state of happiness	Clean, secure environment
Removal	Child is abused and neglected	Child is not "safe" (checklist)
Placement	With the child's extended family first	Any available foster or adoptive home
Reunification	As soon as possible; active efforts	Only if deemed necessary; reasonable efforts
Adoption	With the child's extended family; only as a last resort. Safety and permanence with those considered "mine" and "like me."	Soon ... <to be out of the system> safety/permanence first, reunification last

Basically, in the Indian perspective, strengthening families strengthens the culture, and a family cannot be strong if the child is not part of it. According to the ICWA, "There is no resource that is more vital to the continued existence and integrity of Indian tribes than their children" (ICWA, 1978). From an Indian perspective, children are most permanently stable and safe when they are emotionally and psychologically connected to their culture and in the care of those with whom they have a natural bond. This is the *spirit* of the Indian Child Welfare Act.

However, the uneven application of the ICWA indicates serious gaps in practice knowledge in child welfare. Moreover, child welfare texts and social work journal articles often fail to include implications of social policies for tribes. For example, a recent article for social workers on the Multiethnic Placement Act and the Interethnic Adoption Provisions failed to mention the implications of these acts for the Indian Child Welfare Act (Brooks, Barth, Bussiere, & Patterson, 1999). This omission occurred in spite of specific provisions in the legislation regarding the ICWA. Furthermore, an informal analysis by these authors of model social work curricula revealed very little content on American Indians. This chapter attempts to clarify the policies and philosophical dilemmas that are often encountered and begins by offering principles of culturally responsive practice.

An Overview of Competencies Needed for Culturally Responsive Practice

Donning a new pair of moccasins and dancing a new way brings benefits to **all** children. It also challenges individuals and systems to acquire new knowledge, skills, attitudes, and values. Workers at every level must become aware of institutional and policy barriers to change, and establish creative alliances for change. We must be open to the opportunities and uncertainties that accompany such personal, organizational, and systems transformation. Unfortunately, there are no easy answers and no quick fixes—no cookbook approaches to Indian child welfare practice—that are simultaneously transformative and culturally responsive.

There are, however, a number of competencies and relational aspects of practice that will benefit practitioners in very practical ways wherever they may be in Indian Country. Many of these competencies, particularly those within the knowledge and policy domains, are addressed in greater depth in this chapter. In the authors' view, these competencies can be categorized into three areas:

- **Foundational values** needed for successful practice with American Indian individuals, families, and communities

- **Basic relational skills and attitudes** that are more likely to promote positive and trust-building relationships with American Indian peoples

- **Knowledge domains** that include familiarity with local systems, policy and institutional barriers to change, and laws that affect American Indian children and families

Table 3 lists competencies within each category that we consider crucial for effective practice.

Table 3:   Competencies for Culturally Responsive Practice

Foundational Values	Basic Relational Skills and Attitudes	Knowledge Domains
• Respect for one's own culture • Self-awareness of one's own biases • Recognition of the ongoing realities of racism and marginalization of American Indian peoples • Appreciation of diversity and difference • Respect for the right to self-determination • Acknowledgment of the expertise of individuals, families, and communities to recognize and solve their own problems • Belief in the inherent worth and dignity of all individuals • Valuing of culture as a source of strength and empowerment • Unwavering commitment to social justice	• Being respectful, humble and willing to learn • Being aware of the dynamics of power and privilege in helping relationships • Being patient and tolerating silences • Allowing time for trust to develop • Keeping commitments • Listening to the stories of oppressive history • Affirming the trauma, grief and loss associated with colonialism and forced assimilation • Validating the strengths and resiliency in survival • Negotiation and conflict mediation	• Knowing how to assess for Indian ancestry • Assessing for co-occurring needs of individuals and families • Fostering helpful collaborations within and between helping agencies • Understanding the role of tribal sovereignty • Being aware of the implications of devolution on federal trust responsibility to Indian tribes • Understanding the spirit, intent, and content of the Indian Child Welfare Act (ICWA) and its relationship to the Adoption and Safe Families Act (ASFA) • Knowing how welfare reform and adoption law reforms affect American Indian child welfare practice

The Legacy of Colonialism

It is important to recognize that the majority of models of practice reflect the dominant power paradigm of colonialism (Duran & Duran, 1995). This system of political, economic, and social domination serves those at the center of power and marginalizes or devalues others. Colonialism is based on racial superiority and therefore promotes prejudice and discrimination against minorities and, in particular, people of color. Dehumanization of the colonized people justifies exploitation, oppression, and control of those deemed inferior. The oppressed are often blamed for the conditions which follow internalized shame and negative self-image. Colonialism's success requires cultural genocide and assimilation, including the elimination of history in Indigenous voices (Yellow Bird & Chenault, 1999).

When the people are no longer aware of the history of trauma and loss, the results are confusion, hopelessness and a sense of continuous grief and powerlessness. For indigenous peoples, the legacy of deliberate federal policies of extermination, expulsion, exclusion, and assimilation has left them with serious doubts and apprehension about their capacity for self-governance and self-sufficiency. Unfortunately, most past efforts to "help" Indian nations have not addressed the historical grief nor the strengths and resiliency of the people.

The Historical Trauma of Child Removal and Assimilation Policies

In the past, Indian children were removed from their families and traditional communities under the assumption that being Indian and being poor defined risk (Edwards & Egbert-Edwards, 1989). In particular, the removal of Indian children to boarding schools and for placement with non-Indian families left a legacy of distrust of child welfare services by Indian families (Horejsi, Heavy Runner Craig, & Pablo, 1992). Culturally responsive practice with American Indian families includes understanding the historical legacy of child removal under numerous federal policies. Therefore, a family history assessment is basic to understanding the causes of and appropriate intervention for child abuse and neglect.

Assimilation to mainstream American culture and termination of traditional identity was once thought to be the way to remedy the "Indian problem." Assimilation efforts included changing Indian names to European American names, cutting the hair, and requiring military style uniforms (Skinner, 1992). Any expression of a student's native culture, including language, could be expected to be met with extreme and cruel consequences. Severe emotional, physical, and mental punishments were meted out by matrons and teachers in agonizing, concentration camp-like methods. Isolated and lonely, without recourse, it was the child's version of the Indian holocaust. The dismal failure of these policies led to the near decimation of Indian families and created widespread serious problems in tribal communities. The heart wrenching ongoing effects of what is referred to in Indian Country as the "American Indian holocaust" include unresolved grief, loss of culture, and population.

The statistics on poverty, child abuse and neglect, substance abuse, domestic violence, and the general state of mental health is abysmal. Unemployment for American Indian people ranges from about 28% in urban areas to 90% on some reservations (United States Census Bureau, 1999). Some authors estimate that 95-100% of American Indian families are affected by alcohol and substance abuse (Three Feathers Associates, 1989; Horejsi, et al., 1992). Disproportionately high use of alcohol in young adult women is responsible for elevated reports of fetal alcohol syndrome in American Indian/Alaska Native children (MMRW, 1994). Single female headed households account for 27% of American Indian families, versus 17% of families in the general population. Depending on location, high school graduation rates for American Indian children vary from 20% to 40%, or even less. Only about 8% of American Indian people graduate from college. This compares to 14% of African-Americans and 25% of the general population (U.S. Census Bureau, ibid.).

Responding to the American Indian/Alaska Native intensity of needs, whether on or off the reservation, requires skills that encompass awareness of specific tribal history, values and culture as well as an appreciation of the resilience and strengths of each nation.

Policy Competencies Needed for Culturally Responsive Practice

In addition to an appreciation for the effects of historical trauma and grief, an understanding of the unique legal relationship between Indian nations and the federal government is required. This relationship defines Indian child welfare practice. Federal trust responsibility for tribal welfare is determined by a series of treaties that are still in force today.

There is an ongoing dilemma and struggle within Indian nations. One part of the dilemma involves inherent sovereignty and the desire to care for the social needs of their own people. The other part involves federal trust responsibility for services mandated by agreements with tribes in exchange for Indian land. These dilemmas have led to a complex web of federal, state, and tribal bureaucracies and policies through which programs are funded and administered in tribal settings.

Policy Change in an Era of Devolution

Over the past two decades, many programs formerly administered by the federal government have been devolved to local entities such as states, counties, and tribes. A relatively few tribes have been awarded tribal family assistance grants (the tribal block grant that is similar to TANF).

With few exceptions, most tribal people are still served by state programs. Under these circumstances, trust responsibility for American Indian welfare is being shifted *de facto* to states and counties. This creates important legal questions, since treaties which established trust responsibility are between tribes and the federal government and not between tribes and states (National Congress of American Indians, undated). The shift to state authority for welfare programs creates a radical change in government to government relationships.

While some legal issues still need to be addressed, devolution has meant that a significant level of collaboration is now required between state and tribal governments. However, a number of systemic barriers and misconceptions exist that could hinder collaborative relationships. For example, a state's TANF grant is reduced when tribes within that state's geographical boundaries are allocated a tribal grant. Often, states may have the misconception that tribes can and should provide for their own people. For tribes, previous negative experiences with states have often left distrust and resentment. Despite such obstacles, there is some early evidence in at least one state that intergovernmental relations as well as collaboration within tribal service systems have improved under welfare reform (Brown & Pandey, 1999). To advance these new relationships, all social workers need skills that will help facilitate culturally responsive services to American Indian families.

The foregoing section highlights the complexity of issues faced by child welfare workers today. These issues can be intimidating for agencies and practitioners that serve American Indian families. However, we believe that, with patience and experience, all child welfare workers can begin to understand and be culturally responsive in their practice.

An Overview of Policies Affecting Indian Child Welfare Practice

For American Indian people, the heart of child welfare is the appropriate placement of Indian children in need of protection. To be culturally responsive, child welfare practice must include an understanding of the unique legal and cultural implications of policies for tribal people. The Indian Child Welfare Act of 1978, the Temporary Assistance to Needy Families (TANF) program under the Personal Responsibility and Work Opportunity Reconciliation Act of 1996 (formerly AFDC), and the Adoption and Safe Families Act (ASFA) of 1997 are the principal laws which affect Indian child welfare. In addition, the lack of understanding, confusion, and misinterpretation of the Multiethnic Placement Act (MEPA) and Interethnic Adoptions Provision (IAP) amendment may threaten the culturally appropriate placement of Indian children.

While each of these laws is an attempt to remedy serious concerns for the cultural, economic, and social welfare of children, underlying value conflicts and lack of guidance on policy interactions are problematic. Informal agency approaches may lack cultural sensitivity and foreclose dialogue regarding the professional and personal struggles involved in practice with Native families.

The following section analyzes both the positive intent of individual legislative acts and illuminates possible cultural issues and implications with tribal people. Recommendations for individual, agency, policy, and educational practices in Indian child welfare are also addressed.

The Indian Child Welfare Act: ICWA

Of primary importance to all child welfare practice are knowledge and appropriate application of the Indian Child Welfare Act. Prior to the ICWA, there was an inordinately high incidence of removal of American Indian children, with up to 35% of all Indian children removed from families and 90% fostered or adopted by non-Indian families. Serious problems were being recognized among these children, including depression, marginalization, and high rates of suicide in teen years (Indian Child Welfare Program, 1974).

The ICWA sought to remedy these concerns by ensuring tribal control of child welfare while validating the cultural requirements of child development and seeking to protect Indian families and tribes. Speaking from the legal intent, the Act declares, "There is no resource that is more vital to the continued existence and integrity of Indian tribes than their children" (25 U.S.C. § 1901). Thus, the ICWA is viewed as a cultural and legal victory in the turn of U.S. federal policy toward Indian nations' self-determination (Hauptman, 1995).

Other goals of the ICWA include prevention of Indian family separation and culturally congruent permanency planning including the requirement of "active" rather than "reasonable" efforts for family preservation. Simmons and Trope (1999) note the areas where the ICWA standards must be met by states as including notice to tribes of state child custody proceedings, standards for the placement of Indian children in foster homes and termination of parental rights, active efforts to provide rehabilitative services to the birth family or Indian custodian, transfer of jurisdiction to tribal courts and full faith and credit for tribal judgments, preferred placements of Indian children with their extended family or other Indian families, and tribal right to intervene in state child custody proceedings (p. 7).

Unfortunately, full compliance with the ICWA has been limited. Two reasons stand out. The first of these is lack of knowledge and subsequent jurisdictional confusion (Thorne, 1997), which is manifested in the uneven application by state courts. In violation of the ICWA, state courts have interpreted the "best interest of the child" standard to deny transfers of custody from non-Indian foster parents to guardians who could be viewed as more appropriate under the ICWA standard (Jones, 2000). A news report in *Indian Country Today* (a leading national Native newspaper) reported that two states had recently strengthened case law in upholding the right of extended family to adopt children under the ICWA. These cases denied the "best interest of the child" argument for adoption by non-Indian foster parents (Melmer, 2000). Questions and further information may be obtained from the organizations listed as "ICWA Resources" at the end of the chapter.

Secondly, and all too common, is the failure to assess for ancestry (Lewis, 1998). Ten years after the ICWA, a study showed a *25% increase* in referrals of Indian children to protective custody (Edwards & Egbert-Edwards, 1989). In 1989, less than one-half of Indian children in state custody were placed in Indian homes, and parental notification was received in only 65-70% of state proceedings. Among these, prevention efforts were recorded in only 41% of the cases (Plantz, 1989).

Indeed, twenty years after the ICWA, American Indian children are still disproportionately represented in child welfare referrals. While American Indian people comprise only 1% of the total U.S. population, American Indian children are 3% of referrals to child protective services (Edwards & Egbert-Edwards, 1998). This referral pattern leaves questions of risk and whether assessments of child safety and referrals for placement are culturally appropriate.

Because of the increasing numbers of Indian children in both urban and reservation areas, it becomes imperative for all social workers to be trained in culturally responsive child welfare practice. In addition, it is important to recognize the higher number of "special needs" American Indian children referred for placement. An enduring legacy of historical trauma is the higher incidence of disabilities, fetal alcohol syndrome, and other chronic health concerns (Johnson, 1992).

About half of all children are now served by tribes (Simmons & Trope, 1999). Many children living on reservations are also served by public welfare agencies that may not be in compliance with the ICWA. A positive tribal response to ICWA referrals from state agencies will be likely to increase public agency compliance. Hence, for the ICWA to be utilized appropriately, improved understanding may be needed within both tribal and public child welfare agencies.

The ICWA sets the standard for practice with American Indian families. However, if not sensitively applied, current reforms in both welfare and child welfare have the potential to "turn back the clock" to pre-ICWA rates of inappropriate out-of-home Indian child placements.

Co-Occurring Needs in Indian Country

Families receiving financial assistance are over-represented in terms of their involvement with child welfare systems when compared with the general population (Shook, 1998). A number of factors have been posed as contributing to the phenomenon, including the possibility of a causal relationship between poverty and child abuse and neglect, a high prevalence of co-occurring needs, and a higher level of "surveillance" of welfare families (ibid., p. 2). Whatever the underlying causal factors, it seems reasonable to assume that welfare reform will impact the child welfare system.

Among American Indian people, poverty is a serious concern that bears a direct relationship to child abuse (Horejsi, Heavy Runner Craig, & Pablo, 1992). Given the co-occurring high incidence of poverty, depression, substance abuse, and domestic violence, it is not surprising that 34.4% of Indian children are at risk for abuse or neglect (National Indian Justice Center, 1998). In addition, serious mental health issues have manifested among American Indian youth.

> Robert Jaycob Jensen was first. The lanky 17 year-old Sioux Indian, who'd been drinking heavily and having run-ins with police all summer, slipped into his family's dank basement last August 30. Over toward the corner, past the rusted-out furnace and broken sewer line, he threaded a braided leather belt over a board nailed between floor beams, buckled it around his neck and hanged himself. On November 16, in the same basement with the same type of belt, Robert's 16 year-old cousin and best friend, Charles Gerry, hanged himself. Three other Indian youths have since taken their lives ... in the five months since Robert's death, 43 reservation boys and girls have attempted suicide. ("Rash of Indian Suicides," 1998).

These factors must be viewed in the context of complex historical stress and disrupted parent-child bonding due to federal government-driven child removal to boarding schools and out-of-home placements (Lewis, 1998; Weaver, 1999; Sachs, Harris, et al., 1999).

American Indians remain the most vulnerable people in the United States today. The complex interaction of historical, legal, economic, and social factors makes the elimination of poverty and child abuse and neglect an enormous challenge. As a result of these forces, American Indian children and families are often found to be in "double jeopardy" by being simultaneously involved with the child welfare and public welfare systems (Briar-Lawson, Lawson, et al., 1999). Such families are likely to be negatively affected by the interaction of current welfare reform and child welfare legislation (ibid.).

Welfare Reform under TANF

Of the policies analyzed here, Temporary Assistance to Needy Families (TANF) is the least compatible with native values. This intensive attempt to revitalize individualism essentially divorces the collective from responsibility for social welfare. For example, under TANF, a high value is placed on <u>personal responsibility</u> in providing for the economic needs of children through employment versus receipt of public welfare benefits. One of the key policy assumptions of TANF is that welfare creates dependence, trapping people in generational cycles of reliance on public assistance instead of fostering attitudes and skills necessary to the achievement of economic "self-sufficiency." Thus, TANF emphasizes the *temporary* nature of financial assistance to *individual* families with dependent children.

To this end, welfare reform aims to end "entitlement" benefits through time limits (two to five years as determined by individual states) and increased employment efforts. TANF requires employment seeking activities in order to keep temporary benefits. While tribal values promote self-reliance and meaningful work, major employment barriers for people on reservations include geographical isolation, lack of transportation, few job opportunities, lower levels of education and training, and lack of reliable child care (Brown, 1998).

According to the National Indian Child Welfare Association (NICWA), unfulfilled work requirements and subsequent loss of welfare income are expected to contribute to increased Indian child abuse and neglect. If increased child neglect is indeed the result of welfare reform implementation, American Indian families are facing a new and very real threat to their survival. For those families who must seek employment away from their reservation, decisions are being made to leave children with relatives where the children may qualify for "child only" TANF grants. Such disruptions in Indian family life are reminiscent of the U.S. "termination" era of the 1950s, when Indian families were "relocated" to seek employment away from home (Cross, 1998b). Thus, the historical wounds of family disruption by federal policy are being reinflicted.

The complex interaction of poverty, abuse, and other co-occurring needs in families is not yet well-understood. Despite dramatic decreases in welfare caseloads, there is no empirical evidence to demonstrate that welfare reform has reduced either poverty or family risk. Families with persistent or multiple problems may become overwhelmed with the stringent requirements and drop out of the program, leaving them even more isolated from potential supports. In addition, there is widespread concern that being sanctioned off TANF may increase the chance that children will end up in out-of-home placements. For example, Terry Cross, Executive Director of the National Indian Child Welfare Association, has predicted that 15,000 new child welfare cases would be initiated with welfare reform (Cross, 1998a).

Understanding the ICWA's Relationship to Child Welfare Reform under ASFA

The Adoption and Safe Families Act (ASFA) of 1997 (P.L. 105-89) attempts to reduce long-term foster care placement and expedite permanency for children in protective care. To expedite placement, ASFA places strict time limits on family preservation efforts. Permanency hearings must occur within 12 months after initial placements in foster care, and concurrent planning for family reunification and permanent placement is encouraged. Petitions to terminate parental rights are mandated after a child has spent 15 of 22 months in foster care. ASFA has changed the emphasis in child welfare from family preservation to child safety and more rapid permanent placement through adoption. Furthermore, states receive financial incentives for adopting children.

Of most concern to American Indian people, the new law has failed to consider the cultural and legal requirements of Indian children. If neglect referrals increase due to new time limits on financial assistance imposed by TANF, parental rights may be jeopardized through the promotion of rapid adoption. Thus, cultural values and ICWA standards are violated. Additionally, substance abuse, a major contributor to child neglect among American Indian families, may require rehabilitation beyond these limits.

What practitioners need to know is that ASFA does apply to *all* children who become involved with federally funded foster care or adoption systems, including those children of Indian nations served by Title IV-B or IV-E plans. Fortunately, whether American Indian children are served by public or tribal agencies, *the ICWA standards must still guide the process*. This means seeking all possible solutions to permanency that will include a child's ties to kin and community and consideration of the cultural development of Indian children. Under ASFA, kinship care is recognized for the first time as a legitimate solution to permanency. However, only adoption is given financial incentives, which is a major cultural flaw of ASFA.

Legally, there is no doubt that the ICWA takes precedence over ASFA (Simmons & Trope, 1999). A policy analysis by NICWA showed that ASFA *should not* legally affect the states' compliance with the "active efforts" requirement of the ICWA (ibid). However, there is *always* potential for the ICWA to be violated by public welfare agencies whose staff may not understand either the spirit or intent of the law. If all states adhered to the ICWA guidelines and all tribes had adequate services, Indian children would be guaranteed better protection. Improved guidance and training on ASFA's interface with the ICWA promise to reduce confusion over application of these policies and increase state compliance.

The Bureau of Indian Affairs guidelines for the application of the ICWA "involve and use the available resources of the extended family, the tribe, Indian social services agencies, and individual Indian caregivers" (Bureau of Indian Affairs, 1989).

It was hoped that these guidelines would activate states and tribes under ASFA toward culturally responsive practice with American Indian children; so far, this has not been fully accomplished. Examples of appropriate application of the ICWA and collaboration between agencies will be included in the last section of the chapter.

ICWA and Adoption Law Reforms (MEPA-IAP)

Because adoption has become the permanency plan for increasing numbers of children under ASFA, the Multiethnic Placement Act of 1994 (P.L. 103-82) and Removal of Barriers to Interethnic Adoption of 1996 (Interethnic Adoption Provisions or IAP, P.L. 104-88) must also be examined for their relevance for tribal children. These laws acknowledge that children are sometimes left for undue periods of time in foster care while systems search for same-race or ethnic homes.

MEPA has made it illegal to deny or delay placement based on race or national origin. IAP strengthened MEPA by empowering the Department of Health and Human Services to impose fiscal sanctions on agencies found to be in violation of the law and allowing individuals to sue in federal court. Thus, while not intended to prohibit or discourage racial matching for placement, the first tenet of the law is adoption into any suitable family. This has sometimes caused conflicts with the intent of the ICWA. In fact, both laws simultaneously require that states make efforts to recruit ethnic foster and adoptive families. If successfully adhered to, this aspect of MEPA and IAP could actually strengthen the ICWA.

Under these adoption reform laws, Indian children *are* recognized as having a distinct political status as tribal members, and thus are not subject to the same racial classification utilized under MEPA. Unfortunately, a common reason for not implementing the ICWA is a failure to determine whether or not children are of Indian ancestry. In addition, when states, or tribes with agreements with states, fail to actively recruit Indian foster and adoptive homes, children who might be served under the ICWA are placed in non-Indian homes.

Under the ICWA, children in protective care should be placed with Indian families. However, tribal systems often lack direct funding for adoption and foster care assistance. Overburdened state systems often lack the resources, knowledge and cultural awareness to actively recruit and train Indian foster and adoptive families. In addition, some national adoption advocates argue that children deserve a stable and loving home, regardless of cultural orientation. These factors can result in the misinterpretation of MEPA-IAP, thus deterring compliance with the ICWA and perpetuating cultural genocide on American Indian people.

Stories of Hope: Examples of Culturally Responsive Practices in Indian Country

American Indians living on and off reservations are finding ways to reclaim their heritage and pride by reaffirming and teaching traditional values, spiritual practices, and native languages. One of the many positive aspects of this movement is a blossoming of culturally based programs which cross ethnic, tribal, state, and even national boundaries. Following are three examples of promising practice innovations in Indian communities.

In Oregon, the Warm Springs Tribe is among Indian nations which have adapted the New Zealand Maori model of family group decision-making to child welfare practice in their communities (McNevins, 2000). The Warm Springs Tribe's Family Unity model honors the capacity of extended families and communities to build on their own strengths and wisdom in creating child protection plans. The goal is in line with the *spirit* of the ICWA—to reduce out-of-home placements where possible and to return children already in foster care to their families.

Firmly embedded within this model is the notion that language matters. "Problems" are reframed as "concerns" and "advice" is reframed as "options." McNevins reports that the values of choice, listening, and respect reflect traditional tribal ways. As such, these practices receive widespread community support. McNevins also notes the model's potential for involving families and community in arenas outside of child welfare, including schools, juvenile justice, mental health, and alcohol and drug treatment programs.

The Wind River reservation people in Wyoming also incorporate the traditional value of respect for all parents and children in services provided through Welcome House. Where immediate help through extended family or other community members may not be an option, Welcome House provides respite care in a nonjudgmental way for parents seeking to protect their children from domestic violence, substance abuse, or other potentially harmful events. These parents are affirmed for demonstrating their love for their children through their desire to protect them and keep them safe. Another traditionally congruent aspect of the program's approach and philosophy is to acknowledge the community's role in contributing to the safety and well-being of children (Noseep & Powell, 1999).

The Southern Ute Indian Tribe of Colorado has created its own community collaboration comprised of professionals and "community consultants" who are elders or current or former service recipients. The "Design Team" includes representatives from social services, education, public health, mental health, substance abuse, and other community programs that serve children and families. At the time of this writing, the Southern Ute Design Team has adopted as its mission the provision of "culturally relevant, supportive, and integrated services to ensure that all Southern Ute children are successful in school and in life."

A new tribally funded private school will donate space to house collaborative services for Southern Ute families and their children. Initially, it will serve children from infants through the age equivalent of third grade. The school's vision combines the elements of education and culture, supporting the traditional philosophy of life as a sacred circle encompassing spirit, mind, and body.

These ambitious ventures have challenged those involved to create a vision of a healthy community that will guide the process and to devote time, energy, and commitment far beyond the scope of usual job descriptions and the hours of an average workday. It has also required courage and honesty to confront aspects of the community that create disharmony, and the willingness to risk and change with no clear-cut guarantees of success. Setbacks, disappointment, and criticism are balanced by a passion for creating a better future for the tribe's children. The process has been truly inspirational to this non-Native consultant.

The knowledge and wisdom gained from such stories bring hope to everyone dedicated to improving the welfare of children. 'Business as usual' is failing young people in communities across the United States. Thirty child welfare systems in the United States are currently undergoing class action litigation for failure to protect children (GAO, 1997). This foster care 'crisis' is characterized by inadequate resources to care appropriately for families referred for neglect and abuse. Too often, children are removed from their homes despite shortages in suitable placement homes. The negative effects on children, families, and communities are caused in part by understaffing, inadequate funding, and high employee turnover. The discouragement of child welfare workers under this burdensome and ineffective system should not be neglected.

In rethinking dominant culture assumptions, child welfare practitioners, agency administrators, educators, and social policy makers may find value in the traditions endemic to many American Indian cultures and in adopting the *spirit* of the ICWA to redefine the best interests of *all* children.

New Moccasins

The future of Indian child welfare depends on culturally responsive practices. Generalist training for social workers includes both direct practice methods and social policy analysis. Therefore, social workers should be in the best position to understand the interaction of historical trauma with poverty and abuse. The knowledge base of all child welfare workers should include an informed interpretation of child welfare laws.

However, culturally responsive practice is more than understanding history, valuing diversity, and complying with policy. In order to contribute to real healing of

Indian nations and historical shame over genocidal policies and practices, all child welfare workers, agencies, educators, and policy makers must consciously struggle toward a *change of heart*. Indian children, families, communities, and nations must be served from the *spirit* of the Indian Child Welfare Act. We all must face the challenges of conflicting paradigms regarding child welfare and affirm that the best interest of all children is to grow up in a nurturing environment knowing who they are, connected to their own history, language, customs, and values.

Optimally, an expanded vision of culturally responsive practice will include strategies that address individual practitioner knowledge, skills, and attitudes; agency cultural competence; culturally relevant education and training; transformative academic research; and political compassion and vision. This will include building tribal capacity for child welfare through reclaiming and strengthening values and processes that affirm and empower wholeness. We all must fight for social justice by confronting policies and practices that promote or enable racial and ethnic inequities.

There is hope for the future of culturally responsive practice with American Indian/Alaska Native peoples. The hope lies in child welfare workers and bureaucrats becoming more responsive to the needs of American Indian children and families and communities. Our suggestion is to replace the "big, ugly clunkers" of distrust and disharmony with "new moccasins" of compassion and understanding.

As authors, we believe our dedication to Indian child welfare work was foretold in this elder's words:

> Soon there will be many books that will tell of our ways and perhaps will shame even those who think us inferior only because we are different. To those who believe in the power of the written word these books will proclaim our cultural worth. It has been done so for other races and their teachings. This is how our young people will bring to you the true image of our native people and destroy the distortion of which we have been the victims for so long. Then we will prosper in all things. From our children will come those braves, who will carry the torches to the places where our ancestors rest. There, we will bow our heads and chant the song of their honor. This is how the void will be filled between the old and the new ways.
>
> Chief Dan George, Squamish elder (1899-1981)

Endnotes

1. At the time of this writing, 558 tribes/nations are recognized by the United States of America, with more than 100 additional applications for recognition in progress; some are state recognized but not federally recognized.

2. The terms, "Indigenous," "Native," "Indian," and "American Indian/Alaska Native" are used interchangeably and capitalized to refer to the first "native" people of this country and their descendants.
3. The term, "Indian Country," is capitalized and used to describe the urban, rural, and reservation areas where the first Native people of this country and their descendants live.

References

Adoption and Safe Families Act (ASFA) of 1997 (P.L. 105-89)

Briar-Lawson, K., Lawson, H., Peterson, N., Harris, N., Derezotes, D., Sallee, A., and Hoffman, T. (1999.) Addressing the co-occurring needs of public sector families challenged by domestic violence, substance abuse, mental illness, child abuse and poverty. Paper presented at Society for Social Work Research, Austin, Texas.

Brooks, D., Barth, R. P., Bussiere, A., and Patterson, G. (1999). Adoption and race: Implementing the multiethnic placement act and the interethnic adoption provisions. *Social Work 44*(2). pp. 167-178.

Brown, E. F. (1998, Apr.). Closing remarks. Welfare reform impacts on tribal social services: A national forum. National Congress of American Indians. April 23, 1998.

Brown, E. F. and Pandey, S. (1999). Implementation of the temporary assistance for needy families (TANF) on American Indian reservations: Early evidence from Arizona. St. Louis: George Warren Brown School of Social Work.

Bureau of Indian Affairs. (1989). Guidelines for State Courts: Indian Child Welfare Proceedings. Washington, DC: Author. November 26, 1989. D.2.

Cross, T. (1998a). Welfare of children: Child abuse and neglect. Presented at the National Council of American Indians Welfare Reform Forum. April 22, 1998. Portland, OR.

Cross, T. (1998b, Jul.). Understanding new and changing legislation - ASFA, ICWA, MEPA - The impact on tribal family preservation. Panel presented at Children's Bureau conference, Family Preservation the Indian Way: Bringing it back. Washington, DC.

Duran, E. and Duran, B. (1995). *Native American postcolonial psychology*. Albany, NY: State University of New York (SUNY) Press.

Edwards, E. D. and Egbert-Edwards, M. (1998). Social work practice with American Indians and Alaskan Natives. In A. T. Morales & B. S. Shaefor (Eds.). *Social work: A profession of many faces*. Boston: Allyn and Bacon.

—. (1994). *Native American Indian values: Their application to children and families*. Unpublished, University of Utah, Salt Lake City.

—. (1989). The American Indian Child Welfare Act: Achievements and recommendations. In J. Hudson & B. Galaway (Eds.). *The state as parent: International research perspectives on interventions with young persons.* Dordreicht, The Netherlands: Kluwer Academic Publishers. pp. 37-51.

George, Chief Dan. (1974, 1990). *My heart soars.* Blaine, WA: Hancock House Publishers.

Gooden, I. H. Personal communication. July 1998.

GAO - Government Accounting Office. (1997). *Foster care: State efforts to improve permanency planning show some promise.* Letter Report, GAO/HEHS No. 97-73.

Hauptman, L. M. (1995). *Tribes and tribulations: Misconceptions about American Indians and their histories.* Albuquerque, NM: University of New Mexico Press.

Horejsi, C., Heavy Runner Craig, B., and Pablo, J. (1992). Reactions by Native American parents to child protection agencies: Cultural and community factors. *Child Welfare, 71*(4). Washington, DC: Child Welfare League of America, Inc. pp. 329-342.

Hunt, D. E., Esquibel, A. B., and Begay, S. J. (1999). Culturally competent family-centered practice with American Indian people. Austin, TX: Family Preservation Institute.

Indian Child Welfare Program: Hearings Before the Subcommittee on Indian Affairs of the Senate Committee on Interior and Insular Affairs, 93rd Congress, 2d Session, 15 (1974).

Indian Child Welfare Act of 1978, 25 U.S.C. § 1901, et al. (1978).

Interethnic Adoptions Provision (IAP): see "Removal of Barriers" below.

Johnson, M. J. (1992). "American Indians and Alaska Natives with disabilities." In P. Cahape & C. B. Howley (Eds.). *Indian Nations At Risk: Listening to the People.* Charleston, WV: ERIC Clearinghouse on Rural Education and Small Schools. pp. 86-92.

Jones, B. J. (2000). The Indian Child Welfare Act: In search of a federal forum to vindicate the rights of Indian tribes and children against the vagaries of state courts. *Pathways Practice Digest.* (March 2000). Portland, OR: National Indian Child Welfare Association, Inc. pp. 1-2, & 5.

Lewis, L. (1998). The impact of cultural differences on the treatment of American Indian sex offenders. Unpublished, University of Utah, Salt Lake City.

McNevins, M. (2000). A family unity & group decision model: The advanced skill of building on strengths. *Pathways Practice Digest.* (January 2000). Portland, OR: National Indian Child Welfare Association, Inc. pp. 1-2, & 5.

Melmer, D. (2000). Montana supreme court uphold ICWA. *Indian Country Today, 19*(41). Rapid City, SD: Indian Country Today. March 29, 2000. A1.

MMWR - Morbidity and Mortality Weekly Report. (1994). "Prevalence and characteristic of alcohol consumption and fetal alcohol awareness." Alaska, 1991 and 1993, 43. pp. 3-6.

Moran, J. A. (1999). Preventing alcohol use among urban American Indian youth: The seventh generation program. In H. Weaver (Ed.). *Voices of first nation people: Human service considerations.* New York: Haworth Press, Inc. pp. 106-126.

Multiethnic Placement Act (MEPA) of 1994 (P.L. 103-82)

National Conference of State Legislatures. (1997). *Welfare and Human Services.* Available: www.ncsl.org/programs/csnr/tribe.htm .

National Congress of American Indians. [undated]. Available: http://ncai.org/indiani9ssues/WelfareReform/WRkellog.htm .

National Indian Child Welfare Association, Inc. (1996). *Cross-cultural skills in Indian child welfare: A guide for the non-Indian.* Portland, OR: Author.

National Indian Justice Center. (1998). *Phase III final report: Child abuse and neglect in American Indian and Alaska Native communities and the role of the Indian Health Service.* Petaluma, CA.

Noseep, F. and Powell, G. A. (1999, Nov.). 'Welcome house' in the community: Safe-haven for children and families in crisis. *Pathways Practice Digest.* Portland, OR: National Indian Child Welfare Association, Inc. p. 3.

Personal Responsibility and Work Opportunity Reconciliation Act of 1996, Temporary Assistance to Needy Families (TANF)

Plantz, M. (1989). Indian Child welfare: A status report. *Children Today.* pp. 24-29.

Rash of Indian Suicides. (1998, Feb. 8). *The Bellingham Herald,* p. A5.

Removal of Barriers to Interethnic Adoption of 1996 (Interethnic Adoption Provisions [IAP], P.L. 104-88)

Sachs, S., Harris, L., Morris, B., and Hunt, D. (1999, Sep.). Recreating the circle: Overcoming colonialism and returning to harmony in American Indian communities. Unpublished paper; presented at the American Political Science Association, Annual Program Meeting, Native Studies Section, Atlanta, Georgia. September 2-5, 1999.

Shook, K. (1998). Assessing the consequences of welfare reform for child welfare. *Poverty Research News 2*(1). pp. 1-13. Available: http://jcpr.org/98winter/index.html

Simmons, D. and Trope, J. (1999). *P.L. 105-89: Adoption and safe families act of 1997. Issues for tribes and states serving Indian children.* Portland, Maine: The National Resource Center for Organizational Improvement, Edmund S. Muskie School of Public Service, University of Southern Maine.

Skinner, L. (1992). Teaching through traditions: Incorporating native languages and cultures into curricula. In P. Cahape & C.B. Howley (Eds.). *Indian Nations At Risk: Listening to the People*. Charleston, WV: ERIC Clearinghouse on Rural Education and Small Schools. pp. 54-29.

Thorne, W. (1997). *Beginning and advanced tracks on ICWA*. Third annual Native American Law Symposium. Salt Lake City, UT: University of Utah, College of Law.

Three Feathers Associates. (1989). The status of American Indian families. *Indian Child Welfare Digest*. August-September. pp. 11-12.

Timas, A. and Reedy, R. (1998). Implementation of cultural-specific interventions for a Native American community. *Journal of Clinical Psychology, 5*(3). pp. 382-393.

Tsoi Goodluck, C. (1993). Social services with Native Americans: Current status of the Indian Child Welfare Act. In McAdoo, H.P. (Ed.). *Family Ethnicity: Strength in Diversity*. Newbury Park, CA: SAGE Publications. pp. 217-226.

United States Census Bureau. (1999). Resident population estimates of the United States by sex, race, and Hispanic origin: April 1, 1990 to October 1, 1999 and other reports. Available: http://www.census.gov/populations/estimates/nation/intfile3-1.txt

Weaver, H. (1999). Indigenous people and the social work profession: Defining culturally competent services. *Social Work, 44*(3). New York: National Association of Social Workers, Inc.

Yellow Bird, M. and Chenault, V. (1999). The role of social work in advancing the practice of Indigenous education: Obstacles and promises in empowerment-oriented social work practice. In K.G. Swisher and J. W. Tippeconnic III (Eds.). *Next steps: Research and practice to advance Indian education*. Charleston, WV: ERIC Clearinghouse on Rural Education and Small Schools.

ICWA Resources

Indian Child Welfare Law Center, 1433 E. Franklin, Minneapolis, MN 55404; telephone 612.879.9165; http://www.glrain.net/icwalc/index.html

National Congress of American Indians, 1301 Connecticut Ave NW, Ste 200, Washington, DC 20036; telephone 202.466.7767; http://www.ncai.org

National Indian Child Welfare Association, 3611 SW Hood St, Ste 201, Portland, OR 97201; telephone 530.222.4044; http://www.nicwa.org

National Indian Justice Center, The McNear Building, #7 Fourth St, Ste 46, Petaluma, CA 94952; telephone 707.762.8113; http://nijc.indian.com

Native American Rights Funds, 1503 Broadway, Boulder, CO 80302; telephone 303.447.8760; http://www.narf.org

Chapter 10
Spiritual Issues in Practice with Vulnerable Children and Families

David Derezotes and Tracie Hoffman

Introduction

This chapter was written as an introductory guide to assessment of and intervention with spiritual factors in practice with vulnerable children and families. Although interest in spirituality reappeared in North American helping professions during the last quarter of the twentieth century, the professional literature remains relatively theory-rich and practice-poor in this important domain. In addition, most of the existing literature on spirituality and practice has focused on direct practice (rather than indirect practice), thus adding to the ongoing and unnecessary duality between micro and macro levels of practice. Because of this, the authors have taken a generalist approach that includes both direct and indirect practice.

Following a section on definitions, the chapter contains a section on transference and countertransference, which is an essential process for the practitioner to understand. Then a discussion of assessment and intervention in micro (or direct) level practice is followed by a discussion of issues in meso and macro (or indirect) level practice.

What Is Spirituality?

The effective practitioner recognizes that there is a diversity of spiritual and religious perspectives and that many clients have strong feelings about how religion has impacted spirituality in their lives. Spirituality can be viewed as an individual dimension of human development, interrelated with the physical, emotional, cognitive, and social dimensions development, which expresses the evolving need for connection with both the human soul and the universe. The Greek root of the word literally means the "breath of life" and thus can be thought of as a process in which the individual may move towards such "higher" states of well-being as altered consciousness, enhanced life purpose and meaning, love for and service to others, and peace of mind (Netting, Thibault, & Ellor, 1990; Canda, 1989; Joseph, 1988; Siporin, 1985).

In contrast, religion can be viewed as a social process involving shared rituals, doctrines, and beliefs that may or may not enhance the spirituality of the individuals involved. The Latin root of the word literally means to "bring together" and thus religion creates an institutionalization of practices and beliefs that utilizes a framework of social roles and formal relationships between people (Netting, Thibault, & Ellor, 1990; Joseph, 1988; Siporin, 1985).

A growing number of social workers have called for the inclusion of spiritual/religious content in social work practice. Six arguments used to support this position include: (1) the United States is a highly religious nation (e.g., Wald, 1992; Gallup & Castelli, 1989; Loewenberg, 1988; Marty, 1980); (2) social work considers all aspects of the client and her ecological environment; (3) social work also originated in religious-based charitable organizations; (4) social work values human diversity, including the variety of religious and spiritual beliefs; (5) spirituality and religiosity are highly correlated with psychosocial well-being; and (6) most social workers already consider spiritual and religious issues in their practice (e.g., Worthington, Kurusu, McCullough, & Sandage, 1996; Derezotes, 1995; Cowley & Derezotes, 1993; Sheridan, Bullis, Adock, et al., 1992; Kilpatrick & Holland, 1990; Netting, Thibault, & Ellor, 1990; Denton, 1990; Loewenberg, 1988; Faver, 1987; Siporin, 1985; Meystedt, 1984; and Marty, 1980).

Utilizing Spiritual and Religious Countertransference in Assessment and Intervention

The first and perhaps one of the most important processes in assessment of spiritual and religious factors in social work is the consideration of spiritual and religious transference and countertransference reactions.

In general, transference and countertransference reactions are examined in any thorough case assessment and can help inform the selection of case interventions (Anderson & Stewart, 1983). To review, a transference is any reaction of the <u>client to the social worker</u> and can include cognitive, affective, physical, psychosocial, and\or spiritual responses. Similarly, a countertransference is any reaction of the <u>worker back to the client</u>. There are <u>always</u> transference and countertransference reactions in every therapeutic relationship. These reactions are usually related to <u>both</u> past experiences and the immediate here-and-now experience. For example, a female social worker may instantly feel a dislike for a male client because (a) the client has traits that remind her of her former husband and (b) because the client himself has other traits that she also dislikes.

Countertransferences can be "positive" or "negative," such as (a) a worker who is angry at client, (b) a worker who is scared of a client, or (c) a worker who is sexually attracted to a client. The countertransference can be part of an ongoing pattern in a particular relationship or can be a one-time occurrence between two people.

Social workers can use transference reactions as part of the case assessment. They often are vestiges of past experience. For example, if a client is immediately untrusting of the worker, the worker considers the possibility that other people may have violated the client's trust in the past.

If the worker is unaware of her countertransference with the client, she may well put her own needs ahead of the needs of the client, without even being aware of what is happening. Effective use of countertransference can be seen as central to social work practice with clients (Hepworth and Larsen, 1986). For example, if a worker came from an abusive home herself, she may have learned to withdraw as a child when she became scared by family conflicts. When that worker sees an abusive family system as a professional, even years later, she could easily slip into the same familiar coping style, withdrawing emotionally from a family when she became scared by their behaviors. Unfortunately, the social worker's fear and need to withdraw may not be in the best interests of the children and the family. The family may actually need the social worker to become actively involved, for example, in providing suggestions for interpersonal boundaries and teaching new conflict resolution skills.

If a social worker is aware of the countertransference, then she can use it as part of the case assessment. In general, the social worker asks the following questions: (1) Is it possible that the client or other people in the client's life feel the same way about the client that I do? (2) If the answer to the first question is yes, then what is it probably like to be the client? (3) Finally, how can I use this information to guide my interventions—what does this client need to heal and grow? For example, a worker finds that she dislikes an abusive husband in her practice. The worker assesses that the client's family may all dislike him also. The worker hypothesizes that the client may well feel very alone in his life and tries to address that in the therapy.

Two common forms of countertransferences can be identified (Anderson and Stewart, 1983). Underidentification is the worker's inability to clearly see who the client is because the client reminds the worker of (a) a person he did not like and/or (b) an aspect of himself he does not like. In an underidentification, the worker may respond from her own experience and needs, instead of out of a sensitivity to the client's experience and needs. For example, a worker who was emotionally neglected by her own parents as a child may tend to withdraw empathy and warmth from the neglectful parents she is now working with.

Overidentification is the worker's inability to clearly see who the client is because the client reminds the worker of (a) a person she did like and/or (b) an aspect of herself she likes or desires to have. The worker may again respond from his own experience and needs, instead of out of sensitivity to the client's experience and needs. For example, the same worker who was emotionally neglected by her parents may overidentify with the daughter of the emotionally neglectful parents she is now working with. In this case, the overidentification with the girl victim by the worker might result in the worker assuming the girl feels the same way she did as a child, instead of seeing her as a separate and unique individual.

Religious and Spiritual Transference and Countertransference

Most clients and their social workers have strong transference and countertransference reactions that are associated with spiritual and religious themes. Since spirituality is such an individual process, social workers will have different spiritual landscapes than their clients have. Workers and clients may have strong responses to such differences. Since the majority of people experience religion as being overall either generally supportive of or detrimental to their spirituality, both clients and their social workers may also have strong reactions to any religious differences that exist between them.

Some authors have emphasized how clinical social workers are continuously confronted with spiritual and religious issues that challenge worker and client values (e.g., Canda, 1989, 1988; Kilpatrick & Holland, 1990; Loewenberg, 1988; and Siporin, 1985). These authors have suggested that the practitioner needs to have a clear understanding of her or his own values and beliefs to reduce the risk of imposing them on her client.

Countertransference reactions may be related in part to positive or negative experiences that the worker had in a church or family setting. In general, several steps can be recommended in working with such experiences.

(1) Awareness: The social worker strives to become more aware of all of her feelings, thoughts, and behavioral intentions. Behavioral intentions are our first "knee-jerk" reactions that we would tend to express either verbally and/or physically. As awareness increases, social workers usually develop an ability to identify such reactions more quickly after they first begin.

(2) Acceptance: The social worker also gradually becomes more accepting of all of her feelings, thoughts, and behavioral intentions/impulses. Self-acceptance, just like self-awareness, is a gradual process that continues throughout the life span; impatience with the process tends to impede it.

(3) Assessment: The social worker uses the countertransference reaction to help her assess the client's own past religious experiences and spiritual development. For example, a social worker is working with a family that has a very controlling, religious father. The worker notices that she does not like the father and hypothesizes that the rest of the family may also dislike his use of religion to control. These insights can help the social worker assess the parent's tolerance for spiritual and religious diversity (see Table 1).

(4) Interventions: The social worker differentially selects an intervention response to the client's transference. In selecting interventions, the worker considers her own comfort level, the client system, and any constraints of the practice setting. There is no evidence that any one theoretical approach to dealing with countertransference is more effective than any other (Garfield and Bergin, 1991).

Table 1. Examples of Some Key Spiritual and Religious Assessment and Intervention Issues in Social Work with Children and Families

Intervention Level	Assessment Issues	Intervention Issues
children (micro level)	(1) has opportunity for religious training? (2) is allowed to have and express unique spiritual experiences?	(1) help child understand parental religion (if any) (2) help child develop and express her own spirituality
parents (micro level)	(1) has religious-based parenting, couple, and overall life philosophies? (2) has spiritual experiences and expressions?	(1) foster parent's own spiritual and religious process (2) help parent apply religion and spirituality to parenting and life
family (micro level)	(1) is religious and spiritual diversity respected? (2) does religion or spirituality impact parenting & life	(1) co-create safe environment that fosters freedom to have or not have religious education and allow for all nonviolent spiritual expression (2) co-create nonviolent and nurturing parenting and family behaviors that fit with family's religious and spiritual traditions
community (meso level)	(1) is religious and spiritual diversity respected? (2) does religion or spirituality impact availability of resources and opportunities or social policies?	(1) co-create safe community that fosters freedom to have or not have religious education and allow for all nonviolent spiritual expressions (2) co-create community dialogue among diverse religious and spiritual communities that foster nonviolence and cooperation

Intervention Methods with Children and Families

In general, the worker begins spiritual and religious interventions by considering the spiritual and religious beliefs and rituals that the client already has. Rather than imposing his own beliefs upon the client, the effective worker utilizes the language, metaphors, and rites that the client is comfortable with. The worker does not assume that a client will have certain beliefs just because that client states she belongs to a particular religion, however. Each client is likely to have his own unique spiritual and religious experiences and language.

From the generalist perspective, the best religious and spiritual social work practice with children and families utilizes assessment and intervention strategies on all three individual, family, and community levels (see Table 1). Such social work values as tolerance of diversity, autonomy of the individual, and nonviolent conflict resolution are applied. Table 1 illustrates some examples of key assessment and intervention issues that the worker considers in practice with children and families. For example, row one illustrates how when assessing children, the worker would try to determine whether the child has had opportunities to study religion (especially if the parents are religious) and whether the child has been given freedom to express her own spirituality at home. The worker might intervene by helping the child better understand the religion of her parents (again, if they have one) or to find ways to express her spirituality. Such interventions would be effective if the worker at the same time also works with the parents, the family as a whole, and the community to increase support for religious and spiritual development and diversity around the child.

Social workers are encouraged to use an eclectic approach to interventions with spirituality and religiosity, which is an strategy consistent with the generalist tradition. Since, clinical research suggests that no one method of intervention is overall more effective than the others (Garfield & Bergin, 1994), the social worker is flexible in applying interventions that best match the needs of the client.

The social worker can apply her skills and knowledge in traditional intervention models to spiritual and religious issues.

Psychodynamic Methods

The purpose of Psychodynamic interventions is to help people gain insight into their past experiences so that they can be freed to better get their needs met today. The social worker can first take a spiritual and religious history of the client and family. Such a history includes not only changing religious affiliations within the family, but various spiritual experiences and convictions as well. Special attention can be paid to how the family deals with spiritual and religious diversity; for example, are family members allowed to disagree about spirituality and have different religious beliefs?

The worker can also do a traditional genogram of the intergenerational family, and add elements of spiritual and religious history to the process. The family can take part in these processes, and in doing so gain insight into where they have come from.

Cognitive Behavioral Methods

The purpose of these interventions is to help people change the way they think and act. The social worker can ask the parents to consider how their religious beliefs impact their parenting methods. For example, the adage "spare the rod, spoil the child" may in some cases be used to justify various discipline methods. The worker can ask the parents what their beliefs are in relationship to their children's spirituality and religiosity. For example, should the parent give the children their religion, allow the children to discover religion on their own, or some combination of both?

The worker can also support family members in changing various behavior patterns using formal body-mind-spirit traditions that might help them. For example, the worker might help a troubled young man study a martial art form like Aikido that emphasizes self-discipline and self-control. The worker might encourage a single parent to learn simple yoga and meditation techniques that teach relaxation.

Experiential Methods

The purpose of these interventions is to help people express their feelings in the here and now. The social worker can ask the children and parents to share honestly with one another about how they feel now about spiritual and religious issues. Many children and adults rarely if ever have the opportunity to talk about spirituality and religion in a safe and accepting environment. Although many parents do give their children a religious tradition to build upon, they usually do not listen to their children's direct spiritual experiences. For example, the worker can ask each child and parent in a family to first draw a picture of their spirituality or spiritual path. Then each member is given time to explain their drawing. Other members are instructed to listen without judgement as each person takes her/his turn sharing.

Case Management Methods

Social workers ideally work collaboratively with local clergy, spiritual healers, and other faith-based helpers in the community to better serve common populations in need. However, recent research suggests that less than 1% of clients are referred by their social workers to clergy and that clergy refer less than 5% of the people they serve back to social workers (Webster, 1997). This same research suggests that relationships between faith-based helpers and social workers are key factors associated with collaboration. Therefore, case management must begin with initial and ongoing efforts by the social worker to build collegial relationships with clergy and healers. Forums can be co-hosted by social worker and clergy coordinators during which dialogues between social workers and faith-based workers are held on various topics.

The social worker also has a responsibility to advocate for clients who are discriminated against or oppressed because of their spirituality or religiosity. In some communities, such clients may be agnostics; in other communities, they may be affiliated with Catholics or Muslim or Pagan faith systems.

Intervention Methods with Specific Populations at Risk

Child Abuse and Neglect

With abusive family systems, the worker can sometimes ask religious parents who are perpetrators to consider what they need to do to make peace with their God. Some of these parents feel excessive guilt and shame about their abusive behavior and they require self-forgiveness in order to move on and become better parents. However, other religious parents believe that their God wants them to use certain discipline methods, regardless of whether society accepts them or not. In such cases, sometimes the parent will respond to different interpretations of their religion, particularly when they come from clergy who belong to their faith. In these situations, the worker may, with the client's permission, want to consult with clergy in the community and refer the client to such clergy when appropriate.

Substance Abuse

One way to look at substance abuse is that it is an attempt to change consciousness or spirituality through chemical means. Family members who abuse substances may benefit from a discussion that focuses upon such spiritual issues in substance abuse. The social worker can also try to help the client find alternative methods of changing consciousness that might fit with the client's own spiritual and religious beliefs. For example, a worker may refer a client who is already interested in shamanic practice to a practitioner who specializes in work with altered states of consciousness.

Mental Health

From some spiritual and religious perspectives, various mental health diagnoses can be viewed from alternative perspectives. For example, a social worker may be working with a single father with moderate symptoms of dysthymic disorder. The worker might explain to the father that his depression could be viewed as a message from his soul, rather than just as a symptom to be fixed. Then the client and worker could explore the meaning of the message and its implications.

Unemployment

The word vocation originally referred to a calling from God. Clients who are between jobs or dissatisfied with their work might want to explore the spiritual and religious issues related to their life work. The social worker may try to help a client explore what she feels her true life calling is. Then the worker may act like a mentor and coach, encouraging the client to work towards her dreams. In essence, the task of the social worker is to lovingly carry the client's dreams for her until the client is ready to carry and realize those dreams herself.

Spirituality, Vulnerable Children, and Family Preservation

In connecting spirituality with family preservation, one adage advances a cure-all claim: "The family that prays together, stays together." This old saying is familiar enough to ring "cliche," yet little empirical work has been done to test its promise. Spirituality and family preservation have been largely ignored (Cowley, 1999), though research has been conducted on spirituality and other dimensions of human well being. For example, several studies have scientifically examined the positive effect of prayer on medical conditions (e.g., Bessie, 1999; Coleman, 1999; Dossey & Vandecreek, 1998). Research has been conducted on the effects of spirituality on the coping styles of the frail elderly and other individuals facing death (e.g., Ley & Corless, 1988; Reese & Brown; 1997; Simmons, 1998). Spirituality has been explored as a positive component in recovery from addictions (e.g., Spalding & Metz, 1997; Collier, 1997). Spiritual well being has been found to be the primary factor for resiliency in "suicide survivors" (Fournier, 1997). The role of spirituality has also been explored in diverse cultural communities (e.g., Canda, Shin, & Canda, 1993; Kawulich & Curlette, 1998; Ramirez, 1985; Schiele, 1994; Singh, McKay, & Singh, 1998), with little emphasis placed on spirituality and familial preservation within such communities.

Certain studies point to the empirical link between spirituality and healing from past sexual and physical familial abuse (e.g., Amos, 1995) but *not* on the prevention or elimination of ongoing familial abuse. One study (Lyster, Russell, & Hiebert, 1995) found that remarrying couples primarily valued the spiritual components of remarriage preparation programs, suggesting the failure of earlier marriages was credited to a lack of spirituality in former unions. However, most accounts of the impact of intrafamilial spirituality are excluded from empirical social work literature (Thayne, 1997). However, much information can be found within the realm of popular, nonacademic, publications. These popular accounts are largely descriptive (Crosby, 1997), instructive (Fuchs, 1996; Mitchell, 1996; Nappa, & Nappa, 1996), and anecdotal (Collard-Miller, 1997) versus experimental or even associational. Thus, we have very little scientific data regarding the potentially causal or associated relationship between of spirituality and family cohesiveness (Cowley, 1999). In order to design effective micro, meso, and macro level treatment interventions, social workers must empirically examine the effect of prayer, spirituality, and religion on family preservation.

The Paucity of Spiritual Social Work Resources for Vulnerable Children and Families

Much of our contemporary rhetoric equates "family" and "religio-spiritual values" and credits these values with the preservation of families (Stanley, 1998). Of course, the popular definition of the "intact nuclear family" does not encompass the inclusive constellation of definitions embraced by the social work profession. The National Association of Social Workers defines a family as "a grouping that consists of two or more individuals who define themselves as a family and who, over time, assume those obligations to one another that are generally considered an essential component of family systems" (NASW, 1982, p. 10). While there has been a call for the incorporation of spirituality in diverse family social work research, literature, and treatment (Prest & Keller, 1993), these interrelated domains have remained largely unaddressed.

Even those families who have historically been championed by social work, and marginalized by larger society, have mainly been left to seek spiritual assistance for family growth outside of the social work profession. Self-help groups and books, along with religiously based publications (Jacobs, 1997), have dominated spiritually inclusive, vulnerable-family preservation strategies. For example, public bookstores offer family-based spiritual literature for helping families with disabled children (Webb-Mitchell, 1993), families who have lost a child (e.g., O'Keefe-Lafser, 1998), family members living with AIDS (e.g., Tilleraas, 1988), feminist family members (e.g., Proctor-Smith, 1995; Winter, 1991), the dying and their families (e.g.,

Davidson, 1994; Mc Nees, 1998), African-American families (e.g., Archibald, 1997; Washington, 1995); other families of color and families from diverse cultural backgrounds (e.g., Roberts & Amidon, 1991; Twohy, 1990; Vanzant, 1996), the chronically fatigued (e.g., Vanderzalm, 1998), homosexual individuals and their families (e.g., Clark, 1991; Glaser, 1991), working mothers (Whelchel, 1999), and families with aging parents (e.g., Mc Kenna, 1994).

Self-help literature also includes a myriad of books to aid couples in building spiritual bonds into relationships (e.g., Cohen, 1996; Kaplan & Prince, 1999; Markway & Markway, 1996; Parot & Parot, 1997); and helping vulnerable parents incorporate spirituality into child-rearing (e.g., Bria, 1998; Cataflo, 1997; Collard-Miller, 1997; Crosby, 1997; Davidson-Jenkins, 1995; Mitchell, 1996; Nappa & Nappa, 1996; van Zwelt, 1998; Wright, 1997). Spiritual self-help books for family social workers and other caregivers are also available at the public book store (e.g., Hutchison & Rapp, 1999; Hunter, 1985; Normile, 1995). Some popular literature even directly addresses spirituality in family practice (e.g., Stroh-Becvar, 1998; Walsh, 1999) but rarely do these books offer insights on how to incorporate the social worker's spiritual framework with those of family clients. Popular spiritual literature for family clients and social workers, respectively, tends to be segregated, and all but ignores the possible synergy of both client and social worker framing their collaborative work in a spiritual framework.

A small body of professional literature includes the therapeutic potential of this synergy. Judah (1985) proposed "The Sacramental Model of Professional Service" in which the worker and individual/child/family clients acknowledge the sacred nature of the helping relationship. Social workers who have integrated their own spirituality in the spectrum of social work practice report increased gratification and effectiveness for both themselves and their clients (e.g., Canda, 1988; Sheridan, 1995; Sherwood, D.A., 1998; Sneck & Bonica, 1980). Graham, Kaiser, & Garrett (1998) propose that spirituality has always been a synergistic factor in effective interventions with vulnerable populations, though practitioners have not historically "named" this "hidden" factor.

Meso-Level Spiritual Interventions for Vulnerable Families and Children

Identifying the spiritual nature of social work can be very powerful, not only in direct, micro practice, but also in meso-level interventions with vulnerable individuals, children, and families (Judah, 1985). In Salt Lake City for example, "family experts" (parent clients) and professionals from Child Protective Services, Workforce Services (TANF), Substance Abuse Agencies, the local school system, and other family assistance departments, joined in an effort to coordinate welfare reform strategies. As an initial exercise, all were asked to pictorially represent their perceptions of their respective vocations in relation to family preservation. Subsequently, in small groups, all participants verbally shared their perceptions. Of interest, family experts and professionals alike shared primarily spiritual convictions about their roles...and notably similar convictions. When asked about their experience, participants reported a new sense of dedication to their work as parents and professionals, as well as an intensified sense of enlightened collaboration with one another (Derezotes & Hoffman, 1998). This sense of "mutual mission" was sustained over two and a half years of monthly family expert/professional meetings.

Spirituality is also being utilized in strengthening friendships (Caltagirone, 1989; Chervin, 1992; Dunne, 1996), thus reinforcing informal child and family support networks. Interestingly, utilizing spiritual exercises for developing extra-familial, interpersonal group support is becoming increasingly common outside the field of social work (Riddle, 1995). Even Corporate America is beginning to recognize the importance of spirituality in strengthening and preserving collegial relationships. Some contemporary recommendations for management include strategies for using the spiritual resources of employees in team building (e.g., Marcie & Crocker, 1997).

Spirituality in Micro, Meso, and Macro Level Social Work Education with Vulnerable Children and Families

Social Work is a profession embedded in ethics and linked to a history of religion and charity. Contemporarily, the National Association of Social Workers' (NASW) "Code of Ethics" is largely composed of arguably spiritual principles, including well-being, service, justice, the worth of the individual, and the importance of relationships (NASW, 1997). Yet, we often tend to cringe, rather than rejoice, at being described as "caring" or "bleeding hearts" by those who perceive such characteristics as inconsistent with professional family practice. Some argue that, as social work attempted to join the ranks of the human "sciences," the profession concurrently sought to distance itself from religious roots in order to gain the sterile respect due an "objective academic discipline" (e.g., Goldstein, 1990; Holland, 1989). This may partially account for the veritable dearth of empirical social work literature dealing with the *impact* of spirituality on micro, meso, and macro family concerns. However, some feel that the quest for scientific purity does not justify, nor necessitate, the exclusion of spiritual or religious issues from the comprehensive spectrum of vulnerable child and family needs which social work educators study and address (e.g., Sistler, 1999).

Divine/Human connection has historically incorporated the micro, meso, and macro perspective (Heschel, 1998). Throughout global history, deities charged with overseeing human affairs have been assigned a range of worldly concerns. For example, the Greek Goddess, "Hestia," was delegated the duties of dealing with mortal pleas for self, family, community, and the earth in general. (Waldherr, 2000).

Similarly, creation and accounts of intercessory practices from around the planet share themes of Divinity managing the spectrum of micro-level individual and family concerns, meso-level issues related to groups of people, and macro-level considerations of the natural world (Roberts, & Amidon, 1991; Strickland, 1997). Extending this ancient mico/meso/macro continuum to contemporary social work curricula, it seems consistent to include family spirituality within a generalist framework (Cowley & Derezotes, 1994).

It is important to acknowledge that the study of individual, child, and family spirituality *is* finding a place in Social Work. The Council on Social Work Education has recently called for the inclusion of spirituality in social work curricula. However, at present, many students report being ill-prepared by schools of social work to deal with spiritual concerns when intervening, at all levels of practice, with vulnerable individuals, children, and families (Kaplan & Dziegielewski, 1999; Joseph, 1988; Sheridan & Hemert, 1999). Similarly, many practitioners report a sense of inadequate training in dealing with these sensitive issues (Derezotes & Evans, 1995).Thus, on micro, meso, and macro levels, it is important that accredited schools of social work, as well as continuing education programs, include generalist course work on spirituality and vulnerable individuals, children, and families.

Macro Level Spiritual Interventions with Vulnerable Children and Families

Many authors have debated the importance of including spirituality in dialogue regarding family social policy (e.g., Goodison, 1992; Hoyt-Oliver, 1998). This inclusion is no longer exclusively a matter of theoretical debate. Hodge (1998), in an article titled, "Welfare reform and religious providers: an examination of the new paradigm," details a radical shift in spirituality and family social policy. Hodge notes the following regarding 1996 federal welfare reform legislation: "The most significant changes are found in Section 104 which redefines the role of religious providers. The new provision grants states the option of contracting with sectarian religious providers on the same basis as any other private provider for the delivery of federally funded services" (p. 24). In Texas and New Jersey, evidence suggests that social services delivered to individuals, children, and families were more effectively provided by "faith-based social work services" (*The Economist 2000*, p. 28) than by "traditional" government social work services. Despite arguments about the separation between church and state, Senator John Ashcroft has initiated federal legislation that would expand the reimbursement of religious services in delivering social services to vulnerable individuals, children, and families. Unfortunately, a study conducted at the University of Utah (Webster, 1996) revealed a very low level of referrals from social workers to clergy and, reciprocally, from clergy to social workers. The study also indicated that collaboration between social workers and clergy, in micro, meso, and macro practice, was infrequent as well. It appears that the time has come when social workers can no longer afford to fight what Kornfeld (1997) terms, "turf wars over mind, body, and spirit" (p. 75). Theoretically, as well as practically, generalist child and family interventions must include the dimension of spirituality. Further, we must foster collaboration between social workers and clergy in work with vulnerable children and families across the micro, meso, and macro dimensions of practice.

References

Anderson, C. A. and Stewart, S. (1983). *Mastering resistance: A practical guide to family therapy*. New York: Guilford Press.

Amos, W. E. (1995). Revisiting the Sins of the fathers: responding to adult survivors of abuse. *Journal-of-Family-Ministry, 9*(1): 43-51.

Archibald, C. M.(Ed.). (1997). *Say "amen": The African American family's book of prayers*. New York City: Penguin Putnam Inc.

Bax, M. (Ed.) (1993) *Power and Prayer: Religious and political processes in the past and present*. Amsterdam: V. U. University Press.

Benningfield, M. F. (1997) Addressing spiritual/religious issues in therapy: potential problems and complications. *Journal of Family Social Work, 2*(4): 25-42, 1997.

Bergin, A. E. and Garfield, S. L. (1994). *Handbook of psychotherapy and behavior change*. New York: John Wiley & Sons Inc.

Brady, M. (1995). *Daybreak: Meditations for women survivors of sexual abuse*. Center City, MN: Hazelden Information and Educational Services.

Caltagirone, Carmen L. (1989). *Friendship as a sacrament*. New York City: Alba House.

Canda, E. R. (1995). Editorial: The reflecting pool. *Reflections, 1*(4): 2-4, Fall 1995.

Canda E. R. (1988). Conceptualizing spirituality for social work: insights from diverse perspectives. *Social Thought, 14*(1): 30-46, Winter.

Canda, E. R. (1988). Spiritual diversity and social work practice. *Social Casework, 69*(4), 238-47.

Canda, E. R. (1988). Spirituality, religious diversity, and social work practice. *Social Casework, 69*(4), 238-247.

Canda, E. R. (1989). Religious content in social work education: A comparative approach. *Journal of Social Work Education, 25*(1), 36-45.

Cowley, A. S., and Derezotes, D. (1993). Transpersonal psychology and social work education. Mimeo. University of Utah, Salt Lake City, UT.

Denton, R. T. (1990). The religiously fundamentalist family: Training for assessment and treatment. *Journal of Social Work Education, 26*(1), 6-14.

Derezotes, D. S. (1995). Spiritual and religious factors in practice: Empirically-based recommendations for social work education. *Arete, 20*(1), 1-15.

Derezotes, D. S. and Hoffman, T. L. (1998). *New century/I.P.E.T. Grants: Utah Design Team—November Quarterly Report.* Graduate School of Social Work, University of Utah. Unpublished Document.

Dossey, L. and Vandecreek, L. (Eds.) (1998). *Scientific and pastoral perspectives on intercessory prayer: An exchange between Larry Dossey, MD, and Health Care Chaplains.* Author.

Dunne, J. S. (1996). *The music of time: Words and music of spiritual friendship.* Notre Dame, IN: University of Notre Dame Press.

Faver, C. A. (1987). Religious beliefs, professional values and social work. *Journal of Applied Social Science, 11*(2), 207-219.

Fournier, R. R (1997). *The role of spiritual well-being as a resource for coping with stress in bereavement among suicide survivors.* Boston, MA: Boston College.

Fuchs, N. (1996). *Our share of night, our share of morning: Parenting as a spiritual journey.* San Francisco, C: Harper/Collins.

Gallup, G. and Castelli, J. (1989). *The people's religion.* New York: MacMillan Publishing Company.

Glaser, C. (1991). *Coming out to God: Prayers for lesbian and gay men, their family and friends.* Louisville, KY: Westminster John Knox Press.

Goodison, L. (1992). *Moving heaven and earth: Sexuality, spirituality and social change.* New York City: New York University Press.

Graham, M. A., Kaiser, T., and Garrett, K. J. (1998). Naming the spiritual: the hidden dimension of helping. *Social-Thought, 18*(4), 49-61.

Goldstein, H. (1990). The knowledge base of social work practice: theory, wisdom, analogue, or art? *Families in Society: The Journal of Contemporary Human Services.*

Hepworth, D. H. and Larsen, J. A. (1986). *Direct social work practice: Theory and skills* (Second edition). Chicago, IL: Dorsey Press.

Heschel, A. J. (1998). *Man's quest for God: Studies in prayer and symbolism.* New York City: Aurora Press, Inc.

Hodge, D. R. (1988). Welfare reform and religious providers: an examination of the new paradigm. *Social Work and Christianity, 25*(1), 24-48.

Hoyt-Oliver, J. (1998). Integrating faith and the study of social policy: translating God's will into earthen vessels. *Social Work and Christianity, 2*(2), 130-144.

Hutchison, J. and Rupp, J. (1999). *May I walk you home: Courage and comfort for caregivers of the very ill.* Notre Dame, IN: Ave Maria Press.

Hunter, R. L. (1985). *Helping when it hurts: A practical guide to helping relationships.* Minneapolis, MN: Augsburg Fortress Pubs.

Jacobs, C. (1997). Essay on spirituality and social work practice. *Smith College Studies in Social Work, 67*(2), 171-175.

Joseph, M. V. (1988). Religion and social work practice. *Social Casework, 60*(7), 443-452.

Judah, E. H. (1985).A spirituality of professional service: a sacramental model. *Social Thought, 11*(4), 25-35, 1985.

Kaplan, A. J. and Dziegielewski, S. F. (1999). Graduate social work students' attitudes and behaviors toward spirituality and religion: issues for education and practice. *Social Work and Christianity, 26* (1), 25-39.

Kaplan, B. and Prince, G. (1999). *Soul dating to soul mating: On the path toward spiritual partnership.* New York City: Berkeley Publishing Group.

Kawulich, B. B. and Curlette, W. L. (1998) Life tasks and Native American perspectives. *The Journal of Individual Psychology, 54*(3): 359-367.

Kirkpatrick, A. C. and Holland, T. P. (1990). Spiritual dimensions of practice. *The Clinical Supervisor, 8*(2), 125-140.

Kirkpatrick, A. C. and Holland, T. P. (1990). Spiritual dimensions of practice. *The Clinical Supervisor, 8*(2), 125-140.

Logan, J. (1995). *Reclaiming surrendered ground: Protecting your family from spiritual attacks.* Chicago, IL: Moody Press.

Loewenberg, F. M. (1988). *Religion and social work practice in contemporary American society.* New York: Columbia University Press.

Kornfeld, M. (1997). Integrating spirituality and psychotherapy: what can happen when we stop our turf wars over mind body, and spirit. *American Journal of Pastoral Counseling, 1*(1) 75-86.

Kreutziger, S. S. (1995). Spirituality in faith. *Reflections, 1*(4): 28-35, Fall 1995.

Krill, D. F. (1995). My spiritual sojourn into existential social work. *Reflections, 1*(4), 57-64.

Leehan, J. (1993). *Defiant hope: Spirituality for survivors of family abuse.* Louisville, KY: Westminster John Knox Press.

Ley, D. C. H. and Corless, I. B.(1988). Spirituality and hospice care. *Death Studies, 12*(2), 101-10.

Lyster, R. F., Russell, M. N., and Hiebert, J. (1995). Preparation for remarriage: Consumer views. *Journal of Divorce and Remarriage, 24*(¾), 143-57.

Marcic, D. and Crocker, C. (Eds). (1997). *Managing with the wisdom of love: Uncovering virtue in people and organizations.* San Francisco, CA: Jossey-Bass Inc., Publishers.

Markway, B. G. and Markway, G. P. (1996). *Illuminating the heart: steps toward a more spiritual marriage.* Oakland, CA: New Harbinger Publications.

Marty, M. E. (1980). Social service: Godly and Godless. *Social Service Review, 54*(4), 457-481.

Mc Kenna, D. L. (1994). *When our parents need us most: Loving care in the aging years.* Colorado Springs, CO: Harold Shaw Publishers.

McNees, P. (1998). *Dying: A book of comfort*. Boston, MA: Warner Books.

Meystedt, D. M. (1984). Religion and the rural population: Implications for social work. *Social Casework*, April, 219-226.

Mitchell, J. (1996). *Home, sweeter home: Creating a haven of simplicity and spirit*. Berkeley, CA: Beyond Words Publishing.

Nakashima, M. (1995). Spiritual growth through hospice social work. *Reflections*. *1*(4): 17-27.

Nappa, M. and Nappa, A. (1996). *52 fun family prayer adventures: Creative ways to pray together*. Minneapolis, MN: Augsburg Fortress Pubs.

National Association of Social Workers. (1982). Changes in NASW family policy. *NASW News, 27*, (2).

National Association of Social Workers. (1997). *NASW code of ethics*. Washington, D.C.: Author.

Netting, F. E., Thibault, J. M., and Ellor, J. W. (1990). Integrating content on organized religion into macropractice courses. *Journal of Social Work Education, 26*(1), 15-24.

Normile, P. (1995). *Prayers for caregivers*. Notre Dame, IN: Saint Anthony Messenger Press.

O'Keefe-Lafser, C. (1998). *An empty cradle, a full heart: Reflections for mothers and fathers after miscarriage, stillbirth, or infant death*. Chicago, IL: Loyola Press.

Parot, L. and Parot, L. (1997). *Becoming soul mates: Cultivating spiritual intimacy in the early years of marriage*. Grand Rapids, MI: Zondervan Publishing House.

Prest, L. A. and Keller, J. F. (1993). Spirituality and family therapy: spiritual beliefs, myths, and metaphors. *Journal of Marital and Family Therapy, 19*(2), 137-48.

Proctor-Smith, M. (1995). *Praying with our eyes open: Engendering Feminist Liturgical Prayer*. Abington: Abingdon Press.

Ramirez, R. (1985). Hispanic spirituality. *Social Thought, 11*(3), 6-13.

Reese, D. J. and Brown, D. R. (1997). Psychosocial and spiritual care in hospice: differences between nursing, social work, and clergy. *Hospice Journal, 12*(1), 29-41.

Rey, Greta. (1996). *For caregivers, with love*. New Bedford, CT: Baker books.

Riddle, C. (1995) *The Pathe to love is the practice of love: An introduction to spirituality with self-help exercises for small groups*. Tallahassee, FL: Findhorn Press.

Roberts, E. and Amidon, E. (Eds.) (1991). *Earth prayers from around the world*. San Francisco, CA: Harper/Collins.

Schiele, J. H. (1994). Afrocentricity as an alternative world view for equality. *Journal of Progressive Human Services, 5*(1), 5-25.

Sheridan, M. J. (1995). Honoring angels in my path: spiritually-sensitive group work with persons who are incarcerated. *Reflections, 1*(4), 5-16.

Sheridan, M. J. and Hemert, K. A. (1999). The role of religion and spirituality in social work education and practice: a survey of student views and experiences. *Journal of Social Work Education, 35*(1), 125-141.

Sheridan, M. J., Bullis, R. K., Adcock, C. R., Berlin, S. D., and Miller, P. C. (1992). Practitioners' personal and professional attitudes and behaviors toward religion and spirituality: Issues for education and practice. *Journal of Social Work Education, 28*(2), 190-203.

Sherwood, D. A. (1998). Spiritual assessment as a normal part of social work practice: power to help and power to harm. *Social Work and Christianity, 25*(2), 80-90.

Singh, M. N., McKay, J. D., and Singh, A. N. (1998). Culture and mental health: nonverbal communication. *Journal of Child and Family Studies, 7*(4), 403-409.

Siporin, M. (1985). Current social work perspectives on clinical practice. *Clinical Social Work Journal, 13*(3), 198-217.

Sistler, A. (1998). Christian reflections on the social work research process. *Social Work and Christianity, 25*(2): 145-153, Fall 1998.

Simmons, H. C. (1998). Spirituality and community in the last stage of life. *Journal of Gerontological Social Work, 29*(2/3): 73-91.

Sneck, W. J. and Bonica, R. P. (1981). Attempting the integration of psychology and spirituality. *Social Thought, 6*(3), 27-36.

Spalding, A. D. and Mertz, G. J. (1997). Spirituality and quality of life in Alcoholics Anonymous. *Alcoholism Treatment Quarterly, 15*(1), 1-14.

Stanley, C. F. (1998). *Protecting your family: Develop the spiritual warfare skills necessary for defending your family*. Nashville, TN: Thomas Nelson Publishers.,

Strickland, T. (1997). *One Earth, one spirit: A child's book of prayers from many faiths and cultures*. San Francisco: CA: Sierra Club Books for Children.

Stroh-Becvar, D. (Ed.). (1998). *The family, spirituality, and social work*. Hagerstown, MD: Haworth Press, Inc.

Thayne, T. (1997). Opening space for clients' religious and spiritual values in therapy: a social constructionist perspective. *Journal of Family Social Work, 2*(4), 13-23.

The Economist. (2000). Faith based social work. 2/12/00. p. 28.

Thornton, E. E. (1977). Spirituality and pastoral care. *Journal of Pastoral Care, 31*(2), 73-96.

Tilleraas, P. (1988) *The color of light: Daily meditations for all of us living with AIDS*. San Francisco: Harper and Row.

Tulku, T. (1994). *The world peace ceremony: Prayers at holy places, 1989-1994*. Berkeley, CA: Dharma Publishing.

Twohy, P. J. (1990). *Finding a way home: Indian and Catholic spiritual paths of the Plateau Tribes*. Author.

van Zwet, J. (1998). *My kids grow and so do I: A parent's toolbox for practical spirituality*. Los Gatos, CA: Ascad Communications, Inc.

Vanderzalm, L. (1998). *Spiritual sunlight for the weary: Meditations for the chronically fatigued.* Colorado Springs, CO: Harold Shaw Publishing..

Vanzant, I. (1996). *Acts of faith: Daily meditations for people of color.* New York City: Simon and Schuster Trade.

Wald, K. D. (1992). *Religion and politics in the United States,* (2nd ed.), Washington D.C.: Congressional Quarterly Inc.

Walsh, F. (1999). *Spiritual resources in family therapy.* New York City: Guilford Press.

Washington, J. M.(Ed.). (1995). *Conversations with God: Two centuries of prayers by African Americans.* San Francisco, CA: Harper Trade.

Webb-Mitchell, B. (1993). *God plays piano, too: The spiritual lives of disabled children.* New York City: Crossroad Publishing Co.

Webster, L. J. (1997). *Clergy-social work interface in the provision of mental health care: Implications for social work practice, education, policy, and research.* Dissertation, Graduate School of Social Work, University of Utah.

Whelchel, M. (1999). *Quiet moments for working women.* Ann Arbor, MI: Servant Publications.

Winter, M. T. (1991). *Woman wisdom: A feminist lectionary and psalter.* New York City: Crossroad Publishing Co.

Worthington, E. L., Kurusu, T. A., McCullough, M. E., and Sandage, S. J. (1996). Empirical research on religion and psychotherapeutic processes and outcomes: A 10-year review and research prospectus. *Psychological Bulletin, 119*(3), 448-487.

Wright, W. M. (1997) *Sacred dwelling: A spirituality of family life.* Leavenworth, KS: Forest of Peace Publishing,, Inc.

Chapter 11
Parenting, Caregiving Stress, and Child Abuse and Neglect

Blanca M. Ramos

Introduction

The aim of this chapter is to examine the stress and coping dynamics of the family caregiving process as they relate to parent/child dyads. A major gap in the caregiving literature is the lack of attention paid to parents, particularly mothers, who provide care for their non-disabled children and adolescents. Studies and practices that frame parenting of children and youth, with its accompanying stressors, in the context of caregiving stress are virtually non-existent. This chapter draws on the abundant literature on elderly caregiving to show parallels between parenting and other types of caregiving as sources of stress. The general argument to be presented is that stress exposure, particularly of an environmental nature such as poverty and discrimination, may have deleterious effects among vulnerable families. Some of these deleterious effects may include the abuse and neglect of children by their parents.

Parenting, even though often deeply rewarding and gratifying, can nevertheless become burdensome, causing major strain and distress to the caregiver (McDonald, Couchonnal, & Early, 1999). The stress associated with caregiving adds an extra dimension to the caregiving experience of a parent caring for a child or adolescent. Caregiving stress can not only have an adverse effect on the caregiver's health and mental health, but can also have a potentially devastating effect on the children who are the recipients of care. Stressed caregivers may not perform their caregiving functions effectively and sometimes may even cause harm to their children. In this respect, family violence (Briar-Lawson, Lawson, & Hennon, et al., in press) is a common response to excessive stress. Similarly, parents who abuse their children often experience high degrees of stress (Bugental, Mantyla, and Lewis, 1989). Thus, social workers and child welfare professionals, in general, need to recognize the magnitude of caregiving and parental stress as a risk factor for parental child maltreatment.

Child maltreatment, which has been a concern of the social work profession since its inception, is today the focus of the public child welfare system where abused and neglected children make up most of the cases in many jurisdictions (Littell & Schuerman, 1999). According to the United States Department of Health and Human Services (HHS), in 1998, state child protective services agencies received about 2,806,000 reports of child maltreatment (HHS, 2000). Although child maltreatment is widespread regardless of race, ethnicity, or socioeconomic status, African

American, poor, and single-parent, female-headed families are disproportionally represented among those reported for child abuse and neglect (Littell & Schuerman, 1999). Parental abuse needs to be understood, therefore, within the context of culturally specific norms as they interact with gender, ethnicity, and socioeconomic factors to influence a parent's caregiving practices, the nature of familial bonds, and parenting styles. At the same time, it is necessary to simultaneously consider external factors associated with ethnic group membership, such as prejudice, discrimination, and employment status.

This chapter begins with a discussion of family caregiving as it relates to parenting for a child or youth. Next, caregiver stress is analyzed using a stress and coping model as a conceptual framework. The model's components are discussed in the context of the specific factors that may contribute to caregiver distress for parents who provide care for their children. Here, discussion is focused on child abuse and neglect as potential outcomes of parental caregiving stress. The chapter concludes with beginning recommendations for new century practice to reframe parental child abuse and neglect as stemming from caregiving stress requiring supports similar to other stressed caregivers.

Caregiving

Family Caregiving

In general, family caregiving refers to the activities and experiences associated with providing care to family members who need assistance to sustain an optimal level of functioning, and for adults and their independence (Pearlin, et al., 1990). It involves the objective or behavioral activities as well as the subjective emotional comfort family members can provide (Aldous, 1994). In fact, Hooyman and Gonyea (1995) argue that defining the phenomenon of family caregiving can be difficult because of the complex nature of care. They further underscore the need to distinguish between the notions of *caring for* and *caring about*, which are usually fused together. While *caring for* entails performing instrumental activities of daily living, such as money management, housework, and transportation, *caring about* involves primarily an emotional connection through the expression of love and affection (Hooyman & Gonyea,1995). The concepts of *caring for* and *caring about* are intrinsic to any close relationship and caregiving is, therefore, embedded in all primary relationships (Pearlin, et al.,1990).

Family caregiving has traditionally been woman's work carried out in the context of gender-role socialization or ideology that defines women as *natural* caregivers. This definition, which is primarily socially constructed, affects the lives of both women and men. Despite recent changes in men and women's family roles, women continue as the primary nurturers, kin keepers, and caretakers of family members.

Women provide the vast majority of family care across the life span in their roles as mothers, wives, daughters, and daughters-in-law (Hooyman & Gonyea, 1995).

Feminist scholars have argued that family caregiving is a women's issue and should be understood within the context of systemic or structural factors. That is, family caregiving should be viewed as an issue that goes beyond focusing solely on the woman as an individual to encompass the influences of society's underlying social, economic, and ideological structures. Pertinent to this discussion is the role of ideology, a society's system of beliefs and values, on family caregiving. For example, the ideologies of "familism" and "separate spheres" are at the root of the popular belief that women's principal responsibility is to provide uncompensated care to dependent relatives. Familism, or the family ethic, functions as a principle of social organization, which defines women's expected work and family behavior, underscoring women's caregiving roles as natural and appropriate. The ideology of separate spheres reinforces the gender-segregated nature of women's caregiving roles in the home (Hooyman & Gonyea, 1995). Since patterns of family caregiving are profoundly influenced by cultural values and beliefs, it follows that the dynamics of caregiving will vary across culturally diverse families. These culturally relative values and beliefs intersect with factors related to gender, ethnic group membership, and socioeconomic class, shaping the caregiving process in numerous ways and giving differential meaning to the caregiver's experience. Latino families, for example, share many similarities with African American and Native American families, while differing significantly from those of Asian and non-Hispanic White backgrounds (Ortiz, 1995).

Parental Caregiving

Family caregiving, which takes place at various stages across the life span, includes the care provided by parents to their children and youth. Although the roles of parenting and parental caregiving are closely related, and often overlap, they need to be distinguished and treated separately. According to Kazak & Kristakis (1994) parenting refers to a parent's commitment to assume a substantial responsibility to socialize, guide, discipline, and provide financial and emotional support for a child. It is a lifelong process that continually changes throughout a child's developmental stages. Parental caregiving, on the other hand, refers to the concrete demands as well as the emotional attachments associated with raising a child. These include nurturing, changing diapers, bathing and clothing, teaching, playing with, and negotiating with other systems involved in the child's well being such as health care, schools, and community agencies. While a parent can be removed from the daily details of child care, a parental caregiver is directly involved with them. The responsibility for parenting can be assumed by many adults from the nuclear and extended family such as the biological parents, custodial and noncustodial parents, and stepparents.

Parenting can also be assumed by other adults outside the family including respite care workers, and teachers (Kazak & Kristakis, 1994).

With regard to parental caregiving, the distinction between the notions of *caring for* and *caring about* noted earlier is also helpful in understanding parental caregiving as a distinct form of family caregiving. Here, the typical concrete tasks associated with providing care for a child are differentiated from the emotional attachment and love that characterize a parent-child relationship. This more objective analysis of the manifold tasks of parenting is more helpful than viewing parenting as a value-laden construct infused with highly emotional connotations. For example, it accommodates the assumption that ineffective, inappropriate, and even harmful parental caregiving behaviors should not necessarily be construed as a parents' lack of love and positive feelings about their children. Likewise, when the objective parental caregiving activities are not confounded with the parents' feelings and emotions about their children, there is a greater opportunity to underscore the extensive number of long hours of unremunerated hard work parents, especially women, perform in their roles as caregivers.

Despite the recognition that family is a vehicle for care of people of all ages (Kane & Penrod, 1995), research that examines family caregiving as it relates to parents caring for their children and youth has been minimal. Most caregiving studies have focused on caregivers of frail elderly family members. Whereas there are related differences in these two care recipient populations, the caregiving process, and thus the caregiver's experience, is very similar. Considering these similarities, the findings from elderly caregiving research can prove useful in understanding the dynamics of parental caregiving. For example, as is illustrated later in this chapter, some parallels can be drawn from the dearth of literature on elderly caregiving with regard to caregiver burden, or stress. Information on the ways caregivers experience the stress and coping processes, the caregivers' risk and protective factors for stress, and interventions to help caregivers prevent or ameliorate the negative impacts of stress, could be readily applied to parental caregivers.

Consequences of Caregiving

Providing family care can have both positive and negative consequences for caregivers and care recipients. While caring for a family member can prove gratifying and rewarding, it can also entail physical, psychological, emotional, social, and financial costs (Hooyman & Gonyea, 1995). With regard to negative outcomes that may stem from caregiving, a number of studies have focused, either explicitly or implicitly, on caregiving as a source of burden and emotional distress (Pearlin, et al.,1990).

Caregiver Stress

Research on family elderly caregiving has firmly established its adverse impact on the caregiver's psychological well-being (Yee & Schulz, 2000). Caregiver stress has been extensively documented among caregivers of physically frail elders or elders with Alzheimer's disease (Kahana, et al.1994). Yet, as noted earlier, research on parental caregiving as a source of distress has drawn little attention. For many parents, caregiving activities often become a source of added burdens, as they have to meet extensive caregiving demands with inadequate, unpredictable formal and informal help. Providing care for their children can prove difficult and challenging to the point that this may threaten individual and family well-being. For example, cultural norms stemming from familism values may exert undue demands and pressures on family members, particularly mothers, with regard to caregiving expectations and responsibilities. Similarly, structural, social, and economic constrictions due to low paying wages, racism, and sexism affect the availability of financial resources which, in turn, greatly influence the parental caregiving experience. Poverty, for example, is a major source of parental caregiving stress. Parents providing care for a child or youth, therefore, may also be at high risk for caregiving stress (Phelps, Belsky, and Crnic, 1998).

The next section examines parental caregiving distress using the stress and coping model as an organizing framework. Factors that may contribute to parental caregiver distress are discussed, particularly as they relate to child abuse and neglect.

Parental Caregiving Stress and Child Abuse and Neglect

This section provides an analysis of parental caregiving distress using a stress and coping model. The rationale for this approach is two-fold. First, most research on distress among caregivers of elderly relatives has been based on this type of model. Second, stress and coping models, such as the one presented here, regard child abuse and neglect as a result of both societal and psychological factors. They emphasize the roles of employment, stress, and isolation in child abuse and view the psychological attributes of the parent as a product of society's social conditions (Starr, 1988). This sociocultural perspective is in direct contrast to earlier medically based approaches, which attributed child abuse and neglect solely to a parent's psychological characteristics. These include personality traits, degree of intelligence, and child rearing attitudes. In this view, child abuse and neglect is defined as a problem of parental "psychopathology" where parents who abuse their children are viewed as "sick" and inherently deficient (Margolin, 1992).

The role of stress as a contributing factor has not been a major focus of research in parental child abuse and neglect. Moreover, even when the significance of stress is acknowledged, parental abuse is still attributed to the parents' personal deficiencies or inadequacies. For example, parents who abuse their children are considered to have "poor comprehension about stress management and anger control because of inadequate or abusive responses to social, emotional, and economic stresses in their family environment" (Hullings-Catalano, 1996). Although a stress and coping model does not fully explain all the complexities of child abuse and neglect, it provides a framework for examining the interrelatedness of parental caregiving stressors and coping resources in the dynamics of child abuse and neglect.

The Stress and Coping Perspective

Theoretical Perspective. Most research on caregiving distress has been based on the stress theory developed by Lazarus and Folkman (1984) and the caregiving stress process model formulated by Pearlin and his colleagues (1990). Lazarus and Folkman's stress theory focuses on cognitive appraisal and coping. Pearlin, et al.'s (1990) model views caregiving stress as a process focusing on the various conditions that may result in personal stress and how they develop, change, and interrelate over time. Drawing from these frameworks, caregiving researchers have generally used stress and coping models that address the following variables: the background and context of stress; the stressors; the cognitive appraisal of stressors as stressful or satisfying; coping as a potential mediator between appraisal and outcomes; and the outcomes or manifestations of stress (Knight, et al., 2000; Lazarus and Folkman, 1984; Pearlin, et al., 1990).

The Concept of Stress. Lazarus & Folkman (1984) define psychological stress as a person-environment relationship that the person appraises as taxing or exceeding his or her resources and endangering his or her well-being. From this perspective, the caregiving experience is a transaction between caregivers and their environments. When the caregiving activities exceed the caregiver's internal and external resources, caregiving becomes stressful (Levesque, Ducharme, & Lachance, 1999). Caregiving can be potentially conducive to persistent stress, as it may, under some circumstances, shift from an ordinary exchange of assistance among closely related people to a tremendous and disparately distributed burden (Pearlin, et al., 1990). In this respect, the caregiving activities associated with parenting are often highly demanding and stress producing making effective parenting difficult. Stressed parents may be irritable, tense, and moody and thus overreact when dealing with their children, which then may lead to abuse (Jones, 1990). For example, research has found high levels of stress among parents who abuse their children, a relationship between stress and parental violence toward children, and high levels of stress associated with inadequate parental childcare (Starr, 1988).

Stress Context Variables. The first component of the stress and coping model includes the variables of caregiver-care recipient relationship and caregiver's characteristics such as gender, ethnicity, and socioeconomic status. The recognition that environmental as well as personal resources influence the caregiving experience is consistent with the general thrust of this chapter. These contextual variables reflect the different structural opportunities and barriers parents can encounter in their roles as caregivers.

Caregiving Stressors. Caregiving stress results from a wide range of stressors associated with the process of caregiving. Stressors, which are at center of the stress process, are any problematic experience, condition, or activity that is threatening, inhibiting, or frustrating to a caregiver (Pearlin, et al., 1990).

The parenting experience is often fraught with caregiving demands stemming from primary and secondary stressors. Based on the categorization of Pearlin, et al., (1990) categorization, primary stressors are those which encompass the demands of caregiving such as a child's challenging behaviors and secondary stressors which are the problems and hardships (Pearlin, et al.,1990). Thus, stressors may stem directly from the role of caregiving as well from other areas of the caregiver's life including work and financial stressors (Chiriboga, Weilier, & Nelson, 1990).

Primary Stressors. *Child's Behavior*—A primary stressor parents encounter involves children's challenging behaviors. As is the case for other types of care recipients, children and youth often exhibit challenging, at times even aggressive and defiant, behaviors as part of their developmental process. As their caregivers, parents face a number of stressors since they are required to continuously supervise and monitor such behaviors while ensuring the safety of their children.

Some researchers have proposed that certain children's behaviors have an effect on their parents and on the quality of care they provide them (Starr, 1988). Although it is not completely clear whether an abused child's behavior is an antecedent or a consequence of maltreatment, there are data that suggest it is a contributing factor (Trickett & Kuczynski, 1991). For example, mothers who abuse their children often report high levels of parenting-related stress. Some of this they attribute to their children's frequent refusal to follow behavioral directives or their low tolerance for their children's challenging behavior (Hullings-Catalano, 1996). With regard to a child's challenging behavior, it is important to consider not only a child's unique characteristics, but also society's child development norms, which may encourage children to be assertive, confident, and outspoken. The resulting behaviors may, sometimes, be perceived by a parent as defiant, unruly, and disrespectful.

Daily Dependencies—A related source of stress among caregivers, in general, involves the levels of dependence on the caregiver to satisfy daily and instrumental needs. The greater the number of caregiving activities and the extent of dependency for each activity, the greater the risk for distress. Similarly, a resistant attitude on the part of the care recipient with regard to receiving assistance may increase the likelihood of stress (Pearlin, et al., 1990). With regard to parenting, children and adolescents are highly dependent on their parents who are charged with the responsibility of ensuring that their most basic needs are met and who must perform hands-on, day-to-day activities such as meal preparation, laundry, and other housework tasks. In some respects, the experience of caring for a very young child simulates that of providing care for a frail, elderly family member. In both caregiving situations, the care recipients require assistance with their daily living activities including bathing, toileting, and eating. During various stages of a child or adolescent's developmental process, parents also have to endure recalcitrant attitudes about receiving care and assistance. With regard to parental abuse, younger children tend to be at a greater risk. Younger children usually spend more time with the caregiving parent, and they are more dependent on them.

Secondary Stressors. The primary stressors identified to this point often produce secondary, equally powerful, stressors (Pearlin, et al., 1990). Parents caring for a child or youth may experience secondary stressors stemming from role strains as well as psychological strains.

Role strain—This relates to the impact of caregiving demands on other roles outside the caregiving situation, such as social, occupational, and economic responsibilities (Pearlin, et al., 1990; Yee & Schulz, 2000). Caregiving duties usually involve limitations on the caregiver's social and recreational life. For example, studies have found that caregiving highly interferes with family and leisure time (Chang & White-Means, 1991). Similarly, parents may yearn for greater participation in social activities, such as hobbies, going to church, attending community functions, and recreational events, that are now curtailed by their child care responsibilities. As found among caregivers of elderly family members, these restrictions in social relations lead to a greater sense of loneliness and isolation among parents caring for children and adolescents (Antonucci, 1985; Hooyman & Gonyea, 1995). Researchers have identified parental isolation as an antecedent factor in the etiology of child abuse (Moncher, 1995). Parents who abuse their children tend to be isolated from potentially supportive social networks (Bugental, et al., 1989). For example, mothers who abuse their children tend to spend little time with friends and relatives and often experience intense feelings of loneliness and isolation (Starr, 1988).

Occupational strains are commonly found among caregivers who are employed outside the home, either by necessity or choice, and are also encountered by parents. They frequently experience pressures and dilemmas at the interface of their caregiving duties and occupational responsibilities that may result in role-overload. In order to meet their dual demands, caregivers are forced to make a number of workplace adjustments resulting in greater vulnerability to caregiving stress (Orodenker, 1990). These accommodations usually include work schedule restrictions, reductions in number of hours worked, and missed opportunities for career development or job promotion (Hooyman & Gonyea, 1995). For example, data have shown that women are more likely to be distracted at work with caregiving worries and to use their sick leave to fulfill caregiving obligations (Kramer & Kipnis, 1995). They are also more likely to give up a job due to caregiving demands and expectations (Fredericksen, 1996) and to experience significantly more stress as a result of difficulties balancing demands stemming from both their caregiving and occupational roles (Orodenker, 1990). Men, on the other hand, have up to 15 more hours each week of leisure time than their wives, generally from successfully avoiding housework and child care responsibilities. It has been proposed that these child care responsibility inequities have implications for gender analysis in child abuse (Belesky and Vondra, 1989).

An additional caregiving stressor involves a caregiver's exposure to economic hardships. Caring for a dependent family member can be financially costly as it often represents a reduction in household income and perhaps, for some poor families, having to struggle to make ends meet. Furthermore, the unpaid care provided to a dependent relative and the lost income associated with a temporary or permanent withdrawal from the workforce are of substantial economic value. Empirical evidence of caregiving financial burdens has come from research with families caring for adults with developmental disabilities and with families caring for adults or elderly with chronic disabilities (Hooyman & Gonyea, 1995).

For parents in their roles as caregivers, economic hardship represents a major source of stress. Financial constraints significantly affect the quality of the caregiving environment for both parents and children. At the same time, poverty and low-socioeconomic status have been consistently linked to child abuse and maltreatment. In fact, poverty is often the best predictor of child abuse and neglect (Lindsay, 1994).

For many caregivers, especially women, employment restrictions represent a powerful source of stress that involves the three types of role strains associated with secondary stressors discussed above. When forced to leave the workforce to fulfill familial caregiving demands, a caregiver loses the income as well as the contact with fellow workers and friends, thus forfeiting the opportunity to find meaningful stimulation and companionship outside the home. Hence, employment restrictions and financial burdens may pose negative consequences economically, occupationally, and socially (Scheyett, 1990). Parental unemployment and lack of equitable and meaningful work are also major sources of caregiving stress and may, consequently, result in parental abuse. Unemployed parents, particularly fathers, are likely to spend more time at home near their children at a time when they may be already experiencing high levels of stress, and potentially deteriorating father-child relationships. Similarly, unemployment may lead to marital discord as a result of displaced anger. This, in turn, may elicit temper tantrums and other difficult behaviors from the children to which parents may respond abusively (Jones, 1996). Although child abuse and neglect occur in families of all social classes and not all poor or economically disadvantaged families abuse their children, economic deprivation is a powerful stressor. For example, data have shown a negative relationship between income and child-parent violence (Jones, 1990; Starr, 1988). Economic hardships, which pose a major threat to the parents' ability to effectively meet their caregiving responsibilities, may evoke a stressful reaction of potential harmful outcomes.

Cognitive Appraisal

Cognitive appraisal plays a powerful role in the stress response levels to diverse stressors. It refers to the evaluative processes that intervene between a stressor and a response. Cognitive appraisal is largely evaluative and focuses on whether an encounter is irrelevant, benign-positive, or stressful, and on specific options or strategies to manage the situation (Lazarus & Folkman, 1984). Here, the stress process is viewed as a relationship that is affected or mediated by a person's cognitive appraisals (Chiriboga, Weilier, & Nelson, 1990). For example, persons with low perceived control may appraise the situation as hopeless, and respond with ineffective emotional rather than problem solving coping strategies. Parents who, in addition to facing economic and social stressors, believe that they have low control over life events, are likely to be exceptionally high risks to abuse their children(Bugental, et al., 1989).

Coping. The concept of coping refers to a person's constantly changing cognitive and behavioral efforts to manage specific stressful demands. These efforts can be problem-focused, geared to manage or alter the stressful situation or emotion-focused, aiming to regulate the emotional response to the situation. Furthermore, it is important to distinguish between coping functions, which refer to the purpose a person's efforts, and coping outcomes, the effect resulting from these efforts. Coping is independent of outcome, as effective coping not only involves problem solving, but also serves other functions, such as allowing a person to accept, minimize, ignore, or simply tolerate the stressful situation. Accordingly, coping strategies need to be considered contextually and non-judgmentally. No coping strategy is inherently better or worse than any other.

The ways a person copes depend greatly on the resources that are available and the constraints that preclude use of these resources in the context of the specific stressful encounter. For example, a parent can draw upon a wide range of resources in order to cope with the multiple demands of daily living. These coping resources are multidimensional and can be of a personal or environmental nature. Although the demands posed by a stressful encounter may often exceed a parent's resources, for many situations, resources are adequate. However, their use may engender further conflict and distress. Constraints that inhibit the effective use of coping resources may derive from personal as well as environmental factors. Personal constraints include unique psychological characteristics and internalized cultural values and beliefs that proscribe certain types of behavior or feelings. Environmental constraints include competition for the same resources and social institutions that thwart coping efforts. Difficulties using coping resources effectively may also arise when a parent appraises a stressful situation as highly threatening (Lazarus & Folkman, 1984).

Personal Resources and Constraints. *Cultural Values and Beliefs—*Despite individual and situational differences, cultural values and beliefs, which determine the appropriateness of certain behaviors and feelings, can serve as powerful psychological resources for coping with caregiving stress (Lazarus & Folkman, 1984). A resourceful parent will possess a number of personal competencies, such as problem solving and social skills, physical well-being, and positive beliefs that serve as a basis for hope. For instance, the belief that outcomes are controllable, coupled with beliefs that encourage viewing oneself positively, may serve as a resource for coping with caregiving stress. Parents holding such beliefs, which are at the core of hope, may be more likely to think positively and to view life experiences in a positive light. Hope makes a positive outcome seem highly feasible and helps sustain coping efforts even under the most difficult conditions.

On the other hand, culturally derived personal beliefs can constrain the use of coping resources. For example, religious beliefs that place the locus of control externally may foster appraisals of helplessness by the caregiver. These fatalistic beliefs may discourage problem solving. Caution needs to be exercised with regard to these types of beliefs when working with persons from diverse cultural backgrounds since the belief in fate is closely linked to a person's world view (Ramos, 1997). For example, the notion of mastery may vary across cultural groups, thus impinging upon the types of problem-solving activities used by diverse parents as coping resources.

Similarly, the degree of adherence to the value of familism, in conjunction with personal beliefs about commitments, may constrain a mother's use of coping resources when faced with value conflicts regarding out-of-the-house full-time employment. A strong adherence to familism may not only prove stressful when she is forced, due to economic necessity, to depart from the gender ascribed caregiving role of a full time mother, but may also inhibit her motivation to utilize available coping resources and initiate and sustain effective coping activities.

The resources upon which a parent can draw to cope with caregiving stressors also include those of a psychological nature, including cultural values and beliefs, such as those that view oneself and one's life experiences positively, reinforcing a sense of personal mastery and placing the locus of control internally. For some families, particularly for those at risk of child abuse and neglect, maintaining a positive outlook in the face of numerous stressors, such as economic hardships and unemployment, can sometimes be difficult. For families from diverse cultural backgrounds, beliefs about the locus of control and mastery may vary from those of dominant society. Sometimes these beliefs may constrain and inhibit opportunities to use coping resources effectively. For instance, parents experiencing stressful situations with a child's challenging behaviors may not seek outside help because they believe that the situation is hopeless. This deterministic attitude precludes them from mobilizing to effect change—they may believe "that's the way it is; there's nothing that can be done to change it." Without appropriate, timely intervention, the problem is likely to escalate, the child-parent relationship may deteriorate, and eventually may result in child abuse.

Environmental Resources and Constraints. Parents can also cope with caregiving stress by drawing upon material resources and social supports from the social environment.

Material Resources—The money and the goods and services that money can buy are often overlooked as crucial factors in effective coping. Research has found a strong relationship between socioeconomic status and stress with persons having money and the skills to use it wisely faring much better than those without financial resources (Lazarus & Folkman, 1984). Thus, parents caring for a child or youth may reduce vulnerability to stress just by having money, even if it is not drawn upon, since monetary resources can vastly increase their coping options in almost any stressful encounter.

By the same token, the scarcity of material resources resulting from larger structural factors in the economy, particularly with regard to employment, can constrain a parent's coping efforts. Poverty and economic marginality place some families at great economic disadvantage due to lack of financial resources. This is particularly the case for female-headed families where mothers are frequently the sole wage earners and for ethnic minority parents who may, as a result of prejudicial and discriminatory structural factors, tend to hold jobs that often do not pay enough to support their families. Hence, the parenting experience can be especially challenging and burdensome for these families. This, in turn, can seriously thwart a parent's effective coping, for example, by limiting accessibility to professional legal, medical, and financial services in adverse situations. Lack of material resources—low income and poverty—are among the best predictors of child abuse and neglect (Bugental, et al., 1989).

Social Support—This environmental resource often plays an important role in buffering caregiving stress. It refers to having someone from whom one receives instrumental support or assistance with tangible tasks, as well as expressive support, which is provided by someone who is caring, trustworthy, uplifting, and a confidant (Pearlin, et al., 1990). In this respect, parents may draw assistance and support to manage their caregiving demands from personal, family, and community resources. A resourceful parent could obtain emotional and tangible support from a spouse, relatives, and professionals. Emotional support can also come from the family by spending time together with those who the share parents' spiritual beliefs and values. With regard to community resources, parents can receive emotional and tangible support from friends and relatives, and can turn to the community for help and services (Patterson & Leonard, 1994). Thus, a strong, supportive social network can help buffer the exacerbation of physical and emotional responses to these stressors (Choi & Wodarski, 1996).

As with other coping resources, at times, a parent may not be able to utilize some readily available coping supports due to personal and environmental constraints. With regard to personal constraints, cultural beliefs about the giving and receiving of help, which greatly influence how a person construes the notion of support, may determine whether social supports will be used fully and effectively. For example, parents who attach a negative connotation to the notion of seeking and receiving help may be less likely to use social supports in a crisis. They may believe that the use of social support is a sign of being needy or helpless, a view that is inconsistent with the broader values of self-sufficiency, independence, and mastery. Likewise, some parents may believe that accepting assistance implies the acquisition of some type of obligation to reciprocate.

Parents who are employed, especially women working outside of the home, may often find themselves exhausted with little free time or energy for social activities as a result of multiple responsibilities stemming from their roles as employees and mothers. For women who work in the house performing domestic labor and whose primary responsibility is providing care for their children as full-time mothers, opportunities to meet people and cultivate relationships are often minimal, leading to loneliness and isolation. Thus, while the caregiving literature consistently singles out social support as a powerful coping resource, caregiving demands and expectations often place caregivers at a disadvantage with regard to availability and utilization of social supports when facing multiple caregiving stressors.

Similarly, data have shown a link between concrete and emotional social support and parenting, recognizing the lack of social support as an antecedent factor in the etiology of child abuse (Moncher, 1995). For example, mothers who abuse their children tend to spend little time with friends and relatives and often experience intense feelings of loneliness and isolation (Starr, 1988). Social isolation, or lack of social support, may increase the potential of child abuse through several mechanisms. As such, parents may not have adequate access to relatives, friends, and professionals who could provide assistance with concrete caregiving tasks, such as child-care services or effective parenting techniques. Likewise, parents may not have someone to address their emotional support needs. Such emotional supports, in turn, could help parents relieve some of the burden associated with parenting (Moncher, 1995).

Caregiving Stress Outcomes

Providing care for a family member can be a source of stress for the family caregiver. Caregiver stress, in turn, can negatively affect the parent's physical and psychological well-being. Some studies have found high levels of anxiety and depression among caregivers. Yee & Schulz, (2000) and others have suggested that caregiving stress may compromise a caregiver's physiological functioning, increasing the risk for health problems (Schulz & Beach, 1999). Research has also shown that caregiving stress may interfere with the caregiver's ability to function effectively at the workplace (Patterson & Leonard, 1994). An additional potential outcome of caregiving stress, as was presented here, is parental child abuse and neglect.

Summary

As previously discussed, the caregiving associated with parenting is often highly demanding and conducive to stress. Parents face a number of daily stressors as they perform their caregiving responsibilities, some of which may represent a major threat to their emotional well-being. Most importantly, though, it is the availability and utilization of personal and environmental resources that determine a parent's ability to cope effectively with parenting stress. Poverty, social isolation, and pressures to uphold familism values that restrict equal distribution of caregiving duties and meaningful, equitable employment may not only limit available coping resources, but also curtail the parents' efforts to draw upon them when needed. When confronted with some adverse situations, these parents, whose emotional well-being has been continuously threatened, may react with anger and frustration, which in turn may lead to aggressive behavior toward their children.

Noteworthy with respect to the dynamics of stress and coping is the clear interrelatedness of certain factors that may operate simultaneously as stressors and constraints to coping. This is illustrated by the role of economic hardships, which not only trigger multiple stressors, but at the same time, limit the availability and utilization of coping resources. With regard to parents at-risk of child abuse and neglect, poverty, socioeconomic status, and unemployment can result in high levels of caregiver stress. At the same time, this lack of monetary resources can severely reduce opportunities and accessibility to formal and informal supports.

This dynamic is important as it may help foster a greater understanding of the potential precarious condition of parents at-risk for child abuse. Oftentimes, the argument is presented that caregiving stressors are inevitable with parenting and faced by all families. There is a tendency, at the same time, to question the inherent competency and individual ability to provide effective caregiving and parenting. Perhaps, in placing a focus on the similarity of the stressors experienced by all families, little attention is paid to the dramatic limitations in availability and utilization of coping resources experienced by some vulnerable, and not as economically privileged, families. Parents who abuse their children tend to experience tremendous levels of caregiving stress and at the same time are victims of some powerful structural social conditions that limit their coping resources (Bugental, et al., 1989).

New Century Practice with Parents

This chapter analyzed caregiving stress in the context of parenting. Child abuse and neglect is seen not as the byproduct of a difficult parent but as the potential outcome of parental caregiving stress. It can be argued that providing care for a child or youth is equally if not more stressful than caring for a frail elderly family member. Thus, there is a pressing need to recognize the role of caregiver stress as a risk factor for parental child abuse and neglect.

Services designed to enhance family functioning should include multisystemic interventions that include maximizing parental caregivers' coping resources. Such resource enhancement must include, among others, day care facilities, parent support groups, educational and empowerment programs, homemaker aids, and caregiver allowances or stipends. Furthermore, in conjunction with these coping resource enhancements, new century practices must also address the roles of employment and the work place in effective parental caregiving. For example, social workers and child welfare professionals, in general, need to be highly skillful in conducting assessments to ascertain such information as how lack of monetary assets may constrain resources to cope with crisis situations or stressful parenting. Currently, screening and identifying parental caregiving stress and coping resources at intake is not always a part of agency practice. For parents in the labor market, professionals must consider the impact of work policies and demands on both the parents' emotional well-being and the quality of parental caregiving. This includes assessing for stressors highly conducive to emotional distress, such as role conflict and role strain, stemming from nonfamily-responsive policies at the work place. Considering that African American, poor, and mother-only families are disproportionally represented among those reported for child abuse and neglect (Littell & Schuerman, 1999), it is essential to take into account culturally specific norms, and racial, ethnic, gender, and socioeconomic factors as they influence caregiving as a source of parental stress.

Yet, interventions and patterns of practice are influenced by a multitude of factors including, but not limited to, societal values (Littel & Schuerman, 1999). Social workers, and child welfare professionals in general, practice in an environment where society's underlying value of familism prescribes that family caregiving for the frail elderly and for children are to be viewed differently. It encourages family care for an elder through social norms such as those of "family solidarity" and "filial responsibility," which appeal to a person's commitment to care for their loved ones as they grow old (Tosel, Smith, & McCallion, in press). Family care for children, on the other hand, is mandated through parenting. Parents are responsible for the care of their children whether they are sick or well and for their socialization into adult roles (Patterson & Leonard, 1994). The distinction between caring for the elderly and caring for children permeates societal views about parenting and the helping professions at various levels as illustrated below.

- Family care for a frail elder is usually treated as a form of altruistic behavior, which generates compassion and sympathy towards caregivers for the typical caregiving demands they encounter during the process of caregiving. Family care for children by parents, on the other hand, is considered an obligation where the caregiving burdens of parenting are not readily recognized. Parenting, rather, is regulated by societal cultural norms, which monitor and sanction the adequacy of parenting practices, such as child rearing, often from an ethnocentric, judgmental, and unsympathetic perspective.

- Society's concern with the well-being of family caregivers of frail elders has led to the investment of a vast amount of scientific resources in the study of stress and coping in elderly caregiving (Kahana, et al., 1994). The well-being of caregivers who are parents has not received similar attention; they have not been recognized as major policy or practice issues.

- The response to a family caregiving crisis varies depending upon whether the recipient of care is a frail elderly person or a child. In the case of elderly caregiving the crisis is often attributed to the caregiver's high levels of stress. Referrals for services are usually channeled through the public and private health systems where caregivers are likely to receive assistance from a supportive, nonjudgmental perspective. When considering a caregiving crisis involving a child, responsibility is often attributed to parents and their inadequacies as well as ineffective caregiving practices. Parents are usually referred to an already overburdened child welfare system, particularly to child protective agencies. Parents are investigated by those who may approach them with a negative stigma and provide services with a "blaming the parent," punitive approach.

- Family members caring for an elder are more likely to have access to concrete services, such as respite care and educational support groups, which in turn may serve to prevent serious caregiver stress. Parents, however, are much less likely to have access to this type of resource and, therefore, are more vulnerable to potentially devastating caregiving stress outcomes. Parents are less likely to have access to services, such as parents anonymous, family support centers, and health education programs, which may serve as preventive measures by alleviating the negative impact of caregiving stressors and increasing their coping resources. As a result, by the time parents enter into child welfare system, their problems are exacerbated, and they face the risk of having their children removed.

- Currently, United States policy makers, including President Bill Clinton, are considering a $3000 allowance for caregivers of frail elderly relatives. This is in line with social policy that begins to recognize the economic value of family caregiving. It is imperative that such allowance provisions are also allocated for parents in their roles as caregivers of children and youth.

This chapter argues that the same supports available to other family caregivers (e.g., parents caring for children with disabilities, caregivers of frail elderly relatives) need to be available to stressed parental caregivers. Currently, stressed parents receive inequitable supports when their risk factors of abuse and neglect are reported to child welfare agencies. More effective outcomes with parents in the child welfare system may depend on new cultural norms regarding parental rights to stress reducing supports. Twenty-first Century policies and practices need to address inequities in treatment of family caregivers based on gender, age, ethnicity, income levels and nature of caregiving responsibilities . There is a need for a major infusion of new resources into child welfare systems for caregiver supports involving mutual assistance among parents, stress relievers for parental caregivers, and more enfranchising rather than punitive approaches. Family support and preservation ideologies need to be infused with reframed views of stressed parental caregivers. Until such reformulations occur, more equitable practice may be impeded.

As society transitions into the 21st Century, cultural norms underlying family caregiving must prescribe that parenting is a form of caregiving, with its encompassing burdens and stressors, just like any other type of caregiving namely that of a frail elderly. Child welfare professionals, policy makers, and researchers must take the lead in promoting cultural norms that dictate more current caregiving practices and, thus, align parental caregiving supports with the needs of 21st-Century families.

References

Aldous, J. (1994). Someone to watch over me: Family responsibilities and their realization across family lives. In E. Kahana, D. Biegel, & M. Wykle (Eds.). *Family caregiving across the lifespan* (pp. 42-68). California: Sage Publications.

Antonucci, T. (1985). Personal characteristics, social support and social behavior. In R. Binstock, & E. Shanas (Eds.). *Handbook of aging and the social sciences* (pp. 94-128. New York: Van Hostrand Reinhold.

Belsky, J and Vonora, J. (1989). Lessons from child abuse: The determinants of parenting. In D. Ciccheti & V. Carlson (Eds.). *Child maltreatment: Theory and research on the causes and consequences of child abuse and neglect* (pp. 153-202). New York: Cambridge University Press.

Briar-Lawson, K., Lawson, H., and Hennon, C. (In Press). Meaningful and gender-equitable work and family well-being. In K. Briar-Lawson, H. Lawson, and C. Hennon with A. Jones (Eds.). *Family-centered policies and practices: international implications.* New York: Columbia University Press.

Bugental, D., Mantyla, S., and Lewis, J. (1989). Parental attributions as moderators of affective communication to children at risk for physical abuse. In D. Ciccheti & V. Carlson (Eds.). *Child maltreatment: Theory and research on the causes and consequences of child abuse and neglect* (pp. 254-79). New York: Cambridge University Press.

Carlson, B. (1997). A stress and coping approach to intervention with abused women. *Family relations,* (46), 291-98.

Chang, C., and White-Means, S. (1991). The men who care: An analysis of male primary caregivers who care for frail elderly at home. *The Journal of Crippled Gerontology,* (10), 343-58.

Chiriboga, D., Weiler, P., and Nielson, K. (1990). The stress of caregivers. In D. Biegel and A. Blum (Eds.). *Aging and caregiving* (pp. 121-38). California: Sage Publications.

Choi, N. G. and Wodarski, J. S. (1996). The relationship between social support and health status of elderly people: does social support slow down physical and functional deterioration? *Social Work Research, 20*(1), 52-63.

Flores-Ortiz, Y. (2000). La mujer latina: From margin to center. In M. Flores and G. Carey (Eds.). *Family Therapy With Hispanics* (pp. 59-76). Needham Heights: Allyn & Bacon.

Frederiksen, R. (1996). Gender differences in employment and the informal care of adults. *Journal of Women and Aging,* (8), 35-53.

Hooyman, N. and Gonyea, J. (1995). *Feminist perspectives on family care: policies for gender justice.* California: Sage Publications.

Hullings-Catalano, V. (1996). Physical abuse of children by parents. In D. M. Bushy (Ed.). *The impact of violence on the family* (pp. 43-74). Needham Heights, MA: Allyn & Bacon.

Jones, L. (1990). Unemployment and child abuse. *The Journal of Contemporary Human Services* (pp.579-586).

Kahana, E., Biegel, D., and Wykle, M. (1994). Conclusion. In E. Kahana, D. Biegel, & M. Wykle (Eds.). *Family caregiving across the lifespan* (pp. 382-85). Thousand Oaks, CA: Sage.

Kane, R. A. and Penrod, J. D. (1995). Toward a caregiving policy for the aging family. In R. A. Kane and J. D. Penrod (Eds.). *Family caregiving in an aging society* (pp. 144-70). Thousand Oaks, CA: Sage.

Kay, L. and Applegate, J. (1990). Men as elder caregivers: A response to changing families. *American Journal of Orthopsychiatry 60*(1), 86-95.

Kazak, A. and Christakis, D. (1994). Caregiving issues in families of children with chronic medical conditions. In E. Kahana, D. Biegel, and M. Wykle (Eds.). *Family Caregiving across the Life Span* (pp. 331-355). Thousand Oaks, CA.: Sage.

Knight, B., Silverstein, M., McCallum, T., and Fox, L. (2000). A sociocultural stress and coping model for mental health outcomes among African American caregivers in southern California. *The Journal of Gerontology, 55B*(3), 142-50.

Lazarus, R. and Folkman, S. (1984). *Stress, appraisal, and coping.* New York: Springer Publishing Company.

Levesque, L., Ducharme, F., and Lachance, L. (1999). Is there a difference between family caregiving of institutionalized elders with or without Dementia? *Western Journal of Nursing Research 21*(4), 472-97.

Littell, J. and Schuerman, J. (1999). Innovations in Child Welfare. In D. Biegel and Blum, A. (Eds.). *Innovations in Practice and Service Delivery Across the Lifespan* (pp. 102-23). Thousand Oaks: Sage Publications.

Margolin, L. (1992). Beyond Maternal Blame: Physical Child Abuse as a Phenomenon of Gender. *Journal of Family Issues, 13*(2), 410-23.

McDonald, T., Couchonnal, G., and Early, T. (1996). The impact of major events on the lives of family caregivers of children with *disabilities. Families in Society, 77*(8), 502-14.

Moncher, F. J. (1995). Social isolation and child abuse risk. *Journal of Contemporary Human Services*, September, 421-33.

Orodenker, S. (1990). Family caregiving in a changing society: The effects of employment on caregiver stress. *Family & Community Health 12*(4), 58-70.

Ortiz, V. (1995). The diversity of Latino families. In R. Zambrana (Ed.). *Understanding Latino Families: Scholarship, Policy, and Practice* (pp. 18-38). Thousand Oaks: Sage Publications.

Patterson, J. and Leonard, B. (1994). Caregiving and children. In E. Kahana, D. Biegel, and M. Wykle (Eds.). *Family caregiving across the lifespan* (pp. 133-58). California: Sage Publications.

Pearlin, L, Mullan J., Semple, S., and Skaff, M. (1990).Caregiving and the stress process: an overview of concepts and their measures. *The Gerontologist*, 583-594.

Phelps, J., Belsky, J., and Crnic, K. (1998). Earned security, daily stress, and parenting: a comparison of five alternate models. *Development and psychopathology 19*, 21-38.

Ramos, B. (1998). *Acculturation and Depression Among Puerto Ricans and Puerto Rican Veterans in the Continental United States.* Doctoral Dissertation. Ann Arbor: University Microfilms.

Scheyett, A. (1990). The oppression of caring: women caregivers of relatives with mental illness. *Journal of Women and Social Work, 5*(1), 32-48.

Schulz, R. and Beach, S. (1999). Caregiving as a risk factor for mortality. *JAMA* *281*(23), 2215.

Starr, R. (1988). Physical abuse of children. In V. Van Hassett, R. Morrison, A. Bellack, and M. Hersen (Eds.). *Handbook of family violence* (pp. 119-55). New York: Plenum Press.

Toseland, R., Smith, G., and McCallion, P. (In Press). Family caregivers of the frail elderly. *Handbook of social work practice with vulnerable populations*. New York: Columbia University Press.

Trickett and Kuczynski (1991). Physical abuse of adolescents. In R. Lerner, A. Petersen, and J. Brooks-Gunn (Eds.). *Encyclopedia of adolescence*, 11 (pp. 780-784). New York: Garland.

U.S. Department of Health and Human Services, administration for children and families. (2000). *HHS reports new child abuse and neglect statistics.* HHS News. Washington, D.C.: author.

Yee, J. and Schulz, R. (2000). Gender differences in psychiatric morbidity among family caregivers: a review and analysis. *The Gerontologist, 40*(2), 147-64.

Chapter 12

What Hurts and What Helps: Listening to Families to Build 21st Century Child Welfare Reforms

Katharine Briar-Lawson and Megan Wiesen

One of the benefits of moving into the 21st Century is the ability to look back at the 20th century. Such retrospection offers a perspective on which practices should and should not be maintained in the 21st Century. This chapter lays out some of the lessons learned in working with child welfare families and from design teams (described in other chapters) in the intermountain west. Exemplars are featured from several other states, including cross-systems collaboration, family-guided and -led services, and attributes of several successful cross systems service initiatives. This chapter focuses on integrating families' perspectives with those of professionals who touch their lives.

The Great Divide

What families say they need, child welfare professionals (all the service providers who work with families in the child welfare system) may be unprepared to provide. Twenty-first-Century practices must deal with the disconnection between family needs and service provider responsiveness. Listed below are examples of the disparity between family's needs and what child welfare professionals are prepared to provide. Some of these disparities help to explain the poor outcomes many child welfare families experience (Briar-Lawson, 1998a).

Families: often see child safety, abuse, and neglect as a family issue
Professionals: often see safety as a children's, not a family system issue

Families: would often prefer to mobilize help from those they consider family
Professionals: often do not have the time and capacity to mobilize and listen to the solutions offered by the family system

Families: may perform 90% of health, education, counseling, small business, justice work and policing, and expect comprehensiveness from helpers
Professionals: often specialize; "I just do risk assessment," "I just license foster care," "I just do drug assessments," and "I just do immunizations"

Families: want to feel enfranchised and supported
Professionals: are sometimes blaming, punitive

Families: often want prevention and earlier intervention services at first blush of need
Professionals: usually offer remedial services after the crisis

Families: often need resources, economic supports to be providers and caregivers
Professionals: often lack capacity to foster income supports or jobs

Families: often seek mutual aid and social support
Professionals: often lack the capacity to mobilize or legitimize the use of non-professional intervention strategies

Families: often require TANF or SSI if not working and lack income supports essential to placement prevention and reunification
Professionals: are often forced to use more intrusive measures, such as adoption or permanent guardianship, if TANF has been terminated and family lacks other income

Families: often want concrete relief and help with stress and exhaustion
Professionals: usually have mostly counseling and parenting classes to offer not respite or related care-giving relief (such as parent aids, homemaker aids) other than foster care

Families: often need concrete resources (e.g., for a car repair, new front door for safety, to go to a recreational program for stress reduction and feeling mainstreamed, a prom dress for a daughter needing to improve her self-image)
Professionals: often lack flexible funds and are forced to redefine or ignore these concrete needs

Families: usually need professionals aligned with their service goals and needs, high quality of treatment
Professionals: usually focus on services provided rather than quality of treatment, which families are experiencing

Families: often bring indigenous knowledge, home remedies, culturally based perspectives, and solutions to problems
Professionals: may be poorly prepared to understand and use indigenous and culturally based knowledge and practices

Families: may want to have their definition of the problem and solutions heard and acted on whenever possible

Professionals: are often required to impose risk assessment tools, court-ordered case plans, and may never elicit family case plan or goals, such as how parents would like things to be better and different

Families: often wish to convene their own case staffings and have interprofessional teams working for them

Professionals: may convene interprofessional teams, sometimes without family present, often to dictate with judgmental attitudes what family should do

Families: often care about their interconnected and co-occurring needs (e.g., substance abuse, domestic violence, childcare, elder care, job retention, disabilities, neglect charges, mental health, child truancy, school problems)

Professionals: may specialize in one area only and may not recognize the interconnections; up to 14 professionals may serve the same family

Families: often seek accountability to their goals and capacities

Professionals: often seek accountability to professionally and court-determined outcomes

Families: may see service providers whose case plans are uncoordinated and contradict each other

Professionals: sometimes make referrals that are paper edicts and do not involve interprofessional communication

Families: may feel injured by investigatory, judgmental, punitive, and contentious approaches

Professionals: often lack skills and capacities to be mobilizers of therapeutic and helping relationships; may normalize adversarial relations with families

Families: may need help with feeling motivated and trusting that if they follow through with services that things will get better

Professionals: may lack time and capacity to motivate and to build sense of family efficacy

Families: often expect that service providers will serve as gateway workers to others in the social and health service system

Professionals: may represent and assess only the part of the problem, the symptom for which they are responsible, may lack skills or mandate to serve as gateway worker

Families: seek services tailored to their unique needs and challenges
Professionals: may force fit families into existing programs

Families: have time-limit-driven mandates for behavioral and related improvements.
The TANF, ASFA clocks drive their need to be given priority treatment and services
in order to retain custody of their children
Professionals: may not even be aware of the ASFA clock nor have openings for
services for many months, may be unable to give child welfare and other public sector
families "first call" on services

Partnerships with Families

It is essential for 21st-century child welfare professionals to find ways to learn from,
and to partner with, family members. Such partnerships are often difficult as
professionals may see child welfare parents in negative lights as "perpetrators" or
non-protective parents. Despite neglect and abuse charges, most child welfare parents
have views and perspectives that warrant professional attention and empathy rather
than disdain and discounting.

Beginning efforts are underway in Utah, New Mexico, Nevada, and Colorado to
address the cycles of maltreatment that public sector families experience in their help
seeking and service mandates. The use of family experts (current and former clients)
as key leaders in design teams (described in other chapters) and in capacity building,
training, and systems change work has proven to be effective in sensitizing
professionals on how they need to change. Family experts have helped to guide design
teams in multiple communities. They provide perspectives on "what hurts and what
helps." In addition, their feedback has given rise to front line workers improving their
own cross professional assessments, interactions and referral processes (Briar-
Lawson, Lawson et al.,1999; Briar-Lawson & Wiesen , 1999).

In one community, for example, a family expert looked at the professional
members of the design team and said, "You all saw me two years ago, haggard,
exhausted with needle tracks in my arms and not one of you asked me if I was doing
drugs." As a result, the design team members became more sensitized to the need for
all to do beginning substance abuse assessment. This same kind of feedback was
offered by family experts in a University of Utah class of evening students involving
child welfare workers in the community, who comprised a parallel kind of design
team. Family expert feedback on the need for more skills in substance abuse led these
students to question why substance abuse courses were not required in the Graduate
School.

This consulting and capacity building role of family expert is the foundation for
the building of occupational and educational ladders with and for them (Briar-
Lawson, Lawson et al., 1999). In Nevada and Utah, several are now in school

working on social work or related degrees. In Colorado, several have been hired full time to improve practices in agencies, such as mental health. Their perspective on what hurts and what helps sets the stage for service providers to address the maltreatment syndromes that affect not just families themselves but front-line workers. This, in turn, has led professionals to reconsider their inadvertent dictatorial style of case planning. In one community, for example, professionals come to design team training and learn how it feels to be a client among service providers in that community. Many leave more prepared to listen to family views rather than impose professional edicts on the family about what they might do to improve their situation.

Other examples of helping experiences involving family experts with a Utah design team can be drawn from the following illustrations. Case example 1: After approximately six months of design team meetings, a family expert shared her frustrations with two of the agencies with which she was involved. After listening to her concerns, members of the team from this agency were able to offer assistance and become personally involved to bring some resolution. Without the relationships developed on the team, the family expert would have had a much more difficult time finding solutions. Case example 2: A family expert told of a dilemma in his community regarding substance abuse and how the training in the group had assisted him in identifying treatment options for a community member.

The Need for Service Plan Alignment

Creative research has been undertaken by Bricker-Jenkins (1996) involving child welfare families. Effective outcomes in child welfare were attributed to the degree of "consensus" between the worker and the family. Parents were more likely to follow through on case plans when they felt honored in their definition of the problems (even if it was an incorrect hypothesis that they put forth). They also felt more inclined to follow through on the worker's case plan once their own was tried.

Relevant findings have been generated from a demonstration project in Hennepin County (Owen, Fercello, et al., 1993; Webber, 1994) . Parents were given a choice to use a child welfare case manager who had funds to address their needs or to use the money themselves in "family" driven case planning. Those who did not use the case manager used their "own designated" funds to purchase memberships at the local "Y" so that they could reduce stress and feel "normal." Such findings helped child welfare professionals recognize that the provision of concrete resources may be a precondition for follow through with other services. They also reinforce the importance of listening to what child welfare families say they want and need and finding ways, to whatever extent is legally and safe for the child and family, to address their needs. If not, relationships may be diminished and parental capacity to feel effective and motivated may be lessened.

Influence of Family Experts in Child Welfare

Designating current or former clients as "family experts" has given them special status and roles in guiding cross- systems reforms in design team work in four states in the intermountain west. Family experts in Utah for example have had an impact on practice and delivery of services in the Salt Lake area. This philosophy has led professionals to seek family friendly ways to design service plans, which more effectively protect children and empower families. For example, design teams were a catalyst to child welfare staff to look at a variety of ways to provide more effective services such as family group conferencing. In family group conferencing, families and those involved with them are being asked to meet together and design their own service plans (Wilcox, Smith, et al., 1991). Parents, family members, friends, and any support people they want to have participate are contacted and asked to attend. A facilitator who is not the primary caseworker meets with the caseworker to determine who else should be invited. Professionals who are working with the family are asked to attend, such as any welfare workers, school teachers, police officers, clergy, and so forth. Strengths, needs, and goals of the meeting are discussed and plans are designed by all present. Professionals are asked to leave as family members then design a plan that protects the children and empowers the family.

Collaboration for and with Cross Systems Families and Children

The rise of collaborative practices and service integration is in part a direct response to the fact that child welfare families are "cross systems clients." Research on effectiveness regarding collaborative practices and outcomes for children and families is spotty (Bickman, 1996). Nonetheless, categorical policy and service strategies have resulted in piecemeal approaches to families. As noted above, families may have as many as 14 service providers all working with various needs, governed by often-conflicting policies, services, and funding streams. For every need, presenting problem or service goal, there may be a different front-line service provider who may be unaware of the case plan of the others. As a result, families may be receiving contradictory and exhausting service mandates.

For child welfare families to be more successful, they must have access to supportive and tailored services (Schorr, 1997). Yet, many community agencies and their front-line service providers do not even recognize or know that they are serving child welfare families or that they are central to effective outcomes for them. Even worse, they may be unaware of Adoption and Safe Families Act (ASFA) time limits so that as the 12-15 month clock is ticking regarding permanency decisions in child welfare, families may be sitting on wait lists or denied access to service because either they or other service providers have insufficient resources to address needs. Anecdotal examples are emerging around the country of child welfare families who have been sanctioned (dropped from the welfare rolls) for "non- participation" or terminated due to TANF time limits. In many of these cases, neither the child welfare nor welfare worker knew that families were being served by the other system. This is in sharp contrast to Colorado Springs, where TANF is being used as the prevention and family preservation arm of child welfare (Berns, 1998). Here, workers in both systems address self-sufficiency and family preservation needs, meeting service goals of their shared families. Preliminary research suggests that TANF benefits are a protective factor for reunification of children with their families (Wells, Guo, & Sloan, 2000). Yet, as states determine who to exempt from time limits and welfare terminations, few have designated child welfare families as a "protected category" (Barkdull, Briar-Lawson, et al.,2000). Thus, time limits in welfare compounded by time limits in child welfare create "double jeopardy" families (Briar-Lawson, Lawson, et al., 1999).

Co-occurring Needs in Public Sector Families: Gateway Practices

Recognition of these jeopardized families and their co-occurring needs compel new practices and competencies. Some of these new competencies involve a core of skills that all service providers must possess as they are potential "gateway" workers for one another's service systems. In fact, they must be able to assess, and, in a preliminary way, address domestic violence, child abuse and neglect, substance abuse, mental health and disability challenges, poverty, unemployment, housing, health, and school problems.

Each service provider, regardless of specialty or service system, is a potential gateway-child welfare professional. Gateway workers may help child welfare families get to services they need by addressing an interprofessional core of assessment questions. This core involves the assessment of stress and its effects on parenting, including abuse and neglect, on children's development, parental depression, and related coping, such as the use of self-medicating behaviors. Gateway probes also explore the presence of domestic violence as well as the need for more resources, such as a job, welfare, child care, transportation, and housing.

Effective collaboration models at the front line involve interagency case planning and staffing in which families present their needs, goals, and barriers. Agency service providers respond by tailoring case plans to families' readiness and capacity to use services and to the safety needs of children and the family. All pool their goals and case plans with a coherent focus on shared outcomes.

Often, natural helpers or parent paraprofessionals are present. They help to foster motivation. They may serve as advocates for the parent and family (Alameda, 1996). They often fill in between the cracks of the service systems (e.g., transportation) so that families are able to follow through on case plans that they have jointly crafted.

It is not uncommon for families to reframe their needs as first requiring concrete resources (Briar-Lawson, 1998a). This concretizing of needs is an essential first step to their being open to and ready to use more complex services and treatment for challenges, such as substance abuse, mental health problems and so forth. Yet, few service providers have concrete resources in their "tool" kit. Thus, families' needs and preferences for where they want to start often go unaddressed. Unaddressed needs cause a gap between service providers and families.

Sometimes natural helpers, parent aids, or parent advocates can mobilize some of these concrete resources (Briar-Lawson, 1998b). This resource mobilization helps to reinforce the sense, whenever possible and appropriate, that families are competent, joint crafters in service plans rather than passive recipients of non-negotiated work plans. Families and family experts can also assist with new program development, service initiatives, and cross-systems changes. The following examples suggest a few ways in which innovations can be jointly crafted by practitioners to be more responsive to child welfare families.

Parent's Anonymous in TANF Offices. In a related University-assisted community collaborative, Parent's Anonymous support groups attempt to foster occupational and employment ladders for TANF families. Parent's Anonymous is a parent-led, practitioner-facilitated, mutual-aid strategy to prevent and address abuse and neglect and delinquency. Parent's Anonymous support groups are being offered in local welfare offices in parts of Utah. Here mutual aid and parent supports to address abuse and neglect and job needs are being addressed simultaneously.

Project Hope. Another example of collaboration in Salt Lake City, which addresses related needs, is the FACT (Families, Agencies, Communities Together) Initiative, Project Hope. Project Hope is a team of professionals who meet regularly to address the needs of children and families who live within their school's boundaries. The Project Hope team includes elementary school staff, a Division of Child and Family Services staff member, a Work Force Services employee, a health team member, a school district employee, a member of a preschool intervention team, a member of mental health, and others who provide services to children and families. These teams meet often, usually at least twice per month, to discuss the needs of families who have volunteered for the program. The collaborative efforts are effective in assisting family members with a holistic approach to problem solving. Other varieties of this type of program also exist. In order to meet the needs of schools who do not receive Project Hope funding, schools are combining and sharing resources, then joining with allied professionals to accomplish the same type of goals.

Child Protection Neighborhood Teams. The neighborhood team philosophy in the Salt Lake area began to materialize over four years ago. Leaders in child welfare emphasized collaboration with other agencies to assist in the protection of children.

More trusting relationships were sought, and new partnerships were formed. In addition, a strengths and needs focus was adopted in working with families. The evolution of the neighborhood model since that time has generated a variety of collaborative relationships that have expanded the ability of the Division of Child and Family Services to protect children.

School-Based Collaboratives. The rise of school based collaboratives and service enhancements represents one of the more promising strategies to build more cohesive, integrated, and comprehensive strategies. In fact, child protection workers in Boise were linked to classrooms and had resources to address abuse and neglect, such as emergency income assistance. As a result, diversion rates into child protection cases were as high as 87% (Tanoury, Saunders, & Lusk, 1996).

Multitrack Systems. Efforts to build multitrack assessment and diversion systems have also involved close collaboration with community service providers. Pilots funded by the Edna McConnell Clark Foundation (2000) have demonstrated beginning effectiveness. In fact, multitrack systems promote alternative responses to low and moderate risk child protection families. This enables child protection workers to focus on the most severe cases. For example, Parent's Anonymous groups and neighborhood run family resource and support centers represent examples of a parent-led or co-led alternative response system to which low and moderate risk families can be referred.

These and other neighborhood and front-line practices need to be aligned with middle manager practices and policies as well as state level policy frameworks. Thus, in Utah, front-line reforms increasing the linking of Parent's Anonymous to design teams and to neighborhood-based child protection teams resulted in legislative efforts to turn such pilots into policy exemplars. As a result, a multitrack bill has passed the legislature, thus fortifying new front-line and neighborhood-based collaboratives, and family service oriented child protection practices.

Partnership Examples from Florida and Ohio

Several initiatives from two states tested the impact of parents hired as paraprofessionals, the use of family centered and guided practices, culturally relevant services, and data-driven change. The programs involved services to parents with one or more substance exposed newborns and two school-based initiatives addressing children's risks relating to school failure, child protection involvement, and family poverty and marginalization (Briar-Lawson, 1998b).

Parents Serve as Paraprofessionals

Parents are trained as social service, teacher, or health aides. They serve as role models since they have often been clients. They are provided an occupational ladder beginning with stipends, then move into full-time jobs. Their new well-being, recovery from substances, violent relationships, depression, and their upward mobility adds credibility to the motivational and related supports they bring to the "target population."

Co-founders of Homebuilders along with a work team have identified the helping skills in family preservation practice. This team has concluded that up to 50% of the tasks required to undertake effective practice can be done by paraprofessionals (Apple, Bernstein, et al., 1997).

Parents Aid with More Intensive Services, Creating Improved Ratios of Service Providers to Those Served

Because parents are involved as case aides, the ratio of worker to families is less problematic. Thus professionals are able to more strategically use their skills and time. Moreover, paraprofessionals can often intervene where professionals cannot. For example, teams of mothers in recovery from crack can show up at 2:00 AM to reach out to a former friend and "crack" user saying... "Let us in; there is still hope for you. We have lost our children to adoption; we are HIV positive. We shared the same crack dealer. Now we are sober. Let us share the same sobriety with you." They can be successful with motivational support where professionals have failed.

Family-Centered Practice

Presenting needs and problems are reframed by the family members in terms of goals and solutions and impediments to those goals. The service providers (parents, professionals) work at barrier busting. This is in contrast to caseworkers and others dictating case plans that may do little to enjoin or enfranchise parents as partners in the case plan.

Strength-Based and Empowerment Strategies

Parents and other family members are seen as having assets. Even with abusive parents, attention to strengths that can be harnessed helps to increase the responsiveness to court-ordered treatments and related mandates.

Culturally Responsive Practices

Many families have home remedies that are culturally and contextually prescribed. Finding a way to understand these and to support their efficacy, when appropriate, builds not only on strengths but recognizes that there may be indigenous inventions that can be fostered. Entering families' cultures humbles the service team as professionals learn the meaning of events in the family and the role of indigenous inventions, some of which may be helpful to other families.

New Norms for Quality Interactions

Because families often feel maltreated by those serving them, high-quality interactions are essential. Thus, relationship building with and advocacy for families sends a message that they have reason to feel empowered and helped rather than hurt and demoralized by the helper. Families may craft "bills of rights" or "quality of treatment and interaction indices" on how they wish to be treated by all professionals. Family advocates, family experts, and others can help design these. They then help to reculture the service delivery process with attention to the dynamics of harm that may undercut services being accessed and utilized. For example, in a school-based service collaborative, service providers were asked to rate their treatment of child welfare families. These 14 service providers rated themselves as warranting a 2 on a 10-point scale with 10 being good and 1 poor. Moving quickly to new norms of interaction and treatment is a requisite to many other improvements.

Intervention Teams as Learning and Change System

As teams of professionals and paraprofessionals work with families, they become learning systems. If one intervention does not work they adopt a "whatever it takes" and "no reject" attitude to find the right solution and strategy. Paraprofessionals are critical to the collection of data on changes. They are able to chart progress, step by step, so that they can see and help steward the change monitoring process.

Data and Family Driven Change and Developmental Research Strategies

Research methods also become part of the change process since the goal is to invent solutions to complex challenges. Research methods thus involve intensive, formative, as well as outcome evaluative practices along with developmental research approaches. Quasi-experimental designs are essential. The research team seizes naturally occurring quasi-experimental conditions. For example, in one school parents, as paraprofessionals, had successfully helped the school move from the worst in absenteeism rates to the best in the school feeder pattern. Thinking that the absenteeism problem was solved, the principal then asked the parents to address other school problems. Once the absenteeism outreach activities ended, the absenteeism rates went up again. When the parents' absenteeism outreach team was redeployed again addressing absenteeism problems, the absenteeism rates went back down. Each withdrawal and then reintroduction of the parent absenteeism team helps to generate data within the context of quasi-experimental conditions. Table 1 delineates selected outcomes and impacts.

High Stake Families and Child Welfare Systems

Developmental research and intervention approaches are based on successive patterns of inventing-testing-retesting solutions to approximate desired goals and outcomes. Parent and family paraprofessional roles help to expand inventive options, capacity, and progress charting. Some of the desired outcomes from three demonstration projects sketched above suggest the promise of these untapped "client" resources.

Given the nature of the challenge now facing child welfare families and their service providers, it seems timely to consider the expansion of the helping professional's repertoire to include those who are the "target" system as the "action" system. For example, time limits in welfare and child welfare creating "double jeopardy" families are compounded now by the introduction of time limits in public housing, medicaid, child care subsidies, and so forth. Other welfare state programs may follow suit, given the climate of managed care. In fact, for every co-occurring need, there may be a service response with its own time limit due either to managed care or related welfare state cutbacks. Increasingly, public sector families first may lose welfare grants, then skid into child welfare and run the risk of losing their children to adoption due to the ASFA clock. Given such high stakes and the potential for compounding harms for child welfare families, it is imperative that more helpful and less hurtful practices be mobilized by practitioners.

The stakes are high not only for child welfare families but the very systems that serve them. Mandates accompanying ASFA now require that states be sanctioned when they have not achieved desirable results relating to seven main outcomes. Many of these outcome domains assume that collaborative and enfranchising practices exist among service providers and between providers and families. Benchmarks and goals are being set for states so that failure to achieve them will be costly. These domains for state performance and increasing improvements include (1) reduced re-occurrence of child abuse and neglect; (2) reduced time for reunification; (3) reduced time to adoption; (4) reduced entry into foster care; (5) reduced incidence of abuse and neglect in foster care; (6) increased permanency for children in foster care; (7) increased placement stability. In addition, states are held responsible for the well-being, including health and mental health and school progress of children in out-of-home care.

Table 1. Selected Outcomes and Impacts

Necessary Conditions	Outcomes Sought	Outcomes Achieved	Policy Impacts
Parents as para-professionals More intensive services, improved ratios of service providers to families	Reduced substance and HIV-exposed newborn children, reduced numbers of "abandoned infants"	Substantially reduced numbers of substance and HIV-exposed newborns; continued grant funding; replications	Host agencies adopt policies to hire para-professionals, create occupational ladders; adopt family-centered practice; empowerment strategies
Family-centered practice	Reduced school absenteeism, "police sweeps," and child abuse and neglect	School absenteeism reduced and academic achievement increases; improvements in family functioning, recognized as the best Title I school in Florida	Flexible funds designated for parent stipends, policies of agencies change (new missions, norms); state and county full-service school model expanded with new school-linked service initiatives; replication in several states; multiple investments by funders
Strength-based and empowerment practices Culturally responsive practices Norms for quality of interaction Intervention teams as learning systems Data and family-driven change; developmental research strategies	Reduced cycles of school failure	Improvements in all aspects of student functioning and school performance	Culturally responsive practice principles adopted; state-launched school readiness centers initiated

Beleaguered child welfare systems (with over 30 facing some kind of child welfare class action lawsuit) now require, more than ever, concerted cross-systems efforts to build more accountable and results-oriented outcomes. Systems and service providers must function interdependently to ensure outcome success and to maximize funds for services and support to families.

While the employment of families, such as current and former welfare and child welfare parents is not a panacea, it is one perspective addressing barriers to success. Some service providers may have normalized poor outcomes for child welfare families for so long that the capacity to understand and mount expedited solutions to these accountability challenges may be impeded. Thus, the inclusion of the family expert, parent paraprofessional perspectives, and problem-solving roles into service delivery systems may be a critical asset. Other resources that need to be further mobilized to join in inventive front-line reforms are field units of students from social work and related disciplines.

Sharing of the Accountability Challenges with Universities

Partnerships among universities, Schools and Departments of Social Work, and child welfare agencies and families themselves need to function as incubators of innovative practice models and service improvements (Briar-Lawson & Wiesen, 1999).Together, University and community child welfare partners can design, incubate, test, and refine interventions so that new helping technologies can be invented. (Briar-Lawson, Schmidt, & Harris, 1997).

Many lessons can be derived from the promise of the family preservation movement. This movement may be less about what could be achieved with placement prevention and reunification strategies and more about the capacity of child welfare systems to promote pilots and experimental approaches to service delivery. Educational preparation programs may need to reinvent public sector practice content to include data- and family-driven, transformational, and related front-line system changes.

Educators across the helping professions may need to grapple with such questions as how many of their students in helping disciplines are prepared to simultaneously assess and address all these predictable challenges among child welfare families, or how many are able to prevent their co-occurrence. That is, if one need or risk factor exists, can they work to prevent the co-occurrence of other predictable "disorders"? Simultaneously, is quality of treatment seen as a key component of effective service delivery? How many students are prepared to mobilize some of their clients to be deputized as family experts, to use TANF and related funds to hire them as paraprofessionals? Alignment challenges of the 21st century include attention to what families need, outcomes for which service systems are being held accountable, and the ways in which we prepare our students to work with families as co-inventors of new practices and service effectiveness.

The first decade of the 21st century can be an historic turning point in the history of human services and reform. Listening to families and co- inventing with them and their professional collaborators are key requisites for testing new more promising and desired changes.

References

Alameda, T (1996) R.A.I.N. Makers: The consumers' voice . In K. Hooper-Briar & H. Lawson, (Eds.). *Expanding partnerships for vulnerable children and families* (pp.46-56). Washington D.C.: Council on Social Work Education.

Apple, K., Bernstein, S.,Fogg, L., Haapala, D., Johnson, E., Johnson, R., Kinney, J., Price, D., Roberts, K., Robinson, K., Steele, T., Trent, E., Trent, V., Smit R.,and Vignec, R. (1997). Walking the talk in the neighborhoods: Building professional/natural helper partnerships, *Social Policy, 27* (4), 54-57

Barkdull, C., Briar-Lawson, K., Johnson-Berry, S., Kelley, N., and Abu-Bader, S. (2000, January). *Criteria for exemption from welfare terminations: Implications for child welfare systems.* Paper presented at the Society for Social Work and Research, Charleston, SC.

Berns, D. (1998). *Working papers on TANF, family preservation and poverty eradication.* Colorado Springs, Co: The El Paso County Department of Human Services.

Bickman, L. (1996). The evaluation of a children's mental health managed care demonstration. *The Journal of Mental Health Administration,23*(1), 7-15.

Briar-Lawson, K. (1998a). Capacity-building for family centered services and supports. *Social Work, 43* ,539-550.

Briar-Lawson, K. (1998b). Innovations in collaborative practices. In J. McCrosky and S. Einbinder,(Eds.). *Universities and Communities: Remaking professional and interprofessional education for the next century.* Westport, CT: Praeger

Briar-Lawson, K., Schmidt, D., and Harris, N. (1997). Partnerships: future visions, lessons learned. *Public Welfare,* Summer.

Briar-Lawson, K., Lawson, H., Derezotes, D., Hoffman, T., Petersen, N., Harris, N., and Sallee, A. (1999, January). *Serving families with substance abuse, mental health, domestic violence, employment challenges.* Presented at the Society for Social Work and Research Conference, Austin, TX.

Briar-Lawson, K. and Wiesen, M. (1999, June). *Model partnerships between child welfare and universities.* Paper presented at the Partnership Symposium, US Children's Bureau, Washington D.C.

Bricker-Jenkins, M. (1996). Personal communication with the author.

Edna McConnell Clark Foundation:
http://fdncenter.org/grantmaker/emclark/pubs.html)

Owen, G., Fercello, C., AuClaire, P., and Batko, P.(1993, December). *Public private collaboration to reduce child maltreatment: An evaluation of Minnesota's family options program*. Paper presented at the Tenth National Conference on Child Abuse and Neglect.

Schorr, L.(1997) *Common purpose: Strengthening families and neighborhoods to rebuild America*. New York: Anchor Books.

Tanoury, T., Saunders, M., and Lusk, M. W. (1996). In Partnership with families, schools and communities: Using Title IV emergency assistance funds. In K. Hooper-Briar and H. Lawson (Eds.). *Expanding partnerships for vulnerable children and families* (pp.46-56). Washington D.C.: Council on Social Work Education.

Webber, M (1996) Personal communication with author

Wells, K., Guo, S., and Sloan, J. (2000, January). *Impact of welfare reform on the child welfare system*. Paper presented at the Society for Social Work and Research, Charleston, SC.

Wilcox, R. Smith, D., Moore, J., Hewitt., Allan, G., Walker, H., Ropata, M., Monul., and Featherstone, T. (1991). *Family decision making, family group conferences: Practitioner's views*. Lower-Hutt, New Zealand: Practitioner's Publishing.

Chapter 13

Gaining the Collaborative Advantage and Promoting Systems and Cross-Systems Change

Hal A. Lawson & Carenlee Barkdull

Introduction

The child welfare system cannot be an island unto itself. It needs services, supports, and resources from other systems. Reciprocally, it needs to give something back to these other systems. All of these systems need to collaborate, especially their professionals. *Interprofessional collaboration* is one key to improved services and better results. Moreover, when professionals and their systems collaborate effectively, they also are able to join forces with indigenous community leaders and the private sector. They are able to promote *community collaboration*, a second key to improved services and better results.

At the same time, professionals and families need to collaborate. Their *family-centered collaboration* is an important component of broad-based, community collaboration, and it may be the most important key to improved services and better results.

Success stories about these three kinds of collaboration, i.e., interprofessional, family-centered, and community collaboration, often have a common theme. Successful collaborative initiatives enjoy leadership from social work in general and child welfare in particular. In brief, your leadership is essential.

Toward this end, this chapter introduces collaboration, starting with the current child welfare context that compels it. Then, past and present barriers and problems associated with collaboration are presented. Next, the basics of collaboration are identified. For example, practical definitions of different kinds of collaboration are provided. Collaboration is contrasted with the other "c-words"—communication, cooperation, co-location, and coordination. Collaboration is then connected to other related concepts, such as service integration, cross-systems change, and community-based systems of care. Facilitators for collaboration are identified in conclusion.

Signs of Need in the Contemporary Context: The Promise of Collaboration, Service Integration, and Systems Change

As a new century beings, there are growing needs for collaboration, systems change, and cross-systems change. For example, a growing number of families challenged by poverty and its companions (e.g., social stigma, unemployment, housing, and food insecurities), are living on the edge of the child welfare system.

For example, according to researchers from the National Center for Children in Poverty, poverty rates for children under age 6 increased more than 12% (from 22.0% to 24.7%) between 1979-1983 and 1992-1996 (Bennett & Li, 1998). A 1998 survey of 30 cities conducted by the U.S. Conference of Mayors over a one-year period concluded that emergency food requests by families increased by an average of 14%; that an estimated 21% of these requests have not been met; and, that, while requests for emergency shelter by homeless families increased 15%, some 30% of these requests have not been addressed effectively. Data like these do not bode well for families or for the child welfare system.

Other families are just above the poverty threshold. Like high poverty families, they also confront daily economic stress and, perhaps, some housing and food insecurities. They may be just one crisis away from a rapid slide into poverty.

The tolerance levels of individuals and families vary considerably. For example, a family living in poverty may be able to weather the kinds of employment and housing stress[es] that overwhelm a family not yet living in poverty. On the other hand, the long-term effects of severe stress and profound insecurities are predictable among all kinds of families. As family stress and insecurities increase, child, parent, and overall family well-being decline. As their well-being declines, a pattern of ripple effects becomes evident in all of the public sector child- and family-serving systems. Indeed, this pattern is evident today in a growing number of vulnerable communities.

Multiple Systems in Crisis and the Promise of Collaboration

To begin with, many child welfare systems are in crisis. In many states, the system is already overloaded. Caseloads are too high to meet child and family needs and to enable workers to feel that they are doing a good job. Indeed, some 30 state systems are operating under court-ordered mandates, in part because of the excessive burdens they shoulder. When child welfare systems are in crisis, professionals at all levels of the system experience the effects. Turn-over rates increase, and morale problems grow. In short, when systems are in crisis, the recruitment, retention, job satisfaction, and well-being of front line professionals, middle managers, and top level supervisors are affected.

In the same vein, many juvenile justice systems mirror the growing crises in child welfare. A growing number of public school systems that serve poor and vulnerable children and youth evidence the same needs. Health and mental health systems are struggling to achieve their goals and objectives for poor and vulnerable children and families, and they also face worker recruitment, retention, and well-being challenges. In brief, *the child welfare crisis is part of a cross-system pattern.*

Leaders in social work and in other helping professions are becoming aware of this pattern. They are realizing that yesterday's industrial age practice strategies, policies, and social institutions, for all of their benefits and strengths, are not responsive to the changing psychological, social, cultural, geographic, political, and economic realities of the global age. They boldly proclaim needs for *interprofessional collaboration, service integration, community collaboration, systems change,* and *cross-systems change* in service of vulnerable children, youth, and families and their surrounding communities (e.g., Bruner, 1997; Dryfoos, 1998; Gardner, 1999; Hooper-Briar & Lawson, 1996; Melaville & Blank, 1993; Schorr, 1997; Tourse & Mooney, 1999). They are promoting these new "buzzwords" and others because they know that changes in practices, policies, and institutions usually depend on innovative concepts. Innovative concepts and new language enable diverse people to think and talk "outside the box" and still communicate effectively.

Bold Promises Versus the Cold Realities

National, state, and local movements to "integrate services" and "improve collaboration" among private and public sector agencies have been among the most significant trends in the human services over the last decade. Integrating services and improving collaboration have been hailed as "systems change." In fact, many such systems-change agendas have been structured from the top down (e.g., O'Looney, 1997; Waldfogel, 1997). Leaders and front-liners in child welfare systems have viewed this trend with optimism and hope, especially ones in beleaguered systems faced with growing needs, more complexity, flat or shrinking resources, increased calls for accountability, and often-disappointing outcomes.

Looking back over the 1990s, it is probably fair to say that many child welfare administrators, middle managers, and line workers who have worked with other professionals and systems to integrate services and collaborate would give these so-called systems-change efforts mixed reviews. Certainly there have been inspiring individual success stories. On the other hand, "collaboration" and its companions have not been a panacea, nor have they lived up to their promise in many communities. Unfortunately, many well-meaning people have formed, or joined, so-called "collaborations" only to find that their time spent in meetings never seems to translate into any real changes in systems or service outcomes (Gardner, 1999). Instead of securing help, and making their jobs better, time toward collaboration and its companions adds to the burdens they carry.

So, leaders and front-line professionals in child welfare as well as in other systems may be understandably suspicious about bold claims to promote collaboration, service integration, systems change, and cross-systems change. In fact, professionals at all levels of the system may be hostile to these proposals. They may view it as "this year's new thing," another change for the sake of change, yet another add-on to already heavy and stressful job descriptions.

Bridging the Great Divide Between Policy Proclamations and Practice

Top-down policy proclamations are important facilitators for every change initiative. Unfortunately, many well-intentioned policy mandates often lose something on the way to front-line practice—if they "had it" in the first place. This special something is specificity, precision, and clarity regarding what needs to be done differently and better, along with when and where it needs to be done, how, under what circumstances, why, and with what results. To put it a different way, this special something, which policy proclamations have been missing, provides the answer to this practical question: How would you know it if you saw it? Or, how would you know if you were doing it right and doing good in the process? Although policy mandates may provide resources, incentives, and rewards, they usually do not proceed much beyond grand proclamations, structured from on high, which in effect announce that, henceforth, thou shalt collaborate and integrate services!

It is wholly understandable that policy proclamations create this great divide. They are enabling mechanisms with high symbolic value. That is, they may promote, permit, encourage, support, and reinforce new programs and practices, but political differences and local diversity effectively prevent policy authors from being as specific, precise, and clear as they might wish to be. Or, policy authors may not know exactly what the new programs and practices will look like. They only know that they want something different and better than what they have today.

As understandable as these tendencies are, the fact remains that they create barriers to effective collaboration. For example, when leaders and front-liners alike are confronted with these policy mandates; when they are not provided with sufficient specificity, precision, and clarity; and, when tailored technical assistance, capacity-building, and systems change supports are in short supply, the great divide between policy proclamations and practices remains. In fact, it may even grow.

Little wonder, then, that many professionals feel as if they are "spinning their wheels" as they try to respond to the requirements of policy proclamations for collaboration, service integration, and systems change. Top-level leaders, middle managers, and front-line professionals alike are required to do new things, but they are not provided all of the learning, development, and improvement supports they need. They are stranded on the practice side of the policy divide. But they should not be criticized and blamed when they demonstrate that they are. Like families in need, these professionals should not be blamed for system-induced barriers and needs, including the shortage of capacity building, responsive technical assistance, and above all, specificity, clarity, and precision regarding what they need to do differently and better, and, how practicing differently and better will improve results for families and working conditions for them.

For example, investigators in a national study of school-related collaboration and service integration asked school and agency professionals two specific questions, which in essence addressed the policy-practice divide (Lawson & Briar-Lawson, 1997). The answers professionals provided illuminated the policy-practice divide.

The dialogue tended to follow this pattern. Question 1: *What's new and different here?* Answer: *We're collaborating and integrating services.* Question 2: *How are things better for children and families?* Answer: *We're collaborating and integrating services.* There are no surprises here. Asked to do new, and perhaps dramatically different things, but provided few specific details about how they would know it if they saw it; and how they would know if they were doing good, professionals responded using the same buzzwords that the policy mandates required. Like families' responses to professionals' assessment protocols, professionals' answers can be treated as presenting needs, which signal underlying, root needs and problems.

Introducing Interprofessional Collaboration and Service Integration

As suggested earlier, there are many different levels and kinds of collaboration. In fact, intricate analyses of collaboration and its related concepts are needed. The problem is, these analyses can be overwhelming; and even worse, they may result in confusion, fear, and strategic withdrawal.

Unfortunate and undesirable responses like these can be prevented. Collaboration can be introduced gradually and appropriately. One kind of collaboration— interprofessional collaboration—provides a good point of departure, because it provides a necessary and effective response to child and family needs.

Families' Co-Occurring Needs

A growing number of individuals and their families evidence co-occurring, or intertwined needs (e.g., Halpern, 1998; Kessler, Gillis-Light, et al., 1997). Two such needs—substance abuse problems and mental health needs—may be the most familiar pair. Their relationship is described by the term "co-morbidity" (e.g., Kessler, Gillis-Light, et al., 1997). However, other such needs co-occur with these two. Where child welfare families are concerned, the complete inventory of co-occurring needs includes poverty, unemployment or under-employment, child abuse and neglect, mental health issues, substance abuse, and domestic violence (Briar-Lawson, Lawson, et al., 1999).

For example, O'Keefe found alcohol and drugs were a serious problem in the home of 72% of battered mothers (1995), while McKay (1994) reported that between 45% and 70% of battered women in shelters reported the presence of some form of child abuse in the home. Forty-seven to 63% of the batterers also abused children, and 28% to 56% of the battered women also abused their children (Saunders, 1994).

As with substance abuse and mental health needs, inter-generational patterns may be evident. Research recently conducted in Utah among long-term welfare recipients found that 60% had been abused as children, or they were in domestic- violence relationships as adults (Derr & Taylor, in press).

Furthermore, these multiply challenged families tend to have more health-related problems. For example, diseases that are preventable (e.g., coronary heart disease) often cause them to die prematurely and tragically (e.g., Felliti, Andra, et al., 1998). Even worse, parents and caregivers may pass along their co-occurring needs to their children. In turn, when these children become parents, they pass along their co-occurring needs to their children (e.g., Kessler & Gillis-Light, 1997). In short, the inter-generational transmission of these co-occurring needs is a paramount challenge.

Families' co-occurring needs may be associated with others in their neighborhood communities. For example, when many families with multiple, co-occurring needs live in the same neighborhood community, this local community often is less safe and secure, and it may breed crime, delinquency, high transience, and more domestic violence, substance abuse, and child abuse and neglect (e.g., Halpern, 1995; 1999). The neighborhood community's characteristics contribute to families' co-occurring needs and challenges, and vice versa.

In addition, these co-occurring needs track into others. For example, a school-aged child in a family system stressed by multiple, co-occurring needs is likely to be viewed by teachers and the principal as having academic and behavioral challenges. Another example: When multiple, co-occurring needs are not detected and addressed, parents tend to lose their jobs, families often become fragmented, and the family system may slide into poverty.

The Assembly Line System of Professions

To summarize: Co-occurring individual and family are intertwined. Find one, and sooner or later, you are likely to find the others. Twin rules for practice follow: (1) When you look for one, be certain to look for the others; and (2) Address one, and sooner—not later—you also must address the others. These twin rules compel social work perspectives and action strategies, i.e., ones that are multi-modal and multi-level. To put it another way, intervention-improvement strategies are required that simultaneously address families' presenting, co-occurring needs, while at the same time preventing the occurrence of other, predictable needs that stem from these current ones. The implication is that professionals and these families need to work together.

Unfortunately, the various people-helping professions (the education professions, nursing, medicine, social work, the various health education and promotion professions, the mental health professions) are not configured to address these co-occurring needs. Like 20th-Century social work, they are industrial age institutions. Just as the modern social work profession has developed its boundaries and boundary markers (e.g., specialized university degree programs, language, knowledge, licenses), so have the others. In fact, the professions often compete with one another over their respective boundaries, including which profession should have jurisdiction over particular individual and family needs (e.g., Abbott, 1988). For example, social workers often compete with clinical psychologists and psychiatrists when they claim jurisdiction over children's mental health needs, and when they assert their qualifications to provide family therapy (e.g., Brint, 1994).

Mirroring the assembly line of the factory, there is a system of professions (McKnight, 1995; Lawson, 1998). Each profession has developed in response to one or more specialized needs or problems. Indeed, one or more professions has developed for every specialized part of the human being, the family system, and the neighborhood community. These professions all provide services. More than this, they have helped define and promote these needs and problems, claiming at the same time that they are too important and complex for everyday people to address and that their profession's members will serve society as they intervene. Reflecting industrial age thinking about machines and their component parts, the professions have assumed that each human need, every family challenge is like a component part of a machine. Each need, problem, or challenge can be isolated for treatment, and when it is fixed, the machine (the human, the family) will work as planned. Specialized organizations, service sectors, policy forums, and university disciplines have developed in response.

Another metaphor illuminates the collaborative challenge for the professions. The professions, along with their organizations, service sectors, policy forums, and university systems, are like specialized silos on a farm. The problem is that the specialized farmers (professionals) do not view themselves as part of the same farm, even though their respective silos are near one another. Nor are these professional farmers equipped to do organic gardening and to promote the cross-pollination of their seeds and crops. This silo problem is a systems problem, and it has ripple effects.

Individuals and families, especially families with co-occurring needs, often get lost among the silos. So, for example, a child welfare family with co-occurring needs is expected to

• Locate child support and transportation services in support of employment

- Find the mental health center and receive mental health counseling

- Go to the substance abuse treatment center and receive substance abuse counseling

- Go to the family support center and receive parent education and training so parents do not continue to abuse and neglect their child[(ren)]

- Find the domestic violence center and receive training for non-violent conflict resolution and power-sharing

- Find the employment counselor and receive job skills and development training

- Meet with the child welfare worker to monitor progress

- Meet with the child protection worker and perhaps appear in court with her

- Go to the school to meet with the principal, counselors, and teachers to address their children's needs

Actually, this list is a simple, limited one. A growing number of families have a longer list. For example, Gardner (1999) describes the challenges of working with some 50 agencies when his family adopted two children.

The consequences of little collaboration among service providers often mean that in day-to-day practice, case plans are rarely coordinated. Often, recipients of services may be asked to follow through with competing or even contradictory expectations and goals, which can negatively affect both the ability and motivation of individuals and families to follow through with case plans. Lack of service recipient follow-through can lead to poor outcomes and demoralized caseworkers, who frequently feel frustrated and ineffective in their roles.

Thus, it is relatively easy to evaluate this industrial age pattern of professions, silos, and service delivery. Clearly, individuals and families with co-occurring needs must travel extensively, and they must make considerable sacrifices to secure services, supports, and resources. Professionals with more power and authority than these families often dictate their needs and wants. Because these professionals are prepared to treat just one need or problem in isolation from the others; because they inhabit their problem- and need-specific silos; because these silos are scattered across a community; because the professions are not convened regularly to communicate with one another and work together; and because the professions even compete with one another for the right to serve the same individuals and families, people in need get caught in the middle of the silos. They may have as many as 14 different professionals in their lives (Hooper-Briar & Lawson, 1994). Even though the family knows all of them, these professionals often do not know each other. Even worse, because they do not communicate effectively and they are not convened regularly to harmonize and synchronize their respective efforts, they often work at cross-purposes. Lacking a common denominator of understanding, knowledge, language, and skills, these professionals effectively display a kind of "trained incapacity" to join forces.

Clearly, this industrial age model is not a good way to serve individuals and families, especially child welfare families with co-occurring needs. Nor does this model serve professionals. The well-being and job satisfaction of professionals in every silo depend in part on their effectiveness with individuals and families. If they are unable to do good work and enjoy the rewards and satisfaction that accompany it, their morale will suffer, their job commitments may wane, and agency turnover rates will increase. In short, no one wins with this industrial age system.

Proposals for interprofessional collaboration and service integration stem from harsh, undesirable, and preventable realities like these. These proposals are designed to benefit everyone—families, professionals, policy makers, and other citizens.

Interprofessional Collaboration

Obviously, professionals serving the same individuals and families need to start communicating regularly and effectively. They need to stop working at cross-purposes, often catching families squarely in the middle. At the very least, they need to cooperate effectively and coordinate their efforts. Simply stated: *Every professional working with the same individual and family needs to be "on the same page."* The idea of interprofessional collaboration derives from this basic need. It necessitates the development of interprofessional teams.

Teams often vary considerably (e.g., Ovretveit, Mathias, & Thompson, 1997). Even so, they have common threads. For example, just as a choir director or an orchestra leader works to harmonize, coordinate, and synchronize the efforts of musicians, and just as an athletic coach must do the same with athletes, so, too, does a team of team of professionals need a collaborative facilitator. Where child welfare families are concerned, this person often is a social worker. When a social worker or another professional agrees to provide collaborative leadership, this person may be called the lead case manager or planner, or the team leader.

With the assistance of the lead case planner or team leader, professionals begin to operate like a team. They agree to place the children and the family at the center of their coordinated team planning, and they make every effort to identify, and respond to, co-occurring needs. Often, they develop behavioral norms intended to improve the quality of treatment and interaction among professionals and among professionals and families (Lawson & Briar-Lawson, 1997). These professionals agree on mutual responsibilities and accountabilities. They agree on who will do what, when, how, under what circumstances, and why. They also agree on how to chart progress and measure results. They are communicating, cooperating, and coordinating their efforts, and, as they do, they make progress toward integrating the services that families receive.

As Figure 1 indicates, teams start with effective, regular communication and build on it as they strive to cooperate and to coordinate services (Lawson & Barkdull, 1999). Indeed, some professionals may even move their offices to the same place (co-location). The assumption is that people who work in the same place will find it easier to communicate, cooperate, and coordinate. In other words, they know that the best way to address the silo problem is to redesign the silos for joint occupancy. So, for example, they may co-locate in a school, a local church, a community health and social service agency, a recreation agency, a neighborhood organization, a police station, or a shopping mall. Accordingly, these service integration arrangements often are called "one-stop shopping" (e.g., Hooper-Briar & Lawson, 1994).

When families' co-occurring needs are involved, teams of professionals may build on their progress related to communication, cooperation, coordination, and co-location. *They may agree to collaborate.* Collaboration includes the other "c-words," but it is more than any one of them. As Table 1 indicates, *collaboration means sharing accountability for results* (e.g., Gardner, 1999; Lawson & Barkdull, 1999). In other words, every member of the team—the social worker, the clinical psychologist from the mental health center, the employment counselor, the child protection worker, the domestic violence specialist, the substance abuse counselor, the community nurse, the school counselor, and other possible team members—knows that no one professional or agency will be successful in addressing the families' co-occurring needs unless the others are also successful. Simply stated, *collaboration as shared accountability for results rests on a solid foundation of mutual interdependence.* Each profession needs the others to succeed. The family needs the professions to succeed. Because they depend so much on each other, professionals and families alike join forces, they collaborate rather than going it alone.

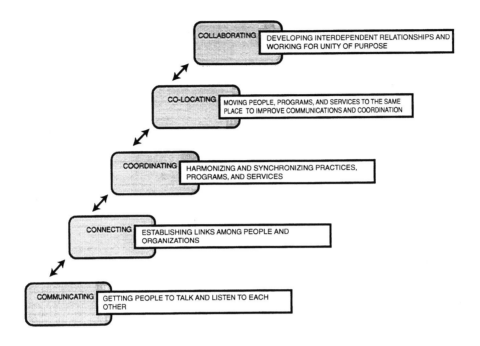

Table 1. The "C-Word Family:" Differences as Choices

Table 1. The Basics of Collaboration

Collaboration is grounded in interdependent relationships. It occurs when individuals, groups, families, professions, and organizations depend upon others' success.   Furthermore, collaboration is   · A method for improving results, not an end or goal in its own right   · Embedded in, and tailored to, local contexts and cultures   · Grounded in understanding of connections and interdependence among characteristics of children, youth, and families and the professionals who serve them   · Cemented by trusting, interpersonal relationships   · Promoted and supported by power-sharing and democratic norms and practices   · Facilitated by shared norms in support of blame-free communications, firm commitments to problem-solving, and improvements in the quality of treatment and interaction all stakeholders experience and expect

Collaboration requires enabling structures, cultures, and processes that promote interdependent planning, evaluation, learning, and development.

For example:

- Shared agreement about problem domain(s)
- Shared aims, values, change principles, and improvement strategies
- Shared results and accountability for them
- Shared commitment to monitoring results and making in-flight adjustments when barriers or stuck-points are identified
- Shared information and resources
- Opportunities for calculated risk-taking, role release, and continuing learning
- Democratized leadership and decision-making structures
- Shared commitments, expressed in inter-agency agreements, to needed changes in policies, organizational structures and cultures, and definitions of "best practices"

Trust can be facilitated by ensuring that

- Norms are proposed for conducting the business of collaborating that everyone agrees to
- An environment of mutual respect and safety is developed in which members are encouraged to be creative, take risks, and explore difficult issues, such as the protection of turf and other barriers to change
- Participating family members and youth should be viewed by the group as resilient experts, as people possessing strengths and aspirations, and as partners in the joint design in all phases of the collaborative's efforts

Service Integration

When professionals are able to collaborate effectively, services are more likely to be integrated. Two catchy phrases have been used to explain and promote service integration. One is "wrap-around services." This phrase suggests that the child and the family system are placed in the middle of interprofessional team planning, and professionals work together, and with the family, to ensure that services are integrated—that is, they are harmonious, synchronized, and produce a mutually beneficial synergy.

The other phrase is "one-stop shopping." This phrase suggests that children and families no longer have to travel extensively to get what they want and need from specialized professionals. Professionals are in the same place; they are co-located. And because they are located in the same place, their collaborative "wrap-around service planning" is facilitated.

Return to the list of co-occurring needs is evidenced in many child welfare families. Especially in urban communities, several specialized professions may need to be convened and co-located to address these needs. By contrast, in rural and frontier communities, generalist practice may be the norm, and the challenge of frequently vast distances separating families from providers when more specialized services are required must be creatively addressed . In brief, place and context weigh heavily in interprofessional collaboration and service integration.

Last, but not least, service integration and interprofessional collaboration initiatives have been noticeably selective (e.g., Briar-Lawson, Lawson, et al., 1999; Halpern, 1999). They have addressed conventional definitions of service needs, but they have not been especially adept at meeting the new requirements associated with the Adoption and Safe Families Act (ASFA) and the employment-related requirements of Temporary Assistance to Needy Families (TANF). Nor have they attended to the needs of "double-jeopardy families" (Briar-Lawson, 1999), i.e., families caught between ASFA's time requirements for placement decisions and TANF's time limits for employment. Interprofessional collaboration and service integration offer the promise of meeting these new century challenges. But they will live up to their promise only if professionals know what to look for and prioritize. Only then will they gain the collaborative advantage.

Enlightened Self-Interest and the Collaborative Advantage

Unfortunately, when collaborative relationships are being formed, facilitators may convey the impression that everyone should put aside their specialized needs and interests. In this environment, it may not be safe to ask and answer two basic, important questions: (1) Why should I, and my agency, participate in this collaborative work? (2) What's in it for me and us? For a host of reasons, questions like these are viewed as the opposite of collaboration. Persons who insist on asking them may be perceived as selfish and unprepared to collaborate.

When such an environment prevails, and when people are unable to ask and address these questions, collaboration is constrained, limited, and perhaps prevented. Busy people with excessive workloads and job pressures simply cannot be expected to attend meetings and participate genuinely unless they have good reason to believe that their attendance and participation will improve their jobs and lead to improved results for children, families, communities, and their agencies.

In brief, when professionals agree to collaborate, share accountability for results, and acknowledge their interdependence, *they are propelled by enlightened self-interest.* They are not selfish or narrowly self-serving. They are enlightened by understanding of their interdependence and the good things that will happen when they invest the time and effort. They are enlightened because they know that by joining forces they gain "the collaborative advantage" (Sarason & Lorentz, 1998).

That is, collaboration improves their professional effectiveness. In turn, their satisfaction increases, their morale goes up, they do not change jobs, and they develop supportive work cultures for newcomers. Figure 2 has been constructed to show these multiple benefits for service providers and teachers (Lawson & Barkdull, 1999) It is one way to think about the requirements for systems change in support of interprofessional collaboration and service integration.

Introducing Systems Change and Cross Systems Change

The preceding brief overview of interprofessional collaboration and service integration paves the way for an introduction of systems change and cross-systems change. Remember the silo metaphor and the assembly line metaphor as you think about these twin changes.

Systems Change

Systems change thus necessitates bridging policy and practice divides. Organizational structures, especially accountability criteria, job descriptions, and supervisory patterns, must be adapted, and work cultures need to change to support collaboration. With collaboration, no one must go it alone.

To put it another way, top-level policies and front-line practices need to be aligned, harmonized, and synchronized. When they are, workers and families enjoy a mutually beneficial synergy. With the virtuous cycle identified in Figure 2, this work of aligning, harmonizing, and synchronizing everyone in the silo is the key to systems change.

Introducing Cross-Systems Change

Cross-systems change entails recognizing that the silos are part of the same farm and working to create firm connections among them. It includes ways to cross-pollinate and create mutually beneficial hybrids. It means sharing the benefits and rewards of mutually beneficial collaboration. In other words, cross-systems change usually means connecting, harmonizing, and synchronizing [child welfare] mental health, juvenile and criminal justice, health, employment services, education, and other policy and sector silos. For example, all might commit to family-centered policies and practices (Briar-Lawson, Lawson, et al., in press) and develop within- and across-silo policies and practices in support of them. Beyond these conventional social welfare sectors are the economic development and business development silos. They may be included in cross-systems change agendas as well.

**Table 2. The Collaborative's Role in Integrating Child
Welfare with Other Important Initiatives**

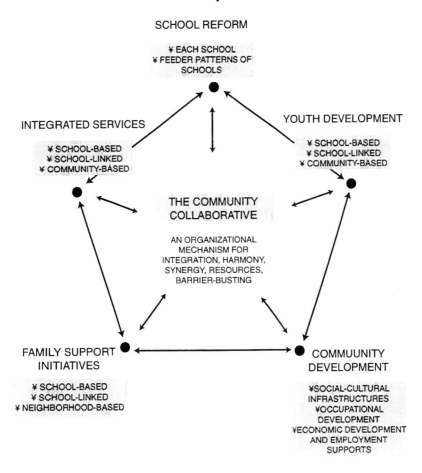

Responsive and Supportive Policy Change

Responsive and supportive policy changes are effected to support and promote collaboration, systems change, and cross-systems change. For example, crisis-oriented service policies that require children and families to demonstrate proof of harm before they can get help may be replaced by preventive policies. Front-line workers may be given flexible dollars, which they can use to do early intervention and prevention with individuals and families in need. Berns (Chapter 3) provides other important examples of how policy change promotes anti-poverty and pro-family work. All such policy changes animate systems and cross-systems change.

Other Kinds of Collaboration

There are four other kinds of collaboration. Each is defined briefly below.

Intra-organizational and Inter-organizational Collaboration

Intra-organizational collaboration entails aligning, harmonizing, and synchronizing workers at all levels in the same agency or school system. For example, large human services agencies that encompass many child welfare and family support functions face the important challenges of getting separate departments and their professionals to collaborate. This is the challenge of intra-organizational collaboration, and it promotes systems change.

Inter-organizational collaboration entails the same kind of work, but it involves two or more organizations. For example, child welfare systems, juvenile justice systems, mental health systems, and school systems can be aligned to address the co-occurring needs of "cross-over kids and their families" (e.g., Lawson & Anderson-Butcher, this book; Cocozza & Skowyra, 2000; Kamradt, 2000).

Collaborating With Families

Proposals for family-centered collaboration often hold the key to systems change, cross-systems change, and new century policies and practices. Family-centered collaboration is described in detail in the next chapter by Briar-Lawson and Harris. The basic idea must be introduced here because it is so important to new century practices and policies.

Advocates for family-centered collaboration are involved in both systems and cross-systems change because they are mounting a strategic attack on the industrial assembly line of the professions (e.g., Alameda, 1996; Alameda-Lawson & Lawson, 2000; Briar-Lawson, Lawson, et al., in press). Their aim is not to disband all of the professions or to deny needs for their specialized expertise. Rather, their aim is to transform the professions and their silos. Although they favor interprofessional collaboration and service integration, these advocates doubt that it will yield all of the benefits that families and professionals need and deserve.

Advocates for family-centered collaboration rest their case on these related claims:

- Families have expertise, and this expertise is an important part of effective solutions to their problems

- Families know what helps and hurts them, and they need to have some "say-so" in what is done, by whom, how, when, where, and why

- Families want and need to develop their capacities to help themselves and each other; they do not want to remain dependent clients

- Professionals need to hear the voices and honor the expertise of every family member, especially the voices of girls and women

- Professionals need to share power and authority with families, making them partners in the design and delivery of services, supports, and resources

Family-centered collaboration thus entails major changes in how individual professions and the assembly line of professions are organized. It requires changes in how professionals treat families. It necessitates changes in professional education and training (see chapter 17). It is a key part of systems change in child welfare and accompanying cross-systems changes. And, it opens the door for broad-based community collaboration—for community-based systems of care.

Community Collaboration

Once individuals and families in need are viewed as having expertise in what they need and want, including what helps and hurts them, then the door is opened for community collaboration. Like family-centered collaboration, community collaboration is based on assumptions about the strengths and the limitations of individual professions and the assembly line of professions. Stated simply, two key assumptions unite these two kinds of collaboration. First: *There will never be enough professionals to meet every child, family, and community need.* Second: *Local community residents—other individuals and families—must be encouraged and supported in assuming joint responsibility and accountability for children's safety and protection, family well-being, and the safety and security of their neighborhood communities.* These related assumptions pave the way for the development of community-based systems of care. Both family-centered collaboration and community collaboration are essential to these systems of care.

Community collaboration requires convening and organizing a community collaborative, or community consortium (Bruner & Parachini, 1997; Farrow & The Executive Committee for Child Protection, 1997; Hooper-Briar & Lawson, 1994; Lawson & Barkdull, 1999; Melaville & Blank, 1993). Figure 3 depicts the sectors that are "at the table" in a community collaborative. These sectors support child welfare, and in turn, child welfare supports them.

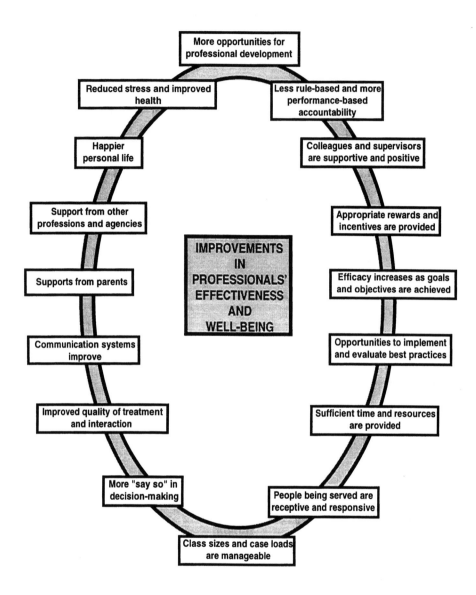

Table 3. Recruiting and Retaining Good People: The Key to Systems and Cross-Systems Change

In brief, community collaboration serves as the umbrella for the other kinds of collaboration—interprofessional, intra-organizational, inter-organizational, and family-centered. These different kinds and levels of collaboration are coordinated, harmonized, and synchronized via community collaboratives.

Table 2 provides concise definitions of the five kinds of collaboration discussed in this chapter. Table 3 provides a list of the skills and abilities needed by new century social workers, collaborative leaders who are prepared to support and promote multiple forms of collaboration, especially community-based systems of care. Table 4 is modified from the research of Chrislip and Larson (1994). It presents other key facilitators for collaboration.

Table 2. Taking a Look at Different Levels of Collaboration

Interprofessional Collaboration
- Happens when two or more people from different professions work together to accomplish the goal of helping a child.
- The professionals may be from the same school or agency, or have different employers.
- By working together toward a common goal, professionals can help one another gain new perspectives, knowledge, and skills.

Interagency Collaboration
- Two or more independent organizations, usually with different missions, develop formal agreements for working together toward a common purpose or goal.
- Good interagency collaboration can make the process of interprofessional collaboration work better, as everyone's roles are clearly defined
- These agreements are frequently in writing (may also be called interagency partnerships).

Intraorganizational Collaboration
- This is necessary in large school systems with many departments, programs, and locations.
- Collaboration may be easier in some ways because the organization holds a common mission or purpose.
- Collaboration may be more difficult in some ways if administrators aren't careful in planning, especially in providing professional development programs and resources for teams of teachers, counselors, social workers, nurses, and psychologists.

Family-Centered Collaboration
- Families, especially parents, are considered full partners with professionals in deciding what kind of services are needed and whether or not the services are actually achieving the desired results.
- Parents, children and families are viewed as experts in what hurts and what helps them—"professional knows best" is not the automatic rule.
- This approach requires both professionals and families to be accountable and responsible in their interactions with one another.

Community Collaboration
- Involves everyone in the community—stakeholders—who are committed to helping improve children's learning, healthy development, and success in school.
- Since all members of the community have a stake—families, professionals, and policy-makers—all kinds of collaboration are needed under this 'umbrella' to make it work.
- The community collaborative helps coordinate, harmonize, and synchronize the operations of schools, youth development programs, community agencies, and neighborhood organizations.

Table 3. Characteristics of Effective Facilitators for Collaboration

- Learns and knows the territory
- Ensures that key stakeholders are at the table
- Has a remarkable ability to scan it for opportunities, benefits, and resources
- Can act as a boundary crosser who can break from the mentality of the organizational chart
- Can build strong networks of social trust among the stakeholders
- Acts in flexible and responsive ways to group needs and changing group dynamics
- Recognizes assets and builds on individual and group strengths
- Understands dynamics involving power, authority, and influence—puts this knowledge to use for everyone's mutual benefit
- Is selfless, altruistic, and modest—never arrogant or self-promoting
- Understands and responds appropriately to diverse cultures
- Takes a wide-angle view of service integration
- Frames needs, problems, challenges, and opportunities in a social-ecological way

Keep in mind that this may not be an exhaustive or complete list for your community. All of the above individuals or groups are likely to share an interest in having students succeed in school. As a result, all are potential stakeholders in your collaboration.

Table 4. Some "Tips" on Planning and Evaluating Collaboratives

Criteria for Successful Collaboration

- The collaborative produces concrete, tangible results
- The timing is good in response to a clear need and stakeholder readiness.
- Stakeholders are sufficiently diverse. One sector and profession does not dominate, and stakeholders view the collaboration process as open and credible.
- High-level, visible leaders in each sector are committed, involved, or both, and they provide legitimacy and credibility. And, because their constituencies are represented in the collaborative, established political authorities support the collaborative, or at the least, do not interfere.
- Over time, stakeholders start to trust each other and become optimistic, and at the same time, mistrust and skepticism decline.
- The collaborative process benefits from strong, facilitative leadership, including trust- and consensus-building, norm development and enforcement, and a results-orientation.
- Small wins, i.e., incremental, interim achievements, and progress markers, are acknowledged and celebrated. These tangible markers help build commitment and keep stakeholders at the table.
- As the initiative evolves and as the collective efficacy of the group increases, the collaborative shifts from specific needs and problems (often narrow and parochial in relation to just one stakeholder group) to broader, more comprehensive concerns.

Key Questions for Stakeholders

- Have stakeholders agreed that there is a problem or need that requires attention? Have they agreed on the definition and parameters of this problem or need?
- Is this problem significantly complex and important? In other words, do stakeholders recognize that none of them can solve it alone, and everyone needs it solved to be successful?
- Have stakeholders agreed to work together? Do they have access to collaborative, facilitative leadership? Have they determined how they will work together effectively? For example, have they developed norms, barrier-busting strategies, and ways to share resources and information?
- Have stakeholders agreed on a implementation plan? Do they view change as linear, in steps, or nonlinear, in interacting phases? Who has oversight for implementation?
- Have stakeholders agreed on the criteria for success (i.e., results, outcomes) and the progress markers? Have they agreed on the measures? On who will measure progress, results, and outcomes?

A Final Note: Enlightened Self-interest and the Collaborative Advantage

Many child welfare staff know what it is to become overwhelmed or to feel "burned out." Effective collaboration addresses self-defeating and demoralizing cycles of failure by promoting a sense of individual and collective efficacy—a "can do attitude"—among workers and the families they serve.

How are efficacy and collaboration related? Through collaboration, people who care about children can be an incredible source of support to one another. Collaborative partners can provide practical help with problem-solving, as well as fresh perspectives and encouragement when a worker feels "stuck," or discouraged. Having others there to reinforce a sense of efficacy—that what we do can and does make a difference—is key to maintaining morale in the face of frequently difficult and stressful work. Indeed, Melaville and Blank (1993) developed the title to their popular guide with this efficacy idea in mind. They called it *Together We Can.*

Helping families to become aware of their own strengths and capacities to solve problems improves efficacy. When efficacy is high, people persist even when they face setbacks and when things do not go smoothly. They are more open to new ideas and to new solutions, and more likely to actively participate and assume responsibility for their case plans.

Put another way, efficacy can be contagious; that is, one person's efficacy can increase another's. There can be many interactive effects. One group's efficacy increases another group's or an individual's or a family's. Improvements in the whole organizational culture can result, promoting beliefs and values that support conditions for the achievement of service recipients *and* human service employees.

Where efficacy is low, the causes can be mapped. Many of the influences of low worker efficacy are outside of the influence and control of agencies. One of the chief benefits of collaboration is that needs and problems outside of the traditional boundaries of agencies can be identified and addressed. Collaboration means that professionals, children, and their families get the help they need through planned connections and strategic interchanges with key community organizations.

When workers across departments, agencies, and professions act as supports and resources to one another, they free up one another's time and energy to do what they do best. It does not mean that everyone is expected to be an expert in everyone else's field. There is still a need for specialization, but there is also a need for workers to develop skills in recognizing and actively looking for co-occurring needs in the families they serve. Having these skills assists workers in providing more timely assistance and intervention to families with the aid of collaborative partners.

Time is a precious commodity these days. It is in short supply for families challenged by ASFA, TANF, and co-occurring needs, and professionals never seem to have enough of it. The collaborative advantage is thus a timely alternative for professionals and families alike. No one should have to go it alone. Enlightened self-interest compels professionals, families, community leaders, governmental officials, and private sector representatives to join forces, promoting and safeguarding the well-being of children and their families and sharing accountability for results.

References

Abbott, A. (1988). *The system of professions: An essay on the division of expert labor*. Chicago: University of Chicago Press.

Alameda, T. (1996). R.A.I.N.makers: The consumers' voice. In K. Hooper-Briar & H. Lawson (Eds.). *Expanding partnerships for vulnerable children, youth and families* (pp. 46-56). Washington, D.C.: Council on Social Work Education.

Alameda-Lawson, T. and Lawson, M. (1999, March). *Parents as the guiding and unifying component for restructuring education support services*. Paper presented at the Council on Social Work Education, San Francisco, CA.

Bennett, N. G. and Li, J. (1998). Young child poverty in the states--wide variation and significant change. In *Early Childhood Poverty Research Brief 1* [On-line]. Available: cpmpcnet.columbia.edu/dept./nccp

Briar-Lawson, K. (1999). Family experts: A missing link in training, curriculum, and cross-systems design. *Child Welfare Partnerships Newsletter*, Council on Social Work Education.

Briar-Lawson, K., Lawson, H., Petersen, N., Harris, N., Derezotes, D., Sallee, A., and Hoffman, T. (1999). Addressing the co-occurring needs of public sector families challenged by domestic violence, substance abuse, mental illness, child abuse and poverty. Paper presented at Society for Social Work Research, Austin, Texas.

Briar-Lawson, K., Lawson, H., and Hennon C., with Jones, A. (in press). *Family-centered policies and practices: International Implications*. New York: Columbia University Press.

Brint, S. (1994). *In an age of experts: The changing role of professionals in politics and public life*. Princeton, NJ: Princeton University Press.

Bruner, C. (1997) *Realizing a vision for children, families and neighborhoods: An alternative to other modest proposals*. Des Moines, IA: National Center for Service Integration, Child and Family Policy Center.

Bruner, C. and Parachini, L. (1997). *Building community: Exploring new relationships across service systems reform, community organizing, and community economic development*. Washington, DC: Institute for Educational Leadership & Together We Can.

Chrislip, D. and Larson, C. (1994). *Collaborative leadership: How citizens and civic leaders can make a difference*. San Francisco: Jossey-Bass.

Cocozza, J. and Skowyra, K. (2000). Youth with mental health disorders: Issues and emerging responses. *Juvenile Justice, VII*(1), 3-13.

Derr, M. and Taylor, M. J. (in press). The link between childhood and adult abuse among long-term welfare recipients. *Children and Youth Services Review.*

Dryfoos, J. (1998). *Safe passage: Making it through adolescence in a risky society.* New York: Oxford University Press.

Farrow, F. and The Executive Session on Child Protection (1997). *Child protection: building community partnerships; getting from here to there.* Cambridge, MA: John F. Kennedy School of Government at Harvard University.

Felitti, V., Anda, R., Nordenberg, D., Williamson, D., Spitz, A., Edwards, V., Koss, M., and Marks, J. (1998). Relationship of childhood abuse and household dysfunction to many of the leading causes of death in adults. *American Journal of Preventive Medicine, 14*, 245-258.

Gardner, S. (1999). *Beyond collaboration to results: Hard choices in the future of services to children and families.* Tempe, AZ and Fullerton, CA: Arizona Prevention Resource Center and The Center for Collaboration for Children, California State University.

Halpern, R. (1995). *Rebuilding the inner city: A history of neighborhood initiatives to address poverty in the United States.* New York: Columbia University Press.

Halpern, R. (1999). *Fragile families, fragile solutions: A history of supportive services for families in poverty.* New York: Columbia University Press.

Hooper-Briar, K. and Lawson, H. (1994). *Serving children, youth and families through interprofessional collaboration and service integration: A framework for action.* Oxford, OH.: The Institute for Educational Renewal at Miami University and The Danforth Foundation.

Hooper-Briar, K. and Lawson, H. (1996). (Eds.), *Expanding partnerships for vulnerable children, youth, and families.* Washington, DC: Council on Social Work Education.

Kamradt, B. (2000). Wraparound Milwaukee. *Juvenile Justice, VII*(1), 14-23.

Kessler, R., Gillis-Light, J., Magee, W., Kendler, K., and Eaves, L. (1997). Childhood adversity and adult psychopathology. In I. Gotlib and Wheaton, B. (Eds.), *Stress and adversity over the life course: Trajectories and turning points* (pp. 29-49). New York & Cambridge: Cambridge University Press.

Lawson, H. (1998). Collaborative educational leadership for 21st century school communities. In van Veen, D., Day, C., and Walraven, G. (Eds.) .*Multi-service schools: Integrated services for children and youth at risk* (pp. 173-193). Leuven/Appeldorn, The Netherlands: Garant Publishers.

Lawson, H. and Barkdull, C. (1999). *Developing caring school communities for children and youth: Integrating school reform and caring communities.* A curriculum guide prepared for the Missouri Department of Elementary and Secondary Education, Jefferson City, MO.

Lawson, H. and Briar-Lawson, K. (1997). *Connecting the dots: Integrating school reform, school-linked services, parent involvement and community schools.* Oxford, OH: The Danforth Foundation and The Institute for Educational Renewal at Miami University.

Lawson, H., Briar-Lawson, K., et al. (1999, April). An empowerment-oriented, interprofessional education and training model for collaboration, organizational development, and policy change. Paper presented at the American Educational Research Association, Montreal, Quebec, Canada.

Melaville, A. and Blank, M. (1993). *Together we can: A guide for crafting a profamily system of education and human services.* Washington, DC: U.S. Department of Education & U. Department of Health and Human Services.

McNight, J. (1995). *The careless society: Community and its counterfeits.* New York: Basic Books.

McKay, M. M. (1994). The link between domestic violence and child abuse: Assessment and treatment considerations. *Child Welfare, 73*(1), 29-39.

O'Looney, J. (1996). *Redesigning the work of human services.* Westport, CT: Quorum Books.

O'Looney, J. (1997). Marking progress toward service integration: Learning to use evaluation to overcome barriers. *Administration in Social Work, 21*(3/4), 31-65.

O'Keefe, M. (1995). Predictors of child abuse in maritally violent families. *Journal of Interpersonal Violence, 10*(1), 3-25.

Ovretveit, J., Mathias, P., and Thompson, T. (Eds.). (1997). *Interprofessional working for health and social care.* London: MacMillan Press Ltd.

Sarason, S. and Lorentz, E. (1998). *Crossing boundaries: Collaboration, coordination and the redefinition of resources.* San Francisco: Jossey-Bass.

Saunders, D. G. (1994). Child custody decisions in families experiencing woman abuse. *Social Work 39*(1), 51-59.

Schorr, L. (1997). *Common purpose: Strengthening families and neighborhoods to rebuild America.* New York: Anchor Books Doubleday.

Senge, P., Kleiner, A., Roberts, C., Ross, R., and Smith, B. (1994). *The fifth discipline fieldbook: Strategies and tools for building a learning organization.* New York: Currency Doubleday.

Tourse, R. and Mooney, J. (Eds.). (1999). *Collaborative practice: School and human service partnerships.* Westport, CT & London : Praeger.

U.S. Conference of Mayors. (1998). Summary: A status report on hunger and homelessness in American cities [On-line]. Available: http://www.usmayors.org

Waldfogel, J. (1997). The new wave of service integration. *Social Service Review, 71*, 463-484.

Chapter 14

Parent to Parent & Family to Family: Innovative Self-Help and Mutual Support

Halaevalu F. Vakalahi and Khadija Khaja

Introduction

Self-help and mutual support groups are the most prevalent formal support groups in America today. These groups are serving over 25 million persons in the United States (Kessler, Mickelson, & Zhao, 1997). Self-help/mutual support was revitalized in the late 1960s and early 1970s as part of the revolt against the professions. Since these early years, self-help/mutual support continues to be a source of de-professionalization (Haug, 1973; Toren, 1974). As part of this revolution was a self-help movement called feminist consciousness-raising (CR), which focused on empowering women to change their lives on their own by recognizing and changing the material and social conditions that entrap them (Rapping, 1997). Today, the self-help/mutual support movement continues to empower women and their families (Salem, Seidman, & Rappaport, 1988).

The partnership among individuals involved in self help/mutual support groups builds on the social work community practice approach in which the "target system becomes the action system." In other words, "clients" who are target systems are not only given help, but are also action systems who are giving help to others. Each "client" is treated as an expert at identifying barriers and conditions that need to be addressed for sustainable and effective change to occur (Foree, 1996; Hooper-Briar & Lawson, 1996; Lipscomb, 1996). Given the accelerated development of self-help/mutual support groups, there may be more help exchanged among self-help groups than within public and voluntary sector social services. A paradigmatic expansion of professional theories and practices is needed to promote and facilitate mutual aid as part of family capacity building and preservation strategy for the next century (Briar-Lawson, 1998; Lloyd & Sallee, 1994).

The purpose of this chapter is to discuss the contributions of self- help/mutual support groups to our society. Self-help and mutual aid have the potential to bring about social change, spiritual leadership, and restructuring of human service practice. Self-help/mutual support groups have contributed enormously to solidifying some of the very real and radical social changes in our society, including combating welfare dependency, school reform, managed care, and improved productivity in the human services (Editors, 1997; Humm, 1997).

Definitions of Concepts Explored

Before proceeding with this chapter, it is important to identify the differences and relationships between self-help and mutual support. According to Burns and Taylor (1998), self-help is defined as the unpaid work that individuals in the same households do for themselves and for each other. Mutual aid is defined as the non-market exchanges of goods and services between people from different households. Mutual aid includes both unpaid (work exchanged for free) and paid (goods exchanged for labor or money) informal community exchanges.

Although, some authors have distinguished between self-help and mutual aid, there are interchangeable relations between these two assistance networks. Using self-help/mutual aid interchangeably, Humphreys and Rappaport (1994) and Nelson, Ochocka, Griffin, and Lord (1998) define such organizations as settings in which individuals with common experiences and needs come together, voluntarily and on an equal basis, to share knowledge, experiences, and supports in an informal and reciprocal manner. Such settings indeed promote non-elite, non-hierarchical, peer power. The underlying values of self-help/mutual include empowerment, interdependent supportive relationships, social change, and learning as an ongoing process.

Principles of Self-Help and Mutual Support

Self-help and mutual support are based on specific principles that are interrelated and need to be integrated. According to Riessman (1997), these principles of self-help and mutual support include (a) social homogeneity, in that group members share a similar condition (e.g., weight control, substance abuse); (b) self-determination, in that group members exhibit desire to help themselves; (c) helper-therapy, in that group members are involved in therapy as they give and receive help (e.g., peer tutoring, peer counseling); (d) strengths-based, in that the focus is on group members' strengths rather than pathology; and (e) services are free and reciprocal.

In applying these principles, Riessman (1997) concluded that self-help/mutual support produces a sense of community and a new kind of productivity. In welfare support groups, people on welfare can help other recipients with issues such as jobs, childcare, health, entrepreneurship, and so forth. It appears that managed care, for all its other problems, could be quite effective if it utilized consumers in self-care and mutual aid groups. Furthermore, it appears that crime could also be further reduced with an advanced system of community policing and neighborhood anti-crime groups. Moreover, public housing works better when tenants manage the operation themselves. Likewise, it appears that cities work best when people with problems are deeply involved in solving their problems. People's engagement creates long lasting solutions and allows individuals to participate in a more democratic society (Katz, 1993; Riessman, 1997).

Self-Help/Mutual Support and Professional Partnerships

The widespread frustration with human services and the search for better solutions present new opportunities to build alliances between professionals and the self-help movement (Nittoli, 1997). Professionals and bureaucrats alone have only solved a portion of problems facing our families. Therefore, there is a need to include more people, more skills, and more resolve at more levels if we are going to make the differences we desire.

Gartner (1997) summarized the strengths of self-help/mutual aid models to include free of charge; not subject to constraints of time, place or format; values experiential knowledge; participants as givers and receivers are equals/peers; and a mutual aid group is seen as a community that is integrated with the natural environment (Bond & DeGraaf-Kaser, 1990). Natural helpers understand their neighborhoods and they know which strategies work and which do not work. Some activities of natural helpers include skills building, providing emotional support, community leadership and networking, and resource acquisition. Likewise, Gartner (1997) indicated that although professionals have biases and limitations, strengths of professionals include accountability, analytic skills, systemic knowledge, and emphasis on training and service-giving ethics. Professionals can supplement the contribution of natural helpers with their skills in grant management, conceptualizing issues, training, evaluation, identification of strengths, fund raising, advocacy, service delivery, problem solving, and mentoring (People Helping People, 1997).

Given these strengths, it seems that harmonizing and integrating indigenous systems of self-help/mutual aid with professional strengths can result in great success and effectiveness. In fact, professional and self-help/mutual support strategies are getting results in communities across the country in areas of welfare-to-work, education, health, and family services (Nittoli, 1997). Specific examples of existing successful professional and self-help collaboration include consumer-led mental health services, self-help groups for women with breast or ovarian cancer, anti-drug abuse program, and school-centered peer groups (Gartner, 1997).

Building on these skills and expertise, in order to be successful in mutual support settings, professionals need to understand the policy foundation of mutual support services and the contribution of mutual support services to resolving social problems. The following section discusses policy foundation, specific social problems, and mutual support services.

Policy Foundation, Social Issues and Self-Help/ Mutual Support

The 1997 Adoption and Safe Families Act promotes the adoption of children in foster care and the Child Abuse Prevention and Treatment Act provides appropriations for community-based family resource and support grants. However, social problems such as mental illness, domestic violence, substance abuse, poverty, and abuse/neglect are all interrelated and interdependent. Therefore, new approaches to family strengthening and preservation must include the cooperation of both families and communities (Madara, 1997; People Helping People, 1997). New training, service, systems designs, and capacity building models are needed to promote family and child welfare goals of safety, protection, empowerment, and reduction and prevention of the impacts of social problems, such as mental illness, domestic violence, substance abuse, poverty, and abuse/neglect.

Community-based services, such as self-help groups, have been endorsed by policy makers as a promising model for restructuring communities inflicted by various social problems (Katz, 1993; Mulroy, 1997; Riessman & Carroll, 1995; Wuthnow, 1994). For example, Parents' Anonymous has been endorsed by the federal government as the benchmark for child abuse and juvenile delinquency prevention and intervention programs. Furthermore, a study by Armstrong (1981) indicated the effectiveness of mutual aid support groups as an intervention tool for parents and children who are at risk for violence and the negative consequences of poverty. Moreover, studies have indicated an association between the presence of social support networks that provide economic and emotional support for families and less risk for child abuse and neglect (Azar, 1991; Belsky, 1993; Mulsow & Murry, 1996; Williams, 1996). In some cases, emotional support may serve as a buffer for the negative consequences of low social economic status (Dukewich, Borkowski, & Whitman, 1996).

Mental Illness and Self-Help/Mutual Support

Self-help/mutual support groups and agencies for mental health clients have grown tremendously during the past 15 years. The value of such groups and organizations in mental health settings has been recognized by both professionals and non-professionals (Christensen & Jacobson, 1994; Mankowski & Rappaport, 1995; Rappaport, 1993). Self-help/mutual aid agencies perceive empowerment of individuals, organizations, and societies as their goal. Such goals are accomplished by helping members obtain needed resources and develop coping skills; providing means of enhancing members' self-concept and lessening the stigma of perceived mental disability; giving members control in the agencies' governance, administration and service delivery; and furthering member involvement in social policy-making

(Humphreys & Rappaport, 1994; Salem, Bogat, & Reid, 1997; Segal, Silverman, & Temkin, 1993).

Currently, there is a rapidly growing body of literature pertaining to self-help/mutual aid and psychiatric consumers (Davidson, Chinman, Kloos, Weingarten, Stayner, & Tebes, 1997; Humphreys, 1996). For instance, Roberts, Salem, Rappaport, and Toro (1999) examined the relationship between giving and receiving help and psychosocial adjustment in a mutual-help group for mentally ill individuals. The most significant finding of this study was that participants who helped others improved in their psychosocial adjustment. Through helping others, participants' feelings of competence increased, and they had the opportunity to develop a more positive, strengths-based perspective.

The National Alliance for the Mentally Ill (NAMI) is a family self-help movement to empower consumers of mental health services. When NAMI was in its formational stages, seventy-one local self-help groups of families of the mentally ill were surveyed to learn something of their composition and strength. About half were independent groups formed by families themselves; the rest were formed by mental health associations or were associated with the American Schizophrenia Association. The independent family groups were larger, more rapidly growing, tended to have regular meetings, and published newsletters. The goals of all seventy-one groups were to provide emotional support, to educate their members, and to engage in consumer advocacy. As the families of mentally ill patients gain power, it is hoped they will insist on more information on treatment, on evidence of efficacy, and justification for costs. Families could lobby the political arena for services they require and challenge the theories of etiology that implicate families in causing or prolonging mental illness (Hatfield, 1981).

GROW Model. The organization GROW is a self-help and mutual support organization founded in 1957 in Australia by former mentally ill patients. In 1978, the first GROW group was founded in the United States. Since then, it has established 100 groups across the United States. GROW is a community treatment alternative consistent with the goal of deinstitutionalization. The organization's conceptual frameworks are based on internal and external resource mobilization and behavior setting theories. GROW organizations focus on community care, economic viability, and grass-roots support. They also seek out political and societal support as well as help from mental health professionals. GROW organizations have three components, including supportive relationships, weekly meetings, and distribution of literature. Individual involvement is encouraged by the creation of group settings that are personal and small in number (Salem, Seidman, & Rappaport, 1988; Zimmerman, Reischl, Seidman, Rappaport, Toro, & Salem, 1991).

Domestic Violence and Self-Help/Mutual Support

Self-help group treatment for males who assault females has been identified as an excellent interaction-based model to help violent men change behavior patterns. Group treatment allows men to describe how they assaulted females from their own perspectives. Men are also given group leadership roles in order to empower themselves and increase their comfort in telling their stories. The mutual aid group process facilitates men facing responsibility instead of denial of their abusive behavior (Gitterman & Shulman, 1994).

Subsequently, victims of violence who often become residents of shelters face a multiplicity of issues. They must cope with life transitions, possibly losing their homes, and having to face interpersonal concerns associated with major changes in a family's circumstances. When goals of advocacy and mutual aid are incorporated into self-help groups, women in shelters appear to cope better. The mutual aid potential is in the sharing of resident frustrations over coping with the shelter's external controls. This creates effective advocacy in suggesting ways of changing shelter rules and procedures that also aid in empowerment of victims of violence (Gitterman & Shulman, 1994).

Substance Abuse and Self-Help/Mutual Support

Self-help/mutual aid recovery approach is one of the major intervention approaches to substance abuse. With the challenges of scarce resources and the gloomy picture of addiction care, self-help/mutual aid organizations can help in the recovery of substance abusers, therefore resulting in less demand for formal professional resources (Humphreys, 1998). Among the many self-help/mutual aid organizations that help substance abusers live substance-free lives are Alcoholic Anonymous (AA), Moderation Management, Narcotics Anonymous (NA), and Women for Sobriety (WFS).

One of the most successful contemporary self-help models and movements is the network of 12-step/anonymous programs. The 12-step movement has grown to be an internationally entrenched, renowned, and influential network of organizations helping members to cope with a mind-boggling array of addictive and/or compulsive behaviors. The 12-step philosophy is based on two assumptions: One's problems are the result of a disease called "addiction," and the "cure" comes from giving one's life up to a Higher Power.

Self-help techniques and principles have been means of providing aftercare services for stabilized methadone maintenance clients. The Clinically Guided Self-Help (CGSH) model emphasized community reintegration and social networking components following a period of primary treatment and demonstrated client stability. The CGSH model allows clients to establish their own agenda of interests and, guided by staff, to engage in a process geared toward maximum participation. The model is clinically based in that staff and participants are engaged in working on current adjustment concerns. The overall goal is to generate the prerequisite skills for successful adaptation of self-help concepts and techniques to the particular needs and interests of individual methadone maintenance programs and clients (Nurco, Stephenson, & Hanlon, 1991).

Young women's self-help support groups are also considered as alternative prevention strategies against the increasing incidence of HIV infection, unwanted pregnancy, substance abuse, eating disorders, and depression. Because previous prevention programs, which were usually school-based, have often failed to address certain adolescent problems, self-help support groups for young women need to be further explored (Azzarto, 1997).

Alcoholics Anonymous Model. The Alcoholics Anonymous Model for Self-Help is described in positive terms of having an effect that no other self-help system had ever obtained. The comprehensiveness of this model and its broad infrastructure and detailed organizational strategy is viewed as creating an atmosphere of concrete help at no cost. The beneficial effects of having control over one's own conditions, the mutual reciprocity of group members, and the empowerment atmosphere creates a strong self-help atmosphere of clear change among members (Riessman, & Carroll, 1995).

Barber and Gilbertson (1998), conducted a study on thirty-eight female partners of heavy drinkers who were randomly assigned either to counseling, self-help, or a waiting list control group. Clients were pre-and post-tested using two self-report measures of distress. Both self-help and counseling were superior to no treatment in producing behavior change in the drinker and in relieving the female partner's level of depression. Self-help therapy is now a realistic option for female partners who either cannot or will not present for treatment.

The Alcoholics Anonymous and Mothers Against Drunk Driving models have been successfully utilized by the self-help movement to enhance the social conditions of various groups and communities. The successes of these models have encouraged people to take part in the self-help movement. As a result, this movement has been recognized by government, philanthropists, and professional helpers as legitimate ways of helping (Gartner & Riessman, 1998).

Poverty and Self-Help/Mutual Support

Self-help/mutual aid traditions have long been strong and prevalent among communities in which individuals are socially and economically deprived (Blair and Endres, 1994; Haughton, Johnson, Murphy, & Thomas, 1993; Meert, Mestiaen, & Kesteloot, 1997). Self-help/mutual aid as an informal form of helping among the poor keeps millions of people off the streets of America and around the world (Ahn & de la Rica, 1997; Cahn, 1999; Thompson, 1998). So much could be learned and applied to the world economies from the informal helping among socially and economically deprived individuals.

Informal helping exists in a variety of settings, including both unemployed and employed individuals (Warren, 1994). Williams and Windebank (2000) conducted a study on self-help/mutual aid practices among 100 households in a deprived neighborhood named Southampton. Self-help/mutual aid was examined as a tool for preventing social exclusion and promoting social cohesion. Participants were from single-earner, multiple-earner, and no-earner households. Findings indicate that participants overwhelmingly relied on self-help/mutual aid not only for economic necessities, but especially for social support. Those who had no earnings received more unpaid help compared to individuals from other households. In spite of the distinct preference for greater amounts of self-help/mutual aid, the authors concluded that constraints such as time, money, skills, and equipment must be resolved in order to fully engage deprived neighborhoods.

The distinct preference for informal helping has led to numerous self-help/mutual aid initiatives. Bok (1988) explored raising the issues of community control and self-help strategies as effective remedies for poverty by utilizing community action agencies (CAAs). As nonprofit agencies, CAAs are unique because all of their strategies have been directed toward maintaining the original mission of the Economic Opportunity Act—to help the poor achieve empowerment and self-sufficiency. Furthermore, community-based initiatives, such as Local Exchange and Trading Schemes (LETS), have been established as powerful tools for developing social supports and promoting mutual aid among deprived individuals and communities (Lee, 1996; Pacione, 1997; Thorne, 1996; Williams, 1996). Moreover, Williams and Windebank (2000) suggested that in order to achieve full engagement among individuals and communities, initiatives like LETS need to be supplemented with structural policies. Examples of policy initiatives include Working Families Tax Credit (WFTC) and Community Service Employment (CSE).

With regard to empowerment of the poor, Fagan and Stevenson (1995) studied an empowerment-based program to improve the parenting abilities of low-income African American men involved in the Head Start program. These African American men developed and participated in self-help groups focusing on having control of one's own destiny; challenging racism; teaching children about violence, sexuality, and substance abuse; and fostering pride in the African American culture. These powerful themes illustrate how self-help groups may be effective in empowering low-income individuals.

Time Dollar Model. A very successful way of combating poverty using self-help principles is the use of Time Dollar barter system in which hours donated become hours banked for reciprocal care and support. In some communities, Time Dollars are honored by local merchants. Thus, the few dollars that families have can stretch farther for the market-based goods that they require. These kinds of programs offer opportunities for individuals to earn currency by helping others. Such programs reinforce reciprocity and trust and often serve as an empowerment tool that may lessen the economic and social stress often resulting in child abuse and neglect. Across the nation, neighborhoods exchange over 100,000 hours of care to meet one another's basic needs. These enable them to make the value of the little income they do have stretch further. It also helps to build trust in communities and among neighborhoods that have become atomized and alienated due to gentrification, housing displacements, job loss, homelessness, and deep and persistent poverty (Cahn, 1997). Certainly, Time Dollar programs have transformed jobless individuals from burdens into assets. In the process of helping others, individuals build their own confidence as well as sharpen their skills (Anonymous, 1998; Cahn, 1999; Thompson, 1998).

The success of Time Dollar programs has swept the nation. A few successful programs are discussed in the following paragraphs. In collaboration with the City University of New York, the Time Dollar Institute developed and implemented cross-age peer tutoring programs for 1,500 elementary school children on the South side of Chicago. The older children tutor younger children. The children earn Time Dollars that they can use to purchase computers and/or accessories for their use at home. In addition to purchasing power, this tutoring program provided role models for younger children and empowerment for tutors. The school reported increase in attendance because students must come to school for tutoring and less bullying after school because tutors take on the responsibility to assure peace (Cahn, 1997).

Similarly, the Superior Court of the District of Columbia established a Time Dollar Youth Court for first time juvenile offenders who committed nonviolent offenses. The jury consists of high school youths having the responsibility to impose sentences ranging from community service and restitution to jury duty. These young people are co-producing peer approval and disapproval, which traditional jury settings are not able to provide. Participating jurors are given the opportunity to earn Time Dollars that can be used to purchase computers or obtain preferential access to summer jobs (Cahn, 1997).

Likewise, Time Dollar programs are beneficial in establishing civic partnerships. The neighborhood of Shaw, Washington, D.C., were seeking pro bono legal services to help deal with the crimes and disorganization in their neighborhood. In collaboration with the Time Dollar Institute, they established a partnership with a law firm who agreed to provide legal services in exchange for hours of volunteer work. The Holland & Knight law firm agreed to exchange one billable hour of legal service for every hour donated in volunteer service by the residents of the Shaw neighborhood. The neighborhood accumulated 375 Time Dollars with which they have purchased $64,000 in legal services. The Time Dollars were earned through "cleaning up trash, planting flowers, taking down license plate of drug dealers, providing safe escort to seniors, tutoring at school, and a variety of neighbor-to-neighbor tasks" (Cahn, 1997, p. 66).

Abuse/Neglect and Self-Help/Mutual Support

Preventing child abuse and neglect through further use of self-help groups continues to be an important goal to achieve. In a study on the use of self-help groups by child abusers, Collins (1978) found that study participants perceived self-help groups as places to learn about rules, expectations, norms, values, attitudes, beliefs and customs regarding proper parenting behaviors. Self-help groups were seen as agents of socialization as they illustrated proper parenting norms for child abusers. Self-help groups also offered opportunities to experience a learning process that influenced role performance and behaviors expected by others, as well as by the child abusers themselves. Peterman (1981), he illustrated the importance of developing self-help parenting groups in poor urban areas as an effective method of intervention.

Similarly, Hegar & Hunzeker (1988) further illustrated that self-help groups for families are an example of effective action-oriented empowerment development strategies for families served by child welfare agencies. They reported that child welfare agencies must be committed to further developing self-help groups for families in order to facilitate families gaining more power, ownership, and responsibility pertaining to parenting decisions. They found that once families became involved with child welfare agencies, they seem to feel disempowered. Thus, self-help groups may be the best method for families to feel empowered again. Likewise, according to Valley, Bass and Speirs (1999), self-help groups could assist child welfare agencies with post adoption programs where families are reunited. By sharing their experiences, these families learn and support one another. They provide hope and inspiration for each other.

Furthermore, Garbarino & Jacobson (1978) suggested that a method to counter abuse is to utilize adolescent peer groups such as the Youth Helping Youth Program. One effective component of the project is the youth self-help group that provides support for maltreated adolescents. Other components include the youth Volunteer Bureau who distribute pamphlets with criteria for identifying maltreatment among peers and suggested steps for help, and a public awareness campaign aimed at increasing youths' awareness of abuse and neglect.

In addition, Leon, Mazur, Montalvo & Rodrieguez (1984) reported that self-help groups could be particularly effective with diverse ethnic families. In their study, they found that self-help groups could be an effective way for Hispanic parents to address the problems and obstacles they encounter. Self-help groups have provided an opportunity for these families to build personal relationships with families of similar concerns and interests, consequently reducing isolation. This model of helping allowed Hispanic parents to establish an environment of trust and enabled families to talk about their parenting anxieties and seek assistance from others in similar situations. Hence, self-help support groups can serve as a positive tool to help diverse ethnic communities become more meaningful participants of human services rather than passive recipients of services.

Parents Anonymous Model. Parents and families are in a prominent position as capacity builders, to take leadership in responding to family needs through self-help programs. Parents Anonymous is the oldest and largest child abuse prevention network in the nation. It is endorsed by federal law as the benchmark for child abuse and juvenile delinquency prevention and treatment programs. Parents Anonymous focuses on strengthening families; responding to diverse family needs; building community partnerships and providing culturally responsive services by integrating values, languages, and strengths of local communities; and creating cost savings across the nation. These weekly free of charge, ongoing mutual support groups are co-led by parents and professionals with the intention of reducing the impact of risk factors and increasing the resiliency of families which may result in preventing child abuse, neglect and juvenile delinquency. In increasing the strengths of families or building protective factors against abuse and neglect, both parents and their children are actively involved in these groups. Being involved in Parents Anonymous, parents and children have opportunities to build on their strengths, learn new skills, improve their self-esteem and social skills, increase their abilities to deal with stress, expand their social support networks, and develop realistic expectations of themselves (Parents Anonymous, Inc., 1996).

Other Relevant Models of Self-Help and Mutual Support

In addition to the models presented above, Maori Family Decision-Making and computer-based group models are emergent methods of helping that merits discussion. These two models are presented below in the context of certain social problems.

Maori Family Decision-Making Model. The Family Decision-Making Model originated in New Zealand among the native Maori people. This model has a cultural base in that, the Maori people developed a culture that included child rearing practices and family decision making, shaped by their relationship to the land. Such a cultural base gives the Maori people the pre-eminent right to be heard, to participate, and to decide what happens to their own.

This model is based on the premise that each family is the "expert" on itself. It exemplifies the significance of indigenous help. Each family has the power to make decisions on itself. The family knows itself better than anyone else does, including those in the external environment. The family is a natural and perhaps, the best place to determine needs and resources for addressing areas of family dysfunction. This model proposes that only in the family can the best decisions be made about the family. This model has been successful in helping families resolve various problems (Wilcox, Smith, Moore, Hewitt, Allan, Walker, Ropata, Monu, & Featherstone, 1991). Although, this model has gained popularity in formal professional settings, its foundation among the Maori people and other Pacific Islanders reflects self-help and mutual support practices.

Computer-Based Group Model. Groups are growing online for the same reason that traditional face-to-face groups have grown; they are meeting unmet needs. Growth in computer-based self-help groups is need-driven. Computer-based self-help groups will increase the linkage of people, ideas, and concerns on national and international levels. Although, there are many benefits of computer-based self-help groups, online networks will contribute to the social isolation of many and to the real prospect of computer addiction for some (Madara, 1997).

The growth of the self-help movement and the rapid expansion of computer communications has led to a variety of computer-based self-help/mutual-aid (CSHMA) groups, including computer-based self-help groups for those with issues related to recovery from sexual abuse. This study found that the potential advantages of CSHMA groups for sex abuse survivors include providing greater access to support, diffusing dependency needs, meeting the needs of those with esoteric concerns, reducing barriers related to social status cues, encouraging participation of reluctant members, promoting relational communication, and enhancing communication of those with interpersonal difficulties. Potential disadvantages included destructive interactions, lack of clear and accountable leadership, superficial self-disclosure, promoting social isolation, limited access to noncomputer-using populations, and lack of research about benefits and user satisfaction (Finn & Lavitt, 1994).

Impacts of Self-Help and Mutual Support

When self-help/mutual-aid networks work, they provide benefits. The benefits of self-help groups are both individual and societal. These benefits include improved coping ability with chronic illnesses and life transitions, friendship and belonging, spiritual renewal, increased political connection, enhanced civil society, and reduced health care resource use (Humphreys, 1997; Kessler, Mickelson, & Zhao, 1997).

Although, methodological limitations in many research studies tend to make it impossible to draw firm conclusions about the impacts and benefits of self-help/mutual support groups, these groups continue to be the most prevalent formal support groups in the United States today (Wuthnow, 1994). The impacts of self-help/mutual aid networks have been due largely to its tendency to promote a sense of community, to provide opportunities for mutual criticism, opportunities to develop effective skills for daily living, to provide role models, and to provide networks of relationships. The financial restraints placed on human service availability have led to an increase interest in self-help/mutual support groups. Practitioners and policy makers hope that self-help/mutual support will reduce the disparity between the need and access to services for individuals with various life problems (Levine & Perkins, 1997).

The child welfare system has increasingly relied on mutual support services to help families feel ownership of their decisions and less isolated from others. For example, many child welfare agencies have parenting support groups developed and implemented by parents themselves. These groups have been successful as families realize they are not alone in needing parenting support. These groups also create a safer environment for families to reach out and be more open to receiving services. Child welfare workers working in self-help/mutual support settings must develop competencies in the following four areas (Briar-Lawson, 1998). Table 1 presents a child welfare worker mutual support services competency list.

Table 1. Child Welfare Worker Mutual Support Services Competency List

1. Definitions related to mutual support/self-help services:

- Understand the definitions and language used to describe mutual support/self-help services.

- Understand the different theoretical frameworks relevant to mutual support/self-help services with families effected by social problems such as substance abuse, domestic violence, mental illness, and poverty.

2. Links between families and mutual support/self-help services:

- Identify and describe the effects of social problems such as substance abuse, domestic violence, mental illness, and poverty on families.

- Identify factors that indicate families at risk for social problems, such as substance abuse, domestic violence, mental illness, and poverty.

- Understand how family psychopathology effects mutual support/self-help services.

3. Mutual support/self-help strategies:

- Outline strategies to assist families experiencing social problems, such as substance abuse, domestic violence, mental illness, and poverty.

- Identify program initiatives aimed at social problems, such as substance abuse, domestic violence, mental illness, and poverty.

4. Cultural competency in mutual support/self-help services:

- Exhibit sensitivity to cultural differences—both from the family and worker's culture.

- Identify how family systems culture interacts with mutual support/self-help services related issues.

- Utilize the strengths and sources of mutual support within the family system's culture.

These four areas of competencies illustrate how child welfare workers can find support for families within the families themselves. This approach ensures the integrity of the family, demonstrating that it is the family who is the expert on their own well-being.

As stated earlier, professionals can play important roles in the success of self-help/mutual support groups. The task is to convince them of their importance and overcome barriers that may prevent professionals from actively participating in the self-help/mutual support movement. Barriers that may need to be overcome include professionals' attitudes and agency policies and procedures that may hinder clients deciding their needs and wants for themselves. Salem, Grant, and Campbell (1998), indicate that successful mutual help in settings such as group homes will require staff's help in enabling voluntary and confidential participation. They found that self-help groups in their study were not successful because staff as gatekeepers control residents' involvement, which is contrary to the self-help concepts of individual and self-selected process.

Summary and Conclusion

As indicated in the literature, self-help/mutual support represents a unique and necessary world view (Humphreys & Rappaport, 1994). The self-help/mutual support movement is fundamentally different from professional help in that it is primarily based on peer control, informality in exchanges of goods and services, mutual giving and receiving, and perhaps, most importantly, it is free of charge.

Current trends show that Americans are increasingly seeking help from self-help/mutual support groups instead of professional settings for problems of daily living. One of the major reasons for the increase in seeking informal help has been scarce resource on both the parts of the help seekers and help providers. In other words, people are less able to purchase help from professionals because they lack the monetary support, and decreasing agency budgets restrain professionals from creating programs with reduced fees or free of charge. The literature has indicated that many households in deprived neighborhoods rely heavily on self-help/mutual aid. In fact, researchers have firmly concluded that full engagement of deprived individuals and communities can be achieved through incorporating and harnessing self-help/mutual support (Williams & Windebank, 2000).

As discussed earlier, the benefits of the self-help/mutual support movement could only be fully realized with both policy and program initiatives. The self-help/mutual support movement has been successfully applied to various social issues and settings, including mental illness, domestic violence, substance abuse, poverty, and abuse/neglect. Likewise, self-help/mutual support principles have the potential to be applied to other social issues and settings. In further developing and maintaining the positive impacts of self-help/mutual support, professionals in child welfare settings must develop sufficient competency levels in self-help/mutual support components and principles. Additionally, there is still a need to further conduct research, develop practice models, and policy based on the self-help/mutual support movement.

The growth of self-help/mutual support has been phenomenal, and the literature seems to suggest incorporating such support into professional settings. As such, researchers have suggested that standard practice among professionals should include recommending that those seeking help should also seek supplemental help from self-help/mutual support groups. With such a framework, self-help/mutual support groups would not be considered a "junior partner" to professionals, but would be considered the "first line of defense" (Humphreys, 1998). As we begin this new century, may we make a new commitment to further cultivate and harness self-help/mutual support as a part of best practices for the New Century.

References

Ahn, N. and de la Rica, S. (1997). The underground economy in Spain: An alternative to unemployment? *Applied Economics, 29*, 733-743.

Anonymous (1998). Stimulating services through time dollars. *In Business, 20*(4), 15-16.

Armstrong, K. A. (1981). A treatment and education program for parents and children who are at-risk of abuse and neglect. *Child Abuse & Neglect, 5*, 167-175.

Azar, S. T. (1991). Model of child abuse: A metatheoretical analysis. *Criminal Justice and Behavior, 18*, 30-46.

Azzarto, J. (1997). A Young Women's Support Group: Prevention of a Different Kind. *Health and Social Work, 22*(4), 299-304.

Barber, J. and Gilbertson, R. (1998). Evaluation of a Self-Help Manual for the Female Partners of Heavy Drinker. *Research On Social Work Practice, 8*(2), 141-151.

Belsky, J. (1993). Etiology of child maltreatment: A developmental ecological analysis. *Psychological Bulletin, 114*, 413-434.

Blair, J. P. and Endres, C. R. (1994). Hidden economic development assets. *Economic Development Quarterly, 8*, 286-291.

Bok, M. (1988). The current status of community action agencies in Connecticut. *Social Service Review, 62*(3), 383-95.

Bond, G. R. and DeGraaf-Kaser, R. (1990). Group approaches for person with severe mental illness: A typology. *Social Work with Groups, 13*(1), 21-36.

Briar-Lawson, K. (1998). Capacity building for integrated family-centered practice. *Social Work, 43*(6), 539-550.

Burdman, M. (1974, Apr.). Ethnic self-help groups in prison and parole. *Crime and Delinquency.* 107-118.

Burns, D. and Taylor, M. (1998). *Mutual aid and self-help: Coping strategies for excluded communities.* York: The Policy Press.

Cahn, E. S. (1999). Time dollars, work and community: From 'why?' to 'why not?' *Futures, 31*(5), 499-509.

Cahn, E. S. (1997). The Co-production imperative. *Social Policy*, Spring, 62-67.

Christensen, A. and Jacobson, N. (1994). Who (or What) can do psychotherapy: The status and challenge of nonprofessional therapies. *Psychological Science, 5*, 8-14.

Collins, M. C. (1978). *Child abuser: A study of child abusers in self-help group therapy.* United States of America: Publishing Sciences Group, Inc.

Davidson, L., Chinman, M., Kloos, B., Weingarten, R., Stayner, D., and Tebes, J. K. (1997). *Peer support among individuals with sever mental illness: History, roadblocks, and a review of the evidence.* Paper presented at the Self-Help Research Pre-Conference, Society for Community Research and Action Biennial Conference, Columbia, South Carolina.

Dukewich, T. L., Borkowski, J. G., and Whitman, T. L. (1996). Adolescent mothers and child abuse potential: An evaluation of risk factors. *Child Abuse & Neglect, 20*(11), 1031-1047.

Editors (1997). The future of self-help. *Social Policy*, Spring, 2-3.

Fagan, J. and Stevenson, H. (1995). Men as teachers: A self-help program on parenting for African American men. *Social Work with Groups, 17*(4), 29-42.

Finn, J. and Lavitt, M. (1994). Computer-based self-help groups for sexual abuse survivors. *Social Work with Groups, 17*(1/2), 21-46.

Foree, S. (1996). Who is this lady called 'Mrs. G' and why does everyone call her for help? One community's story on parent advocacy. In K. Hooper-Briar & H. Lawson (Eds.). *Expanding partnerships for vulnerable children, youth and families.* Alexandria: Council on Social Work Education.

Garbarino, J. and Jacobson, N. (1978). Youth helping youth in cases of maltreatment of adolescents. *Child Welfare, 57*(8), 505-10.

Gartner, A. (1997). Professionals and self-help: The uses of creative tension. *Social Policy*, Spring, 47-52.

Gartner, A. and Riessman, F. (1998). Self-Help. *Social Policy, 28*(3), 83-85.

Gitterman, A. and Shulman, L. (1994). Agents of Change: A Group of Women in a Shelter for Homeless Families. In Mutual Aid Groups, *Vulnerable Populations and the Life Cycle (2nd ed)*, pp. 273-296. Chichester, NY: Columbia University Press.

Gitterman, A. and Shulman, L. (1994). Confronting Responsibility: Men Who Batter Their Wives. In Mutual Aid Groups, *Vulnerable Populations, and the Life Cycle (2nd ed)*, pp.257-271. Chichester, NY: Columbia University Press.

Hatfield, A. B. (1981). Self-help groups for families of the mentally ill. *Social Work, 26*(5), 408-413.

Haug, M. R. (1973). Deprofessionalization: An alternate hypothesis for the future. *Sociological Review Monograph*, December 20, 195-211.

Haughton, G., Johnson, S., Murphy, L., and Thomas, K. (1993). *Local geographies of unemployment: Long-term unemployment in areas of local deprivation.* Aldershot: Avebury.

Hegar, R. L., and Hunzeker, J. M. (1988). Moving toward empowerment-based practice in public child welfare. *Social Work, 33*(6), 499-502.

Hooper-Briar, K. and Lawson, H. A. (1996). *Expanding partnerships: For vulnerable children, youth, and families.* Alexandria, VA: Council on Social Work Education, Inc.

Humm, A. (1997). Self-help: A movement for changing times. *Social Policy*, Spring, 4-5.

Humphreys, K. (1998). Can addiction-related self-help/mutual aid groups lower demand for professional substance abuse treatment? *Social Policy, 29*(2), 13-17.

Humphreys, K. (1997). Individual and social benefits of mutual aid self-help groups. *Social Policy*, Spring, 12-19.

Humphreys, K. (1996). Self-help/mutual aid initiatives by people with psychiatric disabilities. *Community Psychologist, 29*, 9-25.

Humphreys, K. and Rappaport, J. (1994). Researching self-help/mutual aid groups and organizations: Many roads, one journey. *Applied and Preventative Psychology, 3*, 217-231.

Jemmott, F. E. (1997). Self-help and philanthropy: Ready or not, here they come. *Social Policy*, Spring, 53-55.

Katz, A. (1993). *Self-help in America: A social movement perspective.* NY: Twayne.

Kessler, R. C., Mickelson, K. D., and Zhao, S. (1997). Patterns and correlates of self-help group membership in the United States. *Social Policy*, Spring, 27-46.

Lee, R. (1996). Moral money? LETS and the social construction of local economic geographies in southeast England. *Environment and Planning A, 28*, 1377-1394.

Leon, A. M., Mazur, R., Montalvo, E., and Rodrieguez, M. (1984). Self-Help Support Groups for Hispanic Mothers. *Child Welfare, Volume LXI11*(3), 261-268.

Levine, M. and Perkins, D. V. (1997). *Principles of community psychology: Perspectives and applications* (2nd ed.). New York, NY: Oxford University Press.

Lipscomb, A. (1996). Going the distance: A journey. In K. Hooper-Briar & H. Lawson (Eds.), *Expanding partnerships for vulnerable children, youth and families.* Alexandria: Council on Social Work Education.

Lloyd, J. C. and Sallee, A. L. (1994). The challenge and potential of family preservation services in the public child welfare system. *Protecting Children, 10*(3), 3-6.

Madara, E. J. (1997). The mutual-aid self-help online revolution. *Social Policy*, Spring, 20-26.

Mankowski, E. and Rappaport, J. (1995). Stories, identity, and the psychological sense of community. In R. S. Wyer, Jr. (Ed.). *Knowledge and memory: The real story. Advances in Social Cognition, VIII*. Hinsdale, N.J.: Lawrence Erlbaum.

Meert, H., Mestiaen, P., and Kesteloot, C. (1997). The geography of survival: Household strategies in urban settings. *Tijdschrift voor Economische en Sociale Geografie, 88*, 169-181.

Mulroy, E. A. (1997). Building a neighborhood network: Interorganizational collaboration to prevent child abuse and neglect. *Social Work, 42*(3), 255-264.

Mulsow, M. H. and Murry, V. M. (1996). Parenting on edge: Economically stressed, single, African American adolescent mothers. *Journal of Family Issues, 17*(5), 704-721.

Nelson, G., Ochocka, J., Griffin, K., and Lord, J. (1998). Nothing about me, without me: Participatory action research with self-help/mutual aid organizations for psychiatric consumer/survivors. *American Journal of Community Psychology, 26*(6), 881-912.

Nittoli, J. (1997). Self-help and the search for solutions in human services. *Social Policy*, Spring, 68-69.

Nurco, D. N., Stephenson, P. E., and Hanlon, T. E. (1991). Aftercare/relapse prevention and the self-help movement. *The International Journal of the Addictions, 25*(9A), 1179-1200.

Pacione, M. (1997). Local exchange trading systems as a response to the globalization of capitalism. *Urban Studies, 34*, 1179-1199.

Parents Anonymous, Inc. (1996). *Strengthening families in partnership with communities*. The National Organization, CA: Claremont.

Penney, D. (1997). Friend or foe: The impact of managed care on self-help. *Social Policy*, Summer, 48-53.

People Helping People. (1997). Walking our talk in the neighborhoods: Building professional/natural helper partnerships. *Social Policy*, Summer, 54-63.

Peterman, P. J. (1981). Parenting and environmental considerations. *American Journal of Orthopsychiatry, 51*(2), 351-355.

Rappaport, J. (1993). Narrative stories, personal stories, and identity transformation in the mutual help context. *Journal of Applied Behavioral Science, 29*, 239-256.

Rapping, E. (1997). There's self-help and then there's self-help: Women and the recovery movement. *Social Policy*, Spring, 56-61.

Riessman, F. (1997). Ten self-help principles. *Social Policy*, Spring, 6-11.

Riessman, F. (1997). Self-Help New York. *Social Policy*, Summer, 33-34.

Riessman, F. and Carroll, D. (1995). The Special Significance of the Alcoholics Anonymous Model. In *Redefining Self-Help Policy and Practice*, pp.53-81. San Francisco, CA: Jossey-Bass Publishers.

Roberts, L. J., Salem, D., Rappaport, J., and Toro, P. A. (1999). Giving and receiving help: Interpersonal transactions in mutual-help meetings and psychosocial adjustment of members. *American Journal of Community Psychology, 27*(6), 841-868.

Salem, D. A., Bogat, G. A., and Reid, C. (1997). Mutual help goes on-line. *Journal of Community Psychology, 25*, 189-207.

Salem, D. A., Grant, L., and Campbell, R. (1998). The initiation of mutual-help groups within residential treatment settings. *Community Mental Health Journal, 34*(4), 419-429.

Salem, D. A., Seidman, E., and Rappaport, J. (1988). Community treatment of the mentally ill: The promise of mutual-help organizations. *Social Work, 33*(5), 403-408.

Segal, S. P., Silverman, C., and Temkin, T. (1993). Empowerment and self-help agency practice for people with mental disabilities. *Social Work, 38*(6), 705-712.

Thompson, E. (1998). Time Dollar Institute. *Whole Earth, 92*, 53.

Toren, N. (1974). The structure of social casework and behavioral change. *Journal of Social Policy, 3*, 341-352.

Traunstein, D. M. (1984). From mutual-aid self-help to professional service. *Social Casework: The Journal of Contemporary Social Work*, December, 622-627.

Valley, S., Bass, B., and Speirs, C. (1999). A professionally led adoption triad group: An evolving approach to search and reunion. *Child Welfare, 77*(3), 363-379.

Warren, M. R. (1994). Exploitation or co-operation? The political basis of regional variation in the Italian informal economy. *Politics and Society, 22*, 89-115.

Wilcox, R., Smith, D., Moore, J., Hewitt, A., Allan, G., Walker, H., Ropata, M., Monu, L., and Featherstone, T. (1991). *Family Decision Making & Family Group Conference*. Lower Hutt, NZ: Practitioners' Publishing.

Williams, C. (1996). *Keynote address*. National child welfare conference, Memphis, TN: Southern Illinois University.

Williams, C. C. (1996). Local purchasing and rural development: An evaluation of local exchange and trading systems (LETS). *Journal of Rural Studies, 12*, 231-244.

Williams, C. C. and Windebank, J. (2000). Self-help and mutual aid in deprived urban neighborhoods: Some lessons from Southampton. *Urban Studies, 37*(1), 127-147.

Wuthnow, R. (1994). *Sharing the journey: Support groups and America's new quest for community*. NY: Free Press.

Zimmerman, M. A., Reischl, T. M., Seidman, E., Rappaport, J., Toro, P. A., and Salem, D. A. (1991). Expansion strategies of a mutual help organization. *American Journal of Community Psychology, 19*(2), 251-278.

Chapter 15

In the Best Interests of the Child: Youth Development as a Child Welfare Support and Resource

Hal A. Lawson and Dawn Anderson-Butcher

Introduction

The youth development field was a vital part of both urban reform and social work at the beginning of the 20th Century. As the 21st Century begins, youth development is being revitalized, and its scope has expanded. Its aim is to promote the well-being of all children and youth, and it encourages interdisciplinary research and collaborative practice in service of this aim. Leadership programs for youth development are gaining popularity in community agencies and in colleges and universities (e.g., Chaskin & Hawley, 1994; Quinn, 1999). Many of these leadership development programs, especially those in colleges and universities, prepare adults for new roles with children and youth.

However, these leadership programs are not limited to adults. Many concentrate on the recruitment, preparation, and support of young leaders, i.e., children and youth. These youth leaders are viewed as having expertise. For example, the American Planning Association now provides technical assistance materials in support of youth involvement in community planning (e.g., Mullahey, Susskind, & Checkoway, 1999). Youth also provide services and supports to other youth. Vulnerable children and youth may shy away from adults, but they may be willing to listen to, and work with, these youth leaders.

Youth leadership development is, in brief, a complex change strategy. Youth leaders help others, and, at the same time, they help themselves. Often, they develop vocational and educational aspirations in the process (e.g., van Linden & Fertman, 1998). When they are designed in this fashion, these youth development leadership programs share many of the same assumptions as family-to-family and parent-to-parent mutual aid and assistance programs (e.g., Alameda, 1996; Briar-Lawson & Harris, this book; Vakalahi & Khaja, this book; Halpern, 1999). All such programs capitalize on the opportunities and assets associated with indigenous helpers and help-giving networks. All are key components in community-based systems of care.

These emergent youth development programs and accompanying leadership initiatives offer important supports and resources for child welfare professionals and their systems. For example, effective youth development programs and activities promote pro-social skills, and they enable early intervention strategies. In addition, some youth development programs offer both direct and indirect family supports. These supports include child care and supervision, social responsibility training, substance abuse and delinquency prevention, and parenting assistance. Neighborhood- and community-wide commitments to youth development may result in broad-based coalitions and collaboratives, which promote community competence in service of prevention agendas.

The purpose of this chapter is to encourage child welfare leaders and advocates to take advantage of youth development programs and to join forces with youth development leadership initiatives. Key concepts are identified and described, including risk factors, resilience, protective factors, vulnerability, and social competence development. Composites of conventional risk factors and protective factors are provided, and simple, effective practice rules are drawn from these composites. At the same time, cautions are offered about composite lists, especially about risk factors and risk labeling. These cautions signal the importance of social competence development, which simultaneously addresses risk factors and protective factors.

In addition, a new set of risk and protective factors is proposed in this chapter. Most researchers have focused on children, youth, families, neighborhoods, and communities. They have not attended to risk and protective factors related to service design and delivery, or if they have, they have minimized its importance and delegated it to a sub-category. Findings about children and youth in the child welfare system, especially "cross-over kids" who are in other systems such as juvenile justice and mental health, are offered as evidence that service design and delivery issues are either risk factors or protective factors. In fact, youth-serving systems that do not collaborate with other systems and with children, youth, and families may be viewed as "systems at risk." Accordingly, this chapter begins with the concept of risk.

Risk and Risk Factor Assessment

Many professions rely on risk assessments. In fact, the concept of risk has a long history in public health and in medicine. In these professions, as in child welfare, risk connotes an early warning. It means that undesirable events, or results, are likely to occur unless something is done to remove the signs, or indicators, of risk. These signs, or indicators, are called *risk factors*.

Risk assessment and risk factor analysis are predictive tools, which are grounded in statistical probabilities. The underlying logic goes something like this. *If you find at least one of these risk factors, then, sooner or later, you are likely to witness undesirable events and results, which could have been prevented.*

These undesirable events and results often are matters of life and death in child welfare, public health, and medicine. Risk, risk assessment, and risk factor analysis thus promote prevention measures and early intervention strategies, which effectively interrupt and reverse a predicted sequence of events that will cause problems.

In brief, risk factor identification and analysis and, in turn, prevention, and early intervention strategies are crucial practice tools for child welfare professionals. In youth development, as in child welfare, research on risk factor identification and risk assessment tools for youth development are driven by the same compelling need to prevent life-altering and -threatening events and results.

Youth development risk assessment inventories are, however, designed for universal use. These inventories are designed to enable every child to enjoy well-being, i.e., to enjoy healthy growth and development and to assume productive, adult roles and responsibilities in society. Like child welfare risk assessment inventories, youth development inventories are designed to enable prevention and early intervention, perhaps on several fronts.

Risk and Risk Factor Assessment in Youth Development

In the growing field of youth development, an abundance of research explores the predictors, causes, and correlates of problem behaviors in children and youth. Examples of this literature are provided in this section of the chapter, along with a table that summarizes the relevant risk factors.

In the youth development research literature, risk factors are the signs, or indicators, that increase the likelihood that children and youth will evidence personal-social needs and engage in problem behaviors (Durlak, 1998; Hawkins, Catalano, et al., 1999; Jessor & Jessor, 1977; National Crime Prevention Council, 1998; Smith & Carlson, 1997). When these risk factors are detected, there is an increasing probability that delinquency, substance use, teenage pregnancy, and other problem behaviors and outcomes will occur.

Most of this youth development research has been guided by a socio-medical framework, i.e., the same framework used for much of the research in public health, medicine, delinquency, and child welfare. The underlying logic for this framework is reasonable and understandable. Investigators typically start with subjects who evidence problem behaviors and needs. Then these investigators, in essence, back track in these subjects' lives, searching for unusual life experiences or triggering events that account for today's problems and needs (Menaghan, Kowaleski-Jones, & Mott, 1997).

As this research has developed, the range and scope of risk factor identification have expanded. This line of research began with psychological investigations of individuals evidencing need. The question was, in what ways are children and youth evidencing the same need (e.g., substance abusing youth) alike, similar, and different? The initial findings from this line of research prompted investigators to expand their thinking. Then they began to look for co-occurring needs. For example, why are delinquents also substance abusers and how do youth become delinquents and substance abusers? Do substance abusers tend to become delinquents, and do delinquents tend to become substance abusers?

Then the research expanded to include two key factors: (1) children's peer groups and networks, and (2) their family systems (e.g., Haveman & Wolfe, 1995; Parke & Ladd, 1992; Smith & Stern, 1997). More recently, the research has continued to expand to include school-related factors (e.g., Catterall, 1998; Rumberger, 1995), social support networks, and neighborhood characteristics (e.g., Allison, Crawford, et al., 1999; Brooks-Gunn, Duncan, & Aber, 1997; Drake & Pandey, 1996).

Some researchers have determined that a universal focus on <u>all</u> children and youth conceals as much as it reveals. Therefore, they have targeted children and youth in low-income families, concentrating on the multiple dimensions and challenges of poverty (e.g., Brooks-Gunn, Duncan, & Aber, 1998; Lawson, Briar-Lawson, & Lawson, 1997; Seidman, Chesir-Teran, et al., 1999).

Whether focused specifically on poverty, or universally on the well being of all children and youth, the youth development research literature is growing rapidly in every field that serves children and families. Even with today's computer-assisted, information management, and retrieval systems, it has become a daunting challenge to find all of this literature, integrate its findings, and translate these findings into practitioner-friendly, youth risk assessment inventories.

Today, conventional risk factor inventories mirror the complexity and multiple challenges of poverty. They encompass individual, peer, family, neighborhood, school, and community systems. For example, individual predispositions, such as the inability to identify and take cues from, the emotions and feelings of others are risk factors. Peer rejection is a risk factor. The lack of family ties is a risk factor. Long-term unemployment for parents is a risk factor for children. When children do not enjoy strong social bonds at school and experience early difficulties in the classroom, they are "at risk" for school failure and related personal-social needs. Living in an unsafe, destabilized neighborhood is another risk factor. When the neighborhood community lacks strong social norms and enforcement procedures for positive, pro-social behaviors, the children and youth who live there are "at risk."

In short, even though a host of questions remain, risk-related research for youth development has identified multiple factors. Many are related, and some are interdependent. Table 1 summarizes many of these key risk factors (Anderson-Butcher, 2000).

Table 1. Risk Factors Related to Negative Outcomes for Children and Youth

Individual Attributes	Risk Factors
Physiological characteristics	genetics age gender hormonal changes
Temperament or disposition	aggression rebelliousness depression
Favorable attitudes related to drugs, alcohol, sexual activity, and problem behaviors	
Self-constructs	low self-esteem poor interpersonal skills antisocial self-concept
Stressful life events	
Early and persistent problem behaviors	involvement in other problem behaviors involvement in social service systems
Academic failure	grade point average, intellect, and retention at some ages special education absenteeism year in school school dropout school climate

Family Factors	
Family behavior and attitudes toward problem behaviors	
Inappropriate and inconsistent family management practices	
Family conflict	
Family structure	single-parent families poor supervision transiency, instability

Individual Attributes	Risk Factors
Social System Factors	
Lack of connection or commitment to school, family, community, or other organizations	
Peer rejection in elementary grades, social isolation	
Association with peers involved in problem behaviors, norms for problem behaviors	
Societal Factors	
Laws and norms	
Availability of and access to drugs and alcohol	
Economic deprivation and related ethnicity, discrimination, and oppression	
Neighborhood disorganization	

All summaries, including Table 1, offer an important benefit. They identify and integrate a wide array of research and present a composite of key risk factors. On the other hand, the possibility looms that the list of risk factors presented in Table 1 will never be used. That is, by themselves, lists and composites may not hold much meaning for practitioners. When risk factor composites lack meaning, they will not improve front-line practice.

Why are composites such as Table 1 important, and what do they mean for front-line practice? Three responses to this question are in order.

First, the research suggests that problem behaviors among children and youth often co-occur. For example, when young people are gang members, they also tend to have substance abuse needs and engage in premature, and risky sexual behaviors (e.g., Harper & Robinson, 1999). Similarly, young substance abusers tend to evidence school-related problems, and there are accompanying neighborhood risk factors (e.g., Allison, Crawford, et al., 1999). Children in the child welfare system with health and mental health needs are likely to have problems in school and in their family systems (e.g., Silver, DiLorenzo, et al., 1999). The implications for practice are clear: (1) Use the composite in Table 1 to look for other co-occurring risk factors; and (2) Find ways to collaborate with children and youth, their families, and other professions and agencies to address many needs, across several fronts, at the same time.

Second, even if a child or a youth evidences only one risk factor, the predictive value of risk factor assessment must be kept in mind. The research indicates that the risk factor(s) that predict one problem behavior (e.g., delinquency) may be the same factors that predict other problem behaviors, such as substance abuse and school-related problems (Hawkins, Jenson, et al., 1988; National Crime Prevention Council, 1998). Twin practice rules follow. First: Find one risk factor, and, sooner or later, you are likely to find the others. Second: Intervene to address the one risk factor now, but at the same time, implement comprehensive strategies to prevent others.

Third, only rarely does just one risk factor "turn the tide." It is the overall cumulative effect of multiple risk factors that contributes to bad outcomes, i.e., to co-occurring problem behaviors (Boyle and Offord, 1990; Bry, McKeon, & Pandina, 1982; Gordon & Song, 1994; Hill et al., 1998; Jessor et al., 1995; Rutter, 1987a). Unfortunately, it is difficult to predict which risk factors and in what combination will turn the tide for a child and a family. After all, children, youth, and their families vary significantly. Some are able to withstand more stress and hassles than others. Nevertheless, two rules for practice can be derived from this logic. First, the presence of just one risk factor signals needs for immediate action, but it is not a cause for panic because the child is not necessarily in imminent danger. Second, anticipate, and look for variability among children, families, and their communities. Place, context, timing, and the mix of people matter when strategies are selected. In other words, avoid "one size fits all" thinking and interventions.

To summarize, there is growing consensus in the research literature regarding risk factors and clusters of risk factors. These risk factors are associated with problem behaviors and negative outcomes.

The word *associated* is important because it signals a caution. Most of the research on risk factors has identified correlations among risk factors and problem behaviors. To state that risk factors are *correlated* with one another and with problem behaviors is not the same as stating that they *cause* other risk factors and problem behaviors. In fact, determining causation is a messy business, because risk factors co-occur and track into each other. For example, the same risk factor may be viewed as a predictor, co-occurring need, mediator, moderator, and result, depending on the research study and the context in which it was conducted (Kaplan, 1996). Moreover, the research methodologies are not yet sophisticated enough to provide precise causal models. Current knowledge and understanding, while good enough to inform and guide practice in multiple ways, is nevertheless limited. Unfortunately, the same conclusion can be offered in relation to service design and delivery.

Service Design and Delivery as a Risk Factor

To reiterate, the purpose of risk factor identification and analysis is to promote timely, effective, early intervention and prevention strategies. Simply stated, the mere presence of one or more risk factors signals needs for direct, or indirect, service strategies. These strategies may encompass a diverse set of alternatives ranging from natural, community-based supports provided by indigenous helpers to formal interventions provided by professionals, such as social workers, recreation therapists, and clinical psychologists. When service systems work as planned, risks are detected early and effective service strategies are delivered in response. The service providers gain job satisfaction at the same time that children and youth are helped.

In contrast, when the service system does not work effectively, the predicted sequence of events often ensues. One risk factor may lead to another; and in turn, these two risk factors may lead to others. Then problem behaviors and negative results occur. Service design and delivery are implicated here because these problem behaviors and negative results could have been prevented. Three classes of service design and delivery problems may be involved.

First, there may be a design problem. For example, service providers do not know how to identify risk factors and their correlates. Or, providers know how to identify and assess just one risk factor, e.g., substance abuse, because their profession and agency only address this one need. Because they are prepared to notice just one need, they miss others that are just as or more important. Another design flaw: providers are far removed from where children and youth spend most of their time (e.g., schools, recreation agencies, boys and girls clubs), and so they are not afforded opportunities to interact with them, observe them, and do proper assessments of their well-being.

Moreover, design problems are evident when there is an under-supply of service providers in high poverty areas. These areas are likely to exact high tolls on children and families living there (e.g., Lawson, Briar-Lawson, & Lawson, 1997). When there is an obvious under-supply of trained providers, providers often shoulder excessive workloads; this also is a design problem. Furthermore, when service providers lack cultural competence, and they must work with culturally diverse children, youth, and families, a design problem is evident. These design problem examples signal a long list of other possibilities.

On the other hand, the design may be effective, but service delivery and implementation are not. In other words, risk factors are detected⎯a child's needs are known⎯yet, the child does not receive the services s/he and the family need. As with service design issues, countless examples can be provided. For example, a child is assessed in school and referred to community agencies for help, but the providers in the agency do not receive the information, do not follow through, or both. Or, the providers rely on their "pet" intervention strategy, even though it has little or no likelihood of working with the youth evidencing need. Or, the provider works only with one youth, neglecting root causes in the family system, which compel family-centered interventions. Or, the provider offers only psycho-educational training and therapy, neglecting or ignoring clear needs for job development training and school-to-work programs.

Moreover, the child may have multiple risk factors, which require simultaneous interventions promoted through school-family-community agency collaboration. Unfortunately, the providers and the families fail to communicate, let alone collaborate. Or, the provider who is unprepared to understand and respond to cultural and ethnic diversity determines that the youth must be removed from the family and placed in protective custody, or assigned to a residential treatment center. Design, delivery, and implementation problems like these are deterrents to responsive, integrated services for children, youth, and families.

The third class of problems involves both design and delivery. When both design and delivery flaws are evident, children, youth, and their families experience a kind of double jeopardy. For example, state and local policies may prevent service providers from intervening early and effectively because a crisis is not yet evident, or because the risk factors do not correspond to the funding category that is available. Or, providers and their supervisors are unaware of federal and state funding opportunities (e.g., child welfare funding, special education funding, juvenile justice funding), which could support the employment of additional workers and the provision of more effective, comprehensive services. Or, providers and their agencies, including schools and school-based professionals, steadfastly cling to their own missions and goals and fail to collaborate with others who serve the same children and families. Similarly, when universities continue to offer training that does not square with the realities of practice, they cause both design and delivery problems. Both design and delivery flaws are evident in these examples, and the countless others that could be provided.

The point is, when public service systems, including schools, child welfare, juvenile justice, mental health, and health, do not respond; indeed, if they are not positioned or enabled to respond to identifiable risk factors; then children, youth, families, and their neighborhood communities are placed "at risk." Put another way, where these people and their communities in need are concerned, service design and delivery are risk factors. Service systems and their providers do not meet their legal and moral mandates of providing help to people, especially children and youth, in need.

Just as it is unfair and inappropriate to blame vulnerable children, youth, and families for "at risk" environments, so, too, is it unfair and inappropriate to blame individual providers for systems design and delivery problems, which appear to be outside their immediate influence and control. Just as analyses of these "at risk" environments have opened new, comprehensive avenues for research, policy, and practice, the sensitizing concept of "systems at risk" also opens new avenues for research, policy, and practice. For example, it focuses on front line workers' vulnerability to systems design and delivery problems, helping to explain why they burn-out, drop-out, evidence health and mental health needs of their own, and often cannot achieve their goals for actually helping children and youth evidencing need.

As with the person-in-environment focus for examining vulnerable children and youth, this systems-at-risk focus expands the examining lens for research and practice and invites alternative intervention strategies. Psychological perspectives are an imperative, but, at the same time, they are limited. In fact, past-present research and practice have enjoyed limited effectiveness because they have focused narrowly on traits and personality variables of children and youth rather than examining children holistically, or "in the round." Examining children and youth "in the round" must include the systems that serve them and that provide the social arenas and environments for their learning and development. Youth development work, like child welfare work, must be comprehensive and multi-faceted. Both often involve systems and cross systems change.

Children and youth in the child welfare system provide a striking and important example of this line of reasoning. They are in the system because of abuse and neglect. Both abuse and neglect are risk factors, and both also are related to other risk factors. In short, children and youth are in the system, in part, because the needs of their parents and family systems could not be addressed effectively by parents, others in the family system, and providers.

Children and youth in child welfare tend to cross over into other systems, either in the here-and-now or in the future. Similarly, some children and youth in other service systems, especially juvenile justice, mental health, and special education, often come into child welfare. A host of questions remain about these crossover patterns. Recent research has identified important developmental pathways (e.g., Altschuler, 1997; Baron & Hartnagel, 1998; Blome, 1997; Brezina, 1998; Cocozza & Skowyra, 2000; Eamon, 1994; Goerge, Van Voorhis, et al., 1992; Felitti, Anda, et al., 1998; Harper & Robinson, 1999; Inkelas & Halfon, 1997; Jang & Smith, 1998; Loeber, Keenan, & Zang, 1997; Needel & Barth, 1998; Schwartz & Fishman, 1999; Seidman, Chesir-Teran, et al., 1999; Silver, DiLorenzo, et al., 1999; Smith & Stern, 1997; Takayama, Wolfe, & Coulter, 1998). In other words, there are important patterns involving children and youth manifesting need. Although understanding has grown, these developmental pathways are not yet fully understood, and their relationship with "at risk" service design and delivery systems demands more research.

On the other hand, even a superficial reading of this research suggests that these multi-system kids, or "cross-over kids," tend to fall through the cracks. Service providers often do not communicate, and their systems are not positioned to enable them to collaborate effectively. Moreover, a disproportionate number of children and youth in the child welfare, juvenile justice, and special education systems are African-American in some places; Latino in others; and Native American in still others. These identification and placement patterns also suggest systems design and delivery problems. In one sense, both these kids and the providers are vulnerable to "at risk" service systems.

"Cross-over kids" typically present needs that may not be identified; and, if even if they are, they are not addressed effectively. Frankly, reading the research cited above is like reading a tragedy. Funding is available and service providers may want to respond, but in practice, children and youth do not receive the services they need and deserve. In short, all three classes of problems can be located here□service design, service delivery, and both design and delivery. Too many "cross-over kids" end up displaying problem behaviors and evidencing negative results. Service design and delivery problems are risk factors for them. Therefore, helping these kids means also changing " at risk" helping systems. It entails changing service systems into protective factors.

The Limitations of the Risk Language and Framework

The limitations of the risk and risk factor framework in the research literature are accompanied by everyday practice challenges. In practice, risk and risk detection depend on people's judgments and, in turn, their strategic actions (Slovic, 1986). In fact, risk and risk factor identification and assessment connote four related judgments. These judgments are *normative*, *descriptive*, *evaluative*, and *predictive*.

A norm is an agreed upon standard. Normative judgments about risk often mirror personal-professional standards. Because standards and norms are embedded in cultural traditions, *ethnocentrism*□viewing culturally diverse persons through the lens provided by one's culture□is an ever-present limitation.

Risk-related judgments also require descriptive judgments. Observations are challenging enough, but practitioners also must find language and language categories that fit what they have perceived. There are three possibilities for error here: The accuracy of the observations; the choice of words to describe the observations; and, the categorization of these coded observations.

Risk-related judgments are evaluative. Value is the core concept in *e-valuation*. The implication is that every risk assessment (evaluation) is value-laden, not value-free. Its validity is always threatened by the values of the practitioner (evaluator). Training and action-oriented safeguards are needed to expand the gazes of practitioners and deepen their appreciation for diversity. To borrow from Witkin (2000), evaluation hinges on the art and science of noticing. Practitioners and evaluators alike notice some things and not others. In youth development, as in child welfare, practitioners often vary considerably in what they notice and how they decide to intervene. A high risk youth for one worker may be a low risk youth for another. Risk-related evaluations depend on practitioners being able to notice the right things, and they must know why they are the right things for a particular child, at that time, and in that specific context.

The predictive power of risk assessments depends fundamentally on the other three kinds of judgments, i.e., normative, descriptive, and evaluative judgments. For example, limited descriptions, which stem from inadequate evaluations, result in faulty predictions. In turn, decisions regarding when, how, where, and why to intervene are less effective.

The point is, in youth development, as in child welfare, risk and risk factors are not just "out there" waiting to be discovered. People invent and construct "risk" and "risk factors" based on their training, values, and beliefs. Although risk and risk factors provide professionals with some certainty and direction for their work, the fact remains that normative, descriptive, evaluative, and predictive judgments regarding risk, with diverse children and families and in variable contexts, are inherently uncertain. Often, youth development and child welfare practitioners must make all four judgments at the same time. In a growing number of cases where poverty, urban geography, and cultural diversity are evident, these judgments are shrouded in complexity and ambiguity.

Another caution is in order. Although risk identification and risk factor assessment promise help to youth development and child welfare professionals, they also may limit their effectiveness. For example, children and families may be labeled permanently as "at risk" primarily because this is how diverse professionals describe them. The danger looms that children and families begin to define themselves in the same way. In other words, they may begin to see themselves in deficit- and problem-based terms, developing a sense of learned hopelessness and helplessness. The seeds for self-fulfilling prophecies are here in which children and families accept others' labels and expectations and then conform to them.

The danger also looms that children and families are, in essence, blamed for their socially toxic environments, which are outside their immediate control. In other words, children and their families may not be "at risk." Rather, *they are vulnerable to at risk situations, service systems, and environments.* When their environments are the real problem, "at risk" kids, their parents, and families are like victims who are in danger of being blamed for circumstances they did not create and cannot control (e.g., Lawson, Briar-Lawson, & Lawson, 1997; Meenaghan & Kilty, 1993). Furthermore, when risk and risk factors are the only sensitizing practice frames, practitioners may look only for needs, problems, and risk factors. They may overlook, ignore, and neglect other factors that lead to success and good results. Here, it is important to provide another important conclusion from the youth development research. *Despite the presence of one or more risk factors, which may turn the tide for other children and youth, some children and youth are remarkably strong and resilient, and they are able to achieve many of their goals.* In other words, the twin concepts of resilience and protective factors, which are emphasized in the next section of this chapter, are every bit as important as risk factors.

Building Resilience by Enhancing Protective Factors

Resilience is the ability to maintain adaptive functioning in spite of serious challenges or risks (Benard, 1991; Masten & Coatsworth, 1998; Rutter, 1990; Werner & Smith, 1982). Like risk, it involves normative judgments about how well a child or a youth functions effectively. Resilience focuses uniquely on how children, adults, and families achieve success, especially under unfavorable conditions and in challenging circumstances (Reynolds, 1998). So, resilient children and youth overcome apparent adversity, despite the multitude of risk factors they may have or their "at risk" environments. This key sensitizing concept of resilience was developed initially by Dr. Norman Garmezy.

Garmezy (1971) examined children of parents with schizophrenia to determine their risks for developing the illness. His research indicated that having a parent with schizophrenia increased the child's risk for developing this disorder. Despite this prediction, approximately 90 percent of the children Garmezy studied did not develop schizophrenia. As he began to understand this important finding, Garmezy turned to the characteristics of individuals and their environments, focusing on the factors that insulated children against risk and prevented negative consequences. The concept of resilience developed from this research. Resilience applies to children, youth, families, and other individuals who are able to stem the tide against risk factors, which are associated with negative results and problem behaviors.

A related concept, *protective factors*, has developed in concert with resilience. Protective factors are mechanisms, or variables, that help operationalize resilience. These protective factors act to prevent risk factors, and they mollify the effects of risk factors. Protective factors either alter the exposure to risk, or they alter the impact of a risk factor (Rutter, 1985). In short, variable responses among the same kinds of children and youth to the same kinds of risk factors often can be explained by differential protective factors.

Protective factors have many aliases. Protective factors also have been labeled resilience factors, developmental assets (Benson, 1997), compensatory factors, and resource factors (Kaplan, 1996). Regardless of terminology, protective factors help explain why, when exposed to similar stresses, some children and youth overcome challenges and others do not.

Researchers have detected many such protective factors in individuals, their families, and in their environments (Benson, 1997; Davis, 1999; Garmezy, 1985; Hawkins, Catalano, & Miller, 1992; Jessor, Donovan, & Costa, 1991; Jessor, Van De Bos, et al., 1995; Smith & Carlson, 1997; Werner & Smith, 1992). For instance, there are individual attributes such as self-esteem, social skills, autonomy, intelligence, and optimism. Family qualities, such as parental support and family attachment, also have been identified as protective. Moreover, resilience may be promoted through environmental characteristics, such as having pro-social peer groups, being involved in positive activities, and having a caring school and neighborhood. Like risk factor research, the examining lens for protective factors and resilience has expanded over time, moving from Garmezy's initial work with children who had parents with schizophrenia into a wide array of settings and with diverse children, families, and community contexts.

Table 2 provides an extensive outline of the many protective factors identified within the research (Anderson-Butcher, 2000). These protective factors provide opportunities for assessment, prevention, and intervention. In other words, protective factors decrease the likelihood of negative outcomes for children and youth. As with risk factors, relationships among these protective factors are important. In the best circumstances, they tend to co-occur, and the presence of one or more protective factors may predict others. As the number of protective factors increases, the resilience of the child also increases.

Thus, in one sense, it is possible to think of two kinds of cycles. Risk factors comprise vicious cycles, while protective factors comprise virtuous cycles. The challenge for practitioners is clear. They must nurture, create, and strengthen virtuous cycles in substitution for vicious cycles (Lawson, Briar-Lawson, & Lawson, 1997). Optimal practice involves both, not one or the other. Especially where poverty is present, this work requires a dual focus: *Risk and risk factors must be identified and addressed at the same time that protective factors and resilience are assessed to promote strength-based, empowering helping strategies.* Consequently, professionals in youth development and in child welfare must assess both risk and protective factors, and assessment tools must incorporate both.

In other words, risk factors and protective factors may be different, but it is wrong to think about them as dichotomous (Durlak, 1998). That is, it is not one or the other; it is one and the other (e.g., Anderson-Butcher, 2000; Kaplan, 1996). This recent research suggests that it is desirable to think of risk and protective factors as comprising an integrated framework□an asset-vulnerability framework. This new framework highlights needs for improved, integrated assessment tools that help practitioners notice signs of danger, low and moderate risk, vulnerability, protective factors, and signs of resilience in variable, complex, and uncertain practice contexts.

Table 2. Protective Factors Related to the Healthy Development of Children and Youth

Protective Factors	
Individual Factors or Dispositional Attributes	
Physiological characteristics	gender (females more prosocial) age good health
Temperament or disposition	easy going, flexibility sociability and humor
Favorable attitudes, values and beliefs	trust and attachment values for honesty, integrity, caring, responsibility positive attitudes toward school, community, and other agencies, activities, or programs optimism, sense of purpose, positive views of the future, empowerment faith in higher power or religious philosophy achievement motivation
Self-constructs	high self-esteem personal confidence interpersonal skills, such as problem solving and coping self-acceptance self-efficacy, sense of control
Independence and autonomy	
Intelligence	
Active involvement in pro-social activities	participates in extracurricular activities and initiative building activities actively engaged in learning
Law abidance, social responsibility	
Family Factors	
Attachment and connection to at least one parent	
Parental management	discipline supervision clear expectations and boundaries
Parental involvement, especially in schooling	
Parental support	
Presence of fathers	
Nonconflicted relationships	

Social System Factors	
Support factors	adept at gaining support and friendship from adults and others having supportive people in environment presence of and relationship with caring adults (i.e., role models)
Peer factors	attachment to friends involved in prosocial activities having supportive friends from stable families strong social support network positive peer group and relationships
Bonding	opportunities for prosocial involvement within family, school, and community rewards for prosocial involvement within family, school, and community ability and opportunity to contribute to others connection to conventional society, belonging

Societal Factors	
Caring neighborhood and school environment	
Community values youth and believes They are resources	
Neighborhood safety	clear boundaries and expectations

Joining Risk and Protective Factors: Developmental Pathways and the Importance of Timing, Contexts, and Life Course Events

Furthermore, it is all-too-easy to think about risk (and risk factors) and resilience (and protective factors) as static concepts and worry about them only in the here-and-now. The easy route is to do a combined risk and resilience assessment and use the information gained to design helping strategies. In this line of thinking, once the strategies are delivered, and outcomes improve, the job is done. Then practitioners can move on to the next case.

Unfortunately, the easy way is not the best way to proceed. Risk and resilience change over time as the life course developmental experiences of children, youth, and their families may change. Any one of a number of unanticipated events can trigger problems and needs. For example, a job lay-off, a divorce, a premature, tragic death, a move to another school or neighborhood, new friendships that involve gang members⎯these triggering events can change a child's life in a relatively short period of time.

In one sense, risk factors are like a chameleon. They are difficult to detect because they blend into the surrounding environments. The situation is even more complicated. A risk factor in one research study may be a protective factor in another (Kaplan, 1996).

In another sense, risk factors, like protective factors and resilience, are like moving targets. In other words, they are not fixed attributes. They change as life course developmental experiences and surrounding environments change. Both risk and protective factors vary by person, family, and context, both in the here-and-now and over time. In this perspective, any one assessment is like still photography. It is just one snapshot in time, and it does not provide a complete, comprehensive, and lasting picture.

Furthermore, not only are circumstances different for different kinds of young people, but also, their perceptions of these circumstances also vary. Even when their perceptions do not appear to correspond to their surrounding realities, *a youth's perceptions may turn out to be strong protective factors* (Seidman, Chesir-Teran, et al., 1999). This new, important finding adds an unusual dimension to the risk and protective factor literature and to practice that is informed and guided by it. It implies that children and youth need to be asked and that they need to be involved directly in research and practice in their behalf.

Enhancing Social Competence Development

This important finding, like others, points to a key practice strategy. This practice strategy is to develop social competence in youth. Although the connection between social competence and empowerment may not be evident, it is possible and desirable to use empowerment-oriented, strength-based strategies in support of social competence development. In turn, social competence development paves the way for youth leadership development initiatives in which youth are viewed as having expertise in what helps and hurts them; and in knowing what their risk and protective factors are.

Exploring Social Competence

White (1959, 1963) developed the concept of *social competence*. He used this concept to refer to a child's or a youth's sense of confidence that they enjoy some control over their near environments. Several other researchers have built on this definition.

Although some controversy remains about the precise definition of social competence, basic consensus has been achieved. Social competence refers to a pattern of effective adaptation and healthy adjustment (e.g., Elias, 1995; Masten & Coatsworth, 1995, 1998). In brief, social competence involves gaining knowledge, skills, abilities, values, and sensitivities that provide control over life's developmental tasks and challenges; and, it results in achievements and success stories in social arenas, such as school activities, athletics, and peer leadership. These social competence-related success stories replace "rotten outcomes" (Schorr, 1988). Youth with social competence graduate from high school, participate in prosocial activities, and demonstrate goal-directed behaviors related to their future. Socially competent youth evidence multiple protective factors (Elias, 1995).

At a psychological level, social competence includes having the knowledge and the ability to sustain healthy interpersonal relationships. These children and youth exercise good judgment, make sound decisions, and assume joint responsibility for their decisions and actions. They demonstrate social competence when they display appropriate behaviors that are consistent with normative expectations of healthy development. This definition of social competence is well-known, complex, and interaction-based.

Children and youth also need supportive environments that reinforce and promote social competence. In other words, youth development researchers and leaders are learning that social competence development involves more than working with one child or a group of youths. It entails designing supportive environments and activity settings (McLaughlin, 2000). For example, the cultures of schools, families, and youth development agencies must promote clear, appropriate values and norms related to social competence development. Adults working with children in these environments must use language that is appropriate for social competence development. These and other environmental design features are essential for social competence development in individuals. They signal a protective system, one without design flaws. When interactions among psychological and environmental design factors are effective, "pathways toward accomplishment" are developed (Elias, 1995, p. 13).

For instance, social competence has been shown to be an important variable predicting the successful development of children and youth. Its importance in relation to successful academic achievement, healthy adjustment, and desirable social relations, as well as reduced risk for alcohol, drug use, teenage pregnancy, and juvenile delinquency has been noted (Cowen, Pedersen, et al, 1973; Hawkins, Catalono, & Miller, 1992; Hawkins, Jenson, et al., 1988; Moore, Miller, et al., 1996; Rolf, Sells, & Gordon, 1972; Ullman, 1957).

In brief, these positive outcomes are the result of strategies that increase social competence by reducing early risk factors and enhancing protective factors. As social competence is developed and adaptive functioning is improved, risk factors are deterred and protective factors are nurtured (Smith & Carlson, 1997).

To put it another way, social competence increases as virtuous cycles replace vicious cycles. Thus, instead of focusing exclusively on risk and protective factors, practitioners from all fields, especially child welfare professionals, can focus broadly on social competence development. They can target positive goals for youth development by designing interventions that do two things at the same time namely, decrease risk factors and enhance protective factors.

Table 3 presents Elias' (1995) practical social competence assessment and development inventory, which pinpoints specific competencies that children and youth must develop. These direct, practical questions help youth workers identify and describe some of the key elements of social competence development in children and youth. It provides an answer to the most fundamental practice question namely, how would you know social competence development if you saw it?

Table 3. Protective Factors/Social Competencies for Long-Term Adaptation

To what Extent is the Child/Youth
• Able to articulate goals of his or her actions?
• Able to think of more than one way to reach a goal?
• Able to plan a sequence of goal-directed actions?
• Able to realistically anticipate consequences of, and potential obstacles to, actions?
• Able to express a positive sense of self-efficacy (a sense of "I can" and a general optimism about the outcomes of his or her personally initiated actions)?
• Able to express a positive connection and relationship to at least one significant, accessible adult?
• Able to describe participation in and a positive connection to one social group experience (school, club, hobby, peer group; music or art-related instruction; sports; etc.)?
• Able to show sensitivity to his or her own feelings and those of others?
• Able to approach and converse with peers, showing appropriate eye contact, using an appropriate tone of voice, displaying proper posture, and using appropriate language?
• Able to approach and converse with adults, showing appropriate eye contact, using an appropriate tone of voice, displaying proper posture, and using appropriate language?
• Able to manage stressful situations adequately?

• Able to recognize when he or she needs help and effectively seek out that help?
• Able to begin, follow through with, and complete tasks and projects?
• Living with parents or primary caretakers who provide adequate shelter and basic living resources, so not engage in extremes of permissiveness or punitiveness, and have the capacity to contain their own conflict, discord, and disagreements concerning child-rearing?

Social competence is like the picture on the top of the puzzle box of practice. Empowering social competence development strategies, which mollify and prevent risk factors, while enhancing protective factors, are important pieces of the youth development puzzle. This youth development puzzle-solving offers supports and resources for child welfare systems. Assembling the pieces of the puzzle means implementing strength-based, empowerment-oriented, youth development strategies, which promote social competence development and youth leadership. These child- and youth-focused social competence strategies comprise the foundation of many success stories for children, youth, families, and the professionals who serve them.

Furthermore, new youth development leadership initiatives demonstrate that pro-social children and youth, placed in leadership positions and supported accordingly, develop social competence at the same time they promote it in others. That is, youth development, like child welfare, may be enhanced when indigenous leaders are utilized and "natural" helping systems in neighborhood communities, schools, and community agencies are strengthened.

On the other hand, some youth and peer leadership programs actually may encourage delinquency and its associated risk factors. For example, Dishion, McCord, and Poulin (1999) describe the unintended and undesirable consequences of forming groups without fully considering what will happen when older, delinquent youth are placed with younger ones. Delinquent tendencies and behaviors may be reinforced and promoted through subtle group dynamics. Youth development practice will improve as it takes into account peer-related processes and outcomes.

Socially Competent Service Systems

Many social competence development programs for children and youth are designed with a psycho-social focus. In turn, psycho-social intervention strategies support individuals, peers, and families. However, psycho-social perspectives and orientations are not enough, especially where the most vulnerable children and youth are concerned.

Multi-system, "cross-over kids" and their families also need socially competent service systems, ones whose design and delivery enable them to respond effectively to presenting needs. Socially competent systems are designed to enable timely assessment and rapid, effective responses in relation to risk factors and protective factors related to healthy youth development. Based on this assessment, helping professionals connect, communicate, and collaborate with other helping professionals, particularly youth development leaders. Together they promote social competence. Their youth development strategies are culturally sensitive, flexible, strength-based, and "in the round." A "whatever it takes" philosophy is adopted in relation to both early intervention and prevention (e.g., McLaughlin, 2000).

In brief, socially competent systems help children and families in need and, at the same time, promote the well-being and job satisfaction of workers. In other words, service systems can enable wrap-around strategies for both children and workers alike (e.g., Kamradt, 2000). When they do, systems serve as key protective factors for children, families, and workers alike. Jobs get easier and workers do not have to "do it all, alone." Children, youth, and their families benefit. These systems also may promote effective collaboration between youth development and child welfare.

Beyond the Socio-Medical Framework and a Focus on Individuals and Groups

A new approach for youth development research and practice is emerging. Instead of starting with youth and adults with disorders and problem behaviors and then looking backward into their childhood for experiences and circumstances that account for them, this new approach has a different logic. It emphasizes the knowledge, skills and abilities, sensitivities, values, and capacities that every person needs for a health-enhancing childhood and, in turn, a productive adulthood. This research attends to all children and youth, not just those manifesting need, or kids whose resilience and protective factors mollify risk. This more universal approach especially emphasizes the success stories of positive youth development. In addition to focusing on individuals and groups, this new line of research and practice also attends to the youth activities and to the design of the social settings in which these activities are implemented and performed.

For example, Larson (2000), while promoting a new psychology of positive youth development, emphasizes the thousands of ostensibly healthy youth who report that they are bored, feel unchallenged, and lack direction and purpose for their lives. Larson offers the sensitizing concept, *initiative*, to describe what these youth lack and need. Initiative is the ability to start something worth doing and to stick with it. It involves setting goals, implementation planning, putting in the effort, and actually seeing it through (Larson, 2000). Initiative thus is related to social competence development, but it also is qualitatively different.

The development of initiative requires special activities, which meet three requirements (Larson, 2000). To begin with, these initiative-developing activities must be voluntary. Youth must be motivated intrinsically to become involved and stay the course. In other words, their participation in these activities must be self-propelled.

Secondly, youth must be engaged in an environment, or social setting, which brings them into contact with a social-cultural reality outside themselves. That is, the activity must require kids to encounter some part of reality, especially rules, requirements, norms and standards, complexity, and external challenges. Therefore, when they participate, youth experience a social-cultural order. They are not automatically passive when they confront this social order; they redesign it through their engagement. At the same time they learn to follow the rules and adhere to proper procedure, they may design and implement new rules and procedures.

Third, initiative involves *a temporal arc of effort* directed toward a goal (Larson, 2000). In other words, youth are able to commit to participation and stay engaged over an identifiable period of time. Setbacks, unanticipated challenges, and unforeseen circumstances do not deter participation and engagement. Youth keep their "eyes on the prize"—a public performance, a specific goal, the end of a season, or a recording session in a music studio.

Larson (2000) emphasizes two key findings about these three requirements for initiative-building activities. All must be present. In other words, there is an all-or-none phenomenon here. Second, there are not enough initiative-developing activities. Although many activities emphasize one or two of the three requirements, only a few provide youth with all three.

In addition to the importance of the activities, this new approach to positive youth development emphasizes the characteristics of the setting, also called the activity setting (O'Donnell, Tharp, & Wilson, 1993). An extreme example amplifies the importance of the setting. Youth invited to play volleyball in a prison with adult inmates will experience it differently than youth invited to play the same sport, with other kids, in a local boys and girls club. In short, the organizational or social setting weighs heavily on whether youth will participate in any activity; how they will participate, and the outcomes that are likely to result. The design of settings thus emphasizes the norms and values it nurtures, along with those it does not. It includes the provision of a safe, secure environment. And, it lays special emphasis on the characteristics and behaviors of effective youth development leaders (e.g., McLaughlin, 2000; McLaughlin, Irby, & Langman, 1994).

Thus, this new approach complements existing approaches that operate from a different logic—namely, the logic of pathology, disease, and disorder. While this new approach emphasizes a depth psychology (Larson, 2000), arguably it only begins there. This new approach emphasizes the complex interplay among one youth, peers, special activities, youth leaders, and youth development settings--activity settings. Specific to youth development in one sense, this multi-level and -modal approach also offers new avenues for child welfare research and practice. For example, youth in foster care, especially those confronted by the challenges of independent living, have special needs for initiative. Here, as in the more conventional risk and protective factor frameworks, there are important opportunities to unite youth development research and practice with child welfare research and practice.

New Century Youth Development With, and Via, Child Welfare

Youth development, like child welfare, provides a continuum of care and supports. Some youth development initiatives focus on parents (and families). Others focus on parents (families) and the child(ren); these are called "two-generation strategies." Still others focus only on one child, or a group of like children and youth. These child- and youth-focused programs are growing in number. All offer potential supports and resources for child welfare. As in child welfare, the question is not one of youth-focused versus family-centered; both are needed.

Effective social competence development, through youth development programs, is empowering. Participation in these programs, as well as in other extracurricular activities, is linked to decreased academic failure, substance use, and delinquency (Anderson-Butcher, 2000; Holland & Andre, 1987; Larson, 1994; Mahoney & Cairns, 1997; Schinke, Orlandi, & Cole, 1992). Children's involvement in these programs also promotes social responsibility and enhances capacities for independent living. The need for this capacity for independent living is well-established in the child welfare literature and in practice (e.g., Mech, 1994). Its importance is heightened with the recent passage of the federal Independent Living Legislation, which provides enhanced funding supports for child welfare youth in transition to adulthood. Youth development goals are thus child welfare supports and resources. When they are united, both systems become more socially competent.

With this desirable union in mind, child welfare leaders may develop formal partnerships with youth development agencies, such as Boys & Girls Clubs, 4-H programs, Big Brothers and Big Sisters, and YMCA. These agencies provide young people with safe places to "hang-out" that usually are free of violence and gangs. Staff leaders and older teens serve as important role models and provide positive support for and individualized attention to youth participants (Dryfoss, 1998; McLaughlin, Irby, & Langman, 1994). Programs and activities offered develop important life skills, as well as provide supports and resources. Here are some specific examples of programs that may be in place already, and they can be expanded.

- **Boys & Girls Clubs of America** have over 2,300 clubs across the country and serve over three million youth per year. In addition to the recreational programming offered at clubs, youth also can participate in their nationally recognized drug, alcohol, and teen pregnancy prevention program, SMART Moves (Skills Mastery and Resistance Training). Furthermore, they can serve as junior staff members or AmeriCorps volunteers where they may earn stipends or receive college or vocational funding for future education and training.

- **Big Brothers and Big Sisters of America, Inc.**, organizes mentoring programs for youth that come from vulnerable circumstances. Adults and older youth serve as voluntary friends and role models (Burt, Resnick, & Novick, 1997; Fashola, 1998). For instance, in Salt Lake City, Utah, high school seniors serve as mentors and "Bigs" for younger teens that attend the local self-contained alternative junior high school.

- Several after-school programs utilize Hellison's (1985) Social Responsibility Model to teach interpersonal skills to youth within physical education and sport contexts (Hellison, Martinek, & Cutforth, 1996). For instance, **Project Effort**, an after-school program for vulnerable youth in Greensboro, buses youth from the inner city to the local university. Here, university students and past graduates of Project Effort serve as program mentors to younger club members, teaching them social responsibility through recreational activities such as basketball and marshal arts.

- The **New York City Beacons Program** offers school-based after-school programs that outreach to children, as well as provide family services, such as parent education, GED, and ESL classes (Dryfoos, 1999). Youth have opportunities for tutoring, homework assistance, and recreation, and families have access to a range of on-site health and social services.

- Various late night and midnight recreational programs have been organized across the country. Youth involved in these programs are not only afforded opportunities for recreation, but programs also connect youth with various social services, multicultural activities, mentoring programs, and tutoring supports (Witt & Crompton, 1997).

In brief, there are many opportunities for pro-social involvement at youth service agencies. Participants may engage in recreational sports, arts and crafts, and other community programming. More structured services and supports also are provided. These agencies offer educational supports such as tutoring, job training, and homework assistance. Leadership and service clubs provide opportunities for youth to give back to their community, establishing a sense of connectedness and belonging. Moreover, social support groups and skill classes teach vital life skills, such as time management, interpersonal relations, and anger management.

Thus, effective youth development agencies offer strong preventive and early intervention activities and programs. They develop social competence by targeting risk and protective factors. Some also offer important, albeit indirect, family supports, such as child-care and parental assistance. For example, many schools are now providing after school programs. These programs, in essence, provide working parents with affordable, safe child-care. Their children are supervised during the non-school hours. At the same time, problem behaviors, such as delinquency and teen pregnancy, are prevented because kids are supervised. These youth also are involved in healthy developmental activities between the time school ends and the time when their parents are home (e.g., Larner, Zippiroli, & Behrman, 1999).

Furthermore, as kids, especially adolescents, get healthier and learn, they may teach and socialize parents. They also may help their parents get help when they need it. For example, it is not unusual for parents to develop working relationships with staff at a local youth agency, such as a Boys and Girls Club. Compared with some service providers, the staff members may be less intimidating and non-threatening. These staff members have established rapport and trust with kids and their families. In turn, parents may be more likely to seek support and referral. When they do, youth development agencies offer a key family support.

Moreover, when their parents won't get help, and the staff notice that the children are in danger, youth development agencies may act as child protective services. They detect "red flags" and provide monitoring and tracking, as well as report suspected child abuse and neglect.

In short, child welfare services can be much more effective at protecting and nurturing youth by partnering with youth development agencies. These proactive, positive youth developmental strategies, agencies, and programs can help vulnerable children, youth, and their families.

The traditional service plan is altered. Child welfare interventions do not stop at parent education, respite, and mental health therapy. They become preventive and nurturing by targeting risk and protective factors and connecting youth and their families with positive supports and programs aimed at enhancing social competence. For example, a family preservation worker involved in a child welfare system may be working with a family with multiple needs. The parents are in need of parent education or homemaking skills. The kids who have experienced abuse and/or neglect are in need of traditional child welfare interventions, such as social skill development or mental health therapy.

Child welfare workers have more options as they partner with youth development agencies. At the same time, children and youth can be connected with prosocial activities that develop life skills, leadership, social supports, and belonging. Participation also may decrease family stress, because parents worry less about their children's safety when they are not at home. As stress is reduced, the family system tends to become more socially competent.

Child welfare leaders thus may have help link children, youth, and families with youth development opportunities. When child welfare leaders find effective programs, they can replicate them and develop innovative ones. As they do, they will gain additional, broad-based family and community support. Child welfare will no longer be a stand-alone institution in which workers feel they must do it all, alone. Children and families will receive support not only from child welfare systems, but also, from other community agencies that strive to provide opportunities for positive youth development and family support.

Everybody benefits as socially competent systems child welfare and youth development systems join forces. These socially competent systems become protective factors, which promote resilience. When youth development and child welfare leaders join forces, they are safeguarding the well-being of children, youth, and families, while improving the job satisfaction and working conditions of the professionals who serve them.

References

Alameda, T. (1996). The Healthy Learners Project: Bringing the community into the school. In K. Hooper-Briar and H. Lawson (Eds.). *Expanding partnerships for vulnerable children, youth, and families* (pp. 46-56). Alexandria, VA: Council on Social Work Education.

Allison, K., Crawford, I., Leone, P, Trickett, E., Perez-Febles, A., Burton, L., and Le Blanc, R. (1999). Adolescent substance abuse: Preliminary examination of school and neighborhood contexts. *American Journal of Community Psychology, 27*, 111-142.

Altschuler, S. (1997). A reveille for school social workers: Children in foster care need our help! *Social Work in Education, 19*, 121-127.

Anderson-Butcher, D. (2000). *Exploring the relationships among participation in youth development programs, risk and protective factors, and problem behaviors.* Unpublished Doctoral Dissertation, College of Health, University of Utah, Salt Lake City, UT.

Baron, S. and Hartnagel, T. (1998). Street youth and criminal violence. *Journal of Research in Crime and Delinquency, 35*, 166-192.

Benard, B. (1991). *Fostering resiliency in kids: Protective factors in the family, school, and community.* Portland, OR: Western Center for Drug-Free Schools and Communities.

Benson, P. (1997). *All kids are our kids: What communities must do to raise caring and responsible children and adolescents.* San Francisco: Jossey-Bass.

Blome, W. (1997). What happens to foster kids: Educational experiences of a random sample of foster care youth and a matched group of non-foster care youth. *Child and Adolescent Social Work Journal, 14*(1), 41-53.

Boyle, M. H. and Offord, D. R. (1990). Primary prevention of conduct disorder: Issues and prospects. *American Academy of Child and Adolescent Psychiatry, 29*, 227-233.

Brezina, T. (1998). Adolescent maltreatment and delinquency: The question of intervening processes. *Journal of Research in Crime and Delinquency, 35*(1), 71-99.

Briar-Lawson, K. and Drews, J. (1998). School-based service integration: Lessons learned and future challenges. In D. van Veen, C. Day, & G. Walraven (Eds.). *Multiservice schools: Integrated services for children and youth at risk* (pp. 49-64). Leuven/Apeldoorn, The Netherlands: Garant Publishers.

Brooks-Gunn, J., Duncan, G., and Aber, J. (Eds.). (1997). *Neighborhood poverty, volume 1: Context and consequences for children.* New York: Russell Sage Foundation.

Bry, B. H., McKeon, P., and Pandina, R. J. (1982). Substance use as a function of number of risk factors. *Journal of Abnormal Psychology, 91*, 273-279.

Burt, M. R., Resnick, G., and Novick, E. R. (1997). *Building supportive communities for at-risk adolescents: It takes more than this.* Washington, DC: American Psychological Association.

Catterall, J. (1998). Risk and resilience in student transitions to high school. *American Journal of Education, 106*, 302-332.

Chaskin, R. and Hawley, R. (1994). *Youth and caring: Developing a field of inquiry and practice: A report to the Lilly Endowment.* Chicago: The Chapin Hall Center for Children at the University of Chicago.

Cocozza, J. and Skowyra, K. (2000). Youth with mental health disorders: Issues and emerging responses. *Juvenile Justice, VII*(1), 3-13.

Cowen, E. L., Pedersen, A., Babigian, H., Izzo, L. D., and Trost, M. A. (1973). Long-term follow-up of early detected vulnerable children. *Journal of Consulting and Clinical Psychology, 41*, 438-446.

Davis, N. J. (1999). *Resilience: Status of research and research-based programs.* Rockville, MD: Substance Abuse and Mental Health Services Administration, Center for Mental Health Services.

Dishion, R., McCord, J., and Poulin, F. (1999). When interventions harm: Peer groups and problem behavior. *American Psychologist, 54*, 755-764.

Drake, B. and Pandey, S. (1996). Understanding the relationship between neighborhood poverty and specific types of child maltreatment. *Child Abuse and Neglect, 20*, 1003-1018.

Dryfoss, J. G. (1998). *Safe passage: Making it happen through adolescence in a risky society.* New York: Oxford University Press.

Dryfoos, J. (1999). The role of the school in children's out-of-school time. *The Future of Children, 9*(2), 117-134.

Durlak, J. (1998). Common risk and protective factors in successful prevention programs. *American Journal of Orthopsychiatry, 68*, 512-520.

Eamon, M. (1994). Poverty and placement outcomes in intensive family preservation services. *Child and Adolescent Social Work Journal, 11*, 349-361.

Elias, M. (1995). Primary prevention as health and social competence promotion. *The Journal of Primary Prevention, 16*(1), 5-21.

Fashola, O. S. (1998). *Review of extended-day and after-school programs and their effectiveness.* Washington, DC: Center for Research on the Education of Students Placed At Risk.

Felitti, V., Anda, R., Nordenberg, D., Williamson, D., Spitz, A., Edwards, V., Koss, M., and Marks, J. (1998). Relationship of childhood abuse and household dysfunction to many of the leading causes of death in adults. *American Journal of Preventive Medicine, 14*, 245-258.

Garmezy, N. (1971). Vulnerability research and the issue of primary prevention. *American Journal of Orthopsychiatry, 41*, 101-116.

Garmezy, N. (1985). Stress-resistant children: The search for protective factors. In J. E. Stevenson (Ed.), Recent research in developmental psychopathology. *Journal of Child Psychology and Psychiatry, 4*, 213-233.

Goerge, R., Van Voorhis, J., Grant, S., Casey, K., and Robinson, M. (1992). Special-education experiences of foster children: An empirical study. *Child Welfare, LXXI*, 419-437.

Gordon, E. W. and Song, L. D. (1994). Variations in the experience of resilience. In M. C. Wang & E. W. Gordon (Eds.). *Educational resilience in inner-city Americans: Challenges and prospects* (pp. 27-43). Hillsdale, NJ: Lawrence Erlbaum.

Halpern, R. (1999). *Fragile families, fragile solutions: A history of supportive services for families in poverty.* New York: Columbia University.

Harper, G. and Robinson, W. (1999). Pathways to risk among inner-city African-American adolescent females: The influence of gang membership. *American Journal of Community Psychology, 27*, 383-404.

Haveman, R. and Wolfe, B. (1995). *Succeeding generations: On the effects of investments in children.* New York: Russell Sage Foundation.

Hawkins, J., Catalano, R., Kosterman, R., Abbott, R., and Hill, K. (1999). Preventing adolescent health-risk behaviors by strengthening protection during childhood. *Archives of Pediatric Adolescent Medicine, 153*, 226-234.

Hawkins, J., Catalano, R., and Miller, J. (1992). Risk and protective factors for alcohol and other drug problems in adolescent and early adulthood: Implications for substance abuse prevention. *Psychological Bulletin, 112*, 64-105.

Hawkins, J., Jenson, J., Catalano, R., and Lishner, D. (1988). Delinquency and drug abuse: Implications for social services. *Social Service Review, 62*, 258-284.

Hellison, D. R. (1985). *Goals and strategies for teaching physical education.* Champaign, IL: Human Kinetics.

Hellison, D. R., Martinek, T. J., and Cutforth, N. J. (1996). Beyond violence prevention in inner-city physical activity programs. *Peace and Conflict: Journal of Peace Psychology, 24*, 321-337.

Hill, K., Howell, J., Hawkins, J., and Battin, S. (1998). *Childhood risk factors for adolescent gang membership: Results from the Seattle Social Development Project*. Seattle: University of Washington.

Holland, A. and Andre, T. (1987). Participation in extra-curricular activities in secondary school: What is known, what needs to be known? *Review of Educational Research, 57*, 437-466.

Inkelas, M. and Halfon, N. (1997). Recidivism in child protection services. *Children and Youth Services Review, 19*, 139-161.

Jang, S. J. and Smith, C. (1998). A test of reciprocal causal relationships among parental supervision, affective ties, and delinquency. *Journal of Research in Crime and Delinquency, 34*, 307-336.

Jessor, R., Donovan, J., and Costa, F. (1991). *Beyond adolescence: Problem behavior and young adult development*. New York: Cambridge University Press.

Jessor, R. and Jessor, S. (1977). *Problem behavior and psychosocial development: A longitudinal study of youth*. San Diego, CA: Academic Press.

Jessor, R., Van Den Bos, J., Vanderryn, J., Costa, R., and Turbin, M. (1995). Protective factors in adolescent problem behaviors: Moderator effects and developmental change. *Developmental Psychology, 31*, 923-933.

Kamradt, B. (2000). Wraparound Milwaukee. *Juvenile Justice, VII*(1), 14-23.

Kaplan, H. (1996). Toward an understanding of resilience: A critical review of definitions and models. In M. D. Glantz, J. Johnson, & L. Huffman (Eds.), *Resiliency and development: Positive life adaptations* (pp. 1-110). New York: Plenum Press.

Larner, M., Zippiroli, L, and Behrman, R. (1999). When school is out: Analysis and recommendations. *The Future of Children, 9*(2), 4-20.

Larson, R. (1994). Youth organizations, hobbies, and sports as developmental contexts. In R. K. Silbereisen & E. Todt (Eds.), *Adolescence in context: The interplay of family, school, peers, and work in adjustment* (pp. 46-65). Greenwich, CT: JAI Press.

Larson, R. (2000). Toward a psychology of positive youth development. *American Psychologist, 55*(1), 170-183.

Loeber, R., Keenan, K., and Zhang, Q. (1997). Boys' experimentation and persistence in developmental pathways toward serious delinquency. *Journal of Child and Family Studies, 6*, 321-357.

Mahoney, J. L. and Cairns, R. B. (1997). Do extracurricular activities protect against early school dropout? *Developmental Psychology, 33*(2), 241-253.

Masten, A. and Coatsworth, J. (1995). Competence, resilience, and psychopathology, In D. Cicchetti & D. Cohen (Eds.). *Developmental psychopathology: Vol.2., Risk, disorder, and adaptation* (pp. 715-752). New York: Wiley.

Masten, A. and Coatsworth, J. (1998). The development of competence in favorable and unfavorable environments. *American Psychologist, 53*(2), 205-220.

McLaughlin, M. (2000). *Community counts: How youth organizations matter for youth development*. Washington: Public Education Network.

McLaughlin, M., Irby, M, and Langman, J. (1994). *Urban sanctuaries: Neighborhood organizations in the lives and futures of inner city youth*. San Francisco: Jossey-Bass.

Mech, E. (1994). Foster youths in transition: Research perspectives on preparation for independent living. *Child Welfare, LXXIII*, 603-623.

Meenaghan, R. and Kilty, K. (1993). *Policy analysis and research technology.* Chicago: Lyceum Books.

Menaghan, E., Kowalkski-Jones, L., and Mott, F. (1997, Mar). The intergenerational costs of parental social stressors: Academic and social difficulties in early adolescence for children of young mothers. *Journal of Health and Social Behavior, 38*, 72-86.

Moore, K., Miller, B., Sugland, B., Morrison, D. R., Blumenthal, C., Glei, D., and Snyder, N. (1995). *Beginning too soon: Adolescent sexual behavior, pregnancy, and parenthood*. Washington, DC: Child Trends.

Mullahey, R., Susskind, Y., and Checkoway, B. (1999*). Youth participation in community planning*. Chicago: American Planning Association.

National Crime Prevention Council. (1998). *Securing the future for safer youth and communities*. Washington, DC: Author.

Needell, B. and Barth, R. (1998). Infants entering foster care compared to other infants using birth status indicators. *Child Abuse and Neglect, 22*, 1179-1187.

O'Donnell, C., Tharp, R., and Wilson, K. (1993). Activity settings as the unit of analysis: A theoretical basis for community intervention and development. *American Journal of Community Psychology, 9*, 195-232.

Parke, R. and Ladd, G. (Eds.). (1992). *Family-peer relationships: Modes of linkage*. Hillsdale, NJ: Erlbaum.

Quinn, J. (1999). Where need meets opportunity: Youth development programs for early teens. *The Future of Children, 9*(2), 96-117.

Reynolds, A. (1998). Resilience among black urban youth: Prevalence, intervention effects, and mechanisms of influence. *American Journal of Orthopsychiatry, 68*(1), 84-100.

Rolf, M., Sells, S., and Gordon, M. (1972). *Social adjustment and personality development in children*. Minneapolis: University of Minneapolis Press.

Rumberger, R. (1995). Dropping out of middle school: A multilevel analysis of students and schools. *American Educational Research Journal, 32*, 583-625.

Rutter, M. (1990). Psychosocial resilience and protective mechanisms. In J. Rolf, A. Masten, D. Cicchetti, K. Nuechterlein, & S. Weintraub (Eds.). *Risk and protective factors in the development of psychopathology*. (pp. 181-214). New York: Cambridge University Press.

Schinke, S. P., Orlandi, M. A., and Cole, K. C. (1992). Boys & Girls Clubs in public housing developments: Prevention services for youth at risk. *Journal of Community Psychology, 20*, 118-128.

Schwartz, I. and Fishman, G. (1999). *Kids raised by the government.* Westport, CT: Praeger.

Seidman, E., Chesir-Teran, D., Friedman, J., Yoshikawa, H., Allen, L., Roberts, A., and Aber, J. (1999). The risk and protective functions of perceived family and peer microsystems among urban adolescents in poverty. *American Journal of Community Psychology, 27*, 211-238.

Silver, J., DiLorenzo, P., Zukoski, M., Amster, B., and Schlegel, D. (1999). Starting young: Improving the health and developmental outcomes of infants and toddlers in the child welfare system. *Child Welfare, LXXVIII*(1), 148-165.

Slovic, P. (1986). Informing and educating the public about risk. *Risk Analysis, 6*, 403-415.

Smith, C. and Carlson, B. (1997). Stress, coping, and resilience in children and youth. *Social Service Review, 71*, 231-256.

Smith, C. and Stern, S. (1997). Delinquency and antisocial behavior: A review of family processes and intervention research. *Social Service Review, 71*, 382-420.

Takayama, J., Wolfe, E., and Coulter, K. (1998). Relationship between reason for placement and medical findings among children in foster care. *Pediatrics, 101*, 201-207.

Ullman, C. (1957). Teachers, peers, and tests as predictors of adjustment. *Journal of Educational Psychology, 48*, 257-267.

van Linden, J. and Fertman, C. (1998). *Youth leadership: A guide to understanding leadership development in adolescents.* San Francisco: Jossey-Bass.

Werner, E. and Smith, R. (1982). *Vulnerable but invincible: A study of resilient children and youth.* New York: McGraw-Hill.

Werner, E. and Smith, R. (1992). *Overcoming the odds: High-risk children from birth to adulthood.* Ithaca, NY: Cornell University Press.

White, R. (1959). Motivation reconsidered: The concept of competence. *Psychological Review, 66*, 297-323.

White, R. W. (1963). Ego and reality in psychoanalytic theory: A proposal regarding independent ego energies. *Psychological Issues, 3*, 3.

Witkin, S. (2000). Noticing. *Social Work, 45*, 101-104.

Witt, P. A. and Crompton, J. L. (1997). *Recreation programs that work for at-risk youth.* State College, PA: Venture.

Chapter 16
Introducing Child Welfare Neighborhood Teams that Promote Collaboration and Community-Based Systems of Care

Patti Van Wagoner, Rock Boyer, Megan Wiesen, Deb DeNiro-Ashton, and Hal A. Lawson

Introduction

Child welfare professionals are developing exciting practice innovations. These innovations promise to improve results for children and families, and at the same time, they improve workers' job satisfaction and working conditions. Some such innovations help *reform* practices. Others *transform* practices.

The neighborhood-based child welfare team is perhaps the key example of a transformational innovation. It presents a new century practice model. As the name "neighborhood team" suggests, professionals move from the agency to the neighborhood. They form a team, and as they do, they transform their practices. For example, they no longer work alone. The team promotes interprofessional collaboration.

Some teams also promote family-centered collaboration. That is, they view families as experts in what helps and hurts them. These teams make families partners in service planning, delivery, and evaluation. Teams share power with families.

Furthermore, some teams work to develop community-based systems of care (e.g., Farrow & The Executive Committee for Child Protection, 1997). They form multiple partnerships with other neighborhood leaders, religious institutions, agencies, community organizations, businesses, and schools. Teams that accept such a comprehensive vision for their work are truly transformational. Their stories need to be told so that others may benefit from the lessons teams have learned and the models they have developed. Practice-friendly, story telling facilitates replication and scale-up elsewhere.

This chapter presents condensed versions of three such stories, along with key lessons learned. Three team leaders, Patti, Megan, and Rock, are the primary story-tellers. Deb, the fourth author and a school-community developer, worked with Patti. Deb collaborated with Patti's newly formed team, helping to integrate this team with school-based and community-based collaborative service delivery models. Hal, the fifth author, is a university professor. At their invitation, he joined these four experts to help them extract and tell their stories, learn from one another, harvest knowledge, and extend their visions. Their stories draw on their direct experiences, including their formal reports about their progress, barriers, and achievements.

The five authors have used a practice-friendly research method to tell these stories. This method is called collaborative action research (e.g., Lawson, Briar-Lawson, Warner-Kearney, & Ynacay-Nye, 2000). Collaborative action research mirrors many of the changes that accompany the development of neighborhood-based teams. For example, collaborative action research, like neighborhood teams, depends on trusting relationships, mutual respect, and power sharing. With collaborative action research, everyone is a co-researcher and a co-author. There is no dividing line between the researcher and the "subjects." Just as neighborhood teams collaborate in relation to their respective strengths and expertise, so too, do collaborative action research teams draw on each member's strengths and expertise.

Done well, collaborative action research deepens interpersonal relationships, expands trust, enhances learning, and results in rich stocks of knowledge derived from practice. All of these benefits were realized as the team completed its research.

Of course, telling the story effectively presents another set of challenges. The authors have learned again as we have collaborated to write this chapter. Because space is limited, we have had to omit significant amounts of information, including the formal practice model, key change theories, competency domains for effective team practice, and other lessons learned. In brief, this is the first chapter in a longer, more detailed story, one we are continuing to write.

Every compelling story must have a good beginning. A good beginning sets the stage for the chapters that follow. It provides a context. Ideally, readers can identify with the key actors, the context, and the plot that begins to unfold. This chapter thus begins at the beginning.

The Context: Origins of the Neighborhood Team Model

The context for the development of neighborhood teams was a lawsuit (David vs. Michael C. Leavitt) brought against the Division of Child and Family Services (DCFS) by the National Center for Youth Law. Prior to this lawsuit, Utah's Division of Child and Family Services had been a steady, unchanging agency. Staff turnover was low. People left when they retired, or moved. Even in the large metropolitan area of Salt Lake and its suburbs, staff knew each other because at that time DCFS was a relatively small operation. There did not appear to be a need to change services or DCFS.

Then, the crisis arrived with the lawsuit. History shows that crisis and turmoil can bring better and more efficient ways of providing services. Suddenly, the agency was being focused on more than it had ever been in the past. The Governor, legislators, the Director of Human Services, the Director of DCFS, attorneys, and others--all wanted to ensure that DCFS was protecting children and providing the best services possible to Utah's children and families.

This lawsuit was the driving force behind child welfare reform in Utah. DCFS had not received significant increases in funding during the 1980s, despite signs of need. For example, there were increases in reports of child abuse and neglect and a growing number of children were entering the foster care system.

Benefits of the Lawsuit

The benefit of the lawsuit to DCFS was House Bill 265. The bill provided increased funding from the legislature, with the clear aim of bringing DCFS services in line *with* the growing needs. This influx of money was used to employ more caseworkers to meet the needs of increasing caseloads in CPS investigations, In-Home Services, and Foster Care. Along with funding increases, this bill mandated child welfare reform. It outlined specific measures that the Division was required to take in order to change the system.

The Lawsuit Settlement Agreement resulted in a pendulum swing in service provision. Out-of-home placements became more prevalent, and the legal system became more involved in the lives of families. In fact, a growing difference emerged regarding how the child welfare system should respond to the safety needs of children. Many human service professionals believed child protection was best provided with a family-centered approach that looked at the child in the context of the family, assessing risk factors that included immediate safety concerns and the risk for trauma that can result from separating a child from the family.

In contrast, some opponents believed that child protection meant using foster care as the main method of protection. At times, the legal system was used as a means to punish parents and enforce change.

In this contradictory climate, the agency at this time seemed to be reactive and driven by crisis. The changes that were taking place, intended to improve the child welfare services, seemed to create a system focused on compliance with the Settlement Agreement.

Within the first year of child welfare reform, the Salt Lake County region had tripled its workforce. Two-thirds of the workers were new to the child welfare system. Caseworkers were young and inexperienced, most having just completed bachelor degrees in related areas. Many had no background in social work, and they lacked related experience with families. These workers were faced with the challenges of immediate crisis intervention in Child Protective Services (CPS), and they were delegated responsibility for assessing children's safety.

Predictable Problems: Reforming Again and Again and Again

The tools caseworkers had were limited to the ones they received in core child welfare training. New workers were given checklists and expected to complete the paperwork they required for each program area. The assessments these checklists required were sometimes difficult, and workers needed learning and supervisory supports. Unfortunately, they received minimal direct supervision because of the increased demands on the supervisors.

Little wonder that there was an incredible amount of worker turnover. Caseworkers with over six months of experience became the more seasoned employees. The employees who stayed were challenged with burdensome caseloads of 30 or more foster care cases. Employee morale was at an all time low.

The Central Region, which consisted of the largest metropolitan and outlying areas of the Salt Lake City area, was directly under scrutiny. Efforts to manage the growth of the agency had resulted in two types of restructuring. In 1994, the region separated staff into ISF (Intake, Supervision, and Foster Care) teams that gave workers functional roles according to program area (i.e., Child Protective Services, in-home and out-of-home services). These teams were led by mostly inexperienced supervisors. These supervisors had been recruited from line workers when staff numbers increased. The result was that supervisors were overwhelmed with the responsibility of overseeing and understanding heavily procedure-laden policy in all program areas. In short, this was not a formula for success.

Within less than a year, the region was reorganizing again. This time the goal was to build teams. These teams would be formed according to specialized functions--CPS, in-home services, and out-of-home services. Teams were designed to give supervisors and workers the opportunity to become experts in one program area. The idea was to improve both supervision and front-line practice. Accordingly, these teams were segregated in three buildings within the county. One office was comprised of CPS staff, another office with In-Home service staff, and the other with Foster Care staff.

Again, the results were predictable. Services were isolated because the three teams were isolated and located in different places. Families were not receiving timely or consistent support. The agency continued to struggle with the tremendous number of children being placed in out-of-home care.

At the same time, the years of turmoil and change had placed the Division in a position of relative isolation within the community. Under close scrutiny by a Monitoring Panel and under fire in the media, the relationship with the community was tenuous at best.

The Neighborhood Team Model

The Neighborhood Team concept grew out of the need for change that would help DCFS staff and improve how they provided child welfare services. The idea was also to benefit the community by building relationships with key community partners who also had an investment in keeping children safe and strengthening family functioning. In other words, the basic plan was to create community-based systems of care.

DCFS needed to become an integral part of the community and support families, not just intervene when situations became chronic or families were in crisis. Each Neighborhood Team was designated to work with a specific area of Salt Lake County, making it possible to build relationships and partnerships with others in the community. The model would work toward the objectives of connecting families with services that are available in their own neighborhoods and joining with others in the community to work together to build supports for children and families.

We wanted to develop partnerships with schools, mental health service providers, health care providers, law enforcement, church and community groups, foster parents, extended family members, and others to help keep children safe and provide services that would have a positive impact on the family. We needed to become involved in the lives of children at an earlier point of intervention in order to make a difference in family interaction and connect them with community-based support. We were like the families we served. Families could not make changes in isolation and neither could the agency. We wanted and needed the support of the community and opportunities to join with others to utilize the resources available or create accessible services for families within their own neighborhoods.

By moving our core child welfare services to the community, we would be able to build relationships with the families we served and with our community partners. The community would know the child welfare workers that worked specifically with that area. Our partner agencies, such as schools and law enforcement, would be able to work on an ongoing basis with the team rather than with different caseworkers for every family. We hoped to prevent the problems and crises that tear families apart *and cause* children to be removed from their homes by developing relationships between DCFS staff and community partners.

Our aim was for children to be able to remain in their communities while receiving child welfare services. To achieve this goal, we wanted to create foster homes and other formal and informal supports within the neighborhood.

Salt Lake was already divided into three regions. Each region would then be asked to hire one Team Leader to develop a neighborhood model for one of the teams in the region. Once the three Team Leaders were hired, Administration decided to divide the teams by zip code areas. Three advance team areas were chosen due to the neighborhood having some community organization already occurring. The areas were identified as the Jackson team, the Magna team, and the Murray team.

Based on service data, Administration determined the number of caseworkers who would be assigned to the three advance teams. DCFS caseworkers were providing specialized services at the time. These caseworkers were already identified as CPS, foster care, and in-home caseworkers. Thus, each Team Leader was asked to find a specific number of caseworkers from each of the three specialties to begin working on their team.

A state specialist was assigned to work with the Team Leaders. This specialist was designated as a guide and as a link to the state office.

The Team Leaders asked for a lot of autonomy to develop a general neighborhood model along with specific practice principles that may be different for each of the teams. Administration was very supportive of the Team Leaders and their request for autonomy and support. The Team Leaders also strongly suggested that Administration be very outspoken with staff regarding their support for the neighborhood model and their guarantee of its longevity. Staff had experienced quite a few changes since the onset of the lawsuit and felt as though this may just be another temporary whim of Administration. Team Leaders spent a lot of time with staff and the community discussing the neighborhood team philosophy and what it meant in regard to protecting children and helping families.

Team Leaders were given the opportunity to visit an Alabama community kick-off and spend time with various staff throughout the state discussing their neighborhood model of service delivery. The Team Leaders were able to bring back a variety of ideas to help in forming their teams, on how to work with the community, and strategies for working better with children and their families. Alabama child welfare staff had significantly lowered the number of children in foster care by bringing families and community partners to the table and discussing how children could be protected in their homes. Alabama staff also spent a lot of time putting together what they called staff and community kick-offs. These events brought staff together to discuss the neighborhood model of service delivery, and then they brought community partners together to discuss everyone's responsibility regarding child protection.

When the Team Leaders returned to Utah, they began recruiting for their neighborhood teams by talking with staff about what their vision for child protection looked like. They openly discussed the regional plans to have a certain number of staff on each team, answering questions and concerns of staff. A staff kick-off was planned. All staff were asked to attend. The kick-off was held at a park pavilion, and ice-cream was provided. The agenda included a discussion of the vision Team Leaders and Administration had for the neighborhood model of service delivery and the next steps for accomplishing the vision. Staff members were asked to apply for the neighborhood teams. It was also decided that if staff did not apply, then random assignment to the teams would occur.

As Advanced Team Leaders (Patti, Megan, Rock), we became a support system for one another as new territories were explored. To build a Neighborhood Model, we looked at available information on other child welfare agencies in other states and countries that had formed community teams for the provision of services. We reviewed the Patches project in England ("a patch" in England is a neighborhood☐e.g., Smale, 1995). We also examined Florida's Integrated Initiative. A key turning point was the opportunity we were provided to visit Alabama community sites, which had successfully converted to community-based, family-centered services. We learned from them some of the key concepts that would later shape our practice model.

Immediately upon returning from Alabama, we implemented family staffing approaches. We created opportunities to engage families in being a part of Safety Planning, and we engaged them in decision making regarding their children who were at risk of being removed or had been removed from the home. In other words, these family staffing meetings were convened to join with the family, to learn the dilemmas they faced, and to work together for solutions.

We shared a dream that we could make a difference and we could influence our system to become family-centered and involve families in the process of decision making. We had experienced an era of compliance with a Settlement Agreement in which the voice of the family became lost. We wanted to move beyond a compliance-driven system in which paperwork and checklists took precedence over relationship building and family system intervention.

Together, we built upon the initial concept of Neighborhood teams and created a vision in which we would start by bringing our comprehensive child welfare services to the community, providing community-based CPS Assessments, In-Home Services, and Out-of-Home Services. The next step would be to implement early intervention and prevention efforts that would be geared toward strengthening families. The final stage would be establishing a strong connection with families and the community to change the perception that DCFS was the agency that removes children, to an agency for community-based family support.

Families, Agencies and Communities Together (FACT) Initiative

During the early 1990s, the Department of Health, Department of Human Services, State Office of Education, Administrative Office of the Courts, and Department of Workforce Services joined in an interagency initiative to build supports for families that were collaborative, family-centered, community-based, and culturally competent. This was the beginning of FACT legislation in Utah. This statewide initiative implemented Local Interagency Coordinating Councils (LICs) throughout the state of Utah. LICs were formed to bring together agencies to work with families in providing services where gaps in services existed for families with multiple needs. Comprised mostly of administrative staff from multiple agencies, the purpose of these LICs was to allocate resources to support families with co-occurring needs. The allocation of resources included collaboration and joint service intervention between agencies as well as dissemination of funding to families whose own resources would not be able to meet some of their treatment needs. In 1993, the passage of House Bill 39 provided 3.2 million dollars to coordinate services for children at risk.

The FACT model began to establish a relationship and dialogue between schools, homes, and community partners that resulted in greater support for each. Schools were no longer able to meet all the needs of families. There was support within the Division of Child and Family Services, community, and the DCFS partnership with the FACT initiative, which created the vehicle for DCFS community involvement. The Children at Risk (CAR) program was implemented for the purpose of joining the partnership with FACT to work with families who have multiple needs. Workers providing CAR services were connected to key community partners who worked together in the FACT site-based teams.

The focus of these teams was to identify and offer support to families of children, kindergarten through 3rd grade, that were at risk due to environmental, family, health, mental health, academic, and employment concerns. The successful collaboration and relationship building that these interprofessional teams demonstrated helped shape the vision of what a child welfare delivery system could become with community involvement. DCFS was no longer the primary agency to provide child welfare support and services. We recognized that we all needed one another in order to gain support as professionals in working in the human services field. And, families needed service providers to align with their individualized needs instead of providing categorical services that neither fit or helped their situation.

Now that the context has been sketched, the three stories can be told. We start with Patti's and Deb's.

Patti's and Deb's Story: The Murray Community

Murray Community Geographic Information

Murray is adjacent to Salt Lake City, Utah. It is defined as the a hub of Salt Lake County because it is located centrally within Salt Lake County. Murray has approximately 32,000 residents. It is a self-contained community with its own School District and its own electric power company.

Unlike the other nine areas in the state, which were identified for neighborhood team locations, Murray had natural, well-defined boundaries established by the city and school district. It was an ideal location for the Division of Child and Family Services (DCFS) to develop and implement a new model for service delivery.

The community was rich with opportunities for teaming. For example, there was a well-established Crime Council appointed by the Mayor. The Murray School District had implemented an innovative approach to the Families Agencies and Communities Together (FACT) service integration team. Instead of limiting FACT to two school-based teams, the school district had created a team to work with the entire community.

As the DCFS team started working with the community, there was a great amount of support for a new image for DCFS. Some people hoped that it would become an active community agency, while others doubted it would last. Some residents had negative experiences and perceptions of DCFS. They did not trust our agency.

Patti's Story

As I started to negotiate my way through meetings with key players in the Murray community, I realized that the perception that these people would have of DCFS would start with me. If they did not trust me, they would not trust DCFS. I came to them from a position of wanting to learn from them, not as an expert who had all of the answers. It was my goal to find a way for us to work together toward a common goal--strengthening families.

I tried to convey to everyone that I was open to their ideas and suggestions. I wanted them to know that I would always listen. My goal was not merely to create a favorable impression. I was being honest with them and with myself. I wanted and needed to know how they saw DCFS fitting with other agencies and resources in their community. I knew I needed to gain an understanding of the dynamics of the community and find avenues to engage and join with others to support the strengths of the community. I especially needed to know what was working for children and families and what was not. Once I gained this understanding, I could ask the community to help assess what else was needed from DCFS within our role of protection of children and support for families.

In retrospect, I realize that it was my experiences as a Licensed Clinical Social Worker and Intensive Family Preservation worker that gave me a framework for working with the community. For example, in both clinical and community social work practice, there is a need for engaging with others, assessing strengths and needs, providing support and intervention, and working through challenges. The same knowledge, skills, and intervention strategies are needed to be successful in neighborhood teams. The Neighborhood Team's success in Murray can be attributed to the joint efforts between the team and others in the community.

If I were to identify the main factor that influenced Murray Neighborhood Team's success, it would be the partnership that formed between the Murray School

District and the Division of Child and Family Services. I met with several key members of the School District, including the Superintendent, School Board Members, Pupil Services Coordinator, Specialist for At Risk Services, Principals, Counselors, Teachers, etc. The School District was the driving force for implementation of FACT within the schools and in the community. Working with the schools provided the opportunity for dialogue with community partners about our beliefs regarding children and families.

It soon became apparent that, despite our differences, diverse school and community stakeholders shared a common point of reference regarding how services delivery could provide better supports for children and their families. Shared understanding of what would improve services and supports began with past-present successes. In other words, what was already working in the school and in the community provided a point of departure for other new strategies. Like effective community development practice, the neighborhood team model was grounded in the strengths and assets of the community.

My team (and DCFS) worked closely with the school-community FACT team. We collaborated with community partners to implement a continuum of support services for families within the neighborhood. We created a vision for the Murray Neighborhood Team. Our vision was to become full partners with the community to provide prevention and early intervention to families prior to the need for intrusive government agency involvement, especially involvement that would result in pulling families apart.

Our vision was based on our conviction that there was a better way to protect children. We wanted to engage families early and continuously, rather than waiting for a crisis to emerge and then involving DCFS through a Child Protective Services (CPS) intervention. This better way of practicing involved enlisting broad-based community supports for our work on the behalf of children and families. Enlisting these supports meant changing our interactions with the community. By changing the interaction between DCFS staff and the community, the opportunity for prevention planning increased.

Talking about the Neighborhood Team Model

The foundation for change within the DCFS team started with a new way of talking. We talked about the neighborhood model as though it had already been established. This strategic use of language was important as we communicated about our child welfare services. For example, instead of using the word *investigations*, we talked about *CPS assessments*. Instead of maintaining a focus on program areas (i.e., CPS, In-Home, and Foster Care), the language was changed to refer to assessment, intervention, and prevention. In other words, we were less like enforcers who constantly kept families under close surveillance and more like friendly and supportive neighborhood workers who responded to family needs.

In the past, the focus in DCFS was more on how we did things, not what program would fit the family. Our team model was an effort to remove the boxes that are built around programs, boxes which limit access to DCFS as a resource for families and the community. This family engagement process helped establish some flexibility in how we delivered our mandated child welfare services, and it moved us outside the program boxes to work with families in a manner that established the relationship as the key for change within the system.

We started gradually, joining with the Community FACT team by enlisting the support of graduate student interns who could obtain practical experience and were not constrained by caseload sizes or agency policy and practice constraints. With administrative support, a partnership was formed with AmeriCorp to bring a community worker to the neighborhood team. AmeriCorp is a federal program that is build around providing service stipends to volunteers who give a commitment to work with community groups with a common goal. It was bringing these additional team members to work with individuals, children, and families, along with facilitate parenting groups and youth groups that helped us establish a pathway for community service delivery.

The development of the Murray Neighborhood team paralleled the Community FACT team. This grew to an integration of the team into the Community. Workers joined with the team to do assessments with families and provide short-term support. Access to DCFS support services was created by asking how can we work together to support children and families. Instead of waiting for substantiation of abuse and neglect to intervene with families, we based our ability to work with families on strengths of the family, team and community.

There were constraints due to the demands of the mandated services. We had to provide these services and manage caseloads, but at the same time, we worked through these by espousing a belief that, through work with the community in up-front efforts with families, we would reduce the need for our deep-ended services, such as out of home placements. Workers felt supported by the community because they had an avenue for accessing supports for families that did not rely on giving families phone numbers and wishing them good luck or providing case management services through DCFS to access community resources.

The team worked with the Community FACT team to link family with supports. The outcome of many of our CPS assessments with families was that the allegations of child abuse or neglect were not substantiated but the families did have needs that they were challenged to meet on their own. The continuum of support from the neighborhood team changed as we shared responsibility with the community players to protect children and strengthen families.

As the team became part of the community, opportunities to support prevention efforts became more prevalent. Community partners, such as the Boys and Girls club, enlisted us as partners in grants that were used to create mutual support for families. Parents Anonymous support groups for parents were established utilizing team members to facilitate the group along with parent leaders. Neighborhood workers on my team joined with the club to develop and implement groups for youth to prevent unwed teen pregnancy. The workers were excited to move outside their DCFS role and be able to interact with youth in a different way and be role models. These same team members implemented a Safety Program to take into the schools to teach children how to be safe and talk with teachers about risk factors and red flags that could identify children at risk of abuse.

Child abuse and neglect reporting guidelines were shared along with an open invitation to call us and talk about their concerns and invite us to join with the families before abuse and neglect referrals are needed. Early intervention became more of a focus along with provision of mandated services. We were able to establish a community-based neighborhood team that provided the core child welfare services to the community.

We continued to evolve as the agency started to utilize Family Group Decision-Making models to work with families. As we utilized family-centered strategies within our team and focused on building upon the strengths of the family, we started to see a change in how placements were made when children had to be out of their own homes. Families were starting to take a lead by coming together with their extended family members creating opportunities for kinship placement. Community members started to offer to be specific foster care providers when a child they knew needed to be out of their home. Service delivery had changed as a result of being a part of the community.

Four years later, the Neighborhood Practice Model is a work in progress. It will continue to change over time but the basic structure will remain. The central process and belief in the Neighborhood Model is that the relationship we have with the child, family, community partners, and others is the foundation and primary intervention for our work as child welfare professionals.

Changes in the Neighborhood Team and Structure

It was challenging to implement the changes necessary to create Neighborhood Teams. For example, there was resistance to change within the agency because of the fallout from the lawsuit against DCFS.

When the team was structured initially, the DCFS Administration underestimated how much time, work, and supports would be needed for teams to function effectively. The Administration pushed for teams to be "up and functioning" within a few months. In their rush to implement a better model, they unintentionally created some barriers.

For example, the team was comprised of staff members who did not volunteer. They were required to join this "unknown" team, whether they wanted to or not. The DCFS administration also decided the number of workers needed for each team. Murray was assigned 1 CPS worker, 2 In-Home Service Workers, 6 Foster Care Workers, 1 part-time CAR/FACT worker, 2 Supervisors for the line staff, 2 Caseworker Assistants, 1 Senior Caseworker Assistant, 1 Family Preservation worker, and 1 Secretary. In retrospect, my work would have been easier if workers had volunteered. Then, they would have had some idea about what they were "getting into," and they may have brought with them an inclination toward collaboration and team work.

In contrast, my initial workers may have joined my team reluctantly. Each of these team members was used to doing their functional programmatic roles. Workers traditionally reported to their respective supervisors. They were not used to the teamwork approach. Team members had little or no experience with the clinical staffing process we began to develop. They had little or no knowledge of family decision making strategies that gave families some say in what needed to be done. Team members had little prior experience and training with collaboration and working in collaborative teams. They were unaware of other strategies that moved the worker out of isolation in working with families.

Workers reacted predictably. They appeared to be fearful of change, and they were overwhelmed with the thought of doing things differently. They showed needs for safety and security as they faced so many important changes in their work. The Murray Team began to evolve from this point on, and its evolution continues today.

Building the team took a tremendous amount of energy and insight. One of the greatest challenges was to instill hope in the team. A bridge needed to be built between the traditional role of a DCFS worker in delivering child welfare services and a new role and vision.

The team has developed into a group of workers whose focus is on what can be done to support families and to strengthen the safety net for children. Today, instead of functional roles, all of the workers know how to do comprehensive assessments and interventions. They learn to provide the whole continuum of services offered to families from prevention to CPS assessments, to In-Home interventions, and Foster Care when a child needs to be out of the home to remain safe. In other words, their roles have expanded; they have blended once-separate, isolated, and narrowly specialized roles.

These blended roles of the Neighborhood Workers create opportunities to establish a relationship with families and continue to use that relationship as a tool for change. The team needs and develops a supportive infrastructure for these blended, expanded roles. The team's infrastructure provides an environment that encourages and rewards calculated risk-taking; enables mutual supports and joint problem-solving; and encourages the development of new practices and policies.

At the same time, we recognize that we do function with our agency policies and regulations, and we honor them.

In addition, we made a big shift from focusing on caseload sizes alone. We started looking at the families we were serving. We focused on their strengths and needs and identifying strengths of our team in working with them. The supervisor implemented what we now call "a weighted case management structure." We assigned cases according to family's needs and the intensity of services needed. This new structure was designed to ensure that assignments were balanced among team members and that flexibility in service provision would remain.

We changed position descriptions at the same time. Positions were reallocated to create a prevention/early intervention specialist to work with the FACT teams and offer support to other families. The workers and Team Leader became part of the Community FACT team, interfacing and working in teams with other community partners. Teamwork evolved to joint home visits between the Neighborhood Workers and the FACT team members.

In other words, workers moved out of isolation within DCFS and became part of a community team that works together to keep children safe. At the same time, we have tried to involve families in the decision making process at all levels of intervention. For example, the team and the community has used Family Group decision making to engage families in the support services offered through FACT. Similarly, we have used Family Unity meetings to increase the use of kinship care as an alternative to foster care. These processes are used to facilitate permanency for children through reunification, permanent care with relatives, or adoption. Today, the DCFS has implemented the Family Unit model statewide to establish greater family involvement in making decisions about child safety and protection.

There are constraints and challenges in using the Neighborhood Model. For example, we need to gain more support from legal partners, Attorney General, and Guardian Ad Litem, to build a necessary bridge from the community to the court system. Then we can find better ways to facilitate change within family systems when they are involved with the court.

Moreover, the mandates from the agency and the legislature offer challenges for us to be even more creative. The Murray Neighborhood team accepts these challenges and remains focused on maintaining their community connections and providing services in a manner that best meets the needs of the child, family, and community.

We have succeeded in engaging other community partners. Today, some 6 years after we started, Murray community is beginning to work together and is exploring ways for all its members to be included in the neighborhood and locality development efforts. For example, Deborah DeNiro-Ashton and I began to work together closely and effectively to promote this engagement. In the spirit of true collaboration, her story must be woven into mine.

Deb's Story

I have been employed by Murray School District for the past 15 years. I was a schoolteacher for the first eight years. I have the spent the last 7 years as a clinical social worker and community developer. Although my story is about my work as a social worker and community developer, it actually begins with my teaching. My work as a teacher helps explain why I became a social worker.

When I worked as a front-line teacher, I experienced the frustrations stemming from many "systems barriers." I wanted to teach and educate "the whole child," but I could not when many of the children came to school cold and hungry. They were not ready to learn due to home and family issues. As a teacher, I was able to impact positively the children when they came into my classroom; I could see that I was helping them. However, my frustration grew, and so did other teachers', as more and more children came to the school with multiple stressors that impacted their academic success.

The school was unprepared to feed, cloth, and support families. It also lacked the resources necessary to help parents and care givers provide better care for themselves and their children.

From an organizational perspective, the school needed agency and community supports. FACT responded to this need. It started to change the old mind set of major departments and agencies working in isolation and serving only "their" population.

Weaving Together the Two Stories: the Murray Experience with Fact

Similarly, FACT started to change other common practices that were not helpful to workers, or to children and families. For example, the common practice of service agencies was to refer families to other agencies when the worker, the family, or both experienced burn out; or when the family's needs didn't fit within the program offered. Agencies seemed to have rigid mandates. These mandates appeared to serve their administration more than children and families.

FACT's collaborative approach was designed to change the way agencies delivered services and how they treated families. This objective sounded good, and it was needed. But applying it in practice at the school and in the community was extremely difficult. As we began working together, we encountered multiple barriers. These barriers included turf issues, gaps in language and differences in terminology used, and conflicts among people. Our dialogue was often fragmented and unproductive. Professionals often became frustrated with one another, and our frustration had the potential to spill over into the treatment of children and families. All these barriers and others affected how families were served and treated.

It became clear that professionals had a great deal of work to do before they could collaborate effectively. We worked to create a safe environment for open dialogue, an environment in which no one felt defensive and one promoting the goal of serving the entire family through family-centered practices. Starting in 1994, 40 community partners went through a strategic planning process in such a safe environment. This planning process was designed to set the vision and direction for the next five years. We spent an entire day discussing what we wanted for families, identifying barriers, expressing personal frustration for efforts that seemed to not have been making a difference, and learning from one another. For example, we learned that we had more similarities than differences and that our similarities were personal ones, not just professional ones.

We learned that the pivotal point for true collaboration is strong relationships and the trust that cements them. When relationships among service providers were strong enough to work as a team with honest, respectful, and authentic feedback of our individual and group actions, we were ready to collaborate.

We immediately experienced a difference. Most of us were accustomed to working alone, often trying to avoid mistakes and blame. Most of us hadn't experienced such powerful colleague support from a wide variety of individuals with different expertise and training. Cross-training within the team enhanced personal and collective expertise. Members' physical and emotional burnout decreased. There were more people available to work in partnership with families and to serve as collaborative "case managers" of family-directed and -centered services.

The FACT and DCFS teams gained a better understanding of each agency's mission, programs, and practices. As knowledge and understanding grew, better working relationships developed. In turn, systems barriers were eliminated, resulting in families receiving comprehensive and coordinated services.

The image of DCFS has been bolstered and corrected in the process. Misconceptions about DCFS were apparent from the beginning. Now there is a better understanding of the mission of DCFS and the type of intervention they can provide to families. The Neighborhood Team members have built relationships with each school.

Scale-up has commenced in recent years because our work has been so successful. For example, the FACT model was expanded to include all Murray schools. We have developed a central referral process as well as a community walk-in service and information center. This community center was established to provide better access for all Murray residents to gain information about service supports as well as direct services from prenatal throughout the life span.

By co-locating multiple service supports and information in Murray, service delivery has definitely changed. Residents are able to access services in a central location close to their homes, and professional partners provide complex coordination of services among multiple agencies and Family-School-Community Service plans.

Families are joint partners in the development of these service plans. The underlying assumption and belief is that the each family has strengths and when families are given the opportunity, which is their inherent right, to devise and implement their services, long term change can occur. In other words, family-centered collaboration is prized, not just interprofessional collaboration. Agency representatives serve the family and build personal relationships that sustain support and change within the family. Support is voluntary, and it is not restricted by time-lines or eligibility guidelines.

Moreover, community-based systems of support are developing. Individuals and families are assisting their neighbors in accessing support as well as providing expertise, as a team member, in restructuring policy, administrative and service delivery efforts. Thanks to support from a Parents' Anonymous Grant, parents have gained employment within the community and have reported feeling more connected to their community. They report feeling good about being able to "give back" to their community; they feel a stronger sense of belonging.

Community organization and development have emerged from our work. The community development efforts focus on the inclusively and diversity of all community members by learning from one another. Community needs assessments, along with a second round of strategic planning, have created another, more comprehensive vision. When we started our work in 1993, we could not have anticipated the breadth and depth of this vision for broad-based community development and community-based systems of care and support.

Our locality development now focuses on practical application of support for all members. A results-based, data-driven method is being used to map existing resources, gaps and efforts needed to improve conditions community-wide. This group's success is truly based on the relationships established in the early years, as well as new partners from private and public agencies and organizations who want to be part of the community change effort.

Members are beginning to have a voice in communicating their current struggles and are instrumental in changing conditions for themselves and others. In this emergent Mutual Aid model, care givers and care-seekers roles are interdependent and interchangeable. This model provides a holistic approach to re-engineering and equalizing relationships, and in developing responsive policy and services. Kahn (1993) suggests that to be cared for is essential to the capacity to be caring. Residents need to be cared for within the context of their neighborhood and community in meaningful ways that enhances neighbor-to-neighbor connections and reduces isolation.

Our dream for the future is not only to continue our current efforts and expansion process to support Murray residents but also to share what we have learned with others. The cross-community information sharing could bring forth a community treatment and practice model to build stronger neighbor-to-neighbor supports and utilize community resources and organizations to enhance community-wide functioning and well being.

Megan's Story

Background

I began working for DCFS in 1991 after graduating from College with a bachelor's degree in Psychology. I worked as a case manager for foster care and in-home services. After receiving my Master's in Social Work, I spent 2-½ years providing family preservation services with DCFS. After working as a Team Leader for about one year, I then accomplished my goal of receiving an L.C.S.W.

Jackson Neighborhood Team

The Jackson neighborhood area, unlike Murray and Magna, was not a city. The team was defined by the zip code 84116 and used street addresses as boundaries. To most residents, this area is known as Rose Park. The area includes mainly low income, with some middle income families and many apartment complexes. The majority of homes are over 30 years old with a few new subdivisions being built in the outlying areas.

Becoming a Team Leader

When I learned about the concept of the Neighborhood team, and that administration wanted three team leaders to design a model for the Salt Lake area, I was very intrigued and wanted to find out more. As I asked questions and learned that three advance teams would be formed, I was excited about what this would mean for DCFS staff, the families they served, and the community. I allowed myself to dream (little did I know at the time how the dream would be accomplished and expanded).

I thought about what my vision would be for a neighborhood model. I envisioned a community where all of the people who were already working with a family and their children would come together and discuss child protection. Families would be included in service planning and would be strengthened and empowered to protect their children and meet their needs. DCFS caseworkers would partner with schools, police, and communities, and children would be safer and less traumatized because of this. I became more convinced that this was the direction we needed to go in our agency.

I interviewed for the position and was ecstatic when I learned that Patti, Rock, and I had been chosen. The three of us immediately began discussing our vision for the neighborhood model. We were assigned a specialist, Amanda Singer, from the state office to assist us in the process of designing a model of service delivery. Amanda encouraged us to focus on the process and to gather information from other communities that had neighborhood models. She also recommended that we do an assessment of our community's strengths and needs.

Neighborhood Team Formulation

One of my first tasks was to do a community assessment. I began by looking at the programs and services that were already working in the community and helping families. I found a number of programs that I could join with. Examples included a Community Action Team (CAT), a FACT Team, United Way programs, and others. The CAT team included a variety of agencies focused on crime prevention, and this team met weekly. CAT provided an avenue for joining with a variety of community partners and building relationships in which all agencies benefited.

We needed a neighborhood office for our team to work from. I was given authorization to have the State office send out a request for proposals to find a building in the Jackson zip code area. Once we received the proposals, I discussed the options with my team, and we decided on a small office in the upstairs area of a credit union.

One of my most important priorities at this time was to include the team, which I often affectionately called "my team," in most of the decisions. I felt that since we were entering such new territory in child welfare practice, it would be important for all the team members to contribute and help decide what the model should look like in Jackson.

Once the team members were identified, I immediately began having team meetings. This bonding was absolutely essential to the success of the team. CPS assessors, in-home workers, foster care workers, and other team members were all able to build a relationship that assisted in the delivery of services. Case situations were able to be discussed by people with a variety of skills. Transfers from one service to another could be done at weekly staff meetings, or if necessary, at any other time, due to being located in the same building. People who worked in one service area were no longer segregated and were able to get to know those who worked in other service areas. They could now learn more about the jobs those people performed. Morale increased because people felt part of the team and knew their opinions counted. Each team member was influential in decision making.

As the Jackson Team Leader, I directly supervised the two supervisors. As the team evolved, one supervisor supervised two in-home caseworkers, three general CPS investigators, and three sex-abuse CPS investigators. The other supervisor directly supervised five foster care workers, an eligibility technician, a transport technician, and an office technician. This type of organization for our team was ideal as it allowed me to focus on community partnershipping, team building, and being lead team visionary.

Monthly Reports

Patti, Rock and I were asked to provide separate monthly written reports to administration. We were asked to include information regarding our community involvement, team building, team leader needs, and outcomes for the month. We all felt that writing these reports kept us focused on all the differing aspects of our job. Without this constant focus in the beginning, we felt it would have been easy to go back to doing things the way we had done them in the past. As I read over some of my monthly reports, I felt that including some excerpts from them would give a broader picture regarding development of the Jackson team, along with some of the challenges and successes. These reports are presented in Box 1. I have included the entire first report, which was written July 1996. It describes how we got started. You will see that I felt it was extremely important to let administration know how much their support mattered in assuring the success of the neighborhood model. Later excerpts remind me that the process seemed slow at times, but with each success, we were getting closer to our vision which was and always still is before us.

Box 1. Excepts from Megan's Monthly Status Reports

July 1996

The Jackson neighborhood team has been formed. It consists of three CPS assessors, three in-home supervision workers, one family preservation worker, five foster care workers, two eligibility technicians, two transport workers, two supervisors, one team leader, one receptionist, and one secretary. All positions have been filled with the exception of a CPS assessor, an in-home supervision worker, and a supervisor. Also, we will not need a receptionist or secretary until we move into the neighborhood.

The partners we have had contact with in the community have been very supportive and positive about the neighborhood model. The people from the FACT teams and elementary schools that we've met with have invited us to join them in additional meetings once school begins. Valley Mental Health, Utah Groups, and Success by 6 are some of the resources that serve our clients' needs and have discussed ways to partnership with us.

Another group, which is a key part of the neighborhood action coalition, is called CAT Team 1; it serves the Rose Park, Jackson area. We meet weekly with people from a variety of agencies, such as probation, law enforcement, community mobilization specialists, youth and family specialists, and the Mayor's office. This group was organized by the

Mayor's office. It discusses what is going on in the Jackson neighborhood and how to solve community problems.

Family staffings have been held with a variety of workers and the families they serve. These have been successful, positive opportunities to join with families and the community to outline the strengths and needs of a family. Children are being protected and their needs are being discussed along with who is responsible to meet those needs. These meetings are productive for everyone involved.

In regard to any needs I may have concerning the neighborhood team, I am receiving full support and help whenever I need it. Obstacles are being overcome as they arise. We continue to work on team building and morale issues as staff continue to need assurance that they will be supported. We also continue to need a building in the Jackson, Rose Park area. This building will benefit the team personally and help them serve the families more effectively.

My overall assessment of this project is that it is progressing positively. As a team leader, I am receiving tremendous support from all administration. Those in administration have provided us with resources to meet the hefty demands of this task. We have also been given help from many people with specialties who have aided us in our task and have been invaluable resources in making this a successful venture. We are being allowed the time we need to build relationships with the community, which is necessary for success. In addition, we are building relationships within the team, which is also necessary for success. The support we are receiving is essential and very appreciated.

August 1996

One of the significant positive outcomes for August was the Neighborhood Team Implementation Plan that Patti, Rock, Amanda, and I developed. We took the recommendations from the planning retreat we had in July and designed a plan, which includes findings, recommendations, and implementation steps. We presented the plan to administration and are continuing to implement the steps as outlined in the plan.

Another positive outcome was that our neighborhood team staff and I attended the Night Out Against Crime festivities in a Rose Park/Jackson neighborhood. We were able to discuss the neighborhood model and meet many of the families who live in the area. It was a wonderful opportunity to begin building relationships with people who live in Rose Park.

Two of my partners on the CAT team, a law enforcement officer and a law enforcement community affairs person, offered to take me to Rose Park and show me around, so I spent a few hours with them becoming more familiar with the area.

My neighborhood team and I presented at a school district meeting attended by principals, school counselors, and school district personnel from the Jackson/Rose Park area. We discussed the neighborhood model and how we could coordinate services.

My other activities have revolved around planning a CAR (Children At Risk) focus group with FACT members, staffing family issues with various partners, and continuing to develop a well functioning neighborhood team. My team's efforts are resulting in the beginning foundation for many relationships with partners in the community. Each time I meet with a partner, we both acknowledge the need to establish trust between us. We are beginning to build trust through communication materials, and it is growing every day. We are also continuing to receive support from administration which is essential.

Employees are becoming less frustrated as they receive information and feel more settled. Those employees who have not had closure on what they will be doing, such as CAR staff and sex abuse staff, continue to express concern about their own stress and frustrations. I have found that the more information they have about their future, the easier it is for them to do their jobs.

September 1996

North Valley Mental Health invited me to their retreat to talk about the neighborhood model.

I received a request from the Public Employees newspaper editor to do a story about the neighborhood model. The article was positive and other staff from the neighborhood team were also interviewed.

Staff of the Boys and Girls Club, along with Colors of Success and I have met to discuss how we can work together in the neighborhood. I also have been contacting law enforcement at schools and the Salt Lake City Police Department to discuss how we can coordinate our services. I have spent time in the schools with teachers and school personnel and we continue to build stronger relationships.

October 1996

We made progress with CCS (Catholic Community Services) and Volunteer Services. CCS will be facilitating the support group and volunteers will be providing educational assistance to children of the kinship parents. This group will be held at the Boys and Girls club.

I've also been working with other staff to come up with a more efficient, child and family friendly, case transfer process. We have come up with family/neighborhood focused procedures that are also beneficial to staff and the Jackson team will be implementing the process fully beginning December 1. I also have continued to participate in family staffings with my staff and with the schools. I continue to hire and work with new staff.

November 1996

The Jackson neighborhood team should be moving into a building in the Rose Park area during the month of January or February. The team is looking forward to the move as we will be closer to the people we serve. Our community partners are also anxious to have us be located in their neighborhood.

United Way has offered a violence prevention specialist to assist our team in violence prevention. She will be located in our new building with us and will work as a resource for our families.

During the months of October and November, the supervisors in our building met a number of times to go over the settlement agreement in detail. We then provided training to our team members in detail.

My team members are becoming more cohesive and are building relationships with one another and the community. They have pulled together as we are down one CPS worker and have two new in-home workers. Some of my foster care workers are doing in-home cases to help out other team members and others help in various ways. The process of building an effective neighborhood model takes time, commitment, support, and energy from everyone in the agency. We are definitely on our way to a very successful model of working with the neighborhood.

December 1996

Most of the month of December was spent hiring new supervisors and caseworkers for the Jackson team and also for the Salt Lake pod. The other part of December was spent coordinating coverage for team members taking Christmas vacation.

We designed a survey to get feedback on the usefulness of the CAT team and requested suggestions on how our meetings could be more productive. We have all benefited from the weekly meetings and will continue to improve the process so the entire community will benefit.

January 1997

The Jackson team is continuing to be successful in our efforts to reduce caseloads, provide quality services, increase morale within the team, and to work with our community partners effectively. Our foster care caseloads are going down, our CPS caseworkers are linking families with community resources, our in-home workers are remaining busy but are closing cases more quickly. A couple of our foster care workers have taken a few in-home cases when the in-home workers had full caseloads.

We have received positive feedback about our team staff meetings. During our weekly meetings, we give information to staff from administration, staff cases, do case transfers, and provide training to the team on subjects that are of interest to them. We also have guests come frequently to tell us of their program in the community or we have gone to other agency staff meetings to introduce ourselves and talk about how we can work together. Team members have voiced that they enjoy the team meetings and like how they are run. Almost all of our 19 members attend every week.

One of the projects I worked with this month was Project Link. Project Link will be hiring a project coordinator and two school coordinators in the Salt Lake City School district. The coordinator will work with the community to find resources for the children and families who attend the schools. There are ten schools that will be served by Project Link, with five in my area. I have also continued to coordinate with the Salt Lake FACT coordinator. I attend the monthly FACT meetings and monthly CAR (Children At Risk -Project Hope). The CAR worker is assigned to the Jackson team and works in the Jackson and Rose Park elementary schools. She meets with families of children identified through the schools on a voluntary basis.

February 1997

During the month of February, my main project was organizing a meeting with the religious leaders in the Jackson community. We came up with a list of the religious leaders in the community and sent invitations to join a planning meeting with the CAT team. We then followed up with phone calls, and three leaders attended the meeting. We discussed some of the major needs in the community and decided to focus on building relationships and volunteerism. We decided to plan a community fair and invite religious leaders and their congregations. The theme will be "Working together through volunteerism".

March 1997

During March, our CAT team had a follow-up meeting with the religious leaders in the community to discuss our night social. We decided to change the focus slightly and have a resource fair. We will have a variety of booths, including a DCFS booth, where agencies can meet the community members and let them know the resources they offer. We are also going to have some local entertainment from different school groups.

May 1997

The month of May was spent getting ready to move, moving, and taking care of new building concerns once we were at our new location. We moved into our new Jackson building on May 16. Jackson staff have expressed that they are happy to finally be in their building and that they are excited to be located closer to the families they work with and the service providers who work with them.

June 1997

The CAT team Resource Fair was held on June 9 at Riverside Park. It was very successful. We invited a variety of community partners to sit at booths and discuss their services with community residents. We served food and had games and hundreds of residents attended. Some of the partners who were there included the Boys and Girls club, Big brothers and Big sisters, AmeriCorp, Project Link, DCFS, Police department, gang task force, parking enforcement, the community Library, and others. Work Force Services recruited to employ people, the Health Department gave away bicycle helmets for the children, handouts were provided in English and Spanish, and bilingual speaking employees were in attendance. We were asked many times by the children if we would be coming back soon. .

Now that we are in our new building, many of my duties are administrative. Helping the team to run effectively and efficiently are necessary top priorities. Both of the supervisors and I work together and with team members to figure out the best ways to make daily tasks flow as well as possible. The supervisors focus on mentoring, paperwork, and compliance issues with their staff. I focus on how our team can work the most effectively and efficiently with partners and internally. In addition, I meet with both of them regularly to discuss compliance, internal, and external functioning. I have continued to meet, as other team members have, with a variety of community partners.

My recommendations for DCFS concerning the neighborhood model and neighborhood teams are that we continue to go forward with the model, putting as many resources and as much support as is necessary to make the neighborhood teams and the model successful! I believe that the first step in the current part of the process is to ensure that all neighborhood teams have Team Directors. It is impossible for supervisors to supervise, mentor, train, etc. their staff AND coordinate with the community to the extent necessary.

In addition, when neighborhood teams separate into their own buildings, there are many administrative functions that need to be done. When a supervisor is led to these tasks in addition to supervising, they can only supervise a unit, not a team, which can lead to fragmentation. Therefore, I strongly recommend that the support and resources be given to Regional

Directors so they can hire Team Directors for each neighborhood team in their region.

3rd Quarter 1997

As we move along, I am increasingly amazed at the tremendous outcomes from protecting children in this partnership way! Community partners have felt the support of DCFS upper Administration as have the DCFS caseworkers. Morale is increasingly positive as workers realize that their jobs become more doable when they include all of the people involved with a child and family. We have all become more and more aware that financial resources will not continue to grow with the growth of residents and thus the growth of abuse and neglect reports. Eventually, even though there continues to be growth in number of residents, our goal is to have prevention so integrally ingrained in all service agencies that abuse and neglect reports will continue to decrease. The small steps we are taking continue to make a larger effect in the protection of children, and I believe the neighborhood model is at the heart of it all.

The Jackson team members also have found opportunities to help in the community even when they do not have an open case with the family. An example of this is one of our CPS workers has begun coaching a basketball team consisting of 8-9 year old girls from our neighborhood.

1st Quarter 1998

The Jackson neighborhood team continues to work together and with the community to provide a community-centered approach to child protection. Within the team, there is a sense of camaraderie and ownership. Team members work together to solve problems and help children and families. I continuously hear compliments from other agencies and other DCFS employees that our employees go the extra mile, are reliable, do great casework, and help each other out. Team members, through their normal work with schools, law enforcement, mental health, etc., continue to promote a community centered approach of helping children to be safe, meeting children and families needs, and protecting children. We know that we are taking the first necessary steps to reaching an ideal neighborhood model. Partnerships are being formed that allow problem solving. We know that through working together we can solve many more problems and find resources to meet many more needs than we ever could or would be able to on our own.

I also continue to do presentations for different agencies to discuss the neighborhood model and how we can work together to meet the needs of their agency and ours.

It is now March of 2000 and many more lessons have been learned regarding building a neighborhood team model of service delivery. I have learned that it is easy to become stuck in defeatist behavior, focusing on the current crisis and not moving forward. When getting started, it was essential to meet regularly as Team Leaders to discuss our vision and strategies for accomplishing our goals. Writing monthly reports kept us on track and focused. Realizing that we would be on a never ending path of evolution kept us from getting frustrated with how slowly things seemed to be moving at times.

We are currently way ahead of where we were when we began. We not only hold family staffings, we have researched many family models and are currently implementing family unity and family conferencing type models with families. Families are included as part of the service planning team. We have neighborhood teams throughout the entire Salt Lake Valley and all of them have Team Leaders. The community partners have joined the teams and relationships continue to be built throughout the valley. Currently, we face many budget challenges in our Division, and caseloads are increasing due to a hiring freeze. If we allow ourselves to focus on the crisis only, we will waste time and staff morale will decrease.

Administration is encouraging staff to focus on the needs of their teams and devise solutions to meet those needs. The neighborhood model, along with the practice model we have developed along the way, are keeping us grounded. We have built a foundation that will make a huge impact on this crisis and any future problems that may arise.

My current vision is that we will continue to assess our needs and our strengths as an agency and as neighborhood teams. We will recognize the need to be family focused and respectful of the families we serve. We will understand that our goal should be to help children be safe in their homes and that we can't do that without the help of the community. We will continue to hire competent staff who have a desire to learn a variety of skills that will help the children and families they serve. My dream is that we will all continue to dream.

Rock's Story: The Magna Community

My purpose in writing this brief story is to share some of my newfound knowledge and experiences developing and implementing in the community the "neighborhood model" of child welfare. I will share both successes and barriers.

Personal Background and Context

I have my Master's Degree in Social Work. I have worked in Canada (Alberta) and in Utah. I have done both front-line work and administration. I have gained almost 20 years of experience with state-governmental child welfare. I have spent most of these years in supervision, management, and administrative projects.

This neighborhood team model has been one of the most exciting and fulfilling jobs I have ever held. Time and again I asked myself this basic question: "Why has this job been so exciting and fulfilling?" The following story is my first, formal response to this question. It is a brief response, one that does not tell the entire story.

As Megan has said, child welfare professionals in Utah have been working under a legal agreement, which has been in effect since 1994. The Division of Child and Family Services (DCFS) tried several different options, posed various solutions, and piloted alternative methods of service delivery in trying to meet the requirements of this lawsuit. Nevertheless, DCFS was not arriving at the optimal solution to address some of our child welfare needs and barriers. New research and practice, combined with our past successes, pointed to the promise of the "Neighborhood Model: A Team Approach to Child Welfare." This new model was introduced in the state of Utah in early 1996.

This new direction was given full administrative support all the way up to our governor. This broad support is extremely important in the success of this model.

Once we decided on some of our basic roles and responsibilities, we set up a staff kick-off to discuss/sell the new direction and philosophy with all employees in our region. We were very involved in many mini presentations and in face-to-face discussions to sell the staff on this new change. We asked for input and ideas on making this successful.

The Community

Magna has a high population of low-income families. It has a high incidence of sexual abuse, incest, and drug involvement.

The Magna community is made up of approximately 19,000 people. These people are situated on the outskirts of urban Salt Lake City. Although they border on a growing and sprawling metropolitan area, they live and seem to act like theirs is a rural community. This orientation reflects Magna's history, which I needed to understand. For example, it was the main mining town for the Kennecot Copper industry. In short, Magna used to be a town that was clearly different from Salt Lake City. In fact, Magna's political leaders recently tried to become a township again, but they were denied.

Today Magna falls under the Salt Lake City and county government system, which is a source of frustration for residents and leaders. They have two town councils. They were highly suspicious of any outside government intervention.

Building a Working Relationship and Establishing Trust

Thus, the first challenge my team and I confronted when we moved into the community was to develop working relationships with the two councils and establish trust. Today, both councils are involved with child welfare, and they share credit for community and family success stories. The DCFS team and the two councils have worked very well together as a kind of community team for designing and delivering child welfare services.

Once trust was established and working relationships began to develop, the next phases were critical. I had to choose my supervisors and staff. I sold them on the philosophy of team work and true collaboration, especially the creativity and flexibility this new approach would allow as we delivered our child welfare services to the Magna community. Once I had my staff finalized and "on board" with this neighborhood team philosophy, they were excited to get started.

Engaging Residents

We immediately began the process of collaborating and bringing our community partners on board with us. This was a delicate process and needed to be done in phases. Once again, it required building trusting relationships with our partners. We knew that residents had experienced frustration with DCFS. So, we provided opportunities, which allowed residents to vent some of their frustrations with the division. We also asked for input and cooperation on how to deliver our child welfare services in a more effective way in their community.

This community engagement process began with a series of presentations to our two main partners--namely, the schools and the police. We first set up meetings with all the principals, assistant principals, and school counselors. We developed a three-tier pamphlet and handed it out to all our partners. It briefly describes the reason behind the move to neighborhood teams, a little about our philosophy in working with families and partners and a map, names and phone numbers of the three pilot team leaders. It was very beneficial in our initial presentations to our partners.

Today, school professionals continue to help us. They provide us input/feedback, offer their expertise and experience, and the balance so greatly needed in making this community effort successful. We also involved our local police by visiting their community office, doing our presentation with their Staff Sargeant and officers, and gave them a list of all our phone numbers. We invited them to our open house and also invited them to sit on our Magna Case Management Team. They were very excited to work closely with us.

Once we had engaged the schools and the police, we tried to set up several separate meetings and presentations. Together, these meetings and presentations comprised what we called "the community kick-off" to bring on board every possible member of the community. For example, we met with, and did presentations for, the Chamber of Commerce-Business Community, all religious leaders, Law Enforcement, Mental Health, Health Clinics, Housing, CAP (Community Action Program), WIC (Women, Infants and Children) program, Headstart, Evenstart, and the Department of Workforce Services, which is responsible for implementing TANF. We even involved the media. For example, the newspaper did an article on our move into the community and how services would be different and better.

I even felt the need to bring on board the local businesses like the grocery stores, the three main taverns/bars, the flower shop, and the local lawyer and dentist. I went to each place, introduced myself, and gained their support and participation.

Joining Forces and Gaining New Resources

We joined in on the formulation of the new local Magna FACT Council. This council became a major partner in helping write for a Family Preservation grant. After a second try we were successful in receiving $55,000 to help children and families in the Magna community.

From this grant, we hired two part-time Coordinators and formed the Magna Case Management Team, which was made up of all our community agencies. They meet on a weekly basis to discuss needy families and set up plans to help meet their needs and teach them some skills to stabilize their situations. This important work benefited from the input of families and included their voluntary cooperation.

We also met with the two very strong and active community councils and the legislative representatives from the area. They have now become very active members of the Magna FACT Council.

Recruiting and Hiring Staff from the Neighborhood

The team leaders tried to hire staff directly from the neighborhood, who lived and understood the culture and needs of the community. This initiative also helped in establishing trust and a good working relationship. I immediately assigned one staff member to each school in our neighborhood to become familiar with staff and children in that school area. We handed out all our phone numbers and pager numbers so that we could be more accessible and responsive to their needs.

Moving to the Neighborhood

Finally, we positioned our staff in the neighborhood, and we moved all of our staff into our own building there. This move in itself made a huge difference in our working relationship with the community. In other words, this move provided a powerful message about us. It demonstrated our desire to join forces with residents. Residents felt our commitment and dedication to the community. They began to believe that we were there for the long run.

Examples of Successful Outcomes

What difference has the neighborhood team model and philosophy made? Following are some examples.

- We have been able to do more prevention and early intervention work in the neighborhood, especially in the investigative part of the process. *Already there has been a decrease in the number of children being removed from their homes.* In addition, *there has been a decrease in the amount of time children spend in foster care.* Furthermore, *there has been an increase in the number of resources involved up-front in-home services.*

- We have gained more community involvement in helping families deal with family crisis and meeting their needs.

- We have developed our own local parenting class/groups in the schools and in our office. (The team purchased the Love and Logic Training Package and all of our staff were trained on it and two of them now teach the parenting classes.)

- We have been involved in delivering food to needy families, e.g., turkeys on Thanksgiving. While we were doing this, the local newspaper took pictures and did another article on DCFS, which really helped our public relations effort. It helped residents view us as partners, not as cop-like investigators.

- We have gotten involved in Community Action meetings on volunteerism in the evenings. This has resulted in better widespread knowledge of what we do and the services we provide and therefore it has presented areas of interest for the public to get involved wherever they can. We had several people sign a list to volunteer in certain areas. The only barrier with this was that we had to have each person go through a very thorough criminal check. Each volunteer had to be coordinated by our state volunteer coordinator. We are still working on this issue to make it easier and less time consuming for people to volunteer for us.

- We have set up a local clothing closet in our office for needy families. (This closet includes furniture, household items, appliances, hygiene needs, etc.) We also set up a Sub-for-Santa program for Magna, which boosted the existing one already set up by one community person doing it on her own.

- DCFS now helps staff a booth at the local town festival, called Magna Copper Days. We do public relations work at the booth. We also try to recruit volunteers for foster parents, adoptive homes, and help with kids.

- We have enriched our staffing pool. We have hired two part-time Coordinators to run the Magna Case Management Team received from the grant. Also attached to this team, we were successful in obtaining two Evenstart workers to help with outreach work to the Magna families (at no extra cost).

- We have been successful in obtaining the old Webster Elementary School donated by Kennecot Copper, which is a local business partner. It will be set up as a Public "One Stop Shopping Service Center." Many agencies have already committed to move in when renovations are complete. It will be completed in approximately 2 years. This has been a dream of the Magna community for a very long time.

- Primary Children's Hospital submitted and received a grant for a part-time therapist (two days a week) for the Magna Neighborhood only. We were a part of this positive development by helping with the proposal and writing a letter of support. That grant recently added another part-time therapist to the Magna area for one day a week.

- We have successfully served over 120 families and over 150 children in Magna in the past two and a half years.

- We have helped with dental hygiene by buying Fluoride washes and donating those to the schools to give out. We also purchased several cases of Lice kits each year to be donated to any family in need. This is also going out through the local schools, DCFS, CAP, and WIC programs.

- We have provided all kinds of flex funds from the grant to meet families' needs during a crisis situation, and set up training to help eliminate future problems. For example, we have provided for such things as:

  – Food vouchers or food from our food banks
  – Medical Clinic Services (for those without insurance or Medicaid)
  – Pharmacy Vouchers
  – Bus Passes/Tokens
  – Emergency Travel
  – Damage Deposits, Rent, and/or Utilities
  – Car repairs

- Child care, clothing, and furniture
- Insect extermination
- Housing certificates
- Magna Recreation center vouchers (swimming, etc.)
- Many types of counseling, such as parent-teacher consultation, family preservation, eligibility determination for DWS (Dept. of Workforce Services), Medicaid, SSI, WIC, HEAT (A program for subsidized residential heating), Custody/Divorce, Consumer credit, parenting classes and Substance Abuse
- Brought the Immunization van to Magna for free immunizations

- We have also had many in-kind donations from many of the community partners, such as furniture, office supplies, food, shelving, baby clothes and furniture, toys, and building use for meetings. We have even had a home built for a family by coordinating many housing projects and financial institutions

- Staff have worked under better working conditions and experience greater job satisfaction. This is mainly due to better team work within DCFS and externally within the community, more allowance for creativity and flexibility, better use of community resources, greater ability to use social work skills and more involvement of the family in their own treatment planning.

A Personal Transformation

During our collaborative action research focus group work, I was discussing my enjoyment and job satisfaction. I heard myself say I had arrived at a point where I no longer felt like a traditional DCFS employee. I feel so much part of a team within the community, with such a close partnership. I feel like we are our own organization, and we truly help children and families. It was and is a great feeling!

I can only describe this feeling as true, grassroots social work. It's almost like being a member of a family. I've personally never been more satisfied in working for the DCFS. I have been freed from feeling like I have to do it all alone. Now that others are sharing the burden of responsibility and I have others working with me, team members are able to support one another and feel that our work is satisfying and rewarding.

To summarize: This work is exciting and challenging, all at the same time. I have learned so much and will continue to learn every day from this work.

Examples of Outcomes and Lessons Learned

Team leaders were more effective because they benefited from others' experiences and lessons learned. We conclude this chapter by offering examples of lessons learned that might benefit others.

Outcomes

Here are some of the outcomes associated with the three new teams:

- The number of children coming into foster care has been reduced

- Once in foster care, children are reunified more quickly with their families

- Permanency is established more quickly

- The number of kinship placements has increased

- Once the neighborhood team became a presence in the community, direct referrals to the teams increased

- Families are receiving more services from the community

- Employee's satisfaction with their jobs has increased substantially. Employees have built relationships with other employees on their teams and also with professionals outside of their agencies

- There is more community involvement at the onset which provides less isolation for the division and for the community

- More family members, friends, and people from the community are engaged as supports for children and families who are referred to the Division of Child and Family Services

Lessons Learned

We have listed these lessons learned in two tables. Table 1 presents lessons learned about the change process surrounding neighborhood teams. Table 2 presents lessons about teams and team development. These lessons are key examples; they do not exhaust our list.

Table 1. Examples of Lessons Learned About the Development of Neighborhood Teams

- System change at a time when practice is governed by a lawsuit Settlement Agreement brings about feelings of ambivalence and confusion for line staff and supervisors who are just fighting to meet the demands of their job.

- DCFS did not have clearly defined philosophy for practice. Without philosophical cohesion within the Division there was great divergence in how services were provided.

- The resistance to change is present in any organizational change.

- Directives and decisions made by the DCFS administration had a ripple effect on community work.

- Education about who we are and what we are about plays and important role in building relationships and partnerships with other agencies and organizations.

- A strength-based approach incorporates assessment of the strengths and needs of the family, the team, and the community.

- The roles of the workers, supervisors, and support staff need to be clarified and supported.

- Blended roles allow for more support of workers and reduces isolation within the team.

- Flexibility in our roles effects our responsiveness to the needs of families and community partners.

- Try to get as many employees as you can who live in the community you serve. This is really key in establishing that trust. Someone who knows and understands the community culture helps to build trust and can be trusted.

- This is not a short-term project, but staff and Administrators need to know we need patience and it will take time to really make this work successfully. To really see clear results, it might take up to 3-5 years. We cannot rush into any phase of this project. We need everyone to buy off on this philosophy by massaging it slowly but firmly.

- Develop more well planned staff and community "kick offs." It gets everyone excited and thinking about how they can help and be a part of this great movement towards helping families.

- One of the most powerful lessons learned is that we need to involve "family experts" from the community in every aspect of planning and the delivery of services. They must be involved in everything from policy making, to training, treatment planning and decision making for families. They are the ones who have really kept me on track on really remembering why we do this work. Always be open to learning new things, they will teach you much.

- One of the great lessons learned that it is really true that "it does take a whole village to raise a child." The more you involve the community in taking responsibility and accountability for their own families, they really dig in and help and you clearly see more effective progress.

Table 2. Examples of Lessons Learned About Team Building

- It takes more than a mandate to become a team.

- There are three key roles for a Team Leader: Team Building, Administration, and Community Organization.

- DCFS line staff have similar needs to the families that they serve.

- We need to be responsive to the needs of our employees; understand resistance to change, and discover what motivates others.

- The safety and security needs of an employee need to be met in order to build flexibility within the manner they provided services within the team and community.

- A team needs to have an infrastructure (i.e., clinical case consultation and family staffing processes, supervision, mentoring of employees, processes for procuring resources, and administrative support) that supports the mission of the team.

- Being a team player is a choice; some may choose to leave.

- Changes in personnel are opportunities to be creative and innovative. New employees bring a fresh perspective to others as they join with the team.

- Modeling is a valuable tool to use to demonstrate role flexibility and responsiveness to community concerns.

- It's sometimes the differences in how we do things not what we do that strengthens our teamwork with the community.

- It is important to identify the key players in the community to establish relationships and build connections with others.

- Being a community partner requires reciprocity.

- Start where the community is in its process of community building. Join with others who already established collaborative efforts.

- Each community has its own uniqueness. Child welfare service delivery needs to be shaped within each neighborhood to be responsive to that quality that makes the area different from other areas.

- Policy and laws govern "what" we do, but they do not mandate "how" we do it. We have more flexibility within systems than we may perceive.

- A neighborhood model continues to change. Change is an ongoing process that can facilitate growth for the team members.

- Team leaders and managers must teach and support these principles constantly so everyone stays on track.

- The core of everything we do in our work with families and each other as professionals is: "RELATIONSHIP" and building trust between us all.

- We need to really get to know our budgets inside and out and how to be creative and flexible with our resources, within the limits that have been set out for us. This budget "savvy" includes researching and making use of all available grants, donations, setting up clothing/furniture closets, food banks, volunteerism, setting up innovative programs like "time dollar" within your community (see Cahn & Rowe, 1992). Focus on quality of services and creativity with the money you have available to you.

- We need to spend more time on the up-front strategic planning and development of this model, by bringing all staff and administration on board with the neighborhood philosophy and helping them catch the vision. Help staff and the community provide input to the model and be bigger a part of development and implementation.

- Remain positive and enthusiastic about this work and model. It works. It is effective and very satisfying. Keep up this energy, it's very catchy and influential, as well as it brings hope and energy to our families, staff and community partners!

- When we focus on the above lessons and these key principles, we will be successful: (1) Strength-based, (2) Family-centered, (3) Solution-focused, (4) Culturally responsive, (5) Community-based, (6) Safety-focused, (7) Permanency-focused, (8) Shared Accountability, and (9) Collaboration.

This neighborhood team model is a worthy model for any community to develop and create to meet the many complex needs of families. It also meets the needs of professionals who want to use their knowledge and skills, gain supports, and become more effective. Leading these teams is a wonderful job, and it requires the knowledge, skills, and perspectives of professional social workers.

These neighborhood teams promote community-based systems of care. This is really where child welfare needs to go. It needs to be delivered from within each of our communities and neighborhoods. Child welfare is not just about kids in crisis; it is about the welfare of all of the nation's children and their families. Teams are an effective way to promote this important vision and make progress toward achieving it.

Endnote

1. The authors are grateful to Dr. Brenda Smith for her sensitive reading and editorial suggestions.

References

Cahn, E. and Rowe, J. (1992). *Time dollars: The new currency that enables Americans to turn their hidden resource-time-into personal security and community renewal.* Emmaus, PA: Rodale Press.

Farrow, F. and The Executive Committee for Child Protection (1997). *Child protection: Building community partnerships. Getting from here to there.* Cambridge, MA: John F. Kennedy School of Government at Harvard University.

Lawson, H., Briar-Lawson, K., Warner-Kearney, D., and Ynacay-Nye. R. (2000, January). A new model for uniting, harmonizing, and promoting action research, advocacy, systems change, partnerships, and research innovation, dissemination, and utilization. Society for Social Work and Research, Charleston, SC.

Smale, G. (1995). Integrating community and individual practice: A new paradigm for practice. In P. Adams & K. Nelson (Eds.). *Reinventing human services: Community-and family-centered practice* (pp. 59-80). New York: Aldine De Gruyter.

Chapter 17

From Conventional Training to Empowering Design Teams for Collaboration and Systems Change

Hal A. Lawson, Nancy Petersen, and Katharine Briar-Lawson

Introduction

Reflect briefly on all of the new ideas, policies, and strategies that have been introduced in previous chapters. For example, needs have been identified for multiple kinds and levels of collaboration, service integration, systems change, cross-systems change, and results-based accountability. Managed care and capped spending on services have challenged service providers and families. Changes have been required in child welfare because of fresh understanding of families' co-occurring needs. The new requirements associated with the Adoption and Safe Families Act (ASFA) and Temporary Assistance to Needy Families (TANF) have compelled major changes. These examples do not exhaust the list of challenges.

In fact, any such list underestimates the overall challenge. *Every item on the list is in some ways related to others, and all must be addressed at the same time.* In short, the child welfare system confronts massive change.

Massive change always entails learning. Professionals at all levels of the system as well as the families they serve must learn new knowledge and skills, and at the same time, they must "unlearn" others. Agencies must support this individual and group learning. Furthermore, agencies must learn; that is, they must develop organizational structures and cultures in support of organizational learning and continuous quality improvement (e.g., Argyris & Schön, 1996; Senge, Kleiner, et al., 1994). Thus, systems change in child welfare and cross-systems change involving other agencies and public schools depends on new learning, development, and continuous improvement strategies.

Learning-as-change, on such a massive scale, is not easy, and it does not occur overnight. Strategic planning for practice improvement, collaboration, systems change, and cross-systems change will be effective to the extent that it prioritizes this multi-level learning and development. Planning must incorporate much-needed time, resources, opportunities, and supports for learning and improvement. It must involve on-the-job follow-up assistance. It must include responsive technical assistance, effective supervision, mentoring, and both group and organizational capacity-building initiatives. It must incorporate higher education institutions, especially social work education programs, so that their professional education programs and faculty are in step with child welfare agencies and related systems.

Faced with so much novelty, complexity, ambiguity, and uncertainty, everyone in child welfare--front-line professionals, middle managers, top level supervisors, and social work education faculty alike--must "learn their way through" the mazes of complex change. To put it another way, child welfare systems must provide learning-rich work environments in which individuals and groups may take calculated risks. Unlike rigid compliance to legally mandated forms and rules, calculated risk-taking promotes innovation, improvement, and learning. This learning must be targeted and strategic. Because the stakes are so high, it cannot be learning for the sake of learning, which is tied to change for its own sake. Rather, this multi-level learning must be connected firmly to continuous improvements in results for children and families and in the quality of work environments for child welfare professionals.

Furthermore, someone needs to monitor and chart this innovative risk-taking and learning-as-improvement. Best practices derive from them. Child welfare needs to develop stocks of agency and university knowledge about effective learning and successful learning systems, systems that improve results for children and families and for professionals at all levels in the child welfare system.

This chapter describes one such important component in an innovative approach to learning, development, and continuous improvement systems. This component is called a design team model. Although the design team model is related to conventional training and helps guide it, the design team presents a very different approach to learning, development, and improvement. The design team is a mechanism for multiple benefits and complex change. This component fosters collaboration, mutual empowerment, action research, and individual, group, and agency learning, development, and improvement. When higher education institutions are involved, the design team supports agency partnerships and facilitates faculty development. Furthermore, the design team stimulates beneficial ripple effects, or domino effects. As these benefits multiply, they promote systems change and cross systems change.

The chapter progression is as follows. First, the genesis of the design team work, as proposed and developed in a child welfare training grant initiative, is described. Then, design team concept is contrasted with conventional training. Then, a brief overview is provided of key cornerstones in the design team model's theoretical foundation. Next, the model's interactive phases are outlined, and competencies identified by the project's design teams are provided. Key findings and lessons learned are presented. Implications and current developments involving university-related design teams are provided in conclusion.

The Genesis of the Design Team Model: A Four State Child Welfare Training Initiative

In November 1997, a group of university and agency social work professionals from Colorado (Colorado Springs), Nevada (Reno), New Mexico (Las Cruces), and Utah (Salt Lake City) met for the first time to discuss two related grants, which had been awarded to the Graduate School of Social Work at the University of Utah.[1] Katharine Briar-Lawson and Hal Lawson were the principal investigators.

Two Key Purposes and a Mission

The immediate purpose of these grants was to design innovative training programs for front-line practitioners. Training programs were envisioned that would foster new competencies, increase service integration, and build collaborative practices among agencies. These programs were compelled to address the co-occurring needs of families in the child welfare system, at the same time preventing others from entering it. These co-occurring needs included substance abuse, domestic violence, mental illness, poverty, child abuse and neglect, and employment-related challenges associated with Temporary Assistance to Needy Families (TANF). The new requirements for timely placement decisions ushered in by the Adoption and Safe Families Act (ASFA) also compelled new training, including training that helped front line professionals understand families that get caught between ASFA's time lines and TANF's term limits.

A second purpose was to promote timely and effective systems change and cross-systems change in child welfare through an elaborate regional partnership and scale-up plan. The partnership was itself a kind of complex change. It involved universities, especially social work education programs, state agencies, and community partners. Mindful of the diversity among sites and across states, two grants promoted a system for cross-state and site learning, development, and improvement. A regional steering committee was structured to monitor developments and chart progress. Innovations and lessons drawn from one site might not transfer wholesale to others, but promising developments everywhere certainly needed to be shared with others in the region and around the nation.

---

[1] We are indebted to our colleagues who formed this original group, especially David Derezotes, Tracie Hoffman, David Berns, Norma Harris, Delores Nelson, Robyn Ynacay-Nye, Arthur Atwell, Butch Brown, Alvin Sallee, Jonah Garcia, Linda Kean, Rock Boyer, and Megan Wiesen. Others who joined later have been equally instrumental in our learning and development. They include Carenlee Barkdull, Patti von Wagoner, Deborah Hinton, Deborah Ashton, Ellie Pope, Sue Tungate, Myrna Gooden, Deana Kessin, and Deborah Hunt. Above all, we are indebted to all of the family experts who helped each team and the overall initiative.

The evaluation plan emphasized drawing lessons and charting progress from the change journey (Lawson, 1999). Faculty facilitators involved with this work were charged with developing knowledge, skill, and competencies through an new style of engagement called "academically based community scholarship" (Lawson, 1998a; in press). In this style of community-based scholarship, the knowing is in the doing, and faculty need to be in community settings doing forms of action research and other practice-friendly research methodologies.

The steering committee developed the following mission for these grants:

To enable the development of family-centered, culturally responsive, interprofessional knowledge, skills, attitudes, and values that tie the child welfare goals of child protection, permanency, and family preservation to the needs of economic self-sufficiency, mental health, domestic violence, and substance abuse; and to do so in ways that promote collaboration, service integration, and university reforms.

Specific to the grants in one sense, this mission also pertained to many of the challenges child welfare professionals faced. In brief, this was not merely a grant-related "project." It was child welfare work aimed at systems improvement and cross-systems change.

The Initial Impressions of One Facilitator

Nancy Petersen, the faculty facilitator for the Reno, Nevada, site and one of the authors of this chapter, attended this first meeting and led the development of the mission statement. Her impressions, captured through reflective action research, follow. They help to introduce the idea of the design team, and they forewarn readers of predictable reactions to the prospects of dramatic change.

In order to carry out this mission, we were to identify and work with "a design team" at each of our sites, defined as a group of professionals and family experts (service consumers). We were to use their shared expertise and successful interactions to develop collaborative service delivery systems and interprofessional education programs.

Well, some of us left that first meeting feeling a bit anxious and overwhelmed by what sounded to be a very tall order. However, we also felt exhilarated and inspired by a wonderful group of supportive people who seemed to be "on to something," something that sounded like a new approach to the old dilemmas of serving "multi-problem families" in a new era of federally mandated time limits and personal responsibility.

Three years later, the initial design teams have grown and evolved from our initial, tentative steps into a process that those of us involved have described as "life-changing." Some of the design teams developed training; some of them evolved into ongoing system change working groups; some of them have given birth to new design teams in different parts of their state; some of them have had direct impact on the university preservice educational processes and classes offered; and all of them have profoundly affected the personal and professional lives of those involved in ways that are still unfolding. New collaborative relationships were formed and continue to be formed; values and attitudes towards the people we serve and our role in their lives were changed and continue to change; and there is a fundamental recognition of the need for true collaboration and cooperation among all people involved in the social service system, whether they be supervisors, professionals and peers, or the families themselves.

We hope that our experiences will inspire other communities to "pick up the phone" and form their own design teams, knowing that one of the strengths of this model is its absolute integrity and fit to the uniqueness of local communities, their contexts and cultures. While the concrete outcome may not be absolutely clear and predictable at the outset, which admittedly makes for some anxious moments, the effort involved has the potential for, at the very least, changed attitudes and practices on the part of the individuals involved and, at the very most, significant system change across an entire community of service providers.

The discussion now turns to the design team model. The best way to introduce it is to contrast it with conventional training.

Beyond Conventional Training and Back Again

Public schools and child welfare agencies have a lot in common. They need to do a lot more to support one another's efforts (Lawson, 1995; Lawson & Briar-Lawson, 1997: Lawson & Barkdull, 1999). For example, schools that serve high poverty communities have professional turn-over rates that mirror, and exceed, those in child welfare. Many of the same kids that pose challenges for schools also challenge the child welfare system. Most importantly, both schools and child welfare change a lot. In fact, workers feel as if they are changing constantly. Unfortunately, both systems may be changing constantly, but these changes may not result in visible improvements. Both need to become more strategic in the learning and development they target, ensuring that all such changes are tied to improvements for children, families, and workers.

Risking unfair categorization and over-generalization, it is possible to claim that both schools and child welfare frame learning needs and challenges in much the same way. Educators concerned about children's learning emphasize teachers and teaching. Similarly, child welfare leaders planning for change as learning usually focus on their trainers and conventional training.

Planning for conventional training is a good thing to do. Conventional training, offered by experienced trainers sponsored by agencies, non-profit institutes, and higher education institutions, has benefited countless professionals, families, and agencies. As child welfare systems respond to the challenges of massive change, needs for conventional training are increasing.

Evaluating Key Assumptions for Conventional Training

On the other hand, conventional training works best when some twelve key assumptions are justifiable (Lawson, Briar-Lawson, et al., 1999). When they are not, then training isn't likely to be as effective, or successful, as it needs to be. Because the design team model was developed in response to needs that conventional training apparently did not meet, it is useful to introduce and examine quickly just four of the key assumptions underlying conventional training.

To begin with, conventional training requires an expert—the trainer. Then the training process can commence. For, training is basically a one-way information and communication flow. The expert trainer, who knows what is needed and how to do it, conveys her, or his, know-how and know-why to trainees. Many successful apprentice systems operate in the same way, and in short, training is an efficient and effective way to build capacity and share expertise. Important solutions and new practice strategies do not need to be discovered and invented; they merely need to be disseminated and learned.

However, if the trainers are not experts and if they are every bit as challenged as the next person in figuring out what to do to improve practices and policies and change systems, then conventional training is not a viable alternative. This is exactly what happened in the four-state initiative. Everyone quickly faced up to the massive changes that confronted child welfare in all four states, and everyone admitted that they had much to learn. Indeed, nationally recognized experts confessed that, not only did they not have all of the right answers, but also, that they were striving to identify the right questions as the policy and practice environments continued to change dramatically. They also doubted whether budding solutions in one place would work in another.

A second assumption of conventional training is also important to recognize. Conventional training targets individuals. In other words, the theories of teaching and learning for training are derived from research and successful experiences with individuals. In conventional training, the learning of new knowledge, theories, and practices depends on each individual's ability to understand and accept new information and then to apply this information into practice on the job. People learn to see themselves as either smart or challenged, as having "high aptitude" or "low aptitude" for the training, the content, and the tests. They often have to take competency tests--*alone*. And, perhaps most important, individuals are then seen as being responsible for applying the new knowledge and skills to their practice--*alone*.

Leaders in our four-state initiative could not agree with aspects of this assumption about training. No one wanted to promote competition among professionals. All knew that the loneliness and isolation of child welfare professionals is a serious problem, and it should not be perpetuated in training programs. Leaders knew that the sustainability of learning and performance changes hinged in part on follow-up supports and responsive organizational changes.

A third key assumption is that only professionals are qualified to be trainers and trainees. Families are not considered experts, nor are they joint trainers. They are the clients, and their well-being depends on the professionals. In turn, it is then assumed that professionals know, or will come to know through training, what children, parents, and family systems want and need. It shall become apparent that the design team model operates from a competing set of assumptions regarding families. Drawing on Katharine Briar-Lawson's national work with family-centered collaboration and family-centered practice, family leaders were included in the design team mix. When these family experts are recruited from culturally diverse populations, they promote culturally sensitive, competent, and responsive practices.

The fourth key assumption is that the practice improvements and interventions disseminated through the training are generalizable across settings and places and that skills are readily transferable to practice. That is, what works in one place will transfer to another, and training acquired in one place will transfer to another. To put it another way, training content and effective practices are not person-, or "operator-dependent," nor are they "place-, or context-dependent."

In contrast to this conventional assumption, the four states represented in this child welfare initiative evidenced considerable diversity, both within states and across states. For example, frontier communities in Utah and Nevada have with a only a few people within a hundred square miles; they are destined to be different from urban communities with abundant numbers of specialized services. Training for one is not training for the other.

So, the design team model operated from different assumptions. In this model, it is assumed that place matters, i.e., that local contexts and resources weigh heavily in what will work and what won't. It also is assumed that the best way to make services fit and to offer high impact training is to have teams build what they could use on site. For all of the above reasons and others, it was clear to the leaders that, absent better understanding and improved knowledge, skill, and competencies, conventional training would not respond to the massive change needs of child welfare systems.

The Design Teams' Products Feed-Forward into Conventional Training

To reiterate, the plan was not to abandon conventional training or to create a competitor to it. To preview the discussion that comes later, one of the original aims for the design team model was to develop, through an elaborate four-state system for learning, knowledge development, and improvement, the knowledge, skills, and competencies that were needed for conventional training to work. In other words, if the research was not especially helpful, and if agency trainers and university faculty were as needy as the front-line professionals and middle managers, then the only way to proceed was to collaborate in pursuit of the shared need to develop knowledge, understanding, skills, and competencies. The challenge was like designing and building a plane while trying to fly it to an important destination. Teams were required because no individual had all of the answers, and teams needed to design best practices as they served children and families. The design teams thus can be viewed as *practice communities*, i.e., as communities comprised of experts who needed to join forces to learn, develop, and improve results. Their purpose was to address a major void in the practice repertoires and training protocols of child welfare and its related professional systems.

Once the design teams addressed this void, then conventional training would be able to commence again. Indeed, the plan was for design team members to complete their work and then serve as expert trainers. So, the design team model does not compete with, or replace, conventional training. Each guides the other.

Having previewed the design team idea, the model may be introduced. Relevant theoretical cornerstones in its foundation are presented first.

Five Cornerstones for The Design Team Model

Although there are many theories and theoretical frameworks underlying the design team model (Lawson, Briar-Lawson, et al., 1999), it can be introduced and understood by focusing on five key, theoretical cornerstones: empowerment, family-centered collaboration, social learning, action research and learning, and interprofessional education and training. Each is defined briefly below.

From Conventional Empowerment to Mutual Empowerment

As everyone knows, the concept of "empowerment" has received some criticism for being arrogant, self-serving, and patriarchal. Professionals claiming to promote empowerment often assume that the people they serve are needy, dependent, and powerless (e.g., Riger, 1993; Gore, 1993). They create clients at the same time that they claim to empower them (McKnight, 1995).

In contrast, the concept of empowerment in this training model is one of mutual empowerment (Lawson, 1998b). Mutual empowerment depends on a new style of professionalism—namely, a social trustee, civic professionalism (Lawson, Chapter 18). Social trustee professionals can be trusted, and they promote social trust networks with, and among, families. Social trustee, civic professionals are able to imagine what it is like to "walk a mile in the shoes" of children and families in need, and they treat these families in ways that they, the professionals, would like to be treated if they were in these families' shoes. The design team model promotes social trustee, civic professionalism.

Professionals learn to view individuals and families in need as being unique individuals, with assets and strengths. These special professionals also know that their well-being and effectiveness depend in large part upon improvements in the people they serve. In other words, by empowering people in need, these professionals are also empowered. This is the core idea behind mutual empowerment (Lawson, 1998b). When helping is empowering, helpers are empowered.

Individual, or psychological, empowerment is important, but not the only kind. Social empowerment also is prioritized, including ripple effects across several layers—families, groups of professionals, organizations, and communities. All are empowered, and at the same time, empowering. In other words, as they gain power, authority, and action-related competence, they also give it to others, empowering them. A "can-do attitude" spreads quickly through mutual empowerment, and it promotes multiple kinds and levels of collaboration (Lawson, 1998b). It is also contagious. Empowered and empowering people give to their other relationships and organizations what they have learned and experienced. It builds social support networks for the people in need. And finally, this approach targets multi-level system change processes by addressing front-line practice, group norms, supervisory practices, and policy change in a way that addresses the complexity and uniqueness of local cultures and contexts.

Mutual empowerment does not merely promote collaboration. It depends on it. Collaboration requires clear understanding about interdependent relationships, and it entails sharing power and resources in pursuit of shared goals (Lawson & Barkdull, Chapter 13). Professionals thus work to make families *equal partners*, promoting family-centered collaboration.

Family-Centered Collaboration

Family-centered *collaboration* is a key cornerstone (e.g., Alameda, 1996; Briar-Lawson & Wiesen, Chapter 12). This new kind of collaboration is not the same as family-focused and -sensitive practice, which still relies on professionals and assumes that "professionals know best." Family-centered collaboration, and its sister concept, family-centered practice (Briar-Lawson, Lawson, et al., in press), are grounded in social work's strengths-based perspective. They promote cultural competence, because they necessitate power sharing and responsive practices.

Perhaps more than the other theoretical perspectives, the power of this family-centered perspective was brought home quickly and persuasively in the design team process. Four core ideas of family-centered collaboration are (1) Parents and families have expertise and knowledge; (2) Therefore, they need to be partners in deciding what they will do to improve, under what circumstances, when, how, and in what sequence; (3) The voices of all family members need to be heard, especially girls and women, as family relations are democratized; and (4) Mutual aid and family-to-family helping networks may be more effective than top-down, outside-in professional interventions alone.

In contrast to conventional training, former clients--family members who became known as family experts--were included in the design teams. The idea was to promote family-centered collaboration and interprofessional collaboration. The expertise and experience of the family experts on the design teams became invaluable components of the empowerment. For example, they helped professionals learn what it was like "to walk a mile in their shoes." They also helped identify new solutions--what works and why--and, at the same time, to stop and prevent ineffective practices--what hurts and why. Family experts promoted social learning.

Social Learning

This design team model adds social learning to the concept of individual learning. Social learning is an active learning orientation in which participants draw upon their own experience and expertise to co-design their own learning. In the same vein, each brings expertise and an important perspective, enabling them to co-teach. This approach emphasizes the use of skills in everyday, activity contexts and in collaboration with people. The implication is clear: *If you want people to collaborate together in practice, then structure teams that allow them to learn, develop, and improve together.* In other words, empower them, and support them, to build relationships that will work for them--by them--in local contexts. To put it another way, view "training" as the opportunity to structure teams--practice communities--and structure genuine learning and practice tasks that they must address together in the everyday work.

In the case of the design teams, the key is to structure action-oriented learning and development environments. These environments encourage and support design team members in co-teaching and co-learning in relation to new competencies, knowledge, and practice strategies that they must design, implement, and evaluate. In other words, each design team builds its new century strategies at the same time team members learn from one another and develop collaborative, trusting relationships that enable them to work together across diverse systems.

Individual learning is not lost in this design team model. However, people do not have to learn alone, and they do not compete with one another. Team members' learning benefits from the scaffolds provided by their interactions with other team members. Social learning also provides for the social supports that help individuals retain and practice their learning in an ongoing way. So, individual learning and social learning interact in the context of the practice community and the organizational culture (e.g., Salomon & Perkins, 1998; Vygotsky, 1978).

Action Research and Learning

There is a growing body of theory that looks at a "theory of action perspective" (e.g., Argyris, 1996; Argyris & Schön, 1996; Lawson, 1998a; Schön, 1995). It addresses such questions as, How do professionals think in action? How are professionals able to design effectively new practices and policies in their work contexts? Why do they do some things they've been taught, but not others? What are the relative influences of education and work organization on professional action? What are the keys to changing the orientations and actions of professionals to improve their effectiveness? How can their organizations support newcomers? How can professionals continue to learn and improve as they practice?

Very briefly, a few implications from this body of theory apply to the design team model. First, there are often differences between what people say--their espoused theories--and what they actually do--their theories-in-use (e.g., Argyris & Schön, 1996). It is important to identify these differences. When people become aware of them, they are more likely to change, or become more receptive to new ideas and approaches. Several of the design team exercises are designed to highlight differences between espoused theories and theories in use.

Second, the greater the experience and expertise of the professional, the more their practice theories become internalized and even "unconscious." In other words, experts often know and do more than they can say, or write, about themselves and their practices. So, it is important for experienced people to be able to surface, formalize, and share their expertise with others. It also is important that they are given the opportunity to "unfreeze" their taken-for-granted assumptions in a safe environment. The design team model provides such an environment. One person's surfacing, formalizing, and unfreezing processes may be another person's powerful learning; and vice-versa.

Conventional training is not designed to do this kind of work. It barely scratches the surface of professionals' expertise and deeply rooted assumptions. In contrast, co-teaching and -learning focused on everyday practice problems can get at this expertise and these assumptions. Family experts' perspectives are especially powerful ways to address professionals' needs to get "unstuck."

As with mutual empowerment, action theories or theories of action span several levels. They begin with individuals, but they also span programs, organizations, and policies. The design team experiences are structured to promote action research and learning that result in multi-level theories of action and change.

Interprofessional Education and Training

The literature on interprofessional education and training (IPET) provided an important cornerstone. It is a diverse literature. Some of it equates IPET with training for interprofessional collaboration (not family-centered collaboration). In contrast to the Ohio State University with its formal program (Casto & Julia, 1994; Casto, Harshman, & Cunningham, 1998), most universities and colleges have only one course. Much of it focuses on one course in a preservice, university program. This course is typically called Training for Interprofessional Collaboration, and it involves community partners (e.g., Knapp & Associates, 1998).

An increasing number of proposals are being made for interprofessional education and training within the context of broad, sustainable university-community-agency partnerships (e.g., Hooper-Briar & Lawson, 1996; Lerner & Simon, 1998; McCroskey & Einbinder, 1998). The fact remains, however, that the needs of experienced professionals for IPET have not been addressed effectively. Although emphasis has been placed upon the identification of competencies for interprofessional collaboration (e.g., Smith, Culbert, & Deiro, 1998), broad-scale, multi-level collaboration has not been addressed. The design team model was developed in response to this urgent need, promoting at the same time university partnerships and academically-based community scholarship (Lawson, in press).

The Design Team Model's Purposes and Processes

Most simply stated, a design team is a collaborative working group. It has three member categories: family experts; helping professionals, both managers and caseworkers; and a facilitator.

The Idea of Design Teams

This label, design team, is apt for four reasons:

1. The composition of the group (diverse professionals and family experts) represents a new design for teaching, learning, and staff development-support.

2. The design team is expected to "go outside the lines" as needed to invent and pioneer service strategies that improve outcomes.

3. After their work is completed, team members will help other teams, in other places, design their service strategies.

4. These teams may become permanent, self-managed work teams, which provide mutual support and problem-solving assistance for improved outcomes, worker retention, and organizational learning.

In other words, the design teams may become part of new organizational designs for child welfare in particular and the human services in general. They generate new ideas and practices, and they help create new organizational structures and cultures.

Participants' problem-setting and -solving abilities are emphasized. Stronger, trustful interpersonal relationships are targeted in the design team process. The reasoning is simple: *Collaborative practices hinge on healthy relationships, and you are not likely to truly collaborate with someone you do not know and trust.* Participants are expected to negotiate the specific details of the service strategies that will work in their local communities. By placing participants at center stage and responding to their needs, achievements, and situational constraints, opportunities for active learning, mutual teaching, and training-knowledge transfer and knowledge utilization are maximized.

Conventional distinctions between trainers (as *the* experts) and trainees (who need and are present to receive, often passively, trainers' expertise) are irrelevant in this model. This claim does not deny the need for expert training facilitators. Facilitators in this model have other kinds of expertise. As the saying goes, they are "guides on the side" instead of "sages on the stage."

The design team's facilitators structure the action learning environment by providing concrete practice issues and tasks. Participants learn from one another and from the facilitator as they interact. In this model, facilitators are expected to learn along with participants at the same time that they facilitate and observe. They also serve as co-evaluators of this collaborative action learning, harvesting knowledge, skills, and lessons learned.

In other words, the facilitator of each team was not viewed in the conventional sense of being *the trainer expert*, nor were the team members viewed as *trainees,* there to passively receive the trainer's expertise. Instead, the facilitator's role was pivotal in structuring the learning and development process of each team. The facilitator was expected to learn along with the participants at the same time that he or she facilitated and observed the process. The facilitator provided conceptual "tools" to help the team members draw upon, surface, and then share their experiences and expertise with one another; to receive reactions and feedback; to develop new intervention and practice strategies; and to then take them into the real world of practice for implementation.

Within the above parameters, the composition of the design teams varied in the different sites, reflecting the diversity of their participants and the uniqueness of their local contexts. Some teams included only representatives from the major five service sectors, while others expanded their membership to include such services as juvenile justice, education, and police. The number of meetings varied, as did the outcomes. For instance, two teams (Nevada and New Mexico) developed training for their communities and experienced system change in a less formal way, while others (Colorado and Utah) concentrated on formal mechanisms for system change without the providing an actual community training workshop. The average design team meeting took 4 hours (half a day), with a break during the meeting.

Mutual empowerment, social learning, action research and learning, interprofessional learning, and family-centered collaboration were all key processes at work in the design team interactions. People felt empowered at the same time that they empowered others. The design team provided a safe, supportive environment for these interactions. It was especially interesting that focus group interviews conducted at three sites indicated that, for professionals, the interaction with family experts was the most important and critical part of the design team process. True family-centered collaboration, with clients being regarded as experts rather than problems-to-be-solved, was critical in "unfreezing" existing routine practice as well as in developing new practice strategies.

Interacting Phases in the Empowerment-Oriented Model

Eight interacting phases have been identified in the initiation, development and ongoing process of the design teams. It is important to realize that these phases are not necessarily linear but are instead interactive and even circular.

Phase 1:   Gain initial commitments and secure longer term commitments to participate in the design teams in each community setting.

Personal relationships and trust involving the facilitator and other leaders are essential if people are to come. Once they come, interaction must be facilitated in a way that is fun and compelling; otherwise, busy people will not commit the time, effort, and resources that this work involves. The questions, "What's in it for me and why should I come?" must be addressed.

Phase 2:   Develop trust, relationships, and minimize power differences among professionals and family experts.

This part must also be fun and engaging. The idea of families as experts who are also in need of social supports and economic resources related to their well-being is begun here. "Professional knows best" is thoughtfully critiqued and circumstances in which professionals may be part of the problem instead of the solution are identified in a way that is honest and supportive rather than critical or blaming. The interactions and mutual learning lead to solution-based, strengths-based advocacy and helping.

Phase 3:   *Develop sensitivity to diversity and the mutuality of needs and hopes, as well as an understanding of specialized professions and unique families.*

This phase addresses the need to help team members gain a better understanding of what each one does, wants to do, and could do better. An exercise developed by Nancy Petersen looks at "preconceived notions," or stereotypes of professionals and family experts. This exercise can be very helpful if done well and without blame or conflict. Similarly, one that identifies painful experiences that professionals and families alike have had with other agencies was developed in Utah to meet this need. Statements, such as "I didn't know that about you and your work," and "Here's how we can help each other more now that we know and understand each other better," may be very helpful strategies to develop solutions or improvements.

Phase 4:   *Identify and evaluate past-present helping strategies through mutual teaching and learning.*

This addresses the "content" part of the process and is accomplished by means of questionnaires and face-to-face exercises involving what hurts, what helps, and why. Competencies are developed as information is gathered and organized, especially in relation of what to look for (assessment), what to do and what not to do (treatment or casework process), and how to access the most helpful services (referral and resources). These exercises also help stakeholders identify the special qualities of an effective helping professional--a person who knows how to develop relationships by listening, avoiding judgments, and respecting the expertise of the families they serve and who can serve as an effective advocate. The elements of collaboration are identified. Norms for the quality of treatment and interaction are developed, and new helping strategies are designed.

In Nevada, the design team developed competencies relating to the five problem areas and the necessary knowledge about co-occurring needs. The team also developed a list of universal competencies that was developed regarding the characteristics of any professional in the helping services.

Phase 5:   *Move people and organizations beyond past-present practices and co-invent new and better ways to collaborate for improved service organization and delivery.*

This is a crucial phase for people to experience as they move past their "old ways of doing things" and apply their experience of the new model to new ways of providing service. So, for instance, when design team members find they cannot solve a problem or meet needs with the old way of doing things, they need to ask "What will it take or what will we need to do differently to meet the needs in this case?" The design team experience enables team members to move beyond a focus on what individuals do and don't do to focus on service delivery practices, programs, and policies that need to change. In other words, the very experience of learning that we are all in this together, with the best of motives and knowledge, leads us away from blaming the individual to looking at the system itself.

Phase 6:   Deepen commitments and understanding of alternative design models.

This phase involves some review and revisiting of lessons learned and implications for practice. It also involves looking forward to implementation and evaluation of the new strategies and models.

Phase 7:   Refine, improve, and learn through implementation and evaluation.

The design team itself becomes more focused on evaluation, learning, and development. It may choose to make plans for scale-up in other communities, provide training to other groups, and/or begin partnerships with the local university to develop new preservice experiences for future professionals.

Phase 8:   Assume lead responsibilities for training facilitation in other communities and in university preservice professional programs.

Graduates from the design teams, both professionals and family experts, build upon their own experiences to promote and support university preservice professional education. In fact, family experts from the design team have served as guest faculty in university courses.

Key Findings and Lessons Learned

The above section outlines the definition, goals, and processes of the design teams as they were conceived and carried out in Reno, Nevada. Some teams in other sites have followed the same progression (e.g., teams in Colorado). Others have developed similar ones (e.g., other teams in Colorado and teams in Utah). Still others have developed their own progression (e.g., teams in Utah and New Mexico).[2] This diversity is planned. One size does not fit all; every design team must be tailored to its local contexts.

Key Findings

Design teams did promote interprofessional collaboration and family-centered collaboration, but not for every member at the same time. Figures 1, 2, and 3 depict the hypothesized plan. Especially in Reno, Figures 1 and 2 depict what happened to most of the design team members. The policy change suggested in Figure 3 occurred in both Utah and Nevada. On the other hand, some members gained commitments only to interprofessional collaboration through the process, while others gained commitments to family-centered collaboration. Some developed both. At this time, it is impossible to tell what will happen over the long term.

---

[2] For information on these teams, contact the following faculty facilitators. In New Mexico, contact Alvin Sallee (New Mexico State University) and Deborah Hunt (New Mexico Highlands University). In Nevada, contact Robin Yancay-Nye, Director of Training for the State Department of Child and Family Services (Carson City), Nancy Peterson, University of Nevada-Reno, or Stacey Hardy-Desmond, University of Nevada-Las Vegas. In Utah, contact David Derezotes and Tracie Hoffman (University of Utah). For Colorado, contact Arthur Atwell, Director of Training for the State Department of Child and Family Services or Carenlee Barkdull at the University of Utah.

Figure 1. Relationships Among The Key Components of the Design Team

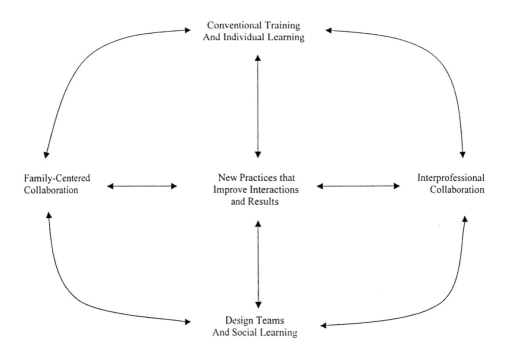

**Figure 2. Key Moments, Processes, and
Results with the Design Team Process**

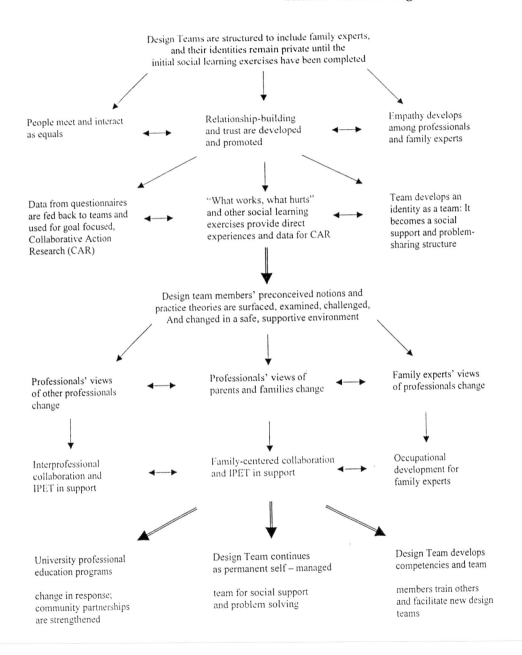

Figure 3. Generative or Multiplier Effects (Documented at One Site)

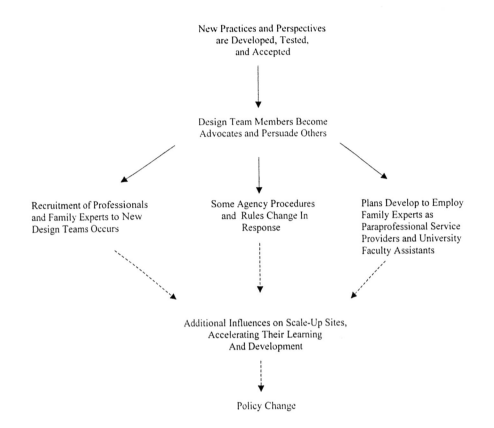

Competency Development

Teams generated competencies, knowledge, and understanding. Tables 1 and 2 are derived from the Reno design team. Table 1 presents specific competencies to meet families' co-occurring needs. Table 2 presents universal competencies, many of which were developed in response to the insightful solutions provided by family experts.

Table 1. A Composite of the Competencies Developed by Design Teams

---

New Quality of Treatment Principles for Public Sector Families

- Families are seen as having expertise regarding what hurts and what helps.
- Families are seen as having perspectives on ways to make services more effective, tailored to their own unique situation.
- Families are given a partnership role in service planning; they may in some cases need to organize the service plan.
- Professionals must respect family perspectives regarding the timing, sequencing, and nature of services that are to be provided or sought.
- Professionals must address the "maltreatment" families experience in the way co-occurring challenges are poorly assessed and service strategies poorly developed.

TANF, Poverty, and Employment

- Has a working knowledge of TANF, including time frames, service plans, and sanctioning processes and is able to use that knowledge to instruct and motivate clients.
- Is able to access TANF services and resources for clients.
- Is able to identify and assess key aspects of work history, work related successes, and aspirations.
- Can identify the interrelationships, including causes and effects, between unemployment and the barriers of substance abuse, mental illness, and/or domestic violence.
- Is able to divert or prevent families from entering the child welfare system by addressing job barriers, including job placement problems.
- Is able to address and mobilize occupational ladders for challenged families.

Domestic Violence

- Recognizes that domestic violence is an issue of power and control, not one of anger management or substance abuse.
- Can assess for pattern of assaultive and coercive behaviors.
- Refrains from asking the victim why they do not leave and when doing so, is cognizant of the high risks and physical threats to them and their children.
- Understands the importance of empowering and supporting the victim to make own decisions and develop own strengths.
- Can help victim identify self-protective factors and develop safety plans.
- Can make appropriate referrals to certified batterers' treatment programs.
- Understands the difference between batterers' treatment and anger management.
- Understands the effects of domestic violence on children, their protective and developmental issues.

Substance Abuse

- Recognizes the disease basis of substance abuse rather than seeing it as a moral issue.
- Recognizes symptoms of the disease as well as stage specific impacts and risks.
- Understands the relationship between substance abuse as an adult and prior victimization as a child, in that alcohol and drugs are a very powerful, and temporarily very effective, means for suppressing painful feelings and memories.
- Can assess and make appropriate referrals for further assessment and treatment.
- Understands stages of recovery, including relapse, and can help client identify relapse triggers, plan alternative behaviors, and a support system.
- Understands the effects of relapse in child safety and is able to assist in planning for safety precautions.

Mental Illness

- Recognizes the primary symptoms of major mental illnesses: depression, bipolar disorder, schizophrenia, post traumatic stress disorder.
- Understands the lifetime impact of mental illness as well as the situationally induced conditions, such as depression after the placement of a child or unemployment.
- Understands medication and compliance issues and these implications for child safety
- Understands case management challenges, including helping people recognize their own symptoms and need for medication

Child Abuse

- Understands the primary goals of child welfare practice, which are to protect children and maintain families when at all possible.
- Can assess increased risk of abuse or neglect of children if any or all of these co-occurring symptoms are worsening.
- Knows the Adoption and Safe Families Act (ASFA) and the new child welfare time frames for termination of parental rights in the event that reunification is not achieved .
- Understands and can practice the family-centered strengths-based collaborative model of practice.
- Understands the issues of culture and diverse coping styles as they mediate and buffer some of the effects of co-occurring symptoms.
- Understands the harmful effects of out-of-home placement on children and the importance of family reunification, when at all possible.
- Recognizes the dynamics of grief and loss and understands how those dynamics affect behavior and attitudes for both children and adults.

Co-Occurring Needs

- Understands that the above problems are often co-occurring and that if one of these is present, one or more of the other needs may also be present.
- Understands that if the above problems are not yet co-occurring, the added stress of unemployment and poverty (loss of TANF payments, for example) may encourage their development.
- Understands that it is critical for the service provider to acknowledge these dynamics, actively assess for the existence of these co-occurring issues, and work to prevent them if they are not yet occurring.

Table 2. Universal Competencies for Working with Individuals and Families

Relationship-Based
Listen, Listen, Listen
Show Empathy
Be Non-Judgmental
Be Compassionate
Respect Me
Ask Me
Hear what I have to say
Allow me to say what I think
Trust Me

Family-Centered, Consumer-Driven
Allow me to make decisions on my own

Strengths-Based, Empowerment
Tell me things that help me feel good about myself
Allow me to make mistakes without bashing me
Give me hope

In other words, the service provider:

- Is kind, caring, and concerned to one another and to the families served.
- Understands that all effective service provision is relationship-based, which is built on listening, understanding, and being empathetic, respectful, and non-judgmental
- Understands that family-centered, consumer-driven practice allows for individual decision-making.
- Communicates without using jargon, initials, abbreviations, or acronyms.

Design Teams and Training

In Reno, the original design team members have developed a mini-design team process, which they have offered in the form of training workshops to the entire service community in Reno. This two-day workshop is facilitated by various members of the original design team, including professionals and family experts. It includes abbreviated versions of exercises done in the original design team that highlight the fundamental importance of relationship in <u>all</u> aspects of service provision, teaching collaboration skills, and encouraging networking. Local service providers teach about their various disciplines. A comprehensive manual of information about the various co-occurring needs and local resources is given out. And, most important, a panel of family experts tell their stories in a way that highlights what has worked and not worked for them.

A conscious effort is made to recruit attendees from as many service sectors in Reno as possible, and the cost is minimal. Thus far, representatives from child welfare, welfare, substance abuse, domestic violence, mental health, housing, public health nurses, juvenile justice, adult probation and parole, family resource centers, and adult services have attended. The workshop was given five times in 1999, to a total of 104 people, and will be given another four times in 2000. In turn, workshop participants may share their experiences with countless others.

A Faculty Design Team

Also in Reno, key leaders from the community design team and the faculty facilitator (Nancy) have developed a university design team. Nancy contacted interested faculty members from eight different departments in the summer of 1999 and invited them to a "faculty design team" to look at ways to incorporate interprofessional knowledge and attitudes into the university's educational program for students preparing to go into some area of human services. That team has been meeting with a core group of interested people from the community design team. In a process similar to the community design team, faculty have been learning from one another about what they teach and identifying the preconceived notions, both accurate and inaccurate, that each held about one another. They have also been hearing from community representatives what they want students to learn before they arrive in the work world, from students what they wished they had learned before going to that first job, and hearing from family experts about "what works" and "what hurts."

At this time, the faculty team has decided to develop an interprofessional course as a group, with group input, support, and buy-in to ensure its relevance to the overall field of human services. This course will emphasize collaboration in relation to co-occurring needs. Nancy and a community design team member plan to teach the course in the fall of 2000.

Findings from Other States

Examples of findings from design teams in other states also are important (Lawson, Briar-Lawson, et al., 1999). When team members were asked to define success after eight or nine meetings, the responses varied considerably and reflected some consistent themes relating to the challenges of this complex change process. Table 3 gives examples of self-reported products and progress markers from the initial four design teams. They include everything from personal growth and development to interagency collaboration, competency development, and changes in agency policy. They also include scale-up sites begun in other sites in the state, and the development of interprofessional courses at the university level. The list is not meant to be exhaustive, for the products and progress markers are "as of this moment."

Table 3. Examples of Self-Reported Products and Progress Markers

Products and Progress Markers
Foundations for both family-centered collaboration and interprofessional collaboration were set in all of the design teams, as indicated by such observations as: • Professionals reported increased empathy and new appreciation for parents' expertise, strengths, problem-solving preferences, and needs. • Professionals reported increased appreciation and understanding of unintended harm caused to parents and families by services provided. • Professionals reported increased appreciation and understanding of the roles and responsibilities of other professionals. • All team members reported improved quality of treatment and interaction between professionals and family experts. • Interpersonal and social supports were developed within the design teams.
Interprofessional collaboration commenced on a small scale, involving two or more design team members and their agency partners.
Family-centered collaboration began to be practiced on a larger scale as professionals from the design teams changed their preconceptions and practices.
Competencies were developed from addressing co-occurring needs of families and, in turn, for interprofessional education and training (IPET) courses and programs.
Existing social work education courses in two universities were modified to include IPET content relevant to co-occurring family needs.
IPET courses were developed, implemented and evaluated at one university.
Design team members in three states planned training programs, two of which have been implemented.
Changes were made in agency policies and practices (e.g., new access lines for families and cross-agency communications were established in one site; intake forms in one neighborhood collaborative have been changed to foster family-centered collaboration).

Products and Progress Markers
Family experts developed occupational plans and received occupational supports through the design team in one site.
Professionals began to plan new work roles for family experts, and team members believe that practices will improve as family experts assume these work roles.
Collaborative action research protocols were developed and piloted, along with new evaluation designs and a new methodology (journey analysis).
Design team members in three states have committed to keep meeting because the team serves as a social support and problem-solving structure.
A scale-up guide for facilitators has been developed and is now being piloted.
Some family experts have participated in national conferences and workshops describing the design team process.
Participation by key administrators in the community workshop developed by the design team in one state (Nevada) led to a recognition of the need for mutual training projects specifically targeted to the welfare and child welfare systems.

Some Key Lessons Learned

The design team model, like the innovative practices, relationships, and partnerships it promotes, is new. Everyone associated with it is still learning. As the familiar saying goes, hindsight gives us 20-20 vision. If we had to do it all over again, we'd do many things differently and hopefully better. Gaining insight through hindsight is a key part of collaborative action research and learning. It is a way to improve, and at the same time, promote new knowledge and understanding. Here, then, are key lessons learned.

In all four states, design teams members expressed a desire for a more clear, concrete set of goals and expected outcomes. Frankly, design teams did not always anticipate, and respond to, a key question that every member brought to the table; namely, what's in this for me and us? This is not selfishness; it is enlightened self-interest (Lawson & Barkdull, Chapter 13). Busy people, professionals and family experts alike, need to gain an immediate sense of how this experience will improve results, making life different and better for them.

Even when more concrete goals were developed, conflicting expectations among individual team members and their agencies still existed. Although these conflicting expectations can lead to hurdles in the group process, the variability of human beings in their receptivity to change, learning and development can also be viewed as an asset. For instance, it can help to prevent "groupthink" (Janis, 1972) and can enrich the process by bringing out the very real dynamics and challenges of real-world change efforts.

Drop-outs occurred across the four states for several suspected reasons, not the least of which was the apparent lack of goals and clear practice outcomes that met the needs of the professionals. Four related lessons learned include (1) The design team process needs to be compressed in time [Note: the original design teams met for at least six months or more]; (2) The goals, timelines, requirements, and commitments for the process need to be clearer at the outset; (3) After trust and collaboration occurs, design team members need to focus upon improvements in everyday, front-line practice and the supports for it; and (4) Design team members need to be given, as the process unfolds, clear choices about possible outcomes for their own efforts, in their own communities, even as they review the work and the outcomes in other communities.

Table 4 provides a list of lessons learned. Lessons learned include both the challenges inherent in the design team process itself as well as those arising from efforts to impact the larger systems. Again, this list is not an exhaustive one.

Table 4. Selected Lessons Learned

Design Team Process
When the design team process is stretched out over a year, family experts are difficult to retain. In some cases, they gain employment and job responsibilities prevent participation on the team. In other cases, the co-occurring challenges that brought them to the attention of services in the first place re-occur, with the result that they are no longer available for participation (substance abuse relapse was a barrier to sustained participation in some cases).
When the design team experience stretches out over a year, and process is perceived as more important than immediate content, or concrete problem-solving, some professionals drop out.
When the design team process does not focus on concrete goals and results, and when data provided are not treated as opportunities for action, design team members get confused. They also become impatient with the learning process and with the facilitator.
The design team process requires a different kind of facilitator, one who is able to structure effective and appropriate learning environments and activities, who can coach and mentor family experts, who appreciates the personal learning opportunities that the design team provides; and who can develop social learning tools that (1) focus team members' efforts and (2) provide data to facilitate collaborative action and research.

Two kinds of time constraints are cited repeatedly across the four sites: (1) too little time is devoted to the design teams; and (2) the faculty facilitators and the principal investigators underestimate the amount of time and supports needed for all of the changes.
Service System Challenges
Family experts and professionals alike are wary of "one size fits all in a one best system" approach to assessment and service delivery. They say that once families are honored as experts, each family must be viewed in context, as a (somewhat) unique case.
Professionals worry about the constraints their home agencies place on the new practices they are developing, and they are especially wary of standardized forms and procedures mandated in states laboring under consent decrees.
Family-centered collaboration, with its values and approaches, may lead to conflict with the career orientations and perceived rewards of some professionals. The challenges of meeting the co-occurring needs of vulnerable families, especially "double jeopardy families" involved in both the welfare and the child welfare systems, entail massive systems changes. These changes cannot be learned and planned all at once. A developmental progression is emerging, one that begins with commitments to interprofessional collaboration, family-centered collaboration, or both. Whether these changes will lead to other, tailored strategies and innovative service designs for meeting families' co-occurring needs remains to be seen.
The development of social work-centered, IPET programs is a dramatic systems design challenge in the academic environment. Faculty development opportunities, resources in support of innovation and learning, and technical assistance and capacity-building are required.
Even though the design team process has "felt" to be a very positive one, with the growth, knowledge, and relationships that have resulted, there is still a danger of collaborating just to collaborate. We must always remember that improved outcomes for the families served is the best indicator of success.

The lessons learned from these first design teams, pioneers as they were, have identified limitations as well as successes. Innovative work is not easy, and complex change is a slow, multi-faceted process. The design teams are in the process of further testing, learning, and development, and it is still too early to make sweeping conclusions and bold claims of miraculous outcomes for the vulnerable families served.

For example, the weakest area for design team members and faculty facilitators alike is employment and employment-related supports. TANF's requirements for work and work-related supports thus compel broad-based capacity-building, including the basic idea that helping parents and care givers get and keep jobs is both a child welfare and related systems best practice issue. In other words, social workers and other helping professionals may not have sole responsibility for job development and supports, but they need to know how to work with other job developers and with the family. They especially need to know how, when, where, and why employment problems and unemployment are root causes for many presenting needs for children and their families (e.g., Briar, 1988; Briar-Lawson, Lawson, et al., in press). Toward this end, employment-related competencies are under development for use with design teams (Briar, 1988).

Toward Paradigm Change?

Clearly, the design team model, and its surrounding cross-state and -site learning, development, and improvement system, have created change, albeit in many different ways. This is not change for the sake of change, but change and learning targeted for improvements. Change happened on an individual level in all sites as actual team participants experienced the design team process and then shared their new insights, values, knowledge, and skills when interacting with peers, supervisors, and families. It also happened on a larger level, with various design teams taking on particular change efforts within their particular communities, inspiring scale-up efforts in other communities. In fact, led by Art Atwell, scale-up is underway statewide in Colorado. Policy change has been documented in Utah and in Nevada (Lawson, Briar-Lawson, Warner-Kearney, & Ynacay-Nye, 2000).

University faculty facilitators changed, and, through their interactions in a regional steering committee (which acts as a umbrella-like design team), facilitators have changed each other as well as the principal investigators. University IPET programs are under development. It appears that, across sites, stakeholders and participants have undergone a kind of "paradigm shift" as they have experienced and then promoted new ways of learning, developing, and, most important, working with individuals and families. Massive change often requires, or promotes, paradigm changes. These changes are always taxing and stressful. However, if vulnerable families and the professionals who serve them benefit from this work, the stresses and challenges of the change journey will be worthwhile.

References

Alameda, T. (1996). The healthy learners project: Bringing the community into the school. In K. Hooper-Briar & H. Lawson (Eds.). *Expanding partnerships for vulnerable children, youth and families* (pp. 46-56). Washington, DC: Council on Social Work Education.

Argyris, C. (1996). Actionable knowledge: Design causality in the service of consequential theory. *Journal of Applied Behavioral Science, 32*, 390-406.

Argyris, C. and Schön, D. (1996). *Organizational learning II: Theory, method, and practice.* Reading, MA: Addison Wesley.

Briar, K. (1988). *Social work and the unemployed.* Washington: NASW Press.

Briar-Lawson, K., Lawson, H., and Hennon, C. with Jones, A. (in press). *Family-centered policies and practices: International implications.* New York: Columbia University Press.

Casto, M. and Julia, M. (1994). *Interprofessional care and collaborative practice.* Pacific Grove, CA.: Brooks-Cole Publishing Company.

Casto, M. Harsh, S., and Cunningham, L. (1998). Shifting the paradigm for interprofessional education at the Ohio State University and beyond. In J. McCroskey & S. Einbinder (Eds.). *Universities and communities: Remaking professional and interprofessional education for the next century* (pp. 54-64). Westport, CT: Praeger.

Gore, J. (1993). *The struggle for pedagogies: Critical and feminist discourses as regimes of truth.* New York & London: Routledge.

Hooper-Briar, K. and Lawson, H. (Eds.). (1996). *Expanding partnerships for vulnerable children, youth, and families.* Washington, DC: Council on Social Work Education.

Janis, I. 1972). *Victims of groupthink.* Boston: Houghton-Mifflin.

Knapp, M. and Associates. (Eds.). (1998). *Paths to partnership: University and community as learners in interprofessional education.* Boulder, CO: Rowman & Littlefield Publishers, Inc.

Lawson, H. (1995). Schools and educational communities in a new vision for child welfare. *Journal for a Just and Caring Education, 1*(1), 5-26.

Lawson, H. (1998a). Academically-based community scholarship, consultation as collaborative problem-solving, and a collective-responsibility model for the helping fields. *Journal of Educational and Psychological Consultation, 9,* 195-232.

Lawson, H. (1998b, July). *Globalization and the social responsibilities of citizen-professionals.* Keynote address, AIESEP International Conference, Garden City, NY.

Lawson, H. (1999). Journey analysis: A framework for integrating consultation and evaluation in complex change initiatives. *Journal of Educational and Psychological Consultation, 10,* 145-172.

Lawson, H. (in press). Beyond community involvement and service learning to engaged universities. *Universities and Community Schools.*

Lawson, H. and Briar-Lawson, K. (1997). *Connecting the dots: Progress toward the integration of school reform, school-linked services, parent involvement and community schools.* Oxford, OH: Danforth Foundation & Institute for Educational Renewal at Miami University.

Lawson, H. and Barkdull, C. (1999). *Developing caring school communities for children and youth: Integrating school reform and caring communities.* A curriculum guide prepared for the Missouri Department of Elementary and Secondary Education, Jefferson City, MO.

Lawson, H., Briar-Lawson, K., Petersen, N., Harris, N., Hoffman, T., Derezotes, D., and Sallee, A. (1999, April). The development of an empowerment-oriented model for interprofessional education and training, collaboration, organizational improvement, and policy change. American Educational Research Association, Montreal, Quebec, Canada.

Lawson, H., Briar-Lawson, K., Warner-Kearney, D., and Ynacay-Nye, R. (2000, January). A new model for uniting, harmonizing, and promoting action research, advocacy, systems change, partnerships, and research innovation, dissemination, and utilization. Society for Social Work and Research, Charleston, SC.

Lerner, R. and Simon, L. (Eds.). (1998). *University-community collaborations for the twenty-first century: Outreach scholarship for youth and families.* New York & London: Garland Publishing.

McCroskey, J. and Einbinder, S. (Eds.). (1998). *Universities and communities: Remaking professional and interprofessional education for the next century.* Westport, CT & London: Praeger.

McKnight, J. (1995). *The careless society: Community and its counterfeits.* New York: Basic Books.

Riger, S. (1993). What's wrong with empowerment? *American Journal of Community Psychology, 21,* 279-292.

Salomon, G. and Perkins, D. (1998). Individual and social aspects of learning. In P. Pearson & A. Iran-Nejad (Eds.). *Review of Research in Education 23* (pp. 1-24). Washington, DC: American Educational Research Association.

Senge, P., Kleiner, A., Roberts, C., Ross, R., and Smith, B. (1994). *The fifth discipline fieldbook: Strategies and tools for building a learning organization.* New York: Currency Doubleday.

Schön, D. (1995). Causality and causal inference in the study of organizations. In R. Goodman & W. Foster (Eds). *Rethinking knowledge: Reflections across the disciplines* (pp. 69-102). Albany, NY: SUNY Press.

Smith, A., Culbert, K., and Deniro, J. (1998). Identifying what collaborative professionals need to know. In M. Knapp & Associates (Eds.). *Paths to partnership: University and community as learners in interprofessional education* (pp. 35-56). New York: Rowman & Littlefield Publishers.

Vygotsky, L. S. (1978). *Mind in society.* Cambridge, MA: Harvard University Press.

Chapter 18

Back to the Future: New Century Professionalism and Collaborative Leadership for Comprehensive, Community-based Systems of Care

Hal A. Lawson

Introduction

The history of social work is intertwined with the history of child welfare. Today, perhaps more than ever before, child welfare needs social work's leadership. It is timely to make strategic inquiries into their joint history. These inquiries yield multiple benefits. These benefits include important lessons learned, inspirational leadership stories, and best practice strategies. Inquiries also yield knowledge and understanding about important losses that have accompanied their changing historical trajectories. Taking stock of the losses is an important step toward meeting the challenges of designing and implementing new century strategies and systems.

This chapter is structured with these challenges, opportunities, and benefits in mind. As its title suggests, the chapter begins by going back to the future. This limited, selective inquiry focuses on a particular style of early professionalism in social work, along with collaborative leadership. It also focuses on the basic idea of democratic citizenship, especially citizens' shared responsibilities for vulnerable children and families and their mutual obligations to one another. These reminders about democracy and democratic citizenship support a key premise: *Both citizens and professionals once collaborated to perform social work, and something important has been lost as the generative idea of "social work" has become restricted to the missions and duties of just one important profession.* Arguably, the most important benefit of going back to the future is to reclaim this compelling vision of collaborative, comprehensive, democratic social work, including the special opportunities, ethical-moral imperatives, and leadership responsibilities social workers have today for promoting this vision and implementing it in child welfare.

In fact, this old century vision is a root for new century plans for comprehensive, community-based systems of care for children, youth, and families. These systems of care are outlined briefly with special attention to the components of a comprehensive intervention and support continuum. Then the analysis turns to key requirements of these systems of care; namely, new century professionalism, collaborative leadership, and citizen engagement. Two styles of professionalism are presented. The preferred style, called social trustee, civic professionalism, is contrasted with an alternative style called mechanical, market-oriented professionalism.

The chapter concludes by presenting opportunities for social work's leaders and child welfare leaders who are not, strictly speaking, social workers to join forces and make history. It is suggested that the dawning of the global age at the beginning of the 21st century brings striking parallels to the dawning of the industrial age at the beginning of the 20th century. As social workers and child welfare leaders join forces to make history, they may re-professionalize child welfare and revitalize social work's professionalization in the process. These exciting possibilities hinge on the political will and determination of leaders in social work and in child welfare, especially their abilities to join forces. The 20th century trailblazers for social work and child welfare provide inspiring success stories of how this important work can be done.

Back to the Future 1: A Tradition of Democratic Professionalism and Collaborative Leadership

One hundred years ago, at the beginning of the 20th Century, the trailblazers for the modern social work profession were hard at work. They were aware that the industrial age was upon them and that their world was changing rapidly. Industrialization, urbanization, immigration, technological development, child labor, and other dramatic changes signaled needs for new approaches to social needs and policies. New institutions were needed, especially ones that responded effectively to the needs of vulnerable children, youth, and families.

Invisible Boundaries as an Asset

The social work profession's trailblazers were a diverse group (Abbott, 1995). In contrast to today's social workers, these trailblazers did not work very hard at trying to identify other, official social workers. Because the profession was in its preliminary, formative stages, these pioneers could not draw on the identity signs and recognition signals today's professionals enjoy. In brief, social work did not have clear, firm boundaries or boundary markers.

Boundary markers include formal university degree programs, specialized language, theoretical knowledge, a code of ethics, credentials and licenses, and professional associations. Because social work's boundaries were not established, nearly everyone who cared about the plight of vulnerable children, youth, and families was welcomed as a kind of social worker.

Furthermore, there were no labor market controls. That is, there were no rules and laws that restricted certain kinds of work, such as child welfare, to licensed social workers. Where uniform standards of quality control are needed and special research, theory, knowledge, and skill are required to perform good work, professions form.

In fact, social work developed as a formal profession in response to these needs and the attendant opportunities they provided. As the 20th century progressed, social work developed its boundaries and boundary markers. For example, a code of ethics, formal education in university programs, research-based practice knowledge, and credentialing systems were identified as key components of best practices with vulnerable children and families. In many states, labor market controls developed, and some restricted certain kinds of child welfare work to social workers. Child welfare systems, in the broadest sense, improved in the process. As systems improved, vulnerable children and families benefitted. Thus, this professionalization of social work was a good thing to do and the right thing to do.

Paradoxically, invisible boundaries and the absence of formal professions also may be viewed as assets. For example, in times gone by, workers and their natural-indigenous community helpers often stepped forward and volunteered because they could not assume that child and family well-being was the welfare state's responsibility, especially social work's or child welfare's responsibility. They could not assume that a family's special presenting needs (e.g., depression, domestic violence) would be detected or "diagnosed" by professionals, who would, in turn, assign the family to another specialized professional (e.g., a clinical psychologist, a domestic violence counselor). Unfortunately, sometimes children's and families' presenting needs were not identified and addressed effectively. Oftentimes, when they were identified and addressed, someone in the local neighborhood community shared responsibility for the success story. Civic engagement by everyday people--being enmeshed in neighborhood and community affairs--was a necessity. This citizen volunteerism was facilitated in part by the absence of formal professions and their professional boundaries.[1]

To put it another way, child and family well-being was not "someone else's problem." In contrast to today, neighbors were less likely to hide from the needs of strangers (Ignatief, 1982). Responsibility had to be shared. It could not be delegated to public service professionals supported by taxes. Help giving was often called "friendly home visiting." In the course of exchanges involving help, former strangers became neighbors and even friends. Contagion, or domino, effects often followed.

People who received help, in turn, gave help and support to others. Mutual assistance and support networks evolved, often reflecting the ethnic and cultural ties that bind and bond. These networks were nested in neighborhood- and community-systems. These networks were the forerunners of today's plans for comprehensive, community-based systems of care.

---

[1] However, the boundaries of privilege and social-economic difference were evident. Many help-givers were from well-to-do-families. Their civic engagement was compelled by religious ideals and a sense of social responsibility that corresponded to the European tradition of *noblesse oblige*, i.e., the responsibilities of an aristocracy to less fortunate people, especially poor people (Boyer, 1978; Bring, 1994).

Where professional and systemic boundaries were visible, social work's trailblazers made it their business to cross the boundaries--to serve as boundary spanners and re-designers. Their boundary work was essential. Absent it, boundaries divided and separated people.

Then, as now, boundaries tended to define difference and suggest "other-ness." Boundaries, both professional and systemic, thus may constrain and even prevent the development of a unified sense of purpose and collaborative leadership, both of which are essential parts of comprehensive, community-based systems of care. In this perspective, the boundary-crossing and--spanning work of early social work leaders was a critical practice tool. It enabled collaborative problem-setting, facilitated culturally-responsive problem-solving, and empowered community leaders to join forces in implementing and evaluating helping strategies (McCarthy, 2000). This important work accounted for many of their success stories.

The Social Work of Collaborative Leadership

Diverse in so many respects, the profession's trail blazing predecessors were alike in some important ways and similar in other ways. Above all, the predecessors were a caring, compassionate group. They shared concern for other people, especially for the most vulnerable among the vulnerable--the nation's children. Many worked tirelessly to secure food, clothing, and safe, secure housing for children and families evidencing need. They worked continuously to protect children and enhance their healthy development. They provided services, developed social supports, and obtained economic resources.

Although some leaders developed the forerunners of settlement houses and worked out of them, these predecessors were not limited to them. They had a "whatever it takes attitude," and this attitude made them inventive and creative. Their work took them to the parks and playgrounds, into schools, inside neighborhood organizations and civic associations, and into religious institutions. As they moved in communities, they gained knowledge and skill about how to enter into new territories. They learned how to cross boundaries and encourage coalitions. Many learned how to blend into local communities. They developed rich stocks of "insider knowledge." They knew how to mine the benefits of neighborhoods and communities and to invest and reinvest them strategically in the same locality. Individuals, families, and neighborhood communities became stronger and healthier as benefits were mined and shared. Virtuous, self-fulfilling cycles of improvement and success stemmed from this strength-oriented, solution-focused, neighborhood-based practice.[2]

Often, these predecessors recruited and mobilized other individuals, families, and organizations to help vulnerable children, youth, and families. They sought help from others because many of these predecessors knew that, when the multiple needs of children and families were concerned, they could not do it all, alone. They may not have had the language, and they could not have known how many formal professions would form over the course of the 20th century. However, they seemed to know intuitively that there would never be enough professionals.

Many sensed that the long-term solution was to create family- and community-based systems of care, which could be integrated with the work they did. In these integrated natural and professional systems, children, youth, families, other residents, and professionals knew one another. They believed that they could count on one another, and so they developed trust in one another. These essential conditions enabled them to offer and receive mutual support and assistance.

A Social Work Vision

Many of these trailblazers were inspired by their religious ideals. Others knew that abject poverty, economic hardship, social and cultural exclusion, and food and housing insecurities were breeding grounds for conflict, violence, crime and delinquency, and even political revolutions. Social work's trailblazers wanted to prevent these social problems, and mindful of European history, they also wanted to prevent ethnic, class, and racial conflicts that might lead to a revolution.[3]

Different in these respects and in others, these trailblazers shared a compelling vision--a societal blueprint--derived from a common call to service. They viewed themselves as "progressive," and their work was a defining feature of the Progressive Era of American history (ca. 1880-1930). In retrospect, this calling could be aptly called *social work* because it was not limited to only one child, or to just one network of families. Although this early, new century social work began with one child in the context of the family, work with a child and a family was set against the backdrop

---

[2] Generalizations like these gloss over significant differences and endemic problems, such as institutionalized racism and ethnocentrism. See Margolin (1997) for a one-sided critique of early social work, including the Janus-faced practices associated with "friendly home visiting." See also Halpern (1999) for a balanced critique of the settlements, including their selectivity and limitations.

[3] Halpern (1999, p. 49), relying on Borris' work, described this orientation as "social control with a conscience."

provided by the local neighborhood community, the city, the state, and the nation. *These trailblazers' calling was social work because its aim was to create a good, just, peaceful, sustainable, and democratic society.* Led by Jane Addams and her strong belief in social justice in a democracy, their calling derived from a sense of social responsibility, which was grounded in ethical-moral imperatives.[4] Help-giving and--seeking thus were framed by implicit and explicit norms for the mutual obligations and responsibilities of citizens from all walks of life. People acted as carriers of these norms, and these norms also were embedded in their neighborhood and community settings. Then, as now, shared normative frameworks were crucial in all collaborative efforts (e.g., Levine, 1998).

Despite predecessors' competing ideas about what needed to be done, how, when, where, and why, they were able to get beyond their differences and work toward a common purpose.[5] United in the pursuit of a common cause that was more important than any one of them, and pursuing a grand vision that was so big that it required every one of them, social work's predecessors were able to collaborate. They collaborated with each other, with other emergent professions, with children and families in need, and with neighborhood and community residents. They accepted shared responsibility for ensuring that differences among diverse people did not prevent effective collective action.

These trailblazers were able to join forces, and as they did, they helped children and families in need. At the same time, they forged the modern social work profession. In other words, the forerunners of the profession simultaneously served themselves as they helped vulnerable children, youth, and families. In this sense, they were self-interested, but not selfish.

Social work's trailblazers were able to collaborate effectively because of *enlightened self-interest.* They were enlightened, but not selfish. They earned the title *social workers* because they always kept their eyes on the grand prize; namely, creating the good, just, peaceful, sustainable, and democratic society. They envisioned a utopian society in which each child's and every family's well-being

---

[4] Margolin (1997, p. 4) provides the reminder that Addams talked about "neighbors" instead of clients, and she refused to keep records. She recognized early two different ethical frames for help-giving and -receiving. With John Dewey, Addams championed what might be called social democratic help giving—albeit with cultural assimilation in mind (Halpern, 1999).

[5] This idea of a common purpose predates the significant differences that emerged as Addams and Richmond gained visibility and were assigned leadership. See Margolin (1997) and Halpern (1999) for incisive analyses of their differences. Margolin concludes that modern social workers may invoke Addams' ideals to justify themselves, but their practice actually corresponds to Mary Richmond's social diagnosis.

would be safeguarded forever. This same compelling vision provides the foundation for the modern idea of comprehensive, community-based systems of care.

Toward Comprehensive, Community-Based Systems of Care

Today, consensus is growing across the nation that the child welfare system needs to improve its operations and its results. Some such improvements can be called *systems reforms*. Reforms involve tinkering within the existing system. For example, reforms include better training, supervision, resource management, and case load assignments. Every one of these reforms is important. These reforms and others respond to emergent needs. These needs include high turn-over rates among front-line workers and their excessive case loads, the disproportionate representation in the system of African-American children and families in some states and of Latinos in others, and the challenges of responding to a growing number of reports of child abuse and neglect. New policies, especially the Adoption and Safe Families Act (ASFA) and Temporary Assistance to Needy Families (TANF), both individually and in combination, also compel systems reforms.

As important as these reforms are, national experts also have concluded that, by themselves, they will not produce the range of improvements needed in the system (e.g., Farrow, 1997). These experts have recommended staying the course with these reforms, while continuing to recognize the good work performed by countless professionals around the nation. However, these experts believe that it is mandatory to introduce *transformational thinking and new century practices*. They know that, in essence,
business-as-usual today will mean results-as-usual tomorrow. There is growing consensus that, for a child welfare system in crisis, results-as-usual is not an acceptable alternative. Results-as-usual will not serve professionals, children and families, or policy leaders.

Transformation thinking and new century practice innovations involve getting outside the "child welfare box." The box does not get ignored, neglected, or abandoned. It gets reconfigured, and it gets stronger, because of its new designs and the stronger foundation on which it rests.

Transformational thinking, new century practice innovations, and the reconfiguration of the child welfare box are founded on eight related claims:

- When the multiple needs and wants of children and their families are considered, the child welfare system cannot do it all, alone

- In turn, there will never be enough trained, competent professionals to meet every child and family need and to respond, in a timely fashion, to every challenge

- Other professionals in community agencies and schools need to assume joint responsibility for the well-being of children and families and collaborate with child welfare professionals and agencies

- Community residents, especially other families, can and should assume joint responsibility for protecting children and supporting families, in turn, promoting community-based systems of care

- Families, broadly defined, need to be partners in service design and delivery because they have expertise in what helps and hurts them (Briar-Lawson & Wiesen, Chapter 12)

- Child welfare professionals, especially social workers, need to assume leadership for promoting community-based systems of care

- It is timely to proceed beyond blaming families and holding them solely accountable for their presenting needs; accountability standards also apply to child and family serving systems and to neighborhood communities (McCarthy, 2000)

- Moreover, it is timely to question whether, and if so when, child welfare can be expected to serve as both the investigative-reporting system and the intervention system, especially when pervasive poverty and its companions are implicated as root causes (e.g., Lindsay, 1994).

Together, these six claims provide a powerful sensitizing framework, one that enables child welfare professionals to get outside the box and develop transformational practices. New opportunities await energetic and visionary leaders.

An Introductory Sketch of Comprehensive, Community-based Systems of Care

Although times certainly have changed, there is considerable merit in the societal vision that social work's trailblazers promoted. Consider it seriously. *At the same time that you think and talk about child welfare, start thinking and talking about the social welfare and well-being of all children and families.* This view, through a wide-angle lens, facilitates a dual focus. It focuses on children and families in the child welfare system, but it also encompasses comprehensive systems of care for every child and family.

These systems are comprehensive in the sense that they are developed in relation to a complete, inclusive intervention and support continuum (described in the next section). For example, these systems encompass the entire spectrum of child and family needs. They build on knowledge about the characteristics of health-enhancing settings in relation to universal standards of child and family well being. They include all of the strategies professionals from child welfare and from other helping systems may consider.

Furthermore, these systems are designed to identify, support, and strengthen existing, indigenous pathways to seeking and receiving help (Vahalaki & Khaja, Chapter 14). In this sense, comprehensive systems also are community-, and neighborhood-based. Professional systems such as child welfare are designed to complement these indigenous systems. Indigenous systems depend on everyday citizens, especially neighbors and friends, who are willing to assume shared responsibility for child and family well-being and neighborhood vitality.

Professionals and their systems are still important. For example, professionals provide services, supports, and resources from external sources as needed. Reciprocally, professionals benefit from these indigenous systems. They receive help from residents, and their jobs are easier and more satisfying because they benefit from indigenous systems of care and support.

With these mutual benefits in mind, planners aim for harmonious relationships among professional systems, especially child welfare, and indigenous systems. For example, neighborhood-based child welfare teams renew connections with local residents and their systems of care (Van Wagoner, Boyer, et al., Chapter 16). Similarly, community policing represents an effort by the justice system to re-establish ties among police offers and local residents. Some school-based models of parent involvement and empowerment are designed to re-establish ties among educators, parents, and residents (e.g., Alameda, 1996), enabling schools to become family-supportive and neighborhood-strengthening organizations (Lawson & Briar-Lawson, 1997). Systems of care are comprehensive when they include and integrate all of these initiatives and yet others.

Alike in their comprehensiveness, these systems also are somewhat unique. Each is tailored to fit its local context. Each builds on local assets while addressing its needs. In this sense as well, these systems of care are community- and neighborhood-based.

In other words, both cultural and structural challenges are involved. Comprehensive, community-based systems of care often start with structural changes--especially the development of pathways to seeking and receiving help. Pathway development is an engineering challenge that requires technical expertise and draws on a growing body of research. For example, pathways to care must be responsive to life course developmental changes, cultural differences, characteristics of the local place, and societal changes.

However, these systems of care require more than technical, research-based expertise about new structures. At the same time resident leaders and professionals collaborate to recommend structural changes, they also promote new cultural practices and norms, including genuine empathy and concern for other people. In other words, systems of care are hollow without caring people, both residents and professionals. To promote cultures of caring and concern, professionals and residents alike may develop new language systems, enabling them to use words that are strength-based and solution-focused, not deficit-based and problem-oriented. They develop shared norms and values, and they make firm commitments to enforcing them. These norms, values, and commitments form the foundation for a comprehensive, intervention and support continuum

An Intervention and Support Continuum

Expansive, wide-angle thinking enables the development of a comprehensive intervention and support continuum. The components in this continuum define some of the essential features in comprehensive, community-based systems of care. This continuum also frames and identifies important strategies and practice tools.

Obviously, children and families already in the system may need *crisis-responsive strategies*. Many crisis-responsive services are mandatory. For example, child protection services are mandated when instances of child abuse and neglect are documented. For better or worse, many lay persons associate child welfare with crises involving children, their parents, and families.

Today, the majority of services in all of the professional sectors remain crisis-responsive. As Weiss and Halpern (1990) describe it, professionals are like ambulance drivers waiting with their professional ambulances at the bottom of the cliff. Their job is to care for people who have fallen off the cliff. These professionals' work is especially difficult because they have to deal with the immediate harm caused by the fall and the long-term harm that pushed these people over the edge.

A comprehensive system must include plans for getting help to people in need before crises arise. For example, children and families living in poverty often demonstrate incredible ingenuity and inspiring resilience. Even so, many manifest one or more serious risk factors. Even if they are not "living on the edge," they may be headed in this undesirable direction. They need timely, strategic *early intervention strategies*.

Early intervention strategies are like early warning systems for weather forecasting and for the military. For these early warning systems to be effective, professionals and community members alike need the equivalent of "radar." Early intervention strategies depend on the timely detection of needs and, in turn, on effective response systems. When early intervention strategies work as planned, families living on the edge are helped to move away from this precarious position.

Others never get near the edge. All such families become stronger and more stabilized, and their children are safeguarded in the process.

In cases where abuse and neglect are detected, early intervention strategies include *mandatory services*. In cases where risk factors are present, but no harms are evident, *voluntary services* can be planned with parents and family systems. Voluntary services can be tailored to specific needs in particular places.

Meanwhile, children and families who are thriving need to stay this way. They will continue to thrive if effective *prevention strategies* are in place. Every strong family can and should benefit from prevention strategies. Oftentimes, these prevention strategies are called *universal strategies*. In the health professions, these universal strategies comprise health education and promotion programs. Like social insurance and entitlement programs (e.g., public schooling for children, social security for retirees), every child and family is eligible and may benefit from them. Similarly, universal family support and neighborhood development initiatives benefit all families and act as prevention mechanisms.

In contrast, *selective strategies*, also called *targeting strategies*, are employed in service of early intervention and crisis-responsive services, supports, and resources. Selective (targeting) strategies pinpoint one child or family, or like clusters of children and families. These selective samples of people often are called "the target population."

In fact, where early intervention is concerned, selective strategies may compel professionals to actively find and recruit children and families on the edge, rather than waiting for a crisis to arise, or waiting for the family to come to the service providers. In brief, *seeking strategies* may replace *waiting strategies*. These new seeking strategies are being pioneered in public health. They derive from growing understanding about how, or indeed, whether people will seek help.

For example, some people living in urban and suburban communities do not know where services are located, and they do not know about some of their needs. Even if they know about their needs, they are unwilling to, in essence, "go shopping" in the community in hopes of finding what they need. Seeking strategies respond to realities like these. Instead of waiting for individuals and families in need to go shopping for services and come to them, professionals use their "radar systems" to identify signs of need, and then they actively seek those children and families with these needs.

Another example: People living in rural and frontier communities also confront special challenges related to access to quality services. Mobile teams of providers who travel in these communities, through "services on wheels" approaches, are using a kind of seeking strategy as they do outreach to these people.

All such seeking strategies depend heavily on local residents. Neighbors, other family members, and friends often are the first to see signs of risk and need. They are able to put professionals on alert, facilitating early intervention. Moreover, local residents, including neighbors, friends, and family members, often are the first line of response. They may be able to help people and families in need "on the spot."

In this context of seeking versus waiting, and of intervening early and doing preventive work, these indigenous helping networks and systems are child welfare resources and supports. For example, child welfare systems often confront vexing challenges, which may seem overwhelming. Professionals are asked to do the impossible because many of the children and the families they are assigned already are in deep crisis.

Neighborhood- and community-based systems of care will enable early detection, and professionals and families alike will benefit from the natural-indigenous supports provided by other residents and their families. Professionals' work can be so much easier, and the family will endure less hardship, if early intervention and prevention strategies are implemented. Clearly, neighborhood-based, indigenous helping systems offer important, effective professional tools for "seeking, intervening early, and preventing." They are a welcome addition to the limited approach of ambulance drivers waiting at the bottom of the cliff to respond to deep crises.

Comprehensive, community-based systems of care frame old and new practice tools. For example, Smale (1995, p. 67) outlines four spheres of professional action for this neighborhood- and community-based work:

- Direct intervention--work carried out in partnership with people in need and residents to tackle pressing problems they identify

- Indirect intervention--work directed to institution-building and broad-scale prevention, the needs for which are signaled by direct intervention

- Service delivery--either through direct intervention or indirect intervention, i.e., professionals give strategies, supports, and resources to community residents, family members, and friends so that they can help the child and the family

- Change agentry--work directed toward changing boundaries, creating new community associations, and building relationships

These four spheres of action are not necessarily segregated. They may become most powerful when they are combined. For example, child welfare professionals may engage the residents of a community in the development of clear, agreed upon norms and standards for child development, security, and protection. In other words, community-based systems of care provide an important opportunity to engage families and resident leaders in important dialogue about the parameters of care and care giving, especially the standards all hold and are willing to uphold for children, parents and caregivers. These standards include the "dos" and "don'ts" of parenting and child development. Developing these norms and standards is itself an educative process, and this process can be contagious in community. Important benefits accompany it.

These norms, standards, and rules can be responsive to the cultural context of the community at the same time they ensure universal quality of care. In other words, they can be tailored to cultural differences, including important differences in Native American, African-American, Asian-American, and Latino communities. At the same time, universal standards are important. Practices that result in abuse, neglect, and harm cannot be justified as "culturally appropriate."

When residents are involved in establishing norms and standards, they also are more likely to assume joint ownership and collaborative leadership for their enforcement. If they do, prevention and early intervention are facilitated. And as they do, the work of child welfare workers is facilitated.

Absent this framework, child welfare workers are forced to act like police officers. Even worse, they are asked to enforce norms and standards that people in need may not have understood, or agreed to, in the first place. Many of the difficulties in child welfare work thus can be prevented when there is comprehensive, community ownership and engagement in the process of developing norms and standards.[6]

The benefits are not limited to child welfare, however. When norms and standards are comprehensive and overlap, other professions and systems benefit, too. For example, effective substance abuse cessation and prevention depend in part on the development of shared communal norms and values about the meaning and importance of healthy behavior. Similarly, school improvement depends in part on the development of community norms of high expectation, achievement, and supportive pathways toward success. Juvenile and criminal justice depend on shared norms regarding safety, security, and lawfulness. In brief, when these norms and standards are framed in relation to comprehensive, integrated indices of child and family well-being and neighborhood vitality, every profession and every service system benefits. Every professional's tool kit expands, and all become more effective.

---

[6] When community residents are engaged and jointly own the development of norms and standards; when the norms and standards are culturally-responsive; and when child welfare workers are "on the same page" as residents and families, considerable progress may be made in addressing a significant problem. This is the problem of the disproportionate representation of ethnic minorities in the child welfare system (and in sister systems such as juvenile justice and special education). In brief, culturally-competent and responsive practice may be facilitated by comprehensive, community-based systems of care.

A Blueprint for Child Welfare: Promoting the Well Being of All Children and Families

Comprehensive, community-based systems of care, framed in relation to an expansive intervention and improvement continuum, offer multiple benefits. Chief among these benefits is a potential blueprint which outlines the contours of a 21st century compelling vision for children and families in general and for child welfare in particular. This blueprint prioritizes harmonious, symbiotic relationships among child welfare, other professional systems, and natural-indigenous person-to-person and family-to-family helping and support networks. In this blueprint, the characteristics of the neighborhood and the community also are targeted for improvement because children and families cannot be supported and strengthened in isolation from where they live.

Notably, in these systems of care, good jobs are important, especially given the policy changes associated with TANF. Similarly, job development is a key part of community economic and social development. In fact, one of the most important lessons learned from the last century is that services must include more than psycho-therapeutic interventions (e.g., Halpern, 1999). They must include job supports, economic development, community organization strategies, pathways to better schooling, and other systems reforms that comprise anti-poverty initiatives (e.g., Bruner & Parachini, 1997).

Community-based systems of care promote multi-level strategies, including micro-practices with a child and the family system, meso-practices with the neighborhood and community systems, and macro-practices with state and national policy systems (e.g., Ellis, 1998). With this blueprint, service providers and community leaders can join forces in identifying existing pathways to care and healthy development. They also can use it to plan, implement, and evaluate comprehensive, community-based systems of care. This blueprint specifies plans for systems change and cross-systems change.

In brief, this blueprint enables comprehensive community planning, along with wise, prudent choices of practice tools and helping strategies by professionals and community residents. It provides a clear sense of purpose and enables a principled approach to rendering and receiving assistance. When diverse professionals and diverse community residents and families share the same blueprint, they can be "on the same page." They can work together effectively and successfully, because each appreciates what the others are contributing and constructing.

Absent this blueprint, one tool is as good as another. In fact, professionals may rely on just one tool, even when other tools are needed. As the saying goes, "if the only tool you know how to use is a hammer, then all of life's problems will look like nails.[7]

Blueprints like these present special opportunities for the kind of collaborative leadership that Progressive trailblazers provided. Leadership must be collaborative because the system cannot be an island unto itself. It needs services, supports, and resources from three other systems: Other professional systems; natural-indigenous neighborhood and community systems; and business, corporate, and other employment systems (because early intervention and prevention in high poverty families starts with good jobs and job supports). Reciprocally, the child welfare system needs to give something back to these other systems.

Both collaborative leadership and community-based systems of care depend on a new style of professionalism. This new style may be called, social trustee, civic professionalism.

Social Trustee, Civic Professionalism and Collaborative Leadership

Yesterday, as today, vulnerable children and families experienced some professional "do-gooders" as intrusive, culturally insensitive, arrogant, controlling, and coercive (e.g, Brint, 1994; Gaylin, Glasser, Marcus, & Rothman, 1978; Halpern, 1999; Margolin, 1997). Some such conflicts may be unavoidable. That is, conflicting perceptions may be endemic in all efforts at doing good and trying to help others. People needing help often do not perceive the need for it, especially when their child, a family member's child, or a friend's child is involved.

For example, they may not share professionals' perceptions of risk and endangerment, and they may not share professionals' and neighbors' views that help is needed. Even if they perceive the need for help, they may not want the kind of assistance that helpers are prepared to provide. In addition, they may resent the professionals' and neighbors' surveillance, viewing it as an invasion of their privacy (Capper, 1996; Knowles, 1996).

In brief, there is a never-ending tension between what helpers are prepared to give and what children and families may perceive, want, and need. Two styles of professionalism develop in relation to this tension. Each creates its own realities in relation to professionals' roles and responsibilities and their choice of helping and support strategies (Lawson, 1998).

---

[7] Apparently, this popular phrase was coined by the famous psychologist, Abraham Maslow, who called it "the law of the instrument." It also is called "diagnostic stereotyping," i.e., fitting children and families to the methods and strategies a professional knows how to use.

Mechanical, Market-oriented Professionalism: The Creation of Clients

One style might be called *mechanical, market-oriented professionalism*. This style of professionalism involves the routine exercise of professional power and authority. The assumption is, professional knows best. In other words, professionals are the experts; families are not. Professionals exclusively know what children and families need. Professionals' assessments, or diagnoses, pave the way for their interventions. Children and families thus depend on the professionals to find out what they want and need. Families cannot be expected to identify their needs and solve their problems without professional assistance. In this style of professionalism, children and families are dependent clients. Professionals wield considerable power and authority over them.

In fact, mechanical, market-oriented professionalism creates clients at the same time that professionals diagnose needs and problems (Cowger, 1998; McKnight, 1995). Professionals in this style do not merely serve. In crass terms, professionals need clients for their livelihoods. As they define needs, they justify their jobs. Little wonder that professionals, operating in this framework, tend not to consider, or use, indigenous helpers and support systems. They assume that expertise about needs, problems, and solutions resides solely with professionals, not with family members and neighborhood residents.

This style of mechanical, market-oriented professionalism is contoured by industrial capitalism and the logic of markets. In one sense, clients are to social and health professionals what customers are to business leaders. Clients and customers comprise markets, and funds gained through these markets enable professionals and business leaders to make a living (McKnight, 1995). In fact, many modern service providers refer to individuals, children, and families in need as "consumers" and as "customers." The ideas of "consumer-guided services" and "customer satisfaction with services" implicates a market-oriented exchange.

Furthermore, when poor people are involved, labeling processes are, too. As Gerry (1999) observes, the poor get services, which are defined and delivered by professionals. In contrast, well-to-do individuals and families get whatever help they need privately, out of the view of others, and absent labels and stereotypes.

Social Trustee, Civic Professionalism

A second style of professionalism is rooted in the Progressive era (Brint, 1994; Sullivan, 1995). It also is associated with the trailblazers for the social work profession, especially in shared ideals of Jane Addams and John Dewey for a style of professionalism congenial to participatory democracy. This style of democratic professionalism may be called *social trustee, civic professionalism* (Lawson, 1998).

Professionals act as social trustees of the common good (Sullivan, 1995). This new professionalism unites the roles of citizen and professional.

Citizen-professionals minister to the needs and wants of other citizens. These professionals practice what they preach. In other words, professionals do not view themselves as privileged persons who are above the people they serve. They are not arrogant, patriarchal, coercive, repressive, or ethnocentric, i.e., seeing others and the world around them through the lens provided by their own culture.

Social trustee civic professionals treat children and families in need in the same way they would want to be treated if they were in the same circumstance. These professionals know how fragile life can be. They know that, absent supports that enable their family systems to thrive, and faced with comparable crises, they might evidence some of the same needs as the family they are serving. Consequently, these professionals are able empathize with families. They understand what it is like to "walk a mile in their shoes."

Social trustee civic professionals operate from a foundation of mutual empowerment (Lawson, 1998). As they empower children and families, sharing power, authority, and decision-making capacities as appropriate, these professionals feel empowered. They gain a "can do" sense of competence, a high sense of efficacy. As children and families are empowered and improve, the professionals feel empowered and their job satisfaction and well-being improve. This is mutual empowerment in action.

Social trustee civic professionals, such as social workers, may perform specialized work in a particular societal sector, such as child welfare, but they do so in relation to a clear, comprehensive vision of the good, just, peaceful, sustainable, and democratic society and its place in the world order. Their profession's missions and conceptions of competent practice, i.e., doing the right things at the right times, for the right reasons and with the right results, are framed accordingly. Regardless of their specific, professional affiliations, all are, in one sense, social workers; and reciprocally, they may benefit from social work's leadership.

Moreover, social trustee, civic professionals prepare children, families, and other residents to help themselves and each other. They strengthen civil society and promote community engagement--especially, mutual concern about the needs of strangers. They protect and promote free spheres of action and association. These fundamental freedoms to act and associate are crucial to the effectiveness of indigenous helping and support systems, and strong democracy is impossible without them. In social work language, promoting citizen engagement and civic association is a powerful form of *indirect practice,* and social trustee civic professionals rely on it.

Like members of a choir who harmonize their voices with others, social trustee civic professionals are able to collaborate, to join forces, and harmonize and synchronize their efforts. As they do, they promote collaborative leadership. Social workers and other child welfare leaders often act as choir and orchestra leaders as they cross boundaries and orchestrate the efforts of professional, family, and resident systems.

Social trustee, civic professionals elevate their social responsibility over narrow self-interests. They are not interested in creating dependent clients. For this reason alone, they can be trusted. And they build social trust networks. They recruit and educate others for social responsibility at the same time they do good work. They purposefully plan for ripple or domino effects. The help they render to one child and family may enable this child and family to help and support for others. *Social trustee, civic professionals build natural-indigenous, neighborhood- and community-based systems of care. And, in turn, these systems of care depend on them.*

Back to the Future 2: A Time of Opportunity as History Repeats Itself

As the 21st Century begins, social workers and other child welfare leaders may go back to the future. Once again, their world is changing rapidly. The industrial age is giving way to the global age, including all of the changes that this great transformation brings (e.g., Lawson, in press a & b). Once again, a growing number of children, youth, families, and their surrounding neighborhood communities are vulnerable to the effects of pervasive changes, and many of these changes appear to be outside of their immediate control. Child and family stress and insecurities are more evident than ever, and, in high poverty communities, they appear to be increasing. As they increase, a pattern becomes evident. This pattern involves all of the child- and family-serving systems, including child welfare, juvenile justice, public schooling, public health, and mental health services. None of these systems may be able to demonstrate that they improve results and satisfy requirements for accountability. When these systems do not collaborate and work at cross purposes (e.g., Lawson & Barkdull, Chapter 13), they unintentionally create situations which constrain and prevent effective problem-solving. Systems get caught in traps of their own making.

One-hundred years ago, social work's founders successfully met multiple challenges like these. They charted a clear course. They successfully met the challenges of developing new concepts (e.g., social diagnosis, settlement house, social casework, coordinated services). They implemented new practices (e.g., assistance strategies that helped the child while supporting the parent and strengthening the family). They promoted new policies (e.g., child labor laws, compulsory schooling laws). They pioneered the development of new social institutions (e.g., child welfare, public schools). Ultimately, their work resulted in the modern social welfare state.

Theirs was not a linear, step-by-step, change and development process. These founders launched their change agenda on several fronts. It unfolded in multiple, interacting phases, at several levels of action—local, regional, state, and national. Like today's practices, their change agenda incorporated and integrated multi-level and multi-modal strategies.

From History-Takers to History-Makers

Social work's founders and their successors benefited from a sense of history. Mindful that their time in history, the industrial age, was pivotal, they refused to fall in line. They were intent on changing the course of human affairs. *They were determined to make history.* They were able to imagine different and better social life worlds for children, youth, families, and themselves, and they had the political will and the know-how to create these social life worlds. They were skilled community and political organizers and mobilizers. To reiterate, they were boundary workers who knew how to cross, extend, and merge the lines that often divide. They developed social work's boundaries as they did new century, 20th-Century, social work (Abbott, 1995; Abramovitz, 1998; Lubove, 1973).

Today a new generation of social work leaders stands on the threshold of a new century. A growing number of needs, many of which are identified, described, and explained in this book, compel an innovative, effective 21st-Century social work. Like their predecessors, this new generation of leaders can benefit from an understanding of history. They know that their time in history--the global age--is a pivotal era. They sense that this is not the time to fall into line. Just as the founders of social work were determined to change the course of human affairs and make their own history, so too, does today's new generation have the same opportunities. *They must have the determination and political will to make their own history.* If so, they will address successfully the emergent, unprecedented challenges of a new century. If they join forces and if they are able to reach basic consensus on the nature and causes of globalization's challenges, their intervention-improvement strategies will be more effective. Their reach will not exceed their grasp. They will develop new century child welfare policies and practices that are simultaneously local, regional, national, and international.

Like the founders of social work, this new generation of leaders needs to exercise their social work imaginations (after Mills, 1969). That is, they must be able to look at existing practices, policies, and social institutions and imagine different and better social life worlds. Like social work's founders, they must be able to set aside their differences, or, at the least, be able to view these differences as opportunities to help each other get outside of their respective "mental boxes" (Senge, Kleiner, et al., 1994). Mindful of growing diversity and difference, they must collaborate effectively. They must collaborate with one another; with other professions; with vulnerable children, youth, and families; and, with broad-based community coalitions.

The Unique Context for New Century Practices and Policies

Indeed, the global age brings unprecedented challenges and needs (e.g., Lawson in press a & b). For example, as transnational corporations relocate their production facilities and new machine technologies (e.g., robotics) replace line workers, millions of low-skilled, assembly line jobs are lost, perhaps permanently. This de-industrialization and the accompanying loss of jobs hit working class families hard. De-industrialization erodes the capacities of entire communities (e.g., Fine & Weis, 1998). Working class African-American families clustered in America's cities may suffer most of all (e.g., Wilson, 1996).

Despite their strengths and assets, local neighborhood communities challenged by globalization evidence urgent needs. Child and family needs are accompanied by neighborhood and community needs. Awareness is growing that there is a new social geography for child welfare practice and policy. So-called "cookie cutter" models and solutions are dangerous because place and context matter in determining what works and what will not. Similarly, community development and collaboration models must take into account the interactions among race and ethnicity, place, and need (e.g., Halpern, 1995).

Meanwhile, the welfare state is being progressively dismantled. At the same time, local businesses, banks, and service institutions, such as restaurants, are forced to compete with Walmart, K-Mart, Staples, Home Depot, Appleby's, McDonald's, Burger King, and countless other, large-scale enterprises. Dubbed "McWorld" by Barber (1996), this growing sameness around the United States and across the world poses new challenges and opportunities. Unprecedented movements of the individuals, children, and families adds to the growing sense of change and instability. Cultures mix and match as people move, resulting in a new poly-culturalism (e.g., Lawson, in press a). No one should underestimate these challenges, least of all child welfare professionals.

On the other hand, common threads run across the 20th and 21st Centuries, and they are visible in the preceding centuries. They provide common grounds, which are fertile for the development of shared purposes and, in turn, effective mobilization for collective action. The seeds for comprehensive, community-based systems of care will grow and prosper in these common grounds. Civic engagement and strong democracy depend on the same seedbed.

So, where might professionals and other citizens find common grounds out of which to grow a sense of common purpose? Once this question is asked, the answers are relatively easy to derive.

Everyone wants children to be safe and secure and to grow up to become healthy adults. They want families to be healthy and strong. They want to be able to lend a hand when others are in need and reciprocally, to be lent a hand from others when they are in need.

Everyone wants neighborhoods and local communities to be safe, secure and vibrant. They do not want to worry about their safety when they step outside their homes. They want their children to play safely and enjoy the outdoors in the same way they did when they were young. They want to be able to know their neighbors and ideally, to trust them and others in the local community. They want to be able mobilize for collective action to fix community problems and meet neighborhood and family needs. They want good jobs for everyone because they know how important meaningful employment is to individuals and families. They want public sector professions and their systems to be successful and to be responsive to them. They want to enjoy the basic freedoms of speech, assembly, press, and religion; and, they want to be free from unjust discrimination, oppression, and repression. They want their equal rights as citizens. And, they want local, state, and national governments to promote and implement appropriate, effective policies, which safeguard their visions for child and family well-being in a good, just, peaceful, sustainable, and democratic society.

Every concerned citizen wants these benefits, values their liberty, and wants to protect universal social insurance and entitlements. Short of living in walled-in, fortress communities, they know that their freedom and well-being hinge on others. They can be recruited to help.

Everyday citizens may not have the formal credentials, and, where the official boundaries and boundary markers of social work are concerned, they may be outsiders. The fact remains, however, that they already do some societal work. *Today, like yesterday, societal and community work is social work.* Everyday people are thus allies for professional social workers. They can do a great deal more. In fact, they must do a great deal more. As economic inequalities grow, and as racial and cultural divides become more problematic, the future of democracy is at stake.

New century social work, like last century social work, thus must be a collaborative, democratic enterprise. This social work is nothing less than the design and construction of social reality. More than merely studying people and society, this social work involves changing them. Professional systems, family systems, neighborhood systems, community systems, state systems, and national systems need to be linked, harmonized, and synchronized, producing a mutually beneficial synergy. Supported and encouraged by this kind of collaborative advantage, child welfare professionals and their systems no longer have to do it all, alone. They may benefit from, and help to create, neighborhood- and community-based systems of care.

As they benefit, so will children and families, especially the most vulnerable ones living on, or near, the edge. With community-based systems of care, the entire intervention and support continuum is transformed from an idealized possibility to an everyday reality. Focused on child welfare in important ways, this voluntary engagement is also a basic requirement of citizenship in a democracy. It necessitates social trustee, civic professionalism and its close partner, collaborative leadership.

A Time of Opportunity for Social Work and Child Welfare

Child welfare professionals and their systems have been assigned society's most important responsibility. They must protect the nation's children and youth, especially the most vulnerable ones, and, at the same time, foster family well- being. When professionals are effective and the system works as planned, vulnerable children and youth gain permanency, stability, safety, and security. Many families are stabilized and fortified. Kids enjoy strong, health-enhancing developmental pathways for learning and growth, pathways that pave the way for productive adult roles. When once-vulnerable kids reach adulthood and become parents, they are able to nurture their own children's well-being and guide them along the same kinds of health-enhancing developmental pathways. In other words, when professionals are effective and the system works as planned, the inter-generational transmission of the needs, problems, and challenges that comprise vulnerability and may result in poverty can be prevented and eliminated.

In this view, *child welfare work is one of the most important responsibilities delegated to any profession.* All other public sector systems, such as education, juvenile justice, health, and mental health, depend in some measure on it. Society's most important responsibility is also its most awesome and challenging one.

Like physicians, nurses, and police officers, child welfare professionals are in "the life and death business." Like these other professionals, they often are asked to work miracles after a crisis already has arisen or when there is already proof of harm. To reiterate, child welfare professionals are asked to strike a difficult balance between the sometimes contradictory roles of enforcer and healer. ASFA adds to this complexity with its requirements for concurrent planning, which itself requires considerable sophistication about family support, family-centered practice, and children's safety, security, and well-being.

Unfortunately, too few laypersons, policy makers, and politicians appreciate this complexity and the attendant difficulty of public sector child welfare. They do not understand how difficult it is to make timely, strategic, and effective decisions that are in the best interests of the child, nor do they understand the broad range of duties assigned to the system and its professionals. They are unable to make the connection between specialized preparation in social work, effective child welfare systems, the well-being of children and families, and the ingredients of a strong, vibrant democracy.

Although outsiders may not fully appreciate all that child welfare professionals do, it is clear to insiders that child welfare work is sophisticated work. It takes a special kind of expert, guided by a social work perspective, to make timely, appropriate, and effective decisions. Child welfare work involves delicate balances between the top priority--the immediate, best interests of the child--and the best possible, long-term solutions for children, families, and society's members. It is the most important kind of social work. It is society's work on the behalf of its most vulnerable members.

These important changes and the benefits identified in the preceding analysis are not likely to eventuate absent changes in what it means to be a child welfare professional. To reiterate, social work's leadership is needed today, more than ever before.

Unfortunately, separate historical trajectories have developed for social work and child welfare. Despite some states' mandates for employing only trained social workers, the national pattern is revealing. Less than a third of child welfare workers are, strictly speaking, social workers. In brief, there is a critical staffing crisis in child welfare, and systems improvement depends fundamentally on solving it (Briar-Lawson, 2000; Briar-Lawson & Wiesen, 2000). Political and market forces help explain part of this disjuncture between social work and child welfare.

In this perspective, social work's professionalization, especially as it relates to child welfare, also needs a critical analysis. However tempting it may be to exempt social work from critiques of the professions and their sway toward mechanical, market-oriented professionalism, the case has been made that this distinguished profession has become part of the problem (e.g., Abbott, 1995; Abramovitz, 1998; Brown, 1998; Lubove, 1974; Rose, 1997; Specht & Courtney, 1997). Once the leader among all of the professions in boundary-spanning, crossing, integrating, the profession's inexorable march toward being a "real profession" in the model of medicine has exacted costs.

As the number of professional boundary markers has increased (e.g., licensing and accreditation systems), social work has begun to look more and more like the other professions in the industrial assembly line system. Gaining prestige in this system of professions has been an important benefit, but it also has exacted costs. Arguably, this profession, like others, increasingly has turned to the psychiatric and psychological disciplines for its knowledge base and language. This increasing social-psychological emphasis reflects and fuels the growing number of social workers interested in mental health services and counseling (e.g., Gibelman, 1999). Many want to work alone, in private practice, as therapists and counselors in the personal troubles and therapy industry (e.g., Abbott, 1995; Rieff, 1966; Specht & Courtney, 1994).

As the psychological lens has ascended in social work, the macro, integrated, sociological, economic, and political lens appears to have declined. As the concern with private practice with relatively well-to-do individuals and families has grown, the special, social work associated with vulnerable children and families and the grand visions that support and safeguard their well-being also have declined. Perhaps reflecting the deprofessionalization of child welfare, new professional opportunities presented by market forces, policy changes, and the desire for higher incomes, today proportionately fewer social workers are oriented toward public sector child welfare (Gibelman, 1999).[8]

As students, market forces, and funding opportunities go, other aspects of the profession's operations may follow. For example, the formal missions of schools, departments, and colleges of social work may change, affording less emphasis on child welfare. Faculty recruitment and research interests also may change, and partnerships with child welfare agencies may decline. In brief, the foundation is laid for the separate historical trajectories for social work and child welfare. Such a separation would have been unimaginable as the modern profession was being forged. When primary, secondary, and tertiary effects of the staffing crisis in child welfare are weighed, this separation represents a significant loss.

New century social work leadership in child welfare must compensate for this loss and others. Keeping the best of professional boundaries and specialization, this new century leadership must respond to the growing challenges, especially the stark realities, of the global age. This leadership is as important in social work education programs as it is in communities and state agencies. It involves the recruitment and training of faculty, especially faculty researchers. It also requires the recruitment and training of social workers for child welfare practice.

This new generation of social work leaders for child welfare, like many of child welfare's current leaders, will need to be creative and inventive. Like the trailblazers for the modern profession, they will need a "whatever it takes" attitude. Seeing challenges as opportunities, they may make history, just as their predecessors did a century ago. History-making social work leaders also gain important opportunities to expand the boundaries of social work as they do the social work of boundary crossing and relationship building.

This important, multi-dimensional boundary work is a best practice strategy. It promotes a 21st-Century vision for the well-being of all children and families. Visions like these are the centerpieces of powerful social movements that produce policy change. And, policy change in the behalf of vulnerable children and families is sorely needed today.

Furthermore, strong democracy and vibrant democratic institutions depend on this kind of new century social work and the improvements it promises for child welfare and related public sector systems. For, just as the strength of a chain depends on its weakest links, so does the strength of American democracy depend on its most vulnerable citizens—its children and youth. Because child welfare and social work attend to the needs of the most vulnerable citizens and oppressed, marginalized populations, both make key contributions to the good, just, peaceful, sustainable, and

---

[8] The relationship between social work's professionalization and child welfare's deprofessionalization is an important, but separate, topic (e.g., Briar-Lawson & Wiesen, 2000). It merits social-historical analysis.

democratic society. However, even when they effectively join forces, they cannot achieve their potential or achieve all that society's members and powerful policy leaders expect. Both social work and child welfare require comprehensive, community-based systems of care in which everyday people and indigenous helping systems are supported and strengthened.

So, professionals and everyday citizens alike must be actively and purposefully engaged in the social construction of reality. All must accept their shared responsibilities for doing new century social work. In striking contrast to mechanical, market-oriented professionalism and its emphasis on monopolizing expertise, social workers acting as social trustee civic professionals may give their expertise to others, recruiting and mobilizing them as partners for collective action.

Paradoxically, by sharing expertise, social workers committed to child welfare also promote themselves and their profession. For, as they share expertise and help people understand their work, everyday people gain understanding about the complexity and sophistication of their work, including the urgency of the life and death decisions professionals must make. Enfranchising others as "social workers" thus promises to support child welfare and promote best practices. At the same time, it promises to revitalize, strengthen, and even expand the professional boundaries of social work.

Endnote

1. I am grateful to Nancy Peterson, Mary McCarthy, and Katharine Briar-Lawson for their criticism.

References

Abbott, A. (1995). Boundaries of social work or the social work of boundaries? *Social Service Review, 69*, 545-562.

Abramovitz, M. (1998). Social work and social reform: An arena of struggle. *Social Work, 43*, 512-526.

Barber, B. (1996). *Jihad vs. McWorld: How globalism and tribalism are reshaping the world*. New York: Ballantine Books.

Briar-Lawson, K. (1998). Capacity building for integrated, family-centered practice. *Social Work, 43*, 539-550.

Briar-Lawson, K. (2000). Personal communication to the author.

Briar-Lawson, K. and Wiesen, M. (2000, June). Effective partnership models between state agencies, the university and community service providers. Paper presented at U.S. Children's Bureau's Invited Conference on Child Welfare, Washington, DC.

Boyer, P. (1978). *Urban masses and moral order in America*. Cambridge, MA: Harvard University Press.

Brint, S. (1994). *In an age of experts: The changing role of professionals in politics and public life.* Princeton, NJ: Princeton University Press.

Brown, R. (1998). *Toward a democratic science: Scientific narration and civic communication.* New Haven & London: Yale University Press.

Bruner, C. and Parachini, L. (1997). *Building community: Exploring new relationships across service systems reform, community organizing, and community economic development.* Washington, DC: Institute for Educational Leadership & Together We Can.

Capper, C. (1996). We're not housed in an institution, we're housed in the community: Possibilities and consequences of neighborhood-based, interagency collaboration. In J. Cibulka & W. Kritek (Eds.). *Coordination Among Schools, Families and Communities: Prospects for Educational Reform* (pp. 299-322). Albany, NY: SUNY Press.

Cowger, C. (1998). Clientilism and clientification: Impediments to strengths-based social work practice. *Journal of Sociology and Social Welfare, XXV*(1), 25-38.

Ellis, R. (1998). Filling the prevention gap: Multi-factor, multi-system, multi-level intervention. *The Journal of Primary Prevention, 19*(1), 57-71.

Farrow, F. (1997). *Building community partnerships for child protection.* Child Protective Clearinghouse: Center for the Study of Social Policy. Washington, D.C.

Fein, M. and Weis, L. (1998). *The unknown city: The lives of poor and working-class young adults.* Boston: Beacon Press.

Gaylin, W., Glasser, I., Marcus, S., and Rothman, D. (1974). *Doing good: The limits of benevolence.* New York: Pantheon Books.

Gerry, M. (1999). Personal communication to the author, October.

Gibelman, M. (1999). The search for identity: Defining social work—past, present, future. *Social Work, 44,* 298-310.

Halpern, R. (1995). *Rebuilding the inner city: A history of neighborhood organizations in the United States.* New York: Columbia University Press.

Halpern, R. (1999). *Fragile families, fragile solutions: A history of supportive services for families in poverty.* New York: Columbia University Press.

Ignatieff, M. (1986). *The needs of strangers: An essay on privacy, solidarity and the politics of being human.* New York: Penguin.

Knowles, C. (1996). *Family boundaries: The invention of normality & dangerousness.* Toronto: Broadview Press.

Lawson, H. (1998, July). *Globalization and the social responsibilities of citizen professionals.* Keynote Address, AIESEP International Conference, Garden City, NY.

Lawson, H. (in press a). Globalization, flows of culture and people, and new century frameworks for family-centered policies and practices. In K. Briar-Lawson, H., Lawson, & C. Hennon with A. Jones (Eds.). *Family-centered policies and practices: International implications.* New York: Columbia University Press.

Lawson, H. (in press b). Introducing globalization's challenges and opportunities and analyzing economic globalization and liberalization. In K. Briar-Lawson, H., Lawson, & C. Hennon with A. Jones, *Family-centered policies and practices: International implications.* New York: Columbia University Press.

Lawson, H. and Briar-Lawson, K. (1997). *Connecting the dots: Progress toward the integration of school reform, school-linked services, parent involvement, and community education programs.* Oxford, OH: The Danforth Foundation and the Institute for Educational Renewal at Miami University.

Levine, M. (1998). Prevention and community. *American Journal of Community Psychology, 26,* 189-206.

Lindsey, D. (1994). *The Welfare of Children.* New York: Oxford University Press.

Lubove, R. (1973). *The professional altruist: The emergence of social work as a career 1880-1930.* New York: Atheneum.

Margolin, L. (1997). *Under the cover of kindness: The invention of social work.* Charlottesville, VA & London: University of Virginia Press.

McCarthy, M. (2000). Personal communication to the author.

Mills, C. (1969). *The sociological imagination.* New York: Oxford University Press.

McNight, J. (1995). *The careless society: Community and its counterfeits.* New York: Basic Books.

Rieff, P. (1966). *The triumph of the therapeutic: Uses of faith after Freud.* Chicago: University of Chicago Press.

Rose, N. (1996). *Inventing our selves: Psychology, power, and personhood.* New York: Cambridge University Press.

Senge, P., Kleiner, A., Roberts, C., Ross, R., and Smith, B. (1994). *The fifth discipline fieldbook: Strategies and tools for building a learning organization.* New York: Currency Doubleday.

Smale, G. (1995). Integrating community and individual practice: A new paradigm for practice. In P. Adams & K. Nelson (Eds.). *Reinventing human services: Community-and family-centered practice* (pp. 59-80). New York: Aldine De Gruyter.

Specht, H. and Courtney, M. (1994). *Unfaithful angels: How social work has abandoned its mission.* New York: The Free Press.

Sullivan, W. (1995). *Work and integrity: The crisis and promise of professionalism in America.* New York: HarperBusiness.

Weiss, H. and Halpern, R. (1990). *Community-based family support and education programs: Something old or something new?* New York: National Center for Children in Poverty at Columbia University.

Wilson, J. (1996). *When work disappears: The world of the new urban poor.* New York: Alfred A. Knopf.